Shojo Beat

Mixed Vegetables

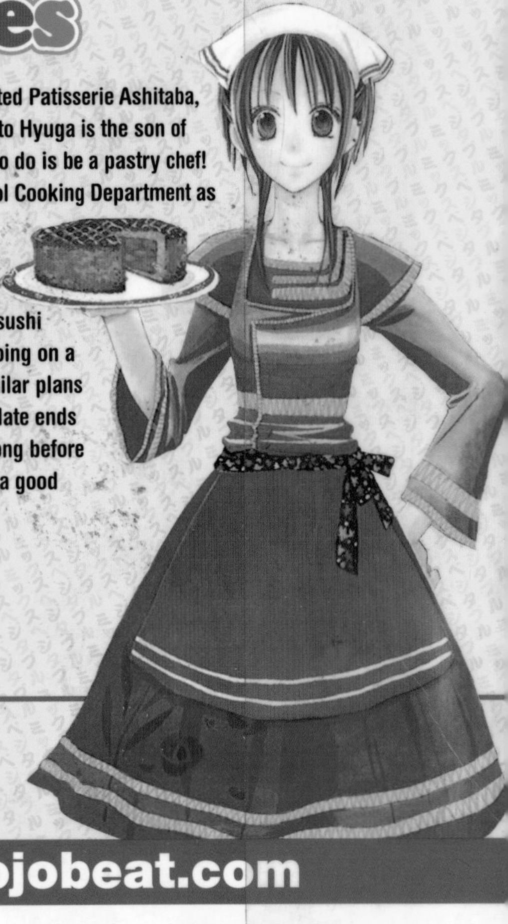

Hanayu Ashitaba is the daughter of the celebrated Patisserie Ashitaba, but all she wants to do is be a sushi chef. Hayato Hyuga is the son of the prestigious Sushi Hyuga, and all he wants to do is be a pastry chef! It's love and leftovers in the Oikawa High School Cooking Department as these star-crossed gourmands do their best to reach their cuisine dreams!

Hanayu thinks her plan to marry into Hayato's sushi family is off to a good start—they're already going on a date! But when it turns out that Hayato has similar plans to marry Hanayu for her patisserie family, the date ends abruptly. Can Hanayu figure out what went wrong before her chance at her sushi dreams, romance, and a good grade on the cake project go out the window?

Can Hanayu create the recipe for happiness?

2

Story & Art by

Ayumi Komura

www.shojobeat.com

$8.99 USA $10.50 CAN

ISBN-13: 978-1-4215-1968-5
ISBN-10: 1-4215-1968-2
50899
9 781421 519685

This book reads from right to left.

VIZ MEDIA

RATED T FOR TEEN
ratings.viz.com

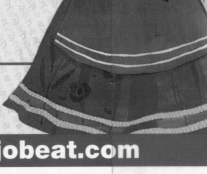

Surprise!

You may be reading the wrong way!

It's true: In keeping with the original Japanese comic format, this book reads from right to left—so action, sound effects, and word balloons are completely reversed. This preserves the orientation of the original artwork—plus, it's fun! Check out the diagram shown here to get the hang of things, and then turn to the other side of the book to get started!

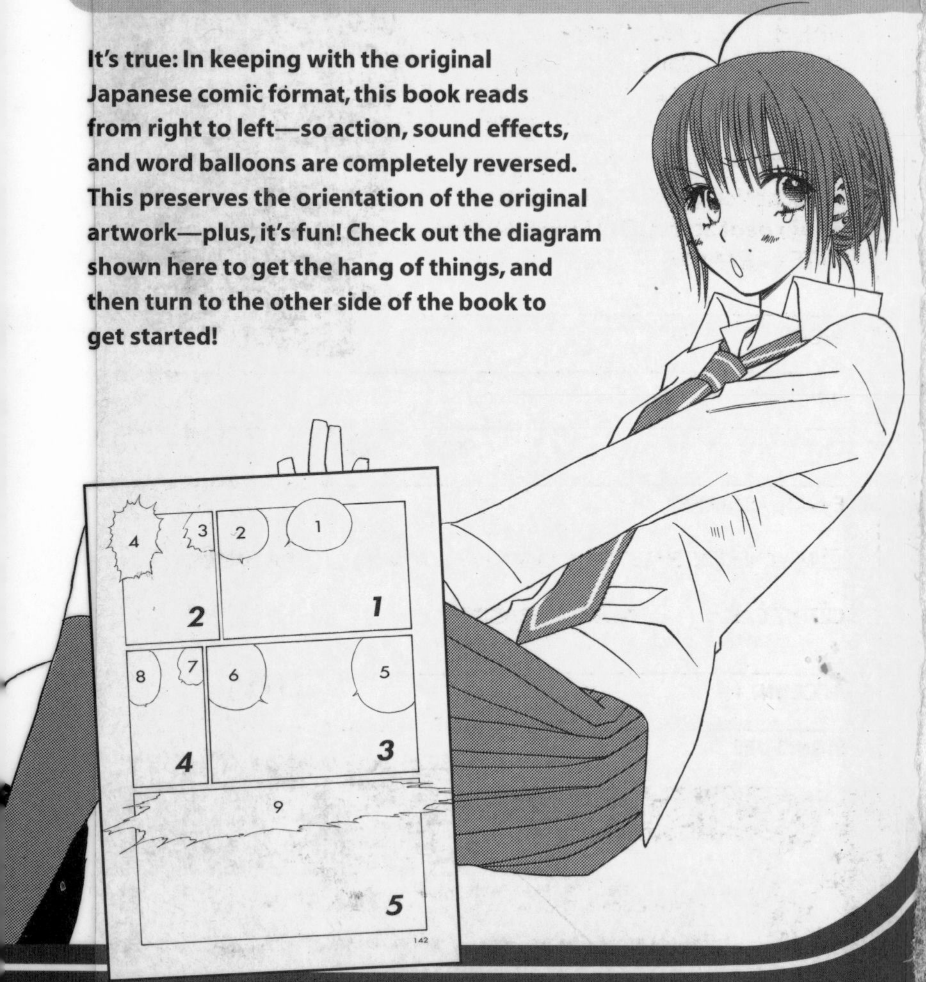

1
2
1
3
4
2
5
6
3
7
8
4
9
5
142

Shojo Beat

Mixed Vegetables

Vol. 2

Story & Art by

Ayumi Komura

Hanayu's classmate; his family owns a famous sushi shop called Sushidokoro Hyuga—but he dreams of being a pastry chef!

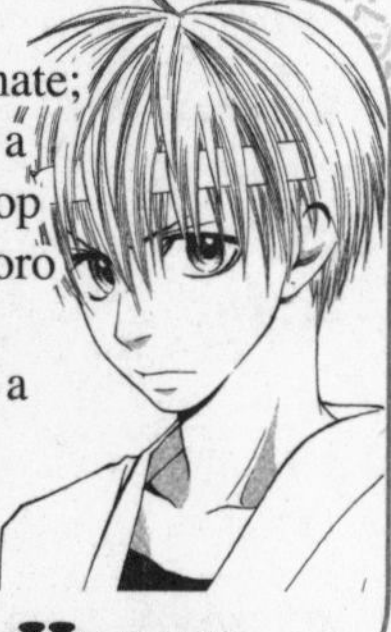

Hayato Hyuga

First-year student in the culinary arts program of Oikawa High School; a baker's daughter who aspires to be a sushi chef.

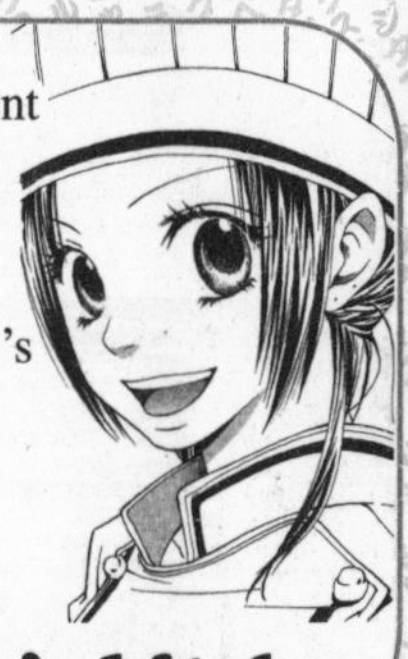

Hanayu Ashitaba

What happened in Volume 1:

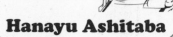

Hanayu thinks that the quickest way to realize her dream of becoming a sushi chef is to marry into a sushi shop family. She cooks up a devious plan to make her classmate, sushi-shop heir Hayato Hyuga, fall for her. Then, out of the blue, Hayato declares his love for her!

They begin dating, but Hanayu is filled with guilt. She tells herself that she must try to return Hayato's feelings. Soon enough she finds that she doesn't need to try to like him—Hanayu is naturally drawn to kind and cute Hayato. Finally, Hanayu realizes her original goal doesn't matter to her anymore, but Hayato does!

Mixed Vegetables

Volume 2
CONTENTS

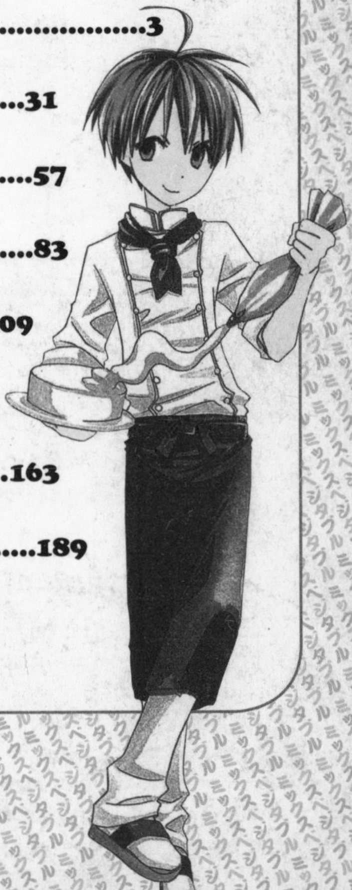

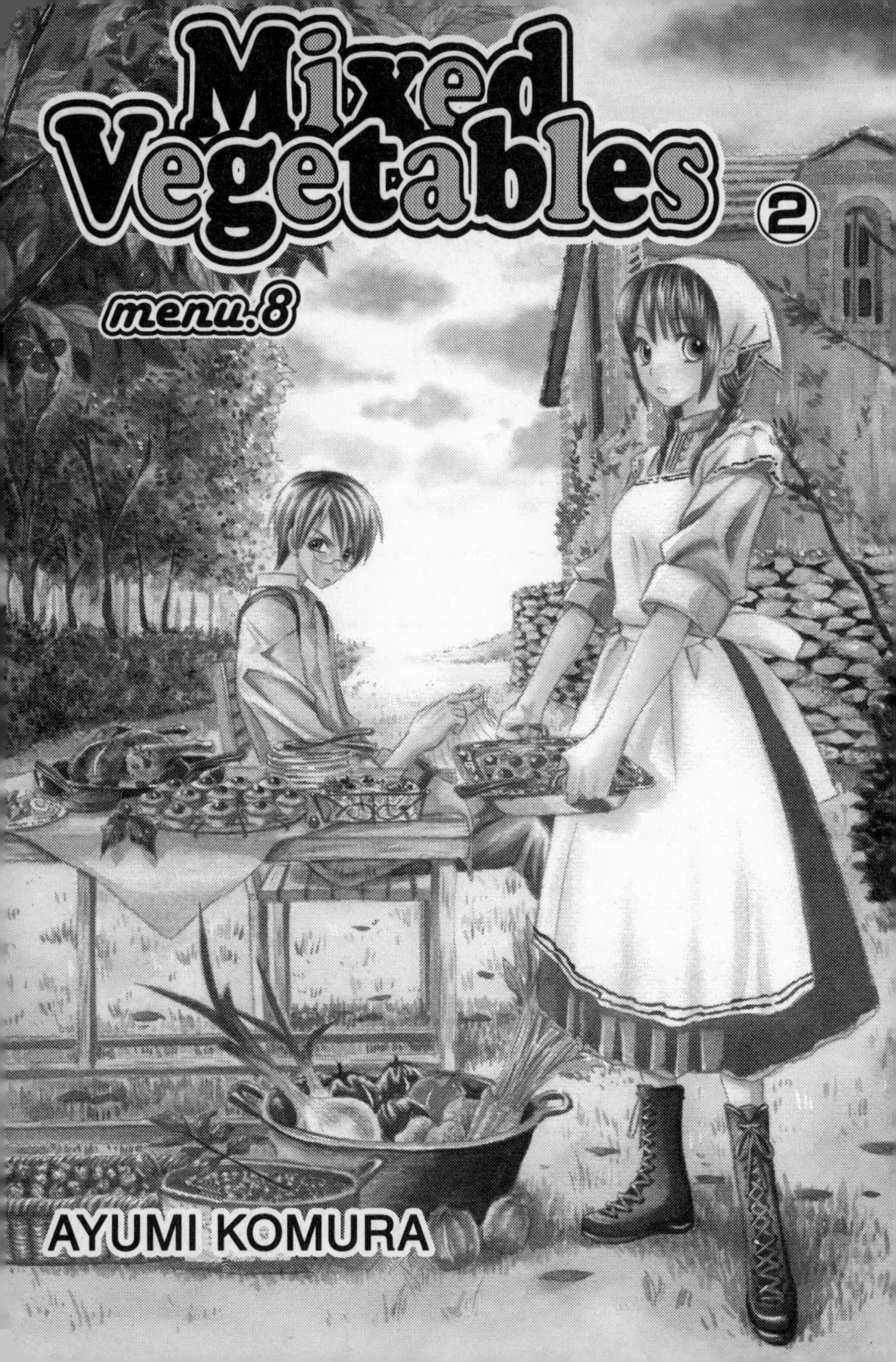
Mixed Vegetables 2
menu.8
AYUMI KOMURA

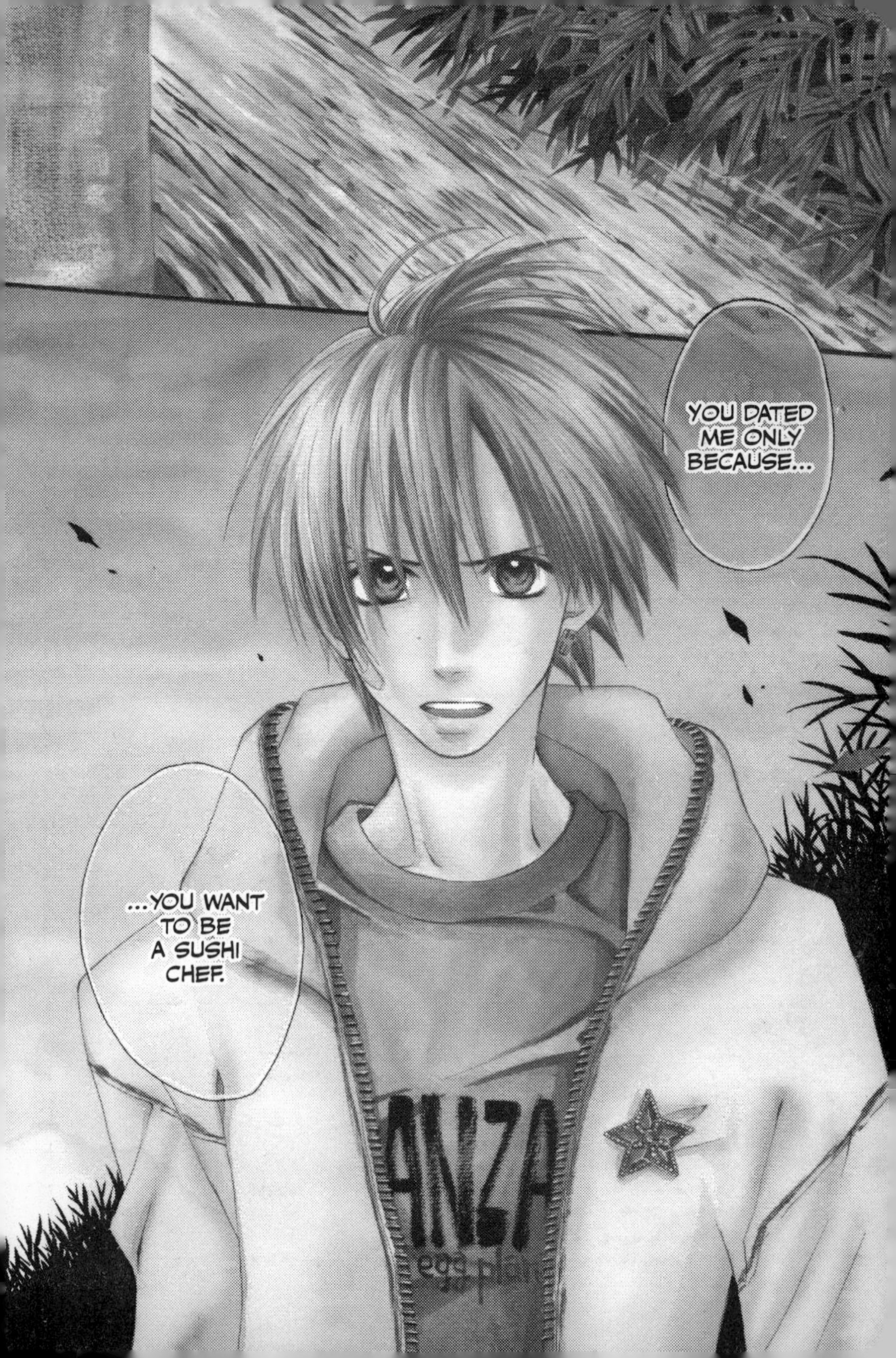
YOU DATED ME ONLY BECAUSE...
...YOU WANT TO BE A SUSHI CHEF.

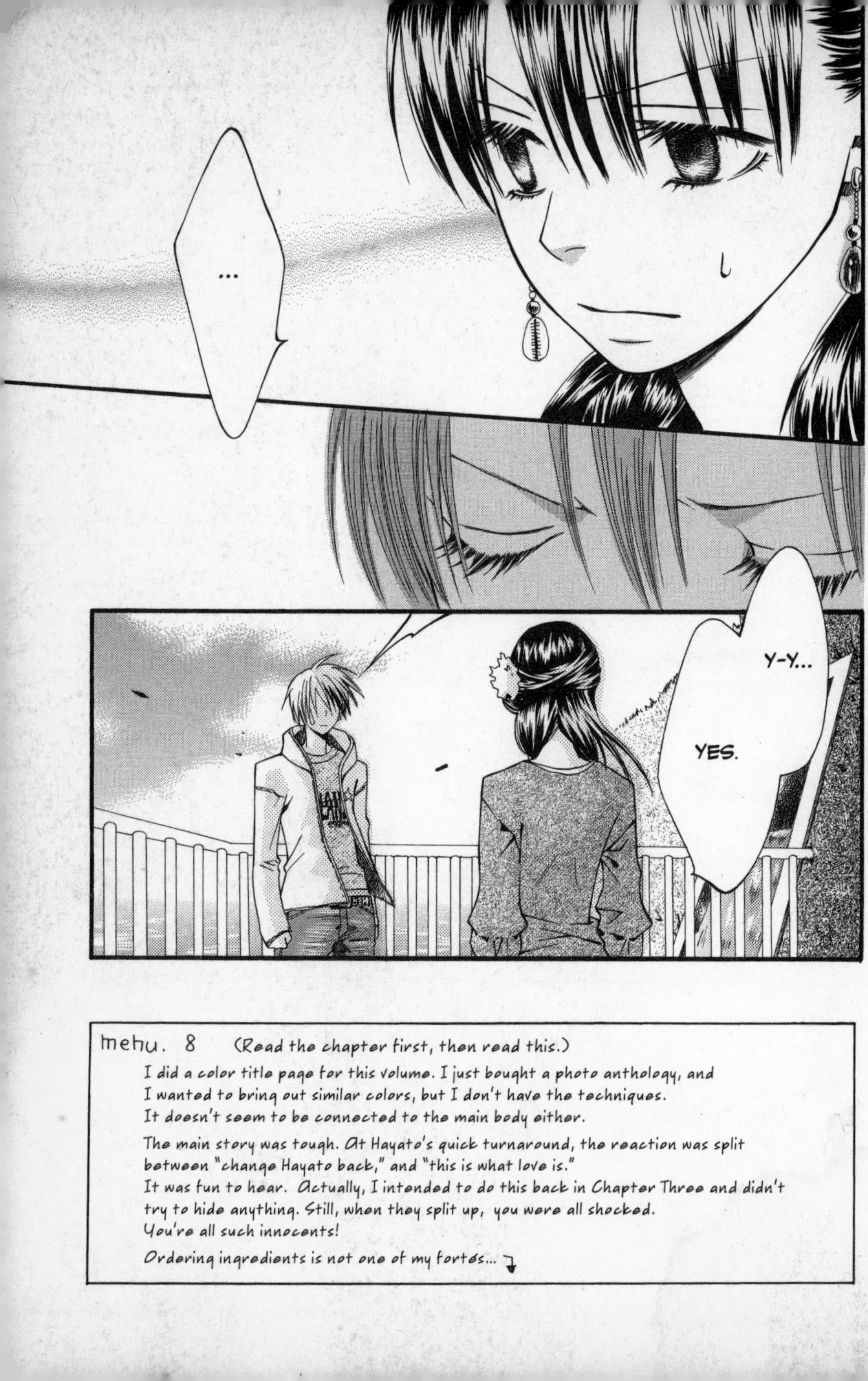
...
Y-Y... YES.

menu. 8 (Read the chapter first, then read this.)

I did a color title page for this volume. I just bought a photo anthology, and I wanted to bring out similar colors, but I don't have the techniques. It doesn't seem to be connected to the main body either.

The main story was tough. At Hayato's quick turnaround, the reaction was split between "change Hayato back," and "this is what love is." It was fun to hear. Actually, I intended to do this back in Chapter Three and didn't try to hide anything. Still, when they split up, you were all shocked. You're all such innocents!

Ordering ingredients is not one of my fortés...

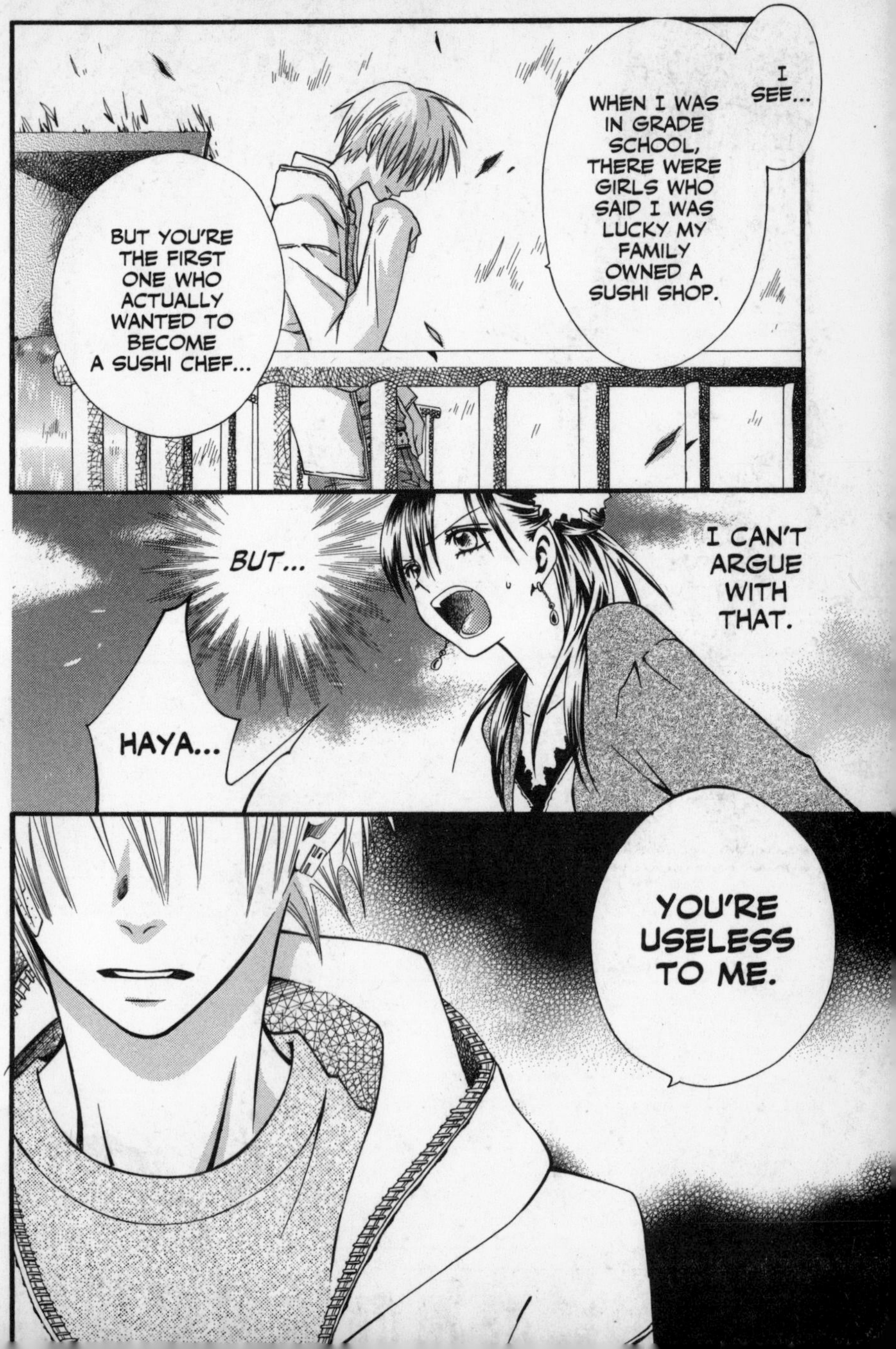
I SEE...
WHEN I WAS IN GRADE SCHOOL, THERE WERE GIRLS WHO SAID I WAS LUCKY MY FAMILY OWNED A SUSHI SHOP.
BUT YOU'RE THE FIRST ONE WHO ACTUALLY WANTED TO BECOME A SUSHI CHEF...
I CAN'T ARGUE WITH THAT.
BUT...
HAYA...
YOU'RE USELESS TO ME.

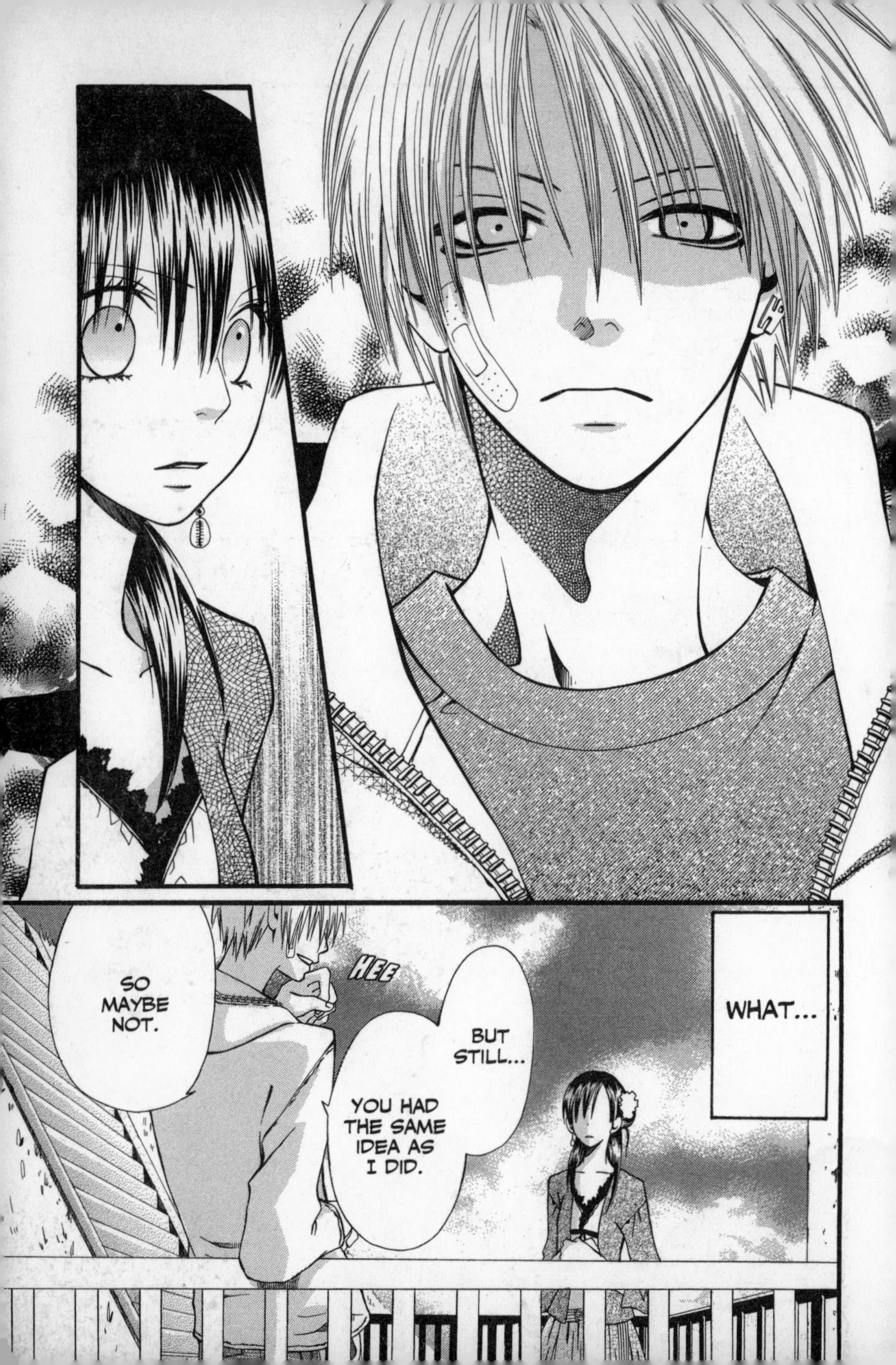
WHAT...
BUT STILL...
YOU HAD THE SAME IDEA AS I DID.
HEE
SO MAYBE NOT.

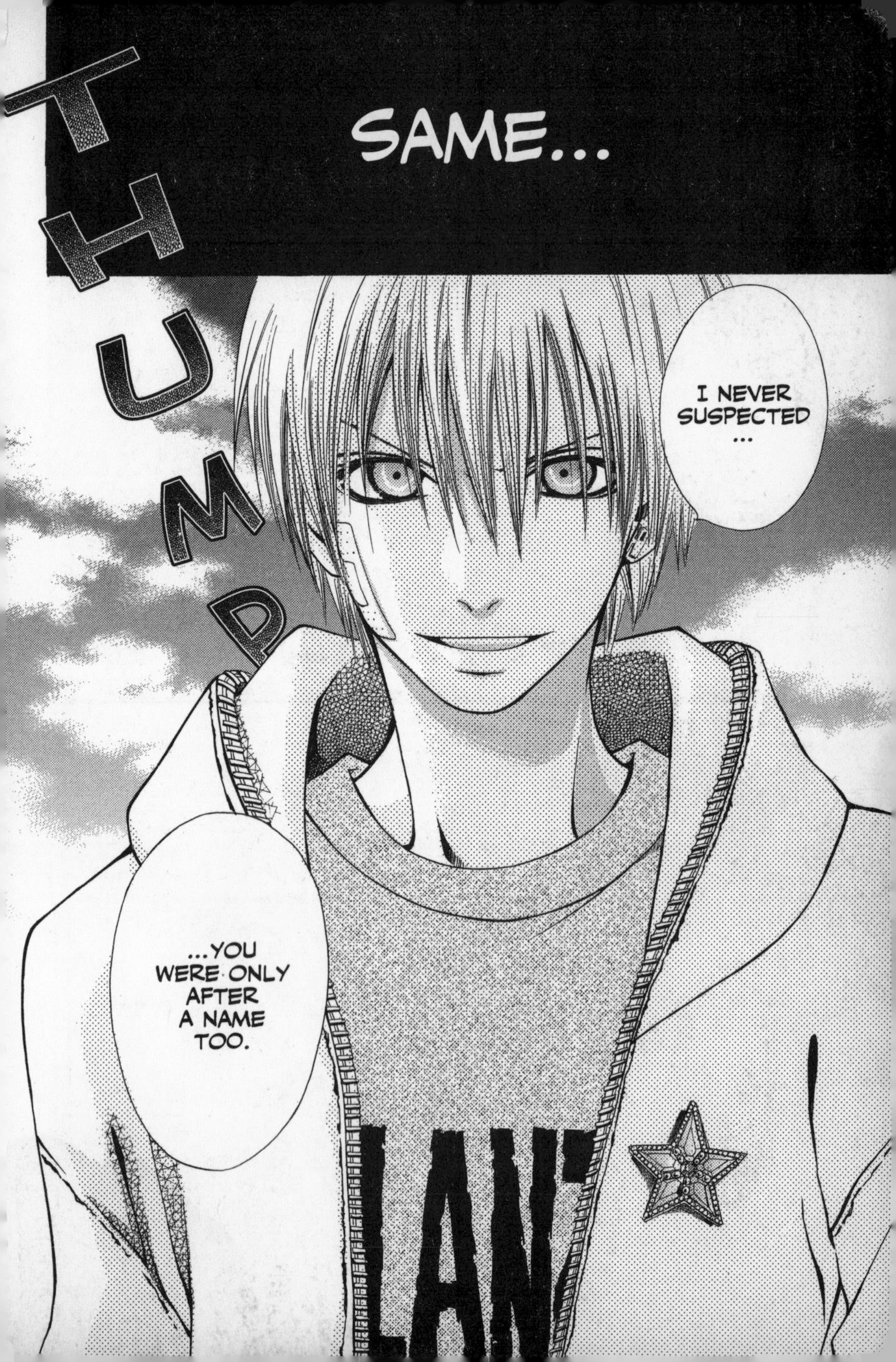
SAME...
THUMP
I NEVER SUSPECTED ...
...YOU WERE ONLY AFTER A NAME TOO.
LAN

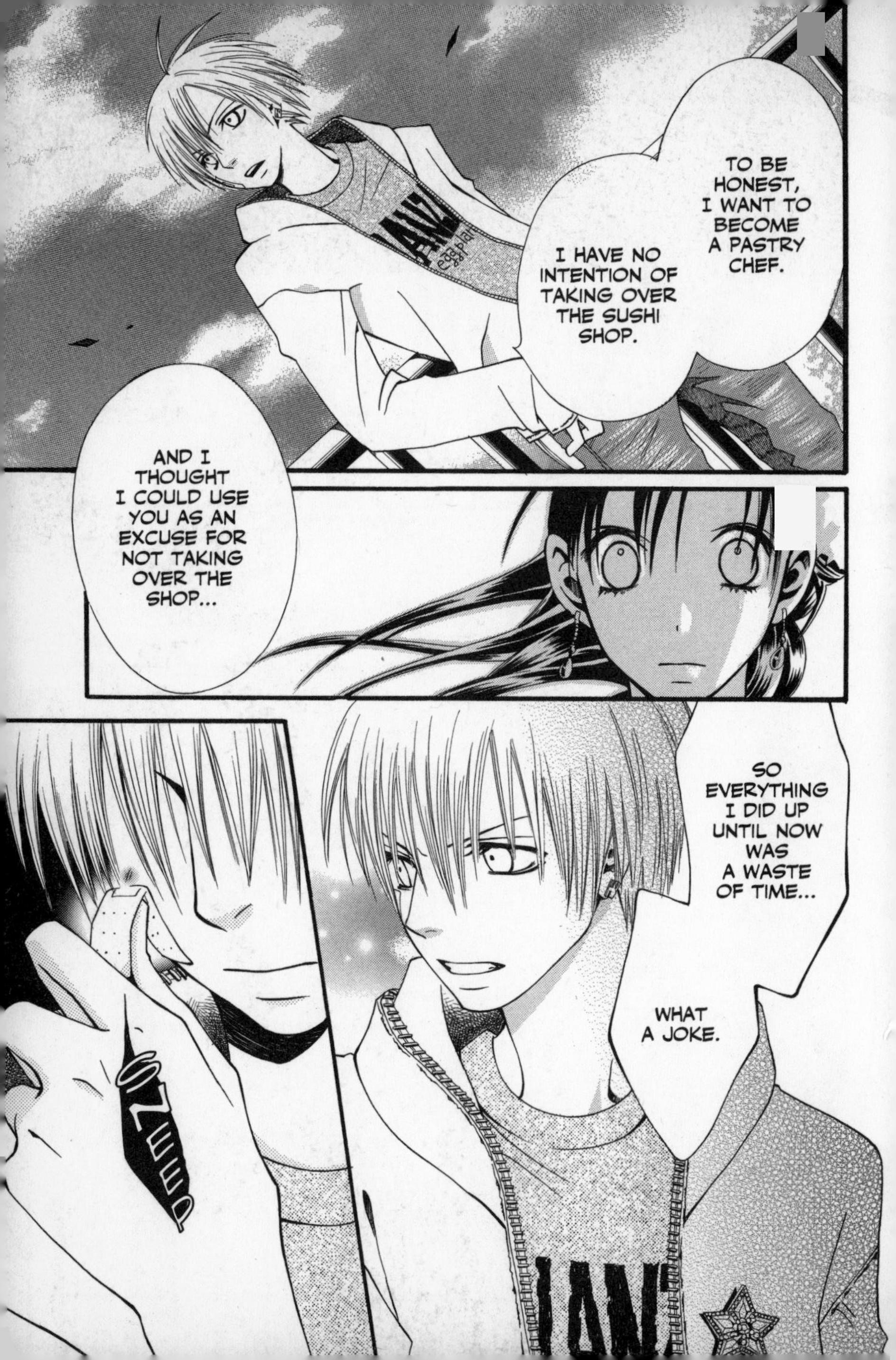
TO BE HONEST, I WANT TO BECOME A PASTRY CHEF.
I HAVE NO INTENTION OF TAKING OVER THE SUSHI SHOP.
AND I THOUGHT I COULD USE YOU AS AN EXCUSE FOR NOT TAKING OVER THE SHOP...
SO EVERYTHING I DID UP UNTIL NOW WAS A WASTE OF TIME...
WHAT A JOKE.

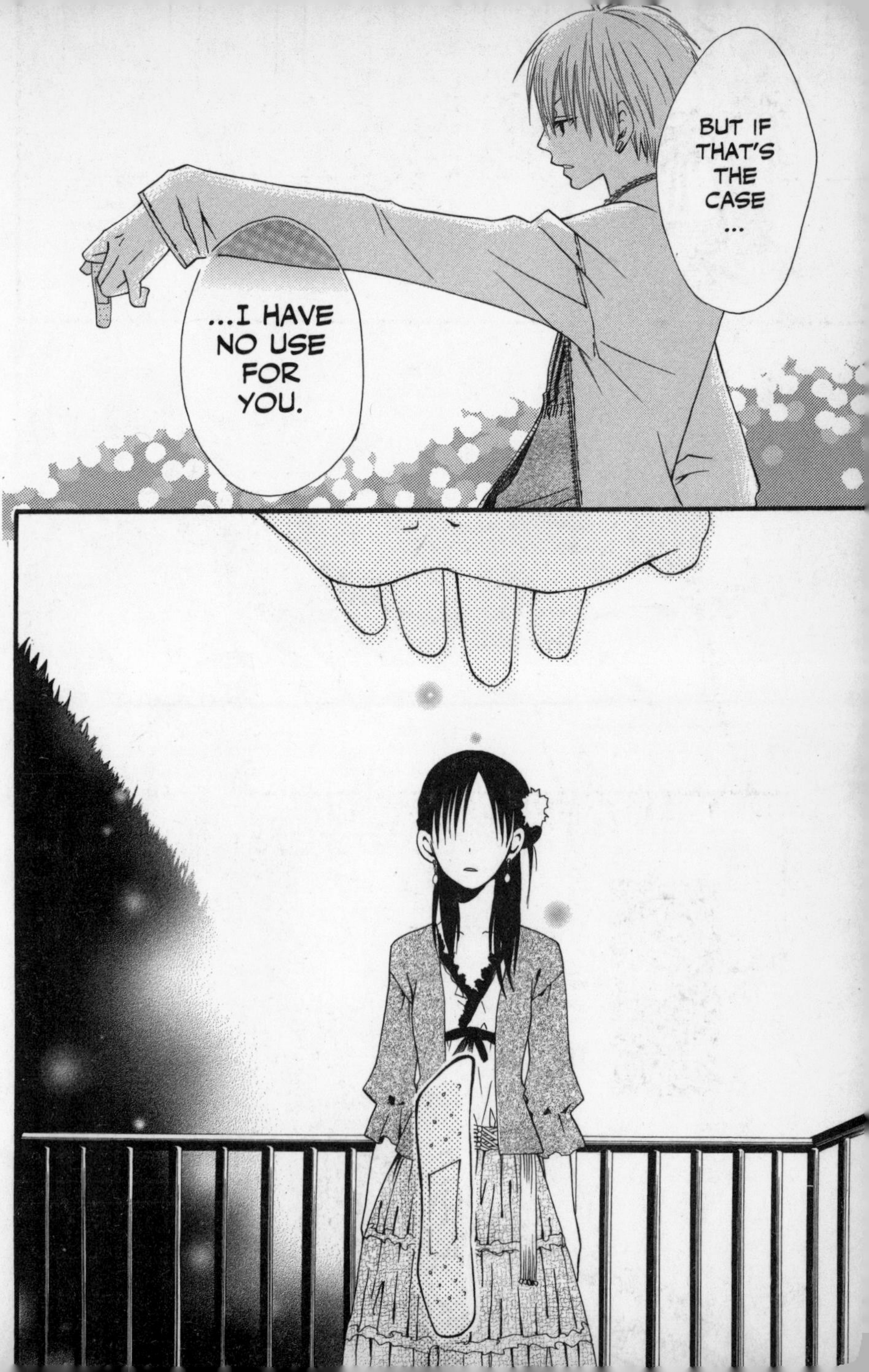
BUT IF THAT'S THE CASE ...
...I HAVE NO USE FOR YOU.

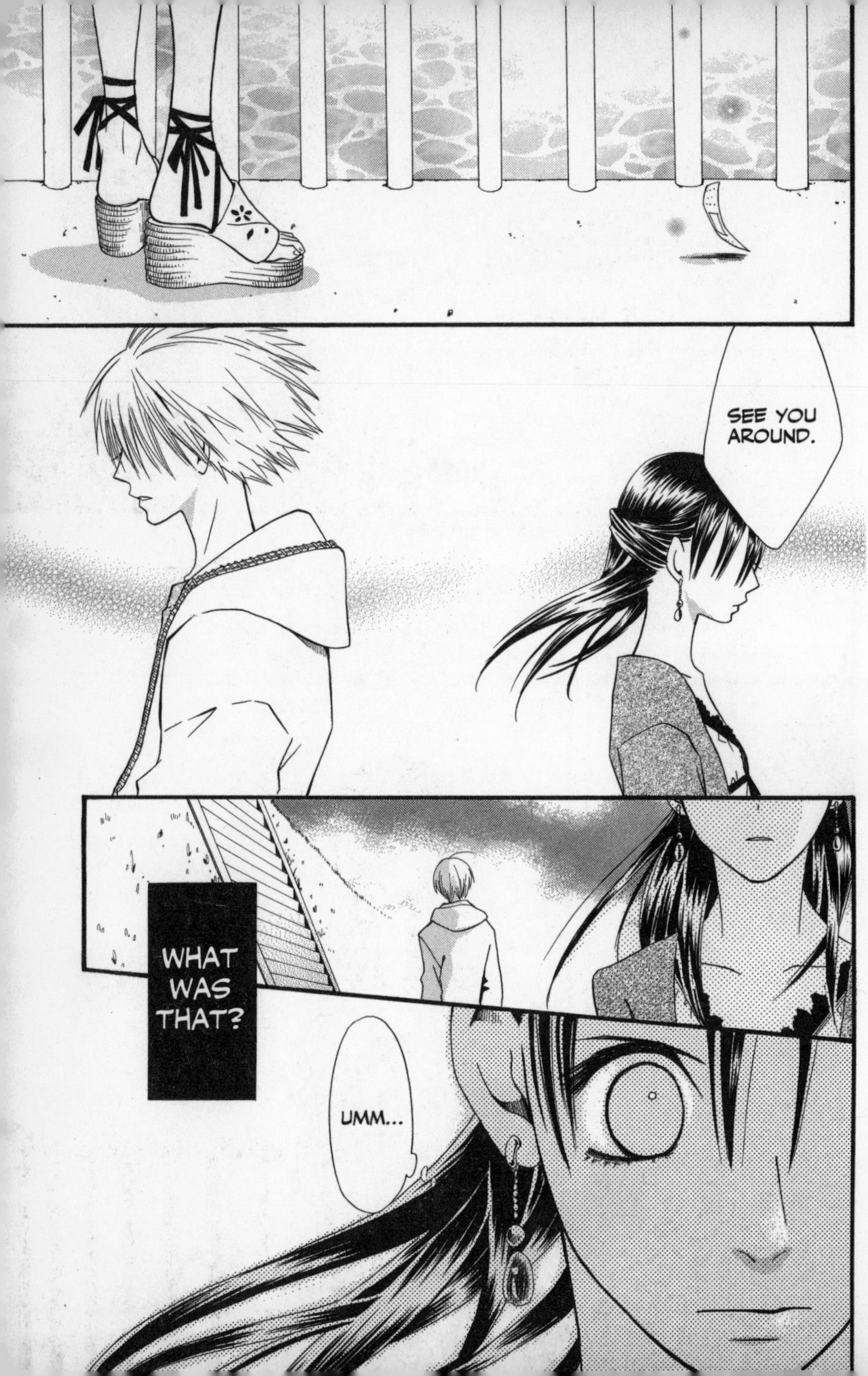
SEE YOU AROUND.
WHAT WAS THAT?
UMM...

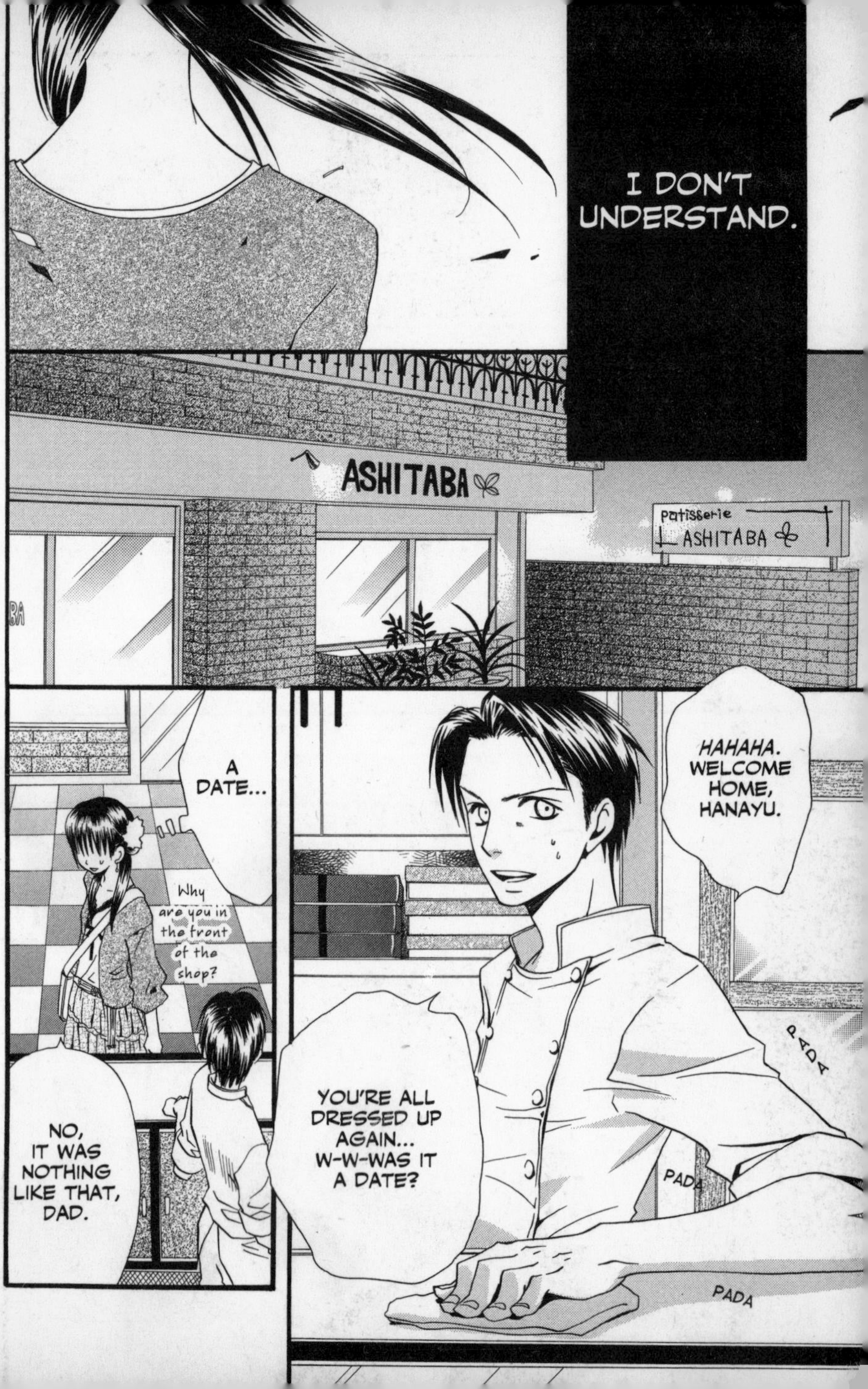
I DON'T UNDERSTAND.
ASHITABA
patisserie ASHITABA
HAHAHA. WELCOME HOME, HANAYU.
PADA
PADA
PADA
YOU'RE ALL DRESSED UP AGAIN... W-W-WAS IT A DATE?
A DATE...
Why are you in the front of the shop?
NO, IT WAS NOTHING LIKE THAT, DAD.

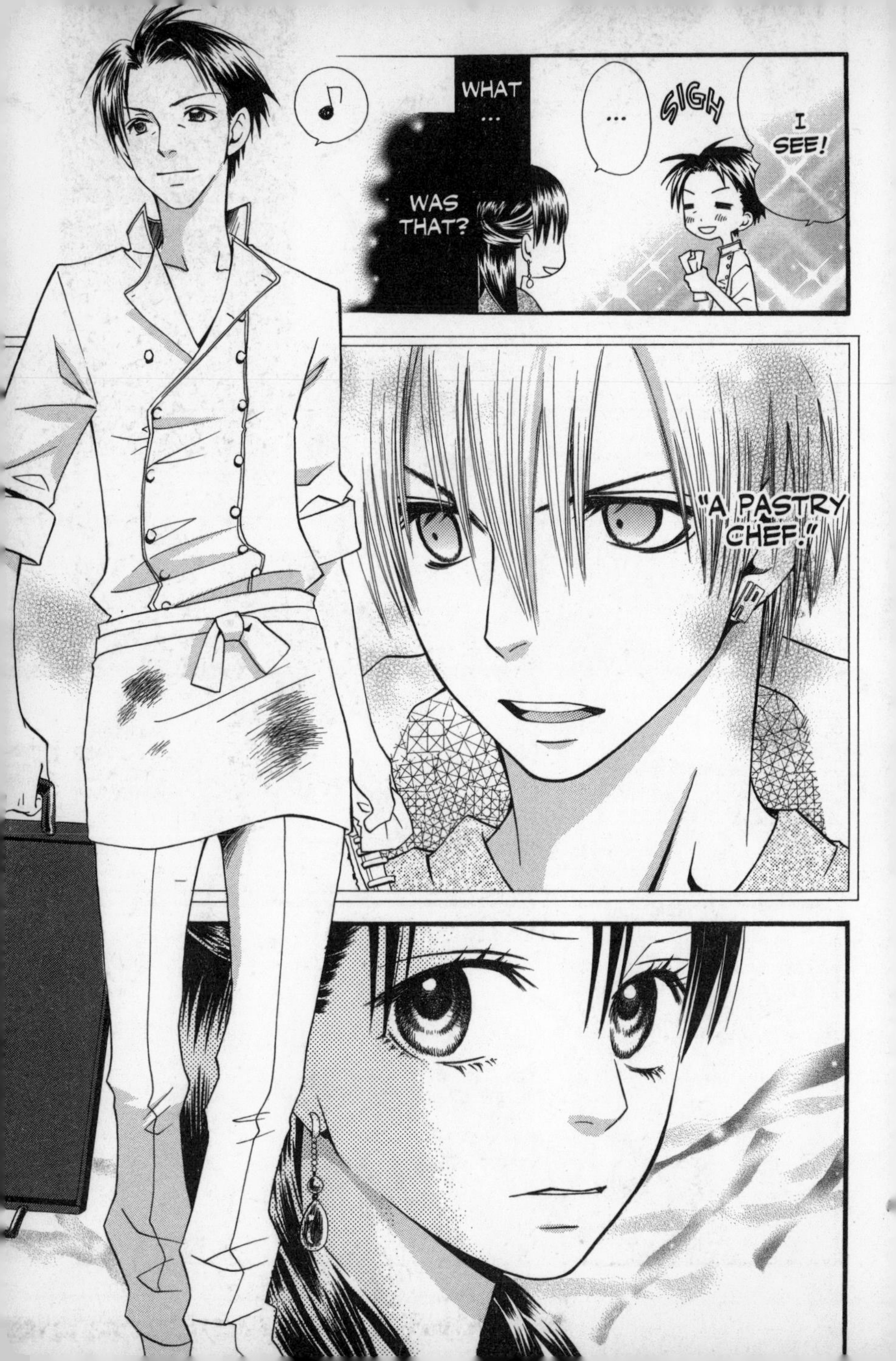
I SEE!
SIGH
...
WHAT ... WAS THAT?
"A PASTRY CHEF!"
♪

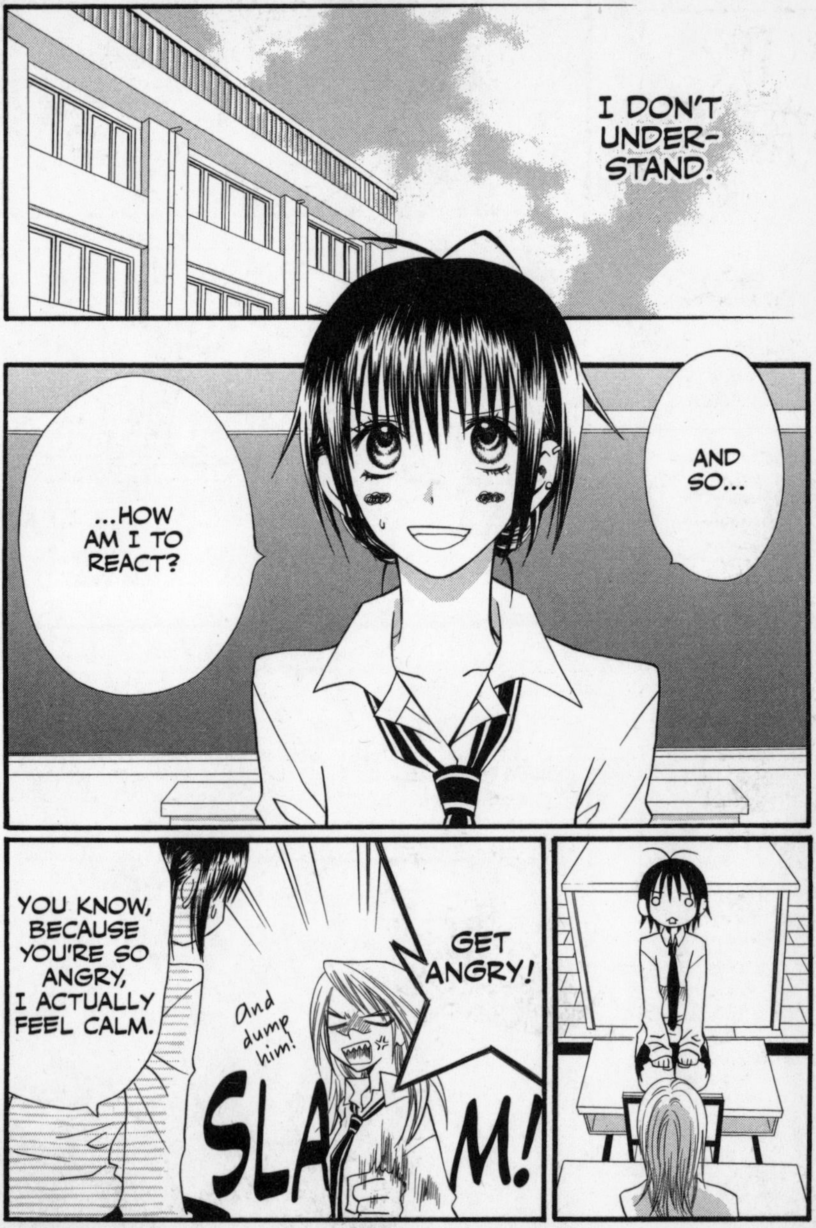
I DON'T UNDER-STAND.
AND SO...
...HOW AM I TO REACT?
GET ANGRY!
And dump him!
SLAM!
YOU KNOW, BECAUSE YOU'RE SO ANGRY, I ACTUALLY FEEL CALM.

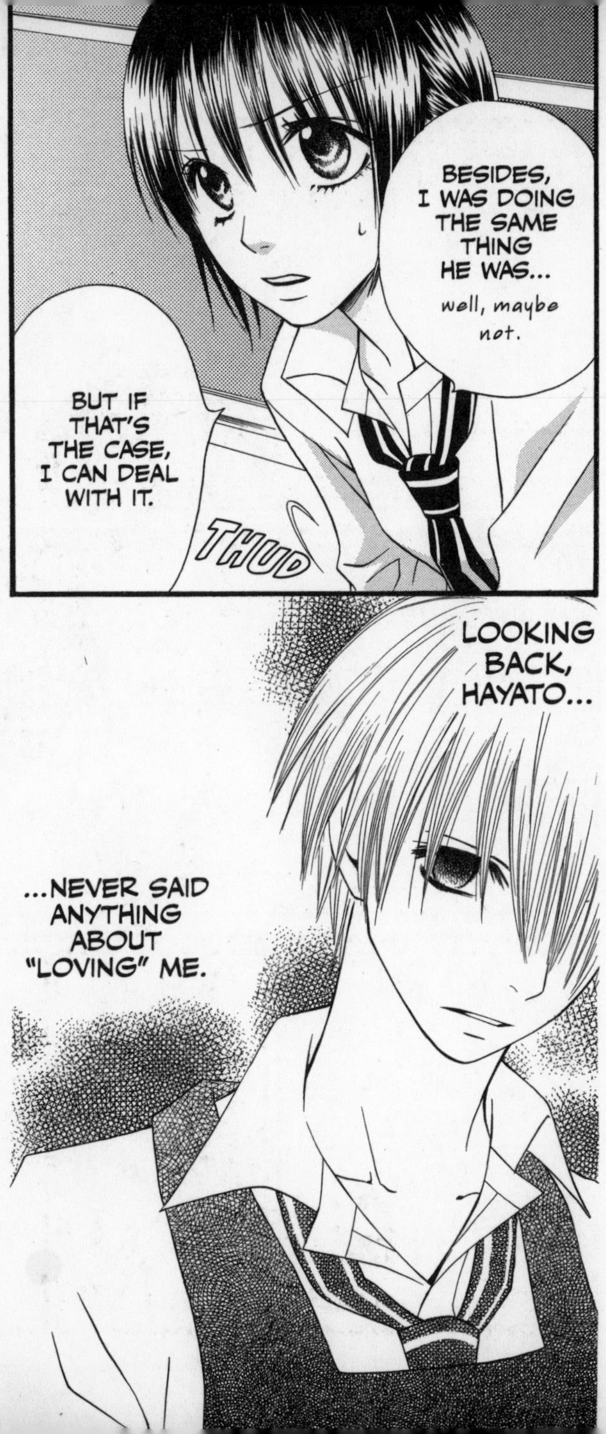
BESIDES, I WAS DOING THE SAME THING HE WAS...
well, maybe not.
BUT IF THAT'S THE CASE, I CAN DEAL WITH IT.
THUD
LOOKING BACK, HAYATO...
...NEVER SAID ANYTHING ABOUT "LOVING" ME.

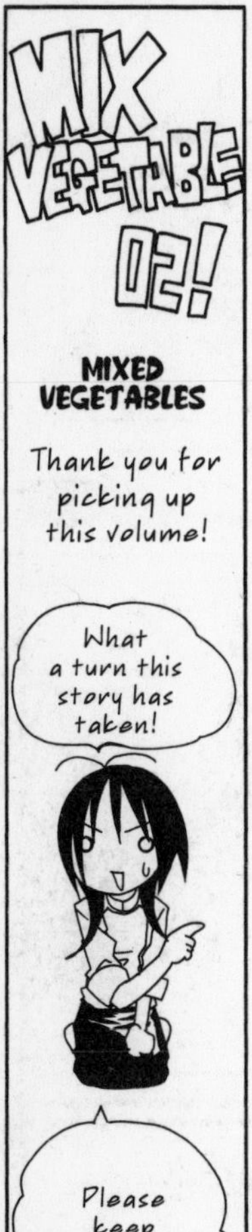
MIX VEGETABLE 02!
MIXED VEGETABLES
Thank you for picking up this volume!
What a turn this story has taken!
Please keep reading!
Keep reading! Keep reading!
Cheer-leading.

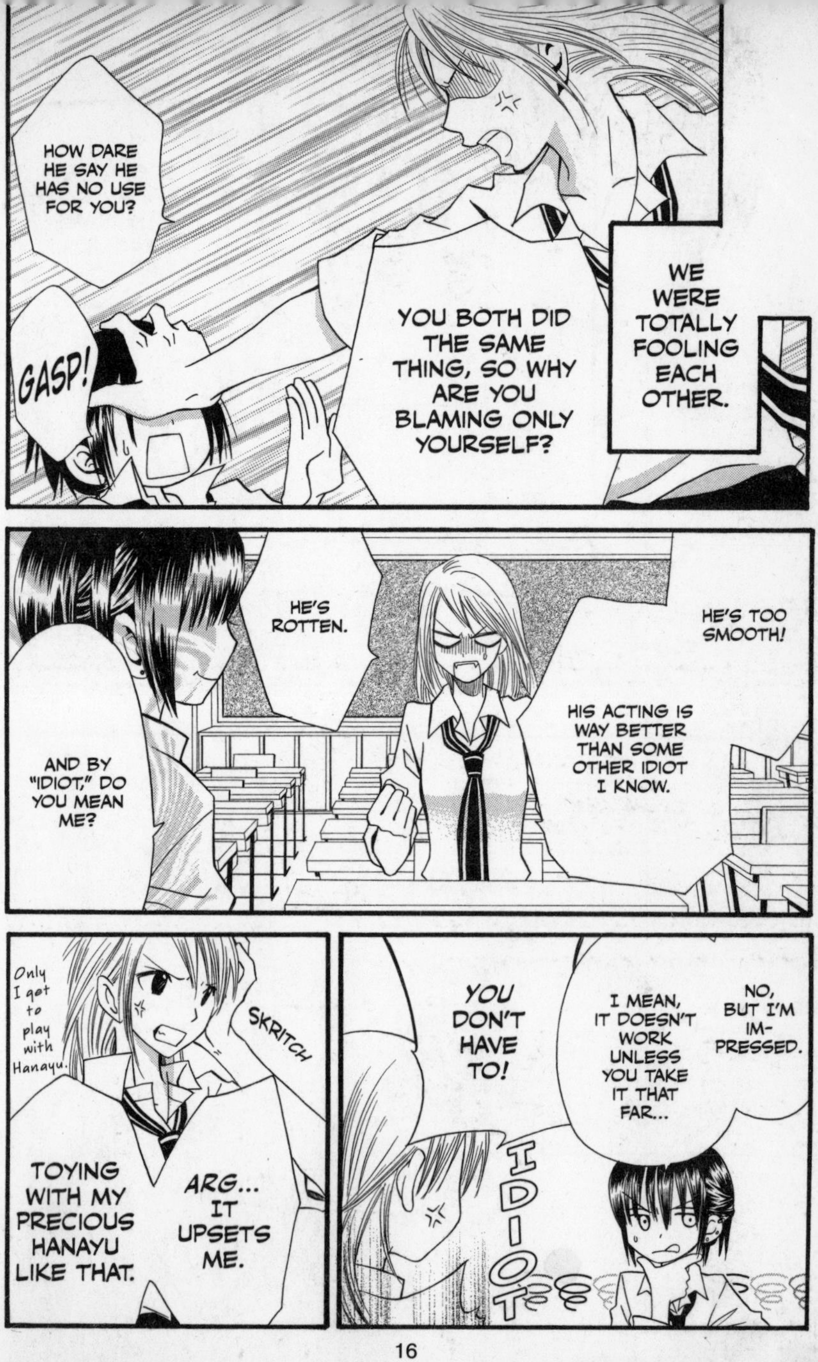
HOW DARE HE SAY HE HAS NO USE FOR YOU?
WE WERE TOTALLY FOOLING EACH OTHER.
YOU BOTH DID THE SAME THING, SO WHY ARE YOU BLAMING ONLY YOURSELF?
GASP!
HE'S TOO SMOOTH!
HE'S ROTTEN.
HIS ACTING IS WAY BETTER THAN SOME OTHER IDIOT I KNOW.
AND BY "IDIOT," DO YOU MEAN ME?
NO, BUT I'M IM-PRESSED.
I MEAN, IT DOESN'T WORK UNLESS YOU TAKE IT THAT FAR...
YOU DON'T HAVE TO!
IDIOT
SKRITCH
Only I get to play with Hanayu.
ARG... IT UPSETS ME.
TOYING WITH MY PRECIOUS HANAYU LIKE THAT.

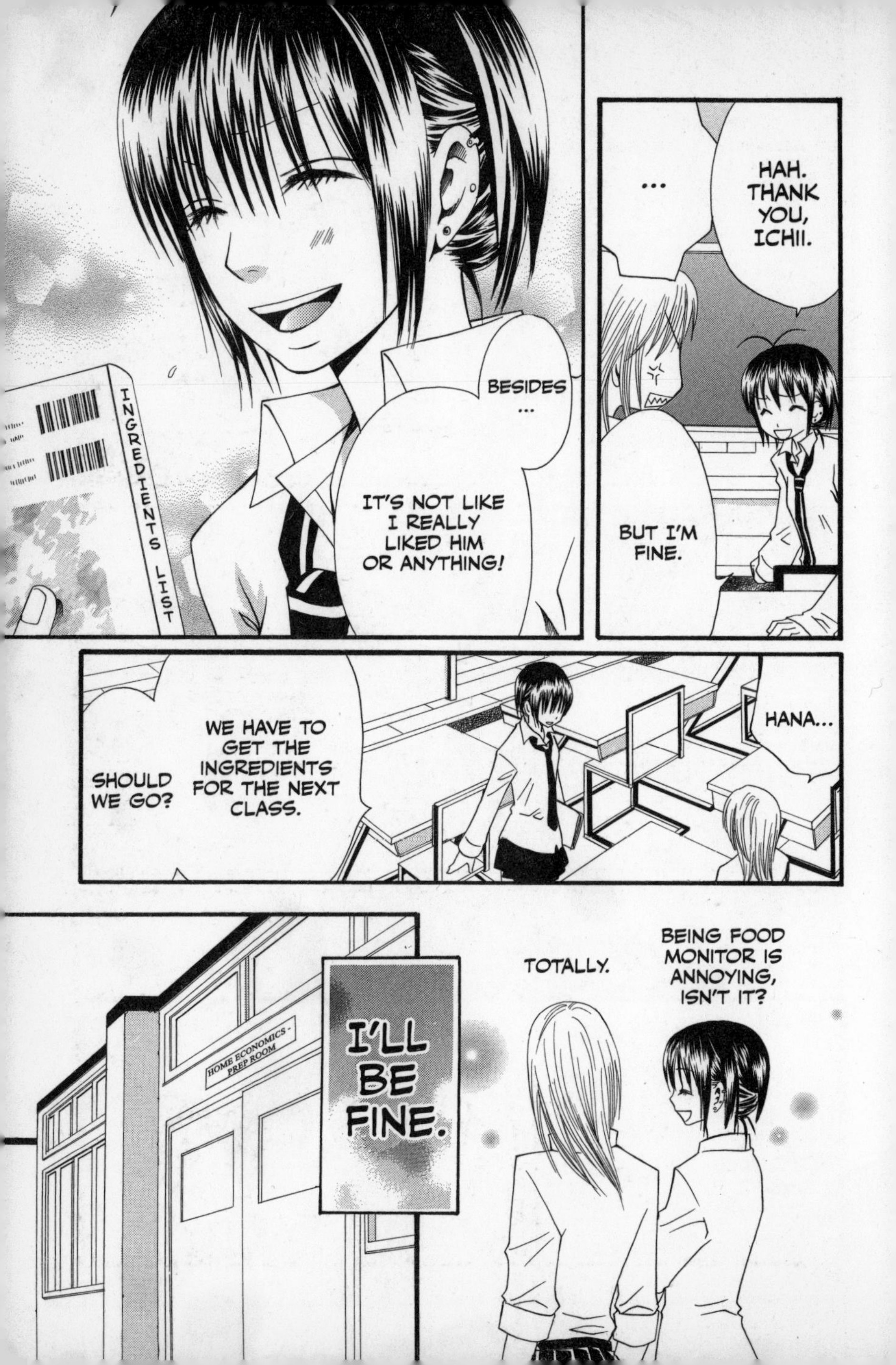
HAH. THANK YOU, ICHII.
...
BUT I'M FINE.
BESIDES...
IT'S NOT LIKE I REALLY LIKED HIM OR ANYTHING!
INGREDIENTS LIST
HANA...
WE HAVE TO GET THE INGREDIENTS FOR THE NEXT CLASS.
SHOULD WE GO?
BEING FOOD MONITOR IS ANNOYING, ISN'T IT?
TOTALLY.
I'LL BE FINE.
HOME ECONOMICS - PREP ROOM

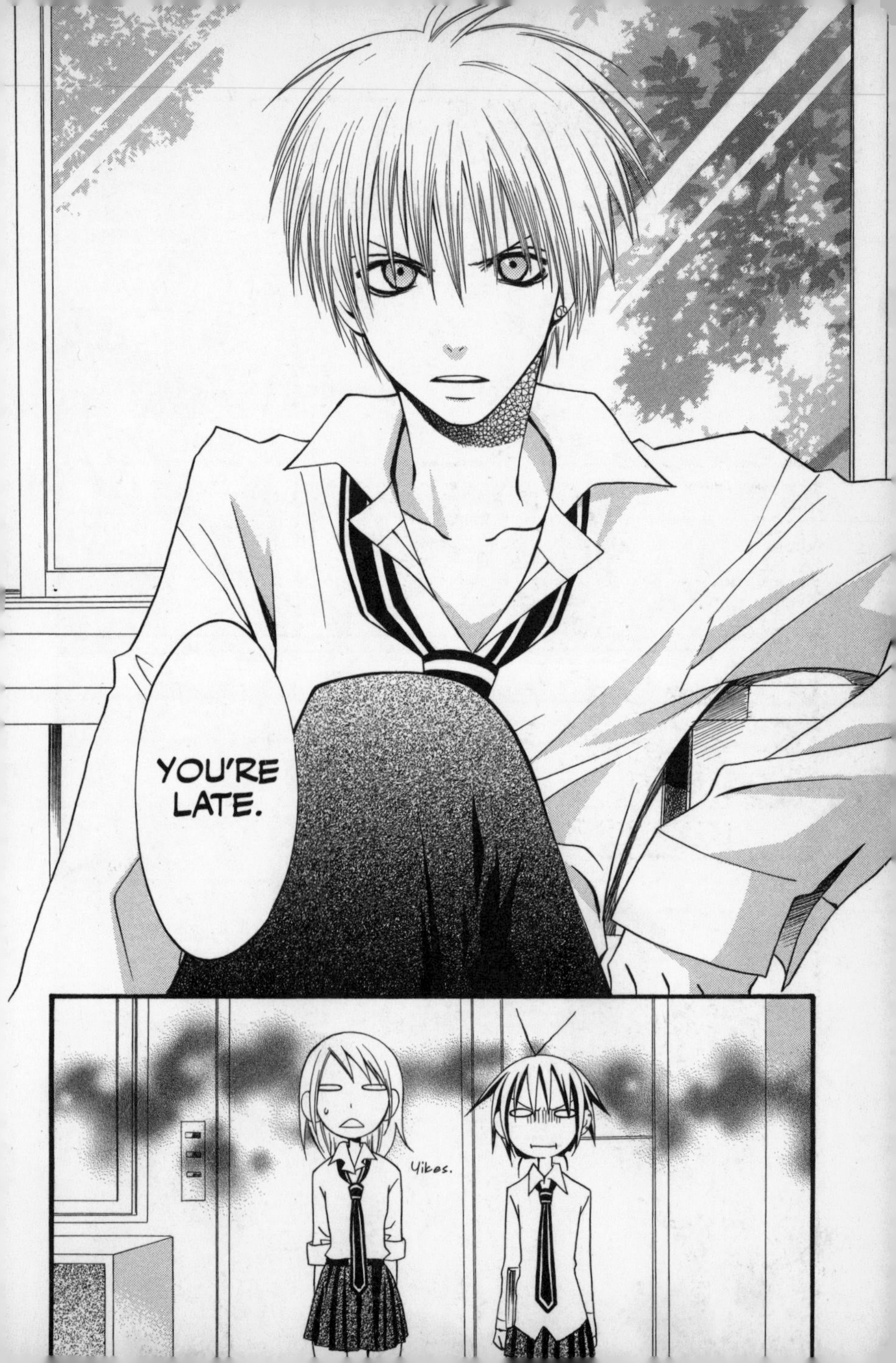
YOU'RE LATE.
Yikes.

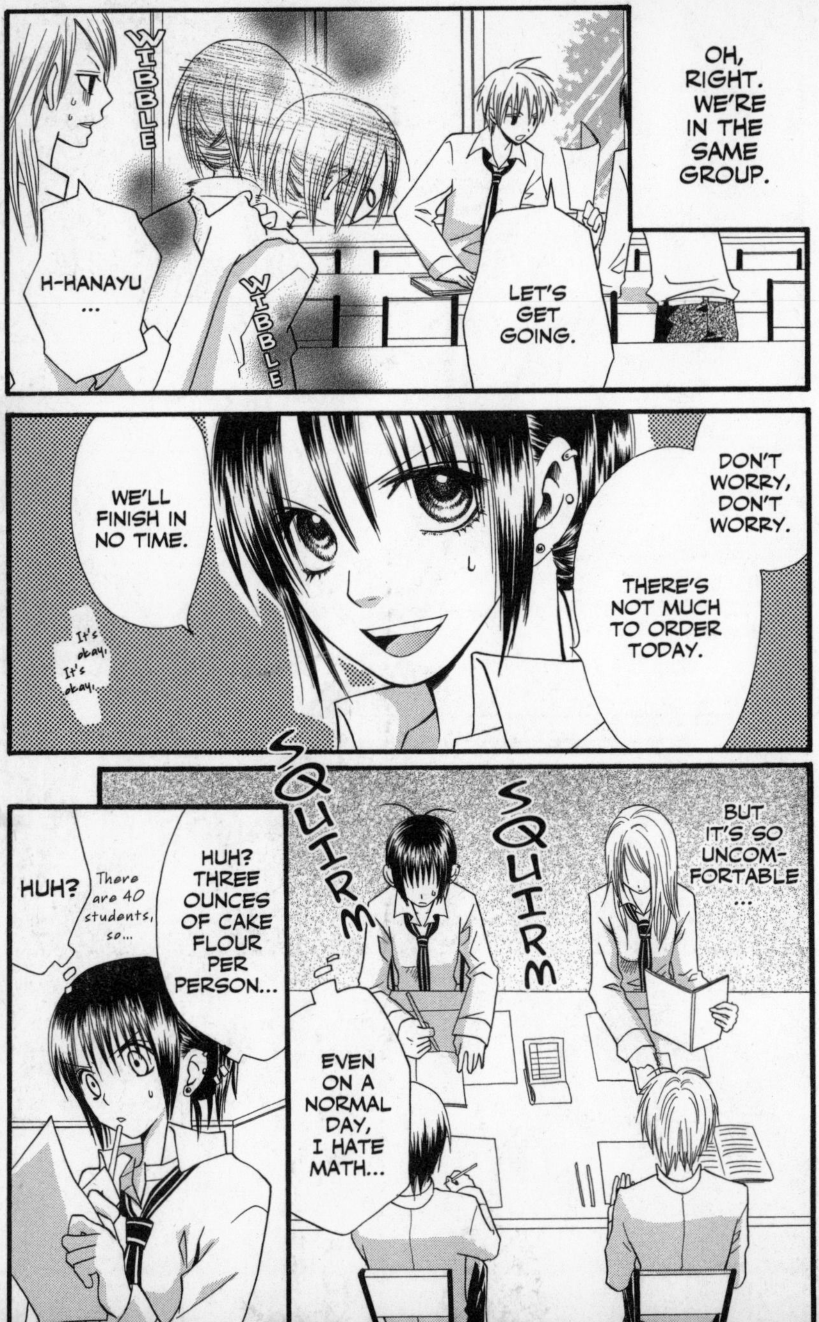
OH, RIGHT. WE'RE IN THE SAME GROUP.
LET'S GET GOING.
WIBBLE
WIBBLE
H-HANAYU ...
DON'T WORRY, DON'T WORRY.
THERE'S NOT MUCH TO ORDER TODAY.
WE'LL FINISH IN NO TIME.
It's okay, It's okay,
BUT IT'S SO UNCOM-FORTABLE ...
SQUIRM
SQUIRM
EVEN ON A NORMAL DAY, I HATE MATH...
HUH? THREE OUNCES OF CAKE FLOUR PER PERSON...
There are 40 students, so...
HUH?

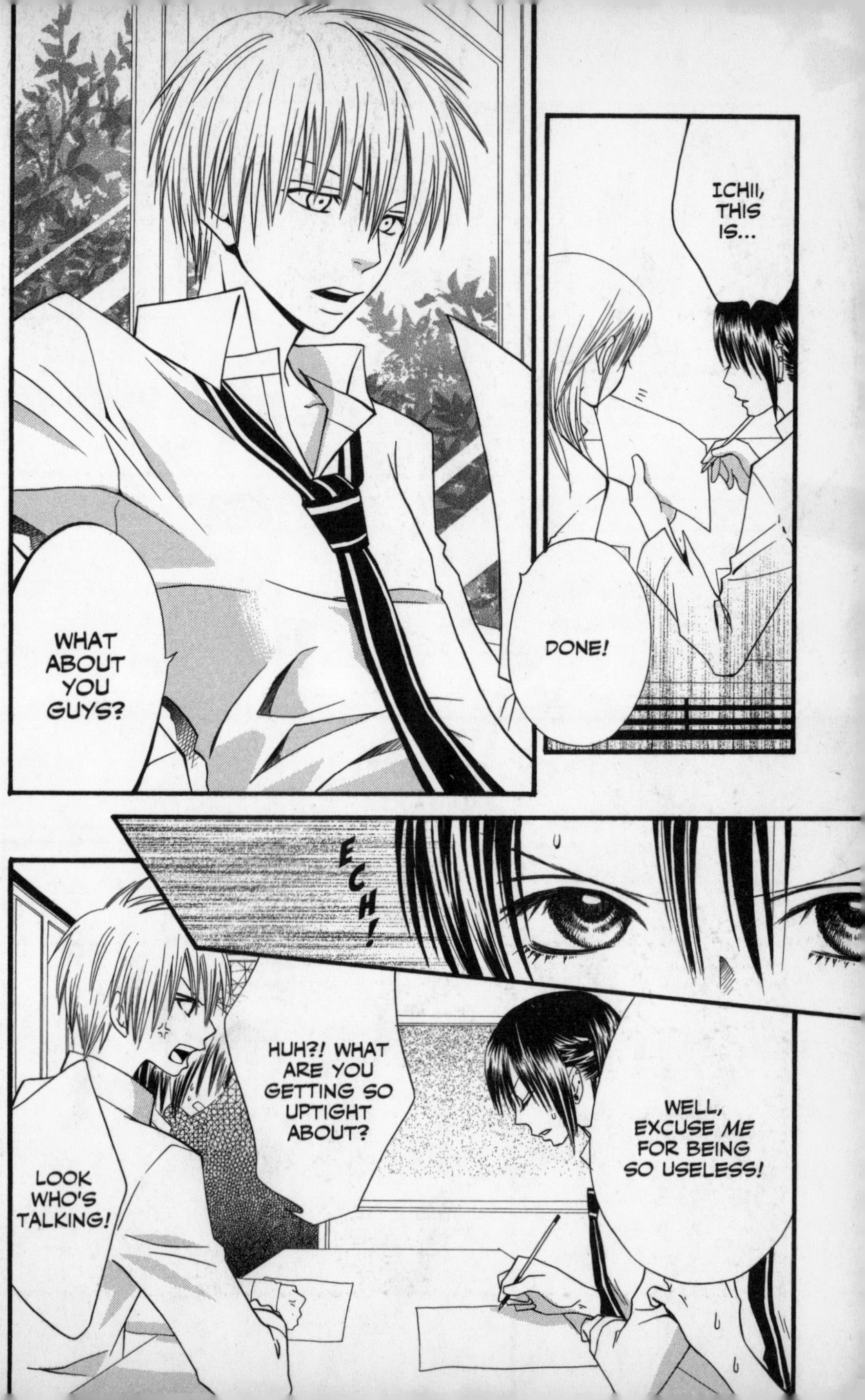
ICHII, THIS IS...
DONE!
WHAT ABOUT YOU GUYS?
ECH!
WELL, EXCUSE *ME* FOR BEING SO USELESS!
HUH?! WHAT ARE YOU GETTING SO UPTIGHT ABOUT?
LOOK WHO'S TALKING!

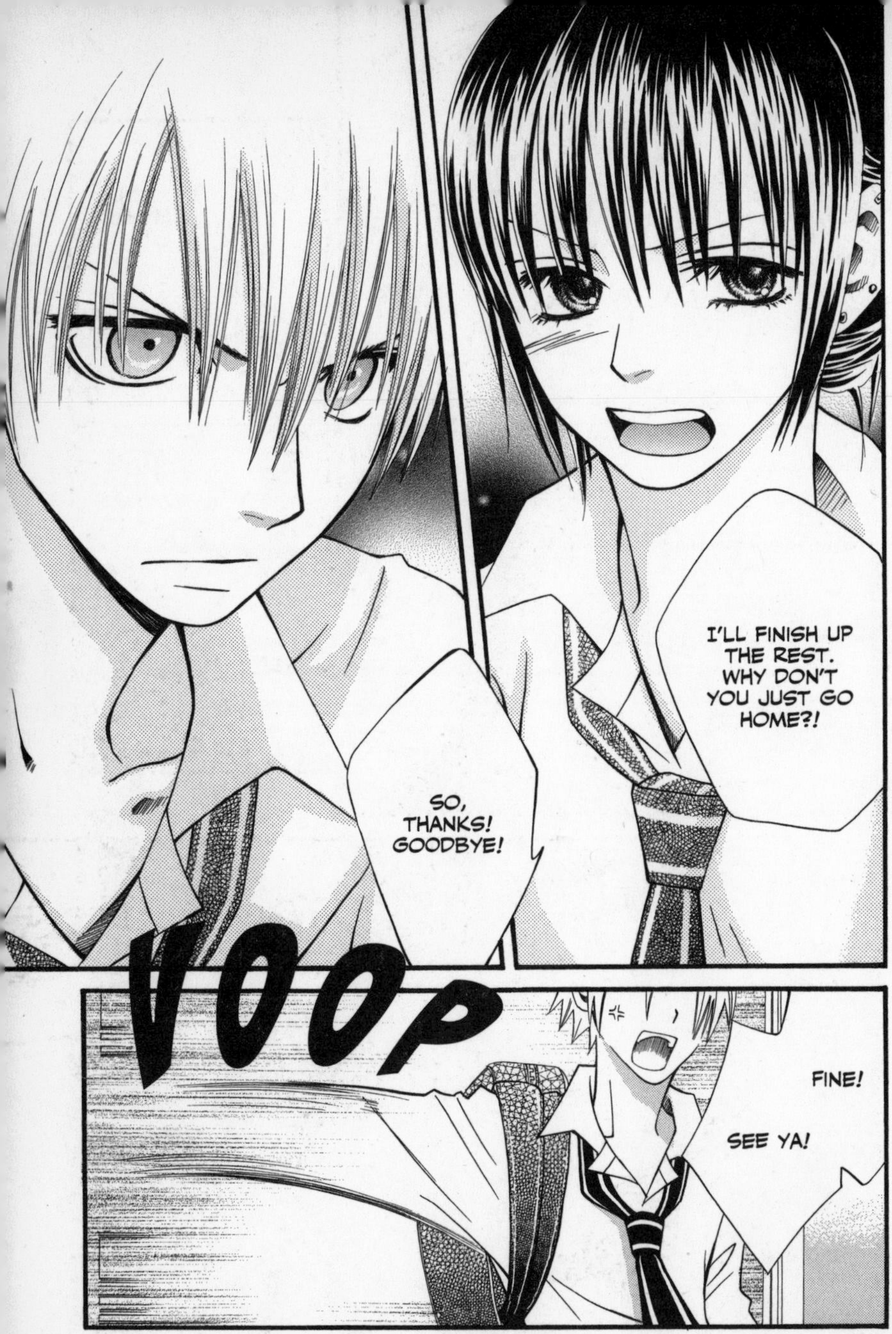
I'LL FINISH UP THE REST. WHY DON'T YOU JUST GO HOME?!
SO, THANKS! GOODBYE!
FINE!
SEE YA!
VOOP

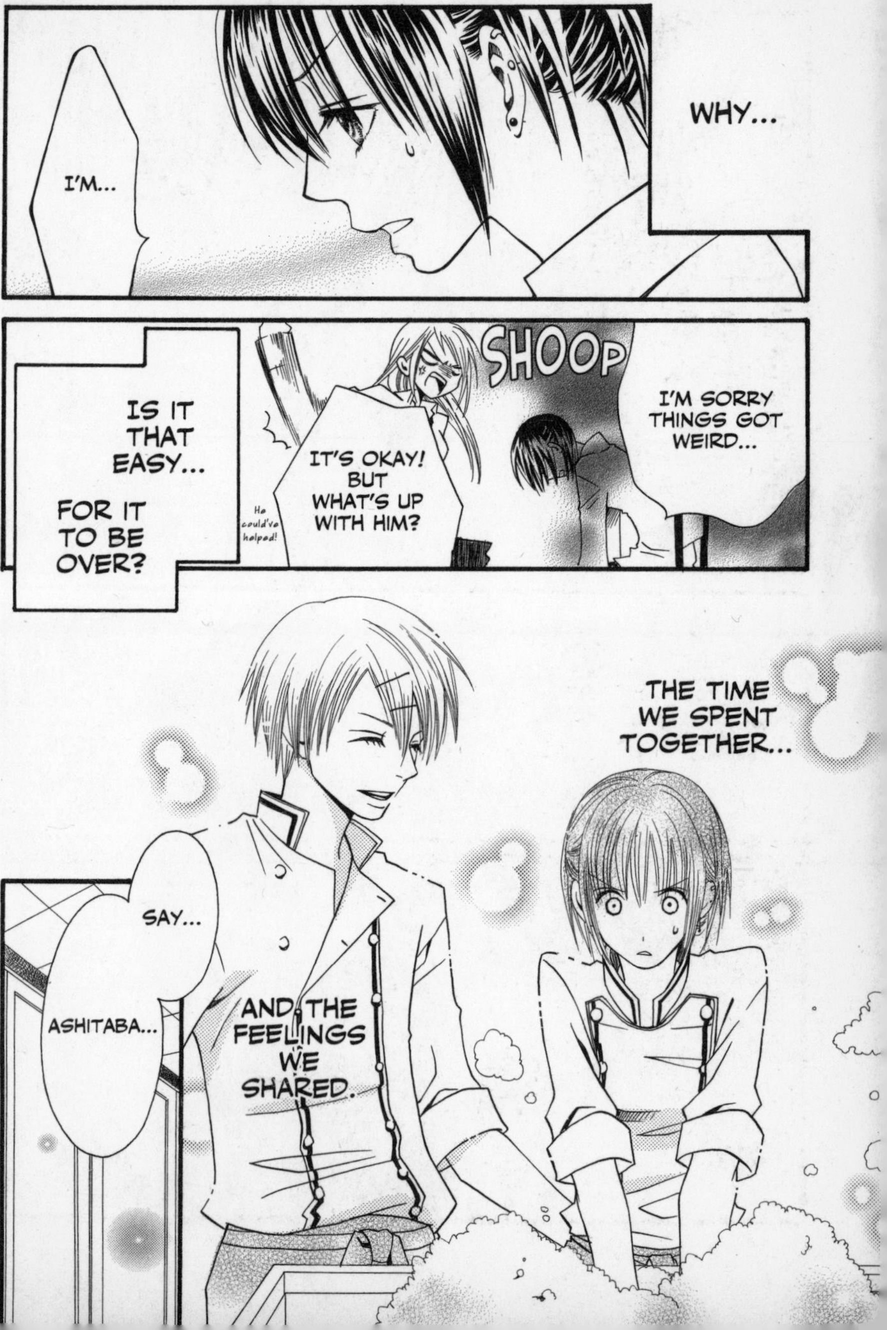
WHY...
I'M...
I'M SORRY THINGS GOT WEIRD...
SHOOP
IT'S OKAY! BUT WHAT'S UP WITH HIM?
He could've helped!
IS IT THAT EASY...
FOR IT TO BE OVER?
THE TIME WE SPENT TOGETHER...
AND THE FEELINGS WE SHARED.
SAY...
ASHITABA...

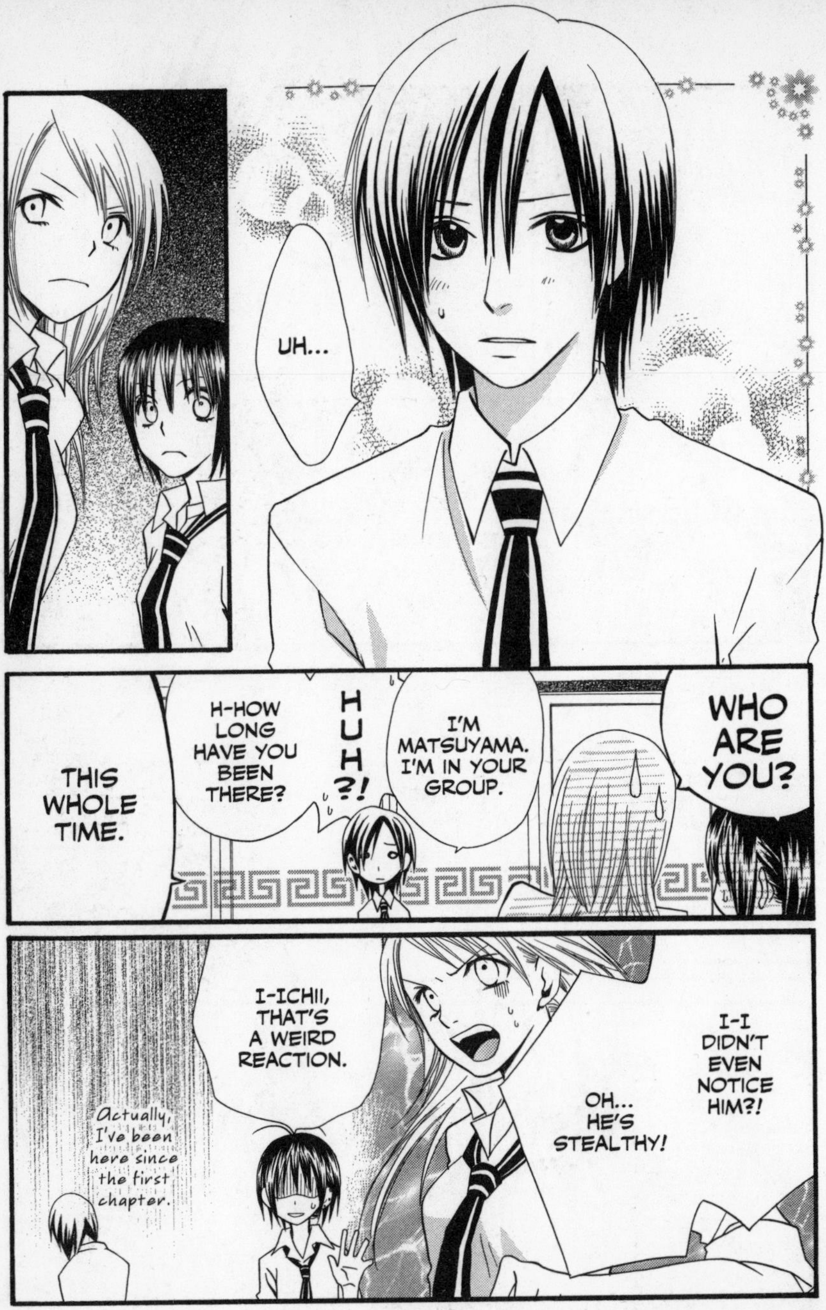
UH...
WHO ARE YOU?
I'M MATSUYAMA. I'M IN YOUR GROUP.
HUH?!
H-HOW LONG HAVE YOU BEEN THERE?
THIS WHOLE TIME.
I-I DIDN'T EVEN NOTICE HIM?!
OH... HE'S STEALTHY!
I-ICHII, THAT'S A WEIRD REACTION.
Actually, I've been here since the first chapter.

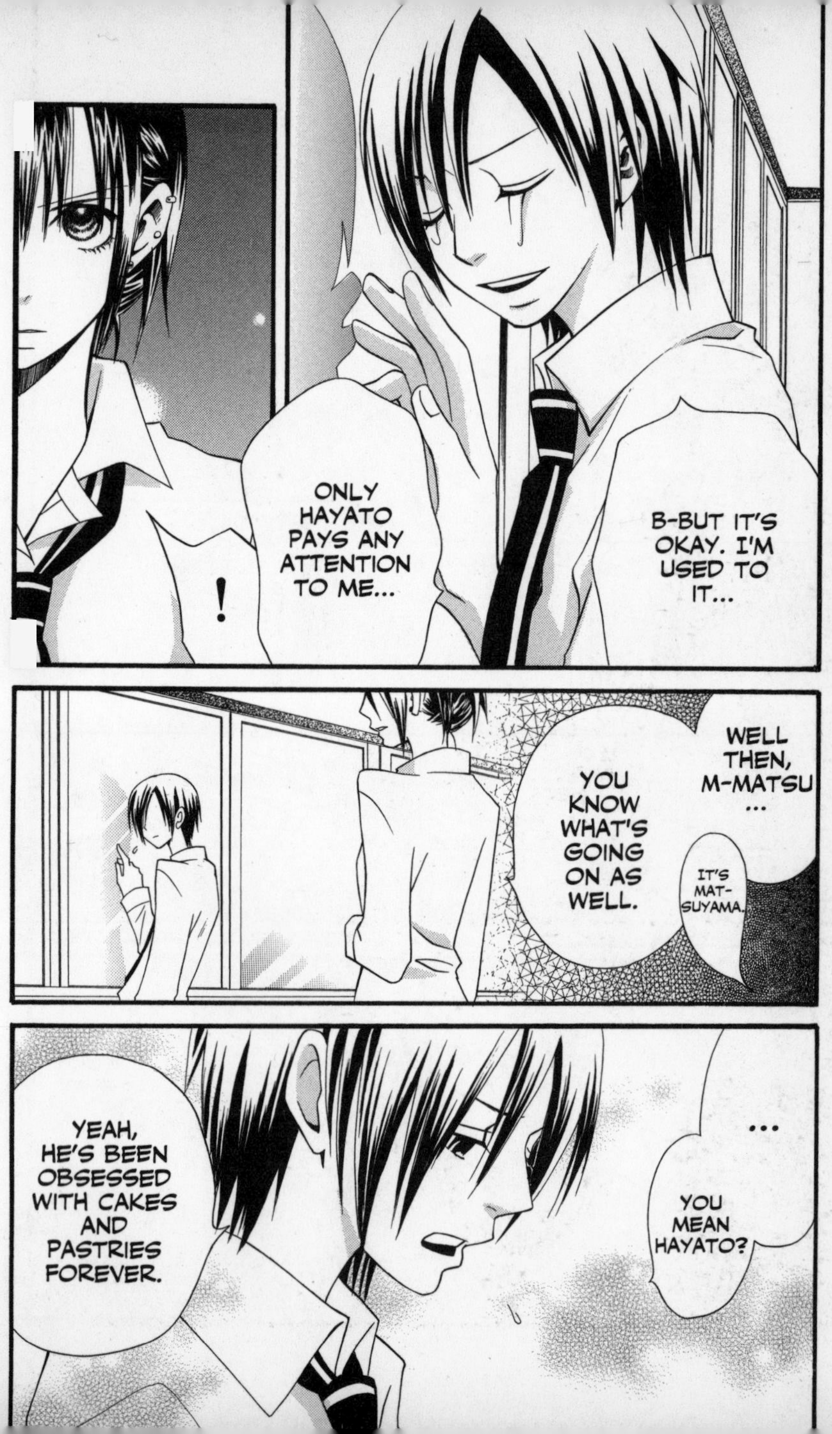
B-BUT IT'S OKAY. I'M USED TO IT...
ONLY HAYATO PAYS ANY ATTENTION TO ME...
!
WELL THEN, M-MATSU...
IT'S MAT-SUYAMA..
YOU KNOW WHAT'S GOING ON AS WELL.
...
YOU MEAN HAYATO?
YEAH, HE'S BEEN OBSESSED WITH CAKES AND PASTRIES FOREVER.

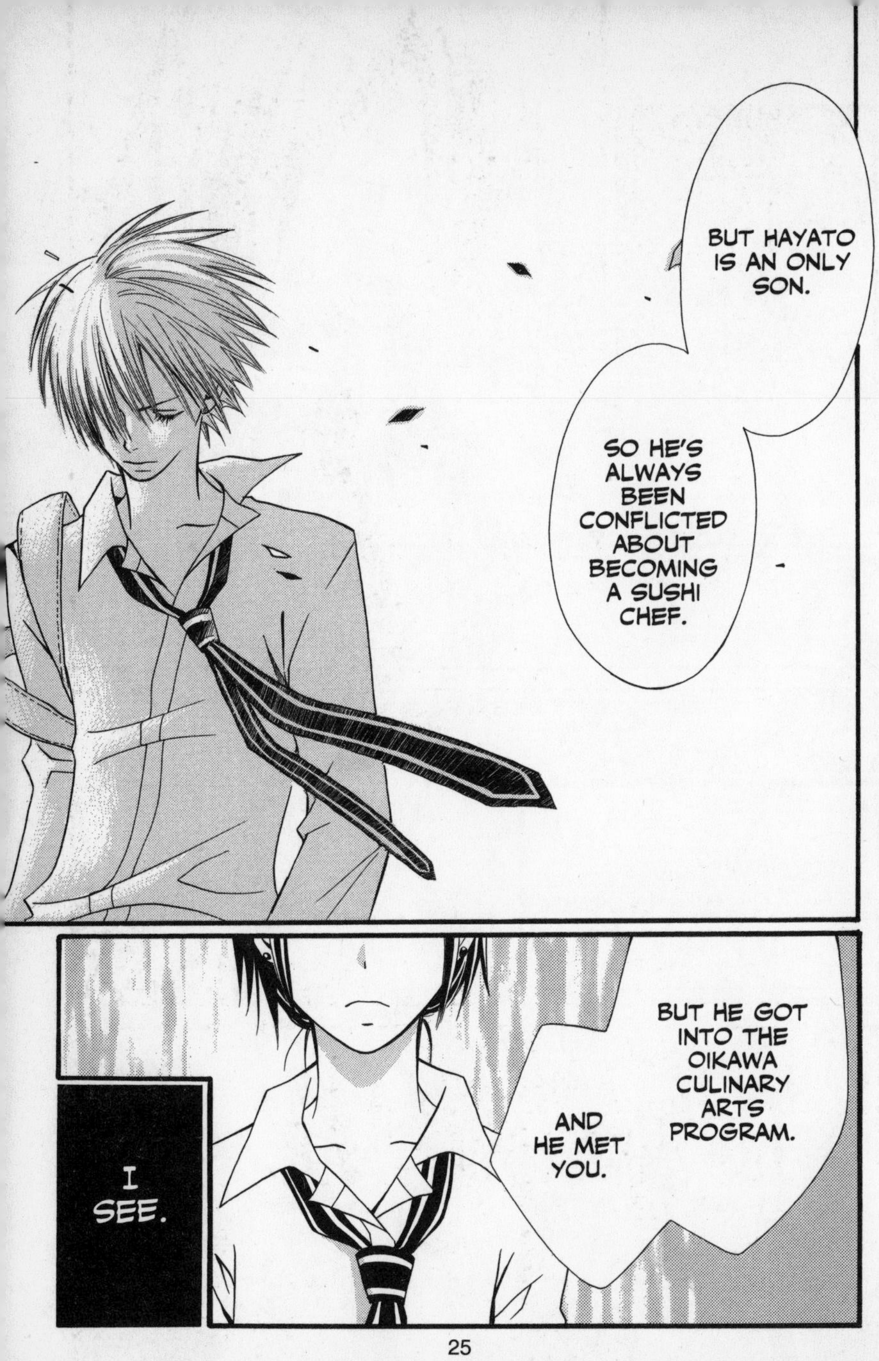
BUT HAYATO IS AN ONLY SON.
SO HE'S ALWAYS BEEN CONFLICTED ABOUT BECOMING A SUSHI CHEF.
BUT HE GOT INTO THE OIKAWA CULINARY ARTS PROGRAM.
AND HE MET YOU.
I SEE.

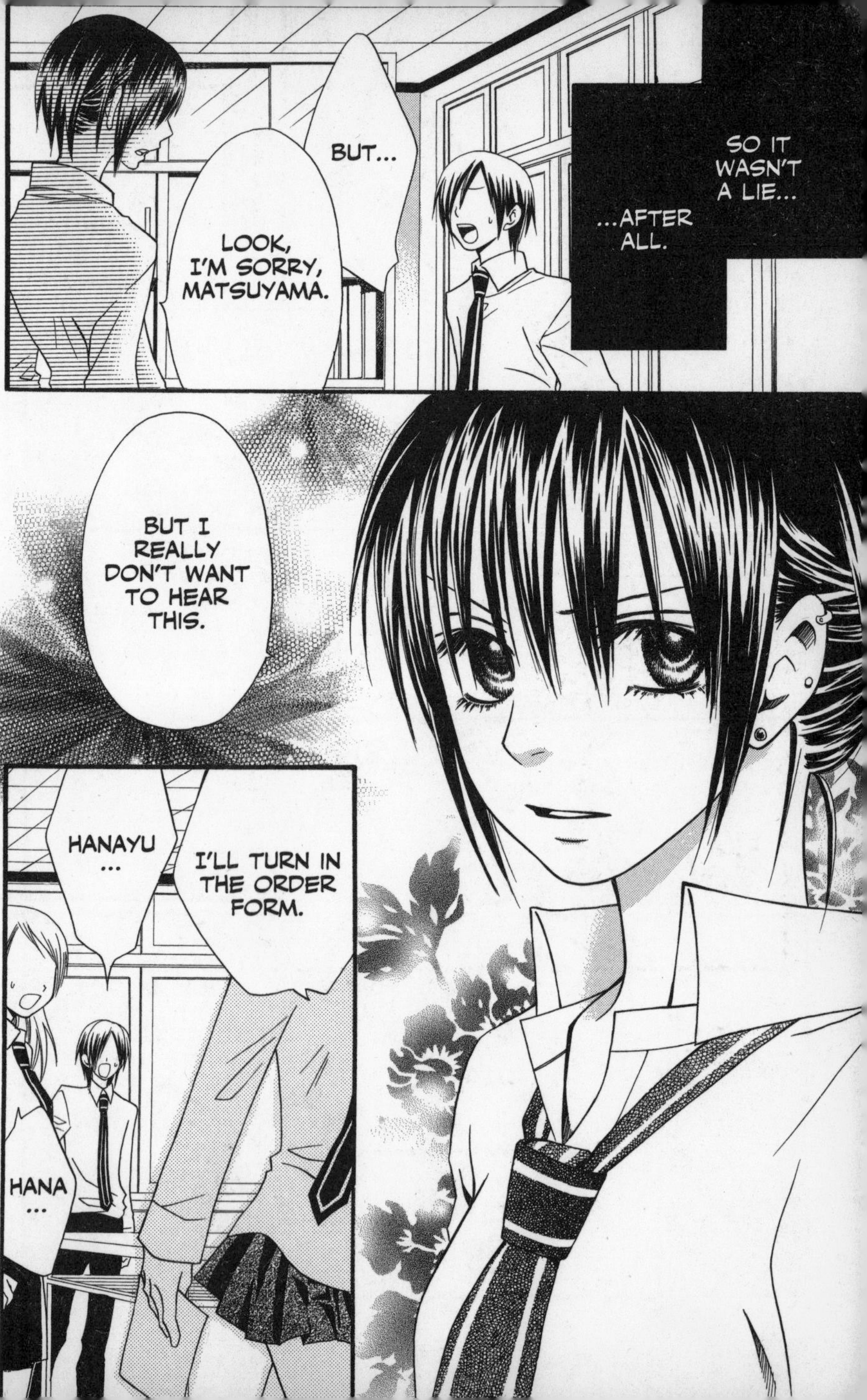
SO IT WASN'T A LIE...
...AFTER ALL.
BUT...
LOOK, I'M SORRY, MATSUYAMA.
BUT I REALLY DON'T WANT TO HEAR THIS.
I'LL TURN IN THE ORDER FORM.
HANAYU ...
HANA ...

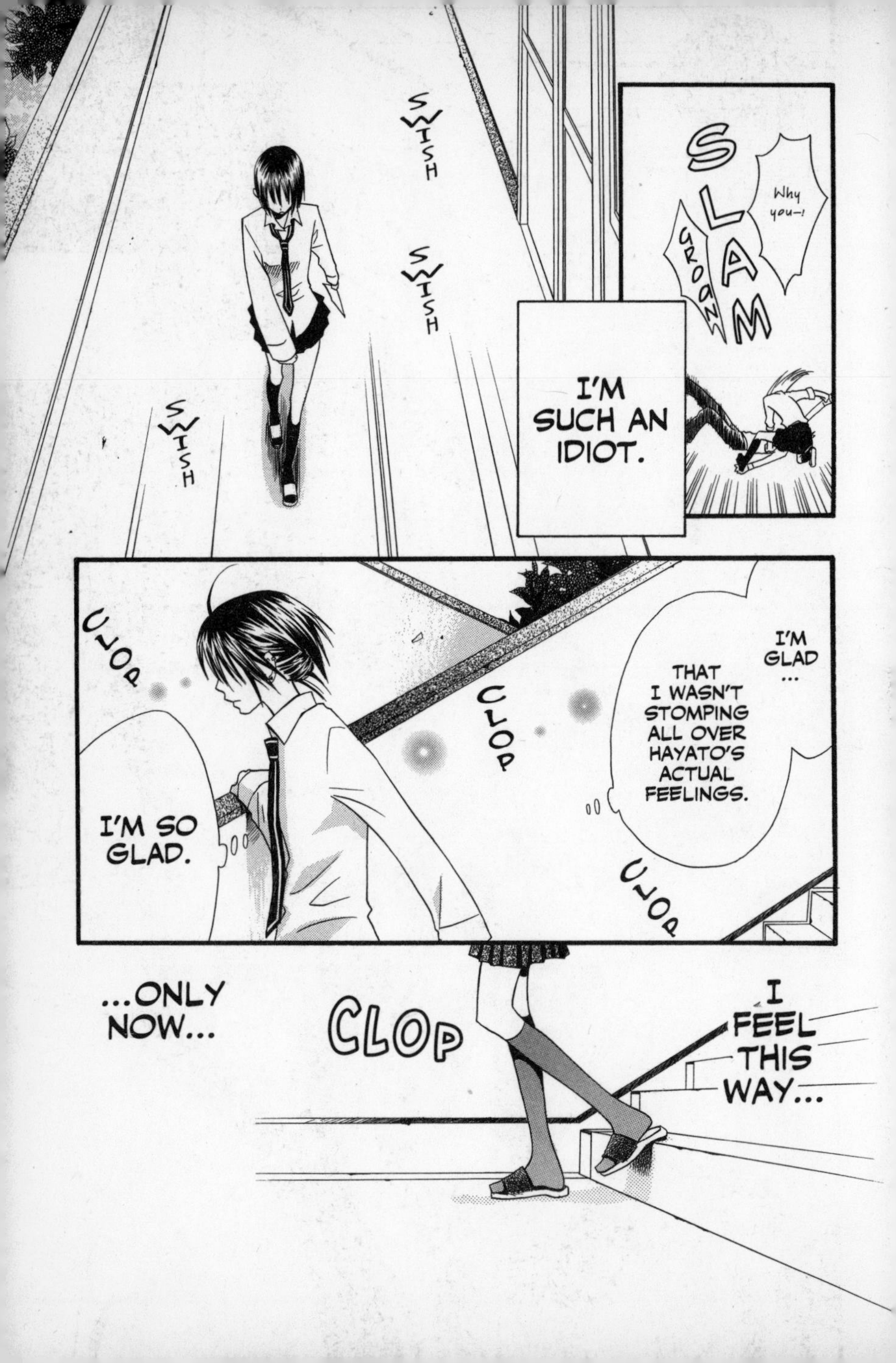
Why you—!
SLAM
GROAN
I'M SUCH AN IDIOT.
SWISH
SWISH
SWISH
I'M GLAD...
THAT I WASN'T STOMPING ALL OVER HAYATO'S ACTUAL FEELINGS.
CLOP
CLOP
CLOP
I'M SO GLAD.
I FEEL THIS WAY...
CLOP
...ONLY NOW...

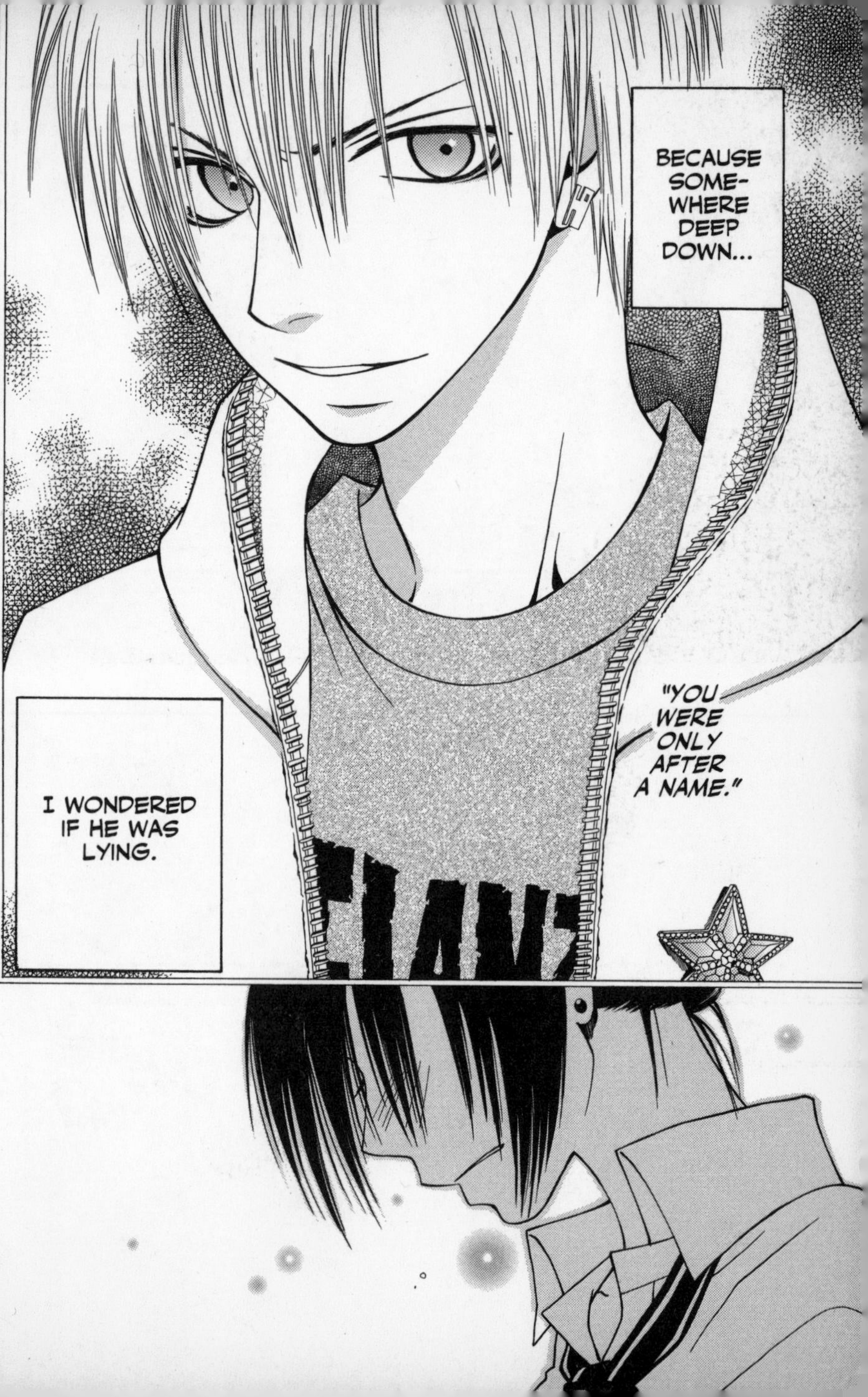
BECAUSE SOME-WHERE DEEP DOWN...
"YOU WERE ONLY AFTER A NAME."
I WONDERED IF HE WAS LYING.

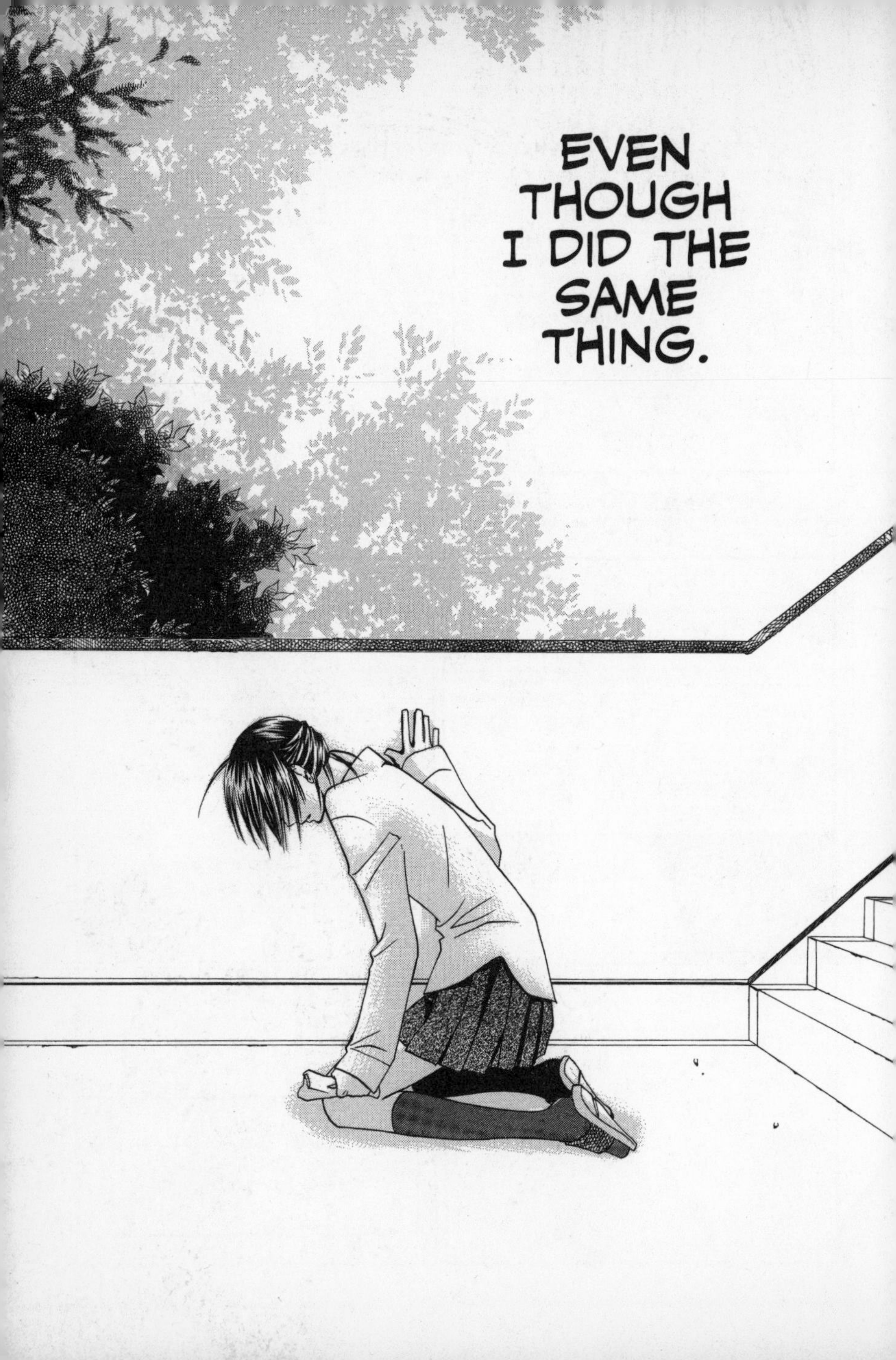
EVEN THOUGH I DID THE SAME THING.

SIDE DISH Mixed Vegetables 1

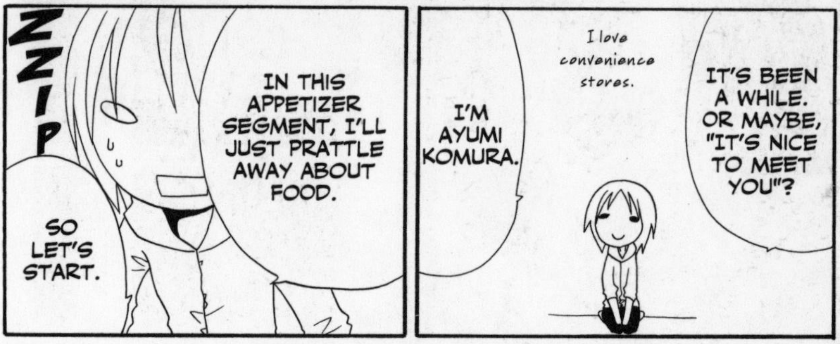
IT'S BEEN A WHILE. OR MAYBE, "IT'S NICE TO MEET YOU"?
I'M AYUMI KOMURA.
I love convenience stores.
IN THIS APPETIZER SEGMENT, I'LL JUST PRATTLE AWAY ABOUT FOOD.
ZZIP
SO LET'S START.

WHAT DO YOU THINK IS THE BEST DRINK TO HAVE WITH CHOCOLATE?

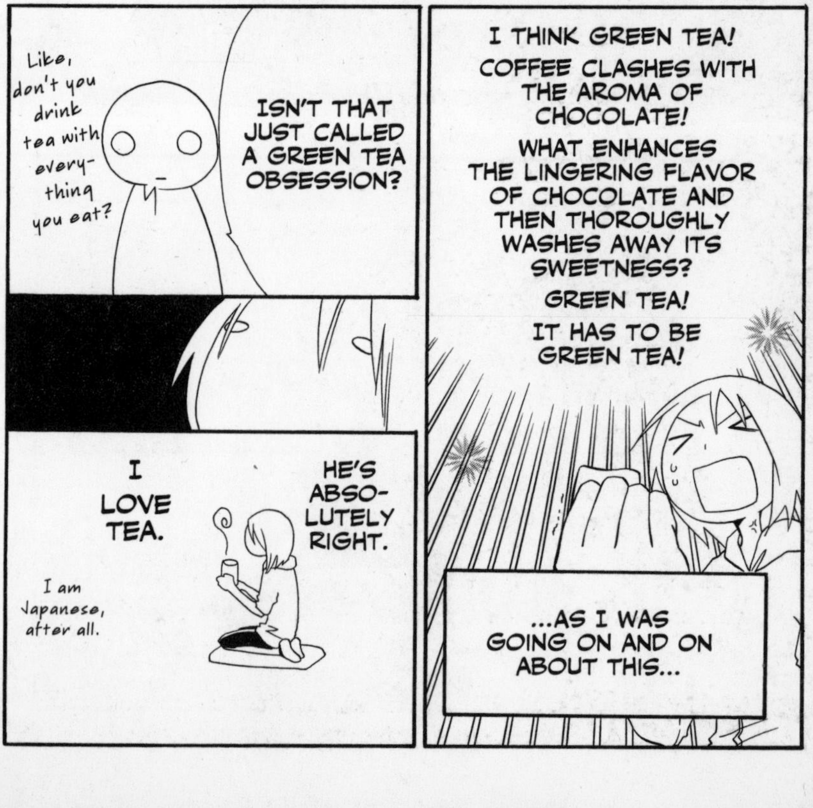
I THINK GREEN TEA!
COFFEE CLASHES WITH THE AROMA OF CHOCOLATE!
WHAT ENHANCES THE LINGERING FLAVOR OF CHOCOLATE AND THEN THOROUGHLY WASHES AWAY ITS SWEETNESS?
GREEN TEA!
IT HAS TO BE GREEN TEA!
...AS I WAS GOING ON AND ON ABOUT THIS...
ISN'T THAT JUST CALLED A GREEN TEA OBSESSION?
Like, don't you drink tea with every-thing you eat?
HE'S ABSO-LUTELY RIGHT.
I LOVE TEA.
I am Japanese, after all.

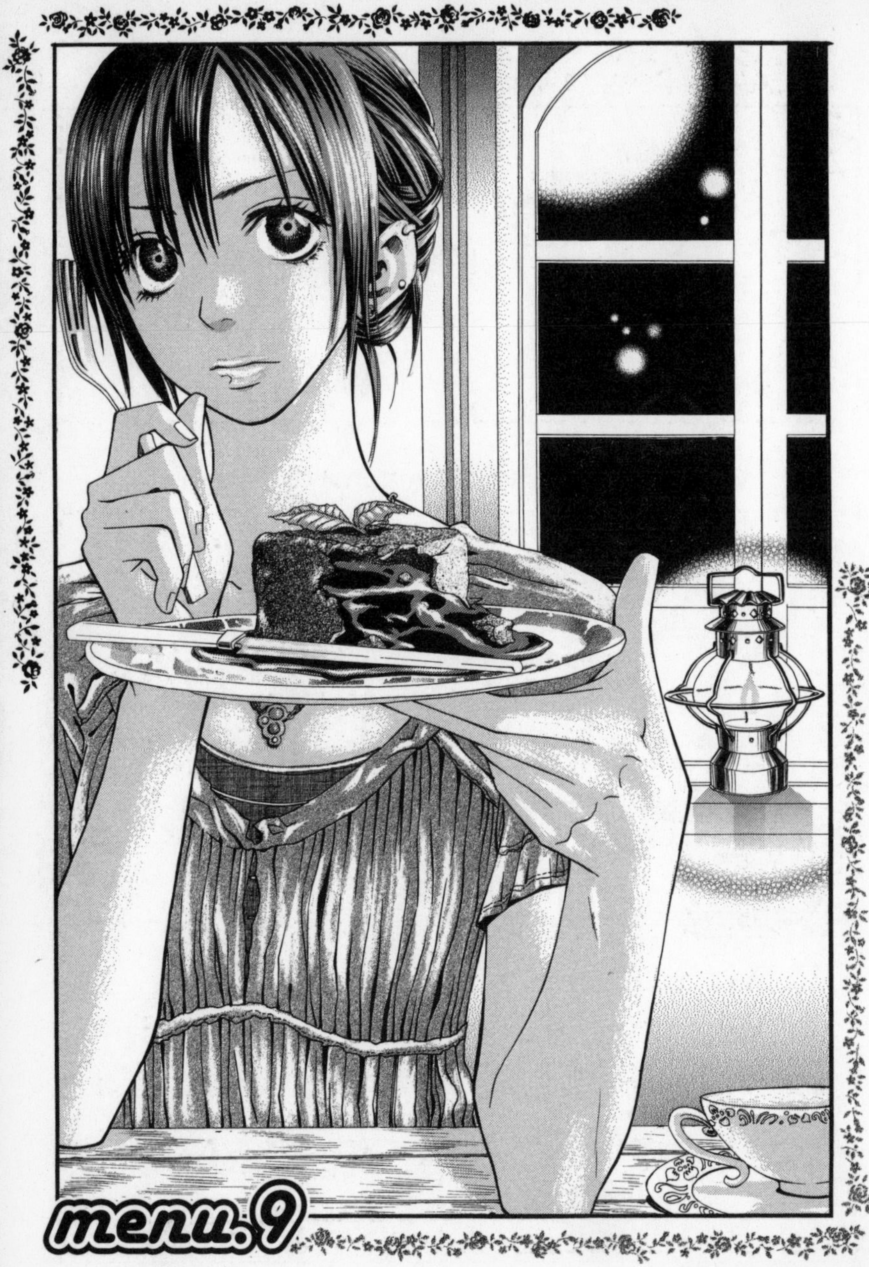
menu.9

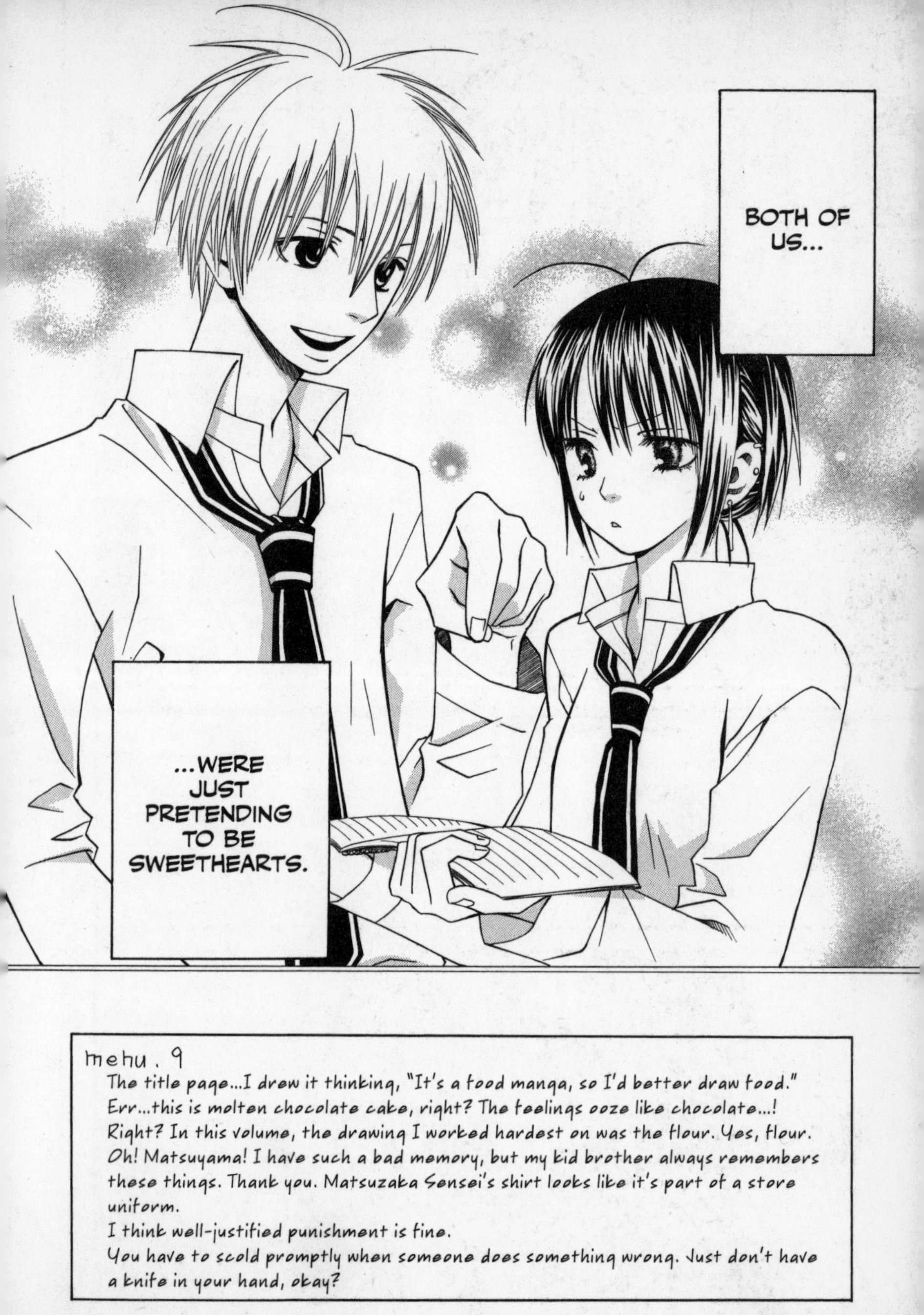
BOTH OF US...
...WERE JUST PRETENDING TO BE SWEETHEARTS.

menu . 9

The title page...I drew it thinking, "It's a food manga, so I'd better draw food." Err...this is molten chocolate cake, right? The feelings ooze like chocolate...! Right? In this volume, the drawing I worked hardest on was the flour. Yes, flour. Oh! Matsuyama! I have such a bad memory, but my kid brother always remembers these things. Thank you. Matsuzaka Sensei's shirt looks like it's part of a store uniform.

I think well-justified punishment is fine.

You have to scold promptly when someone does something wrong. Just don't have a knife in your hand, okay?

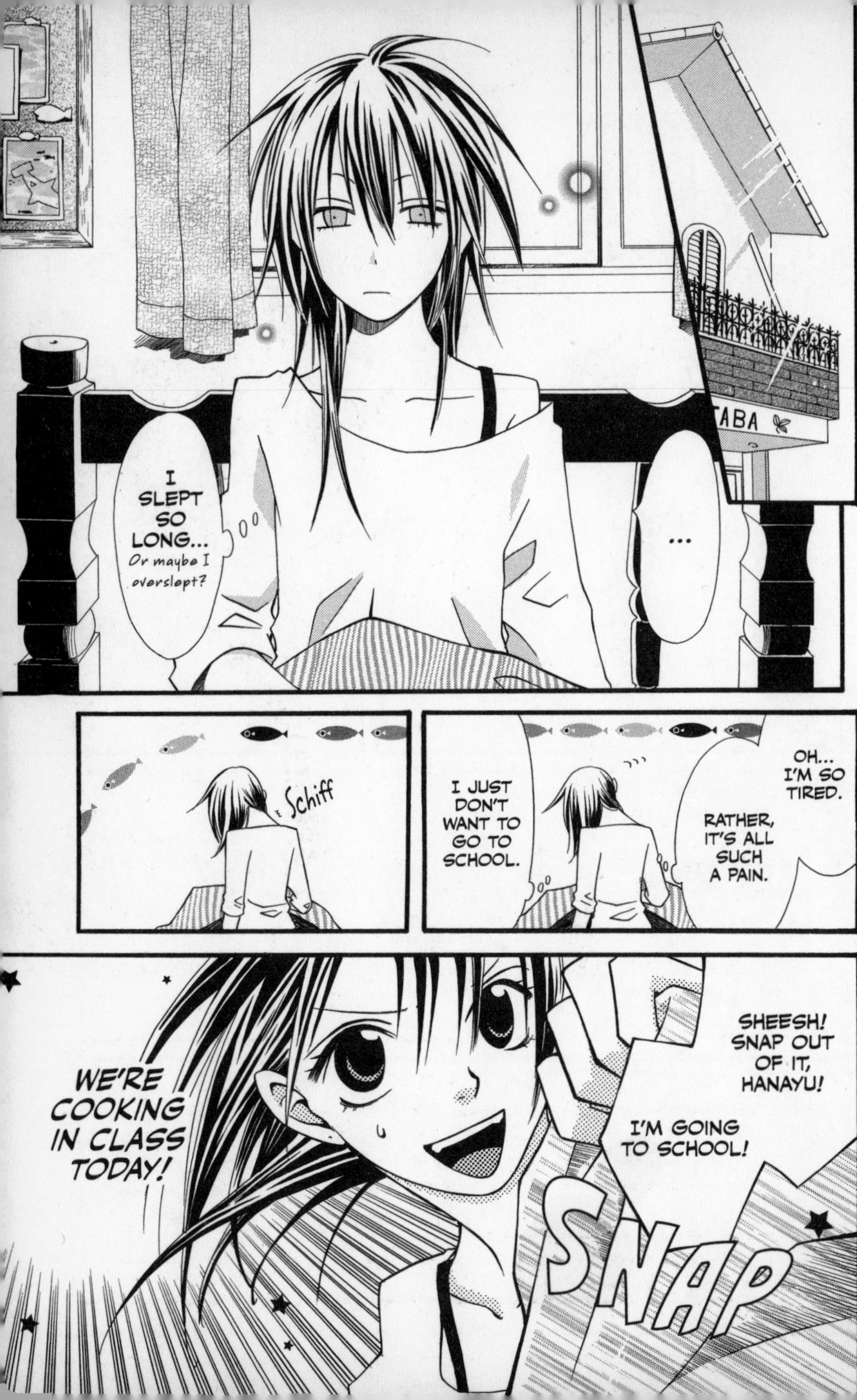
TABA
...
I SLEPT SO LONG... Or maybe I overslept?
OH... I'M SO TIRED.
RATHER, IT'S ALL SUCH A PAIN.
I JUST DON'T WANT TO GO TO SCHOOL.
Schiff
SHEESH! SNAP OUT OF IT, HANAYU!
I'M GOING TO SCHOOL!
WE'RE COOKING IN CLASS TODAY!
SNAP

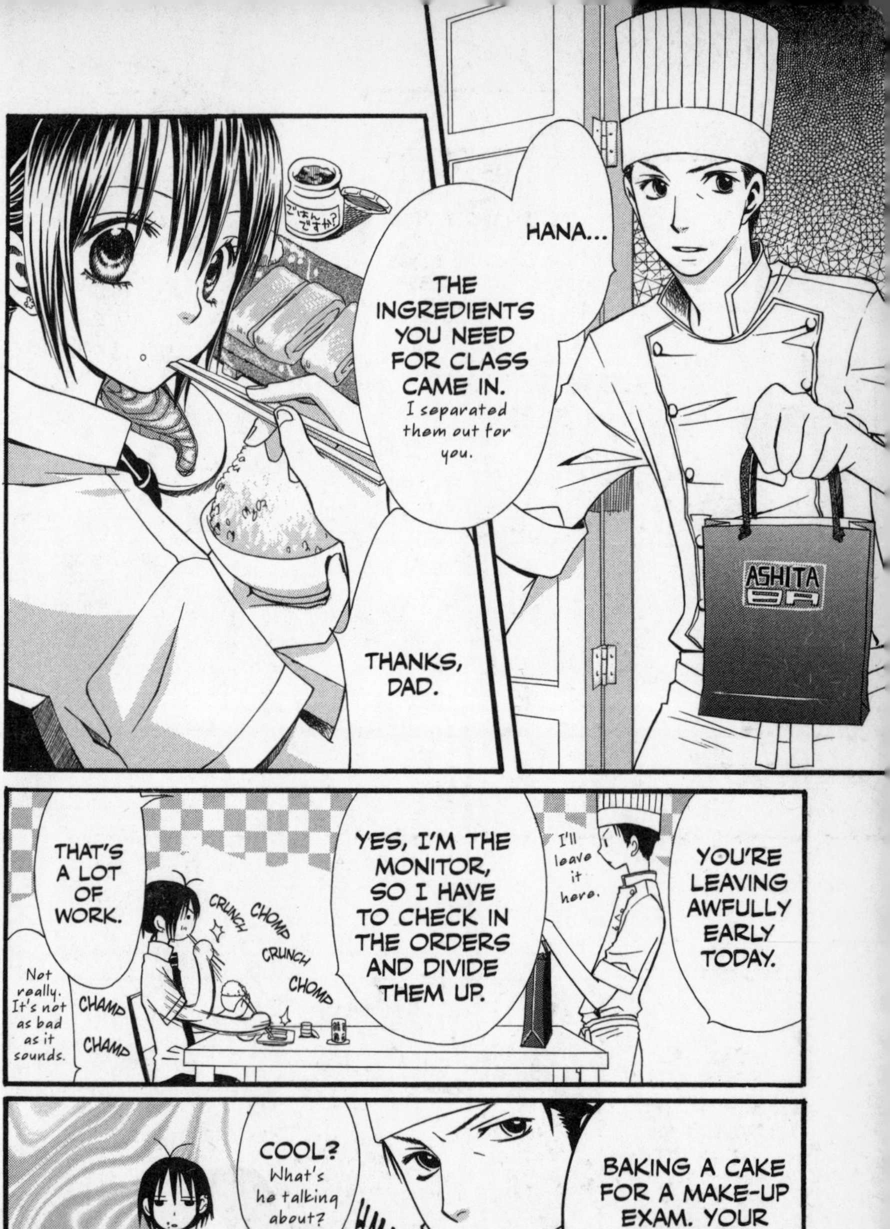
HANA...
THE INGREDIENTS YOU NEED FOR CLASS CAME IN.
I separated them out for you.
ASHITA BA
THANKS, DAD.
YOU'RE LEAVING AWFULLY EARLY TODAY.
I'll leave it here.
YES, I'M THE MONITOR, SO I HAVE TO CHECK IN THE ORDERS AND DIVIDE THEM UP.
CHOMP
CRUNCH
CRUNCH
CHOMP
THAT'S A LOT OF WORK.
Not really. It's not as bad as it sounds.
CHAMP
CHAMP
BAKING A CAKE FOR A MAKE-UP EXAM. YOUR TEACHER'S PRETTY COOL.
HMMM
COOL? What's he talking about?

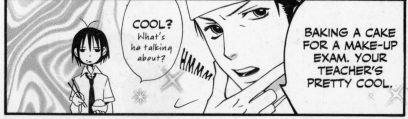

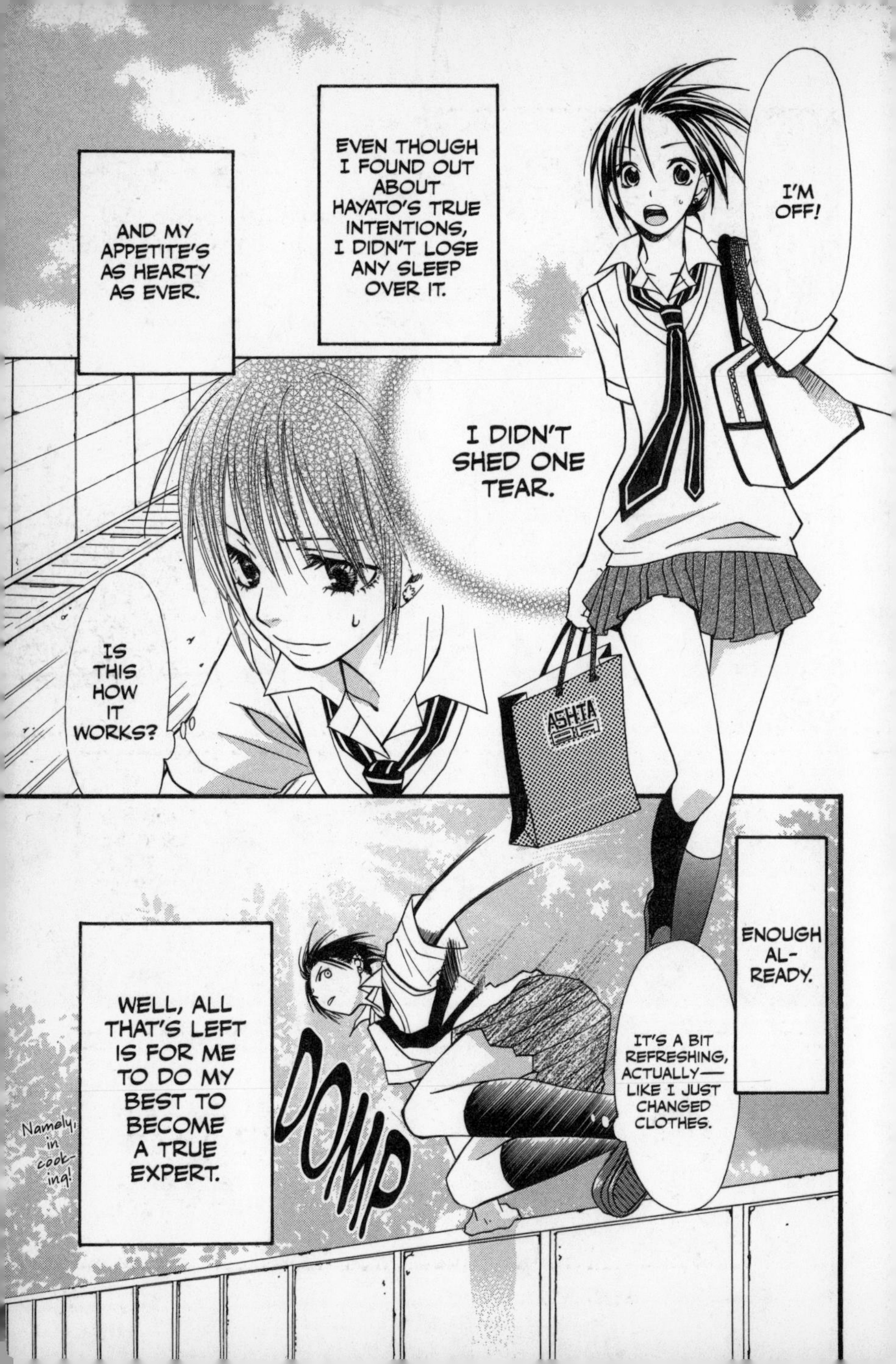
I'M OFF!
EVEN THOUGH I FOUND OUT ABOUT HAYATO'S TRUE INTENTIONS, I DIDN'T LOSE ANY SLEEP OVER IT.
AND MY APPETITE'S AS HEARTY AS EVER.
I DIDN'T SHED ONE TEAR.
IS THIS HOW IT WORKS?
ASHITA
ENOUGH AL-READY.
IT'S A BIT REFRESHING, ACTUALLY— LIKE I JUST CHANGED CLOTHES.
WELL, ALL THAT'S LEFT IS FOR ME TO DO MY BEST TO BECOME A TRUE EXPERT.
DOMP
Namely, in cook-ing!

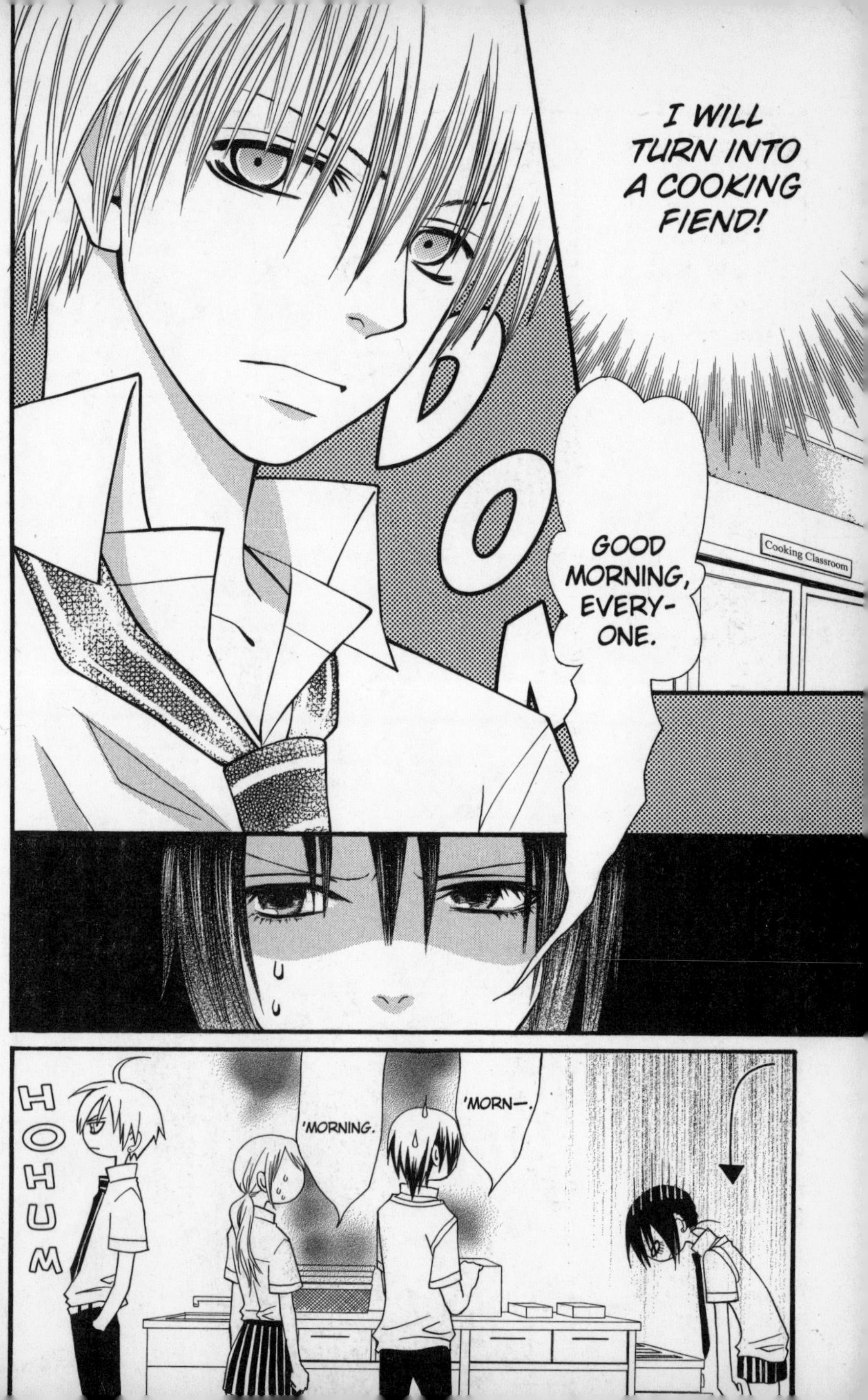
I WILL TURN INTO A COOKING FIEND!
Cooking Classroom
GOOD MORNING, EVERY-ONE.
'MORN—.
'MORNING.
HOHUM

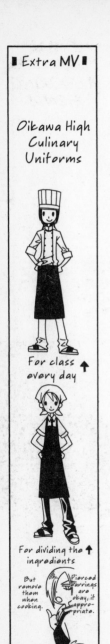

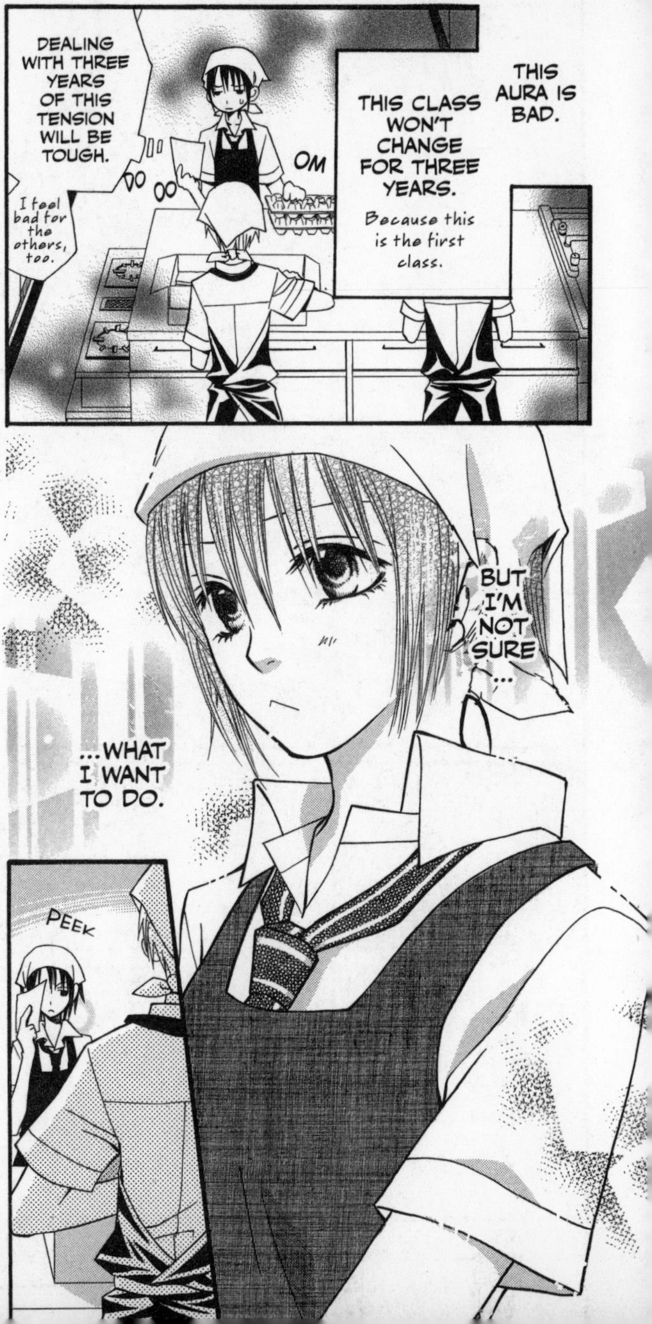
THIS AURA IS BAD.
THIS CLASS WON'T CHANGE FOR THREE YEARS.
Because this is the first class.
OM
DEALING WITH THREE YEARS OF THIS TENSION WILL BE TOUGH.
DO
DO
I feel bad for the others, too.
BUT I'M NOT SURE...
...WHAT I WANT TO DO.
PEEK

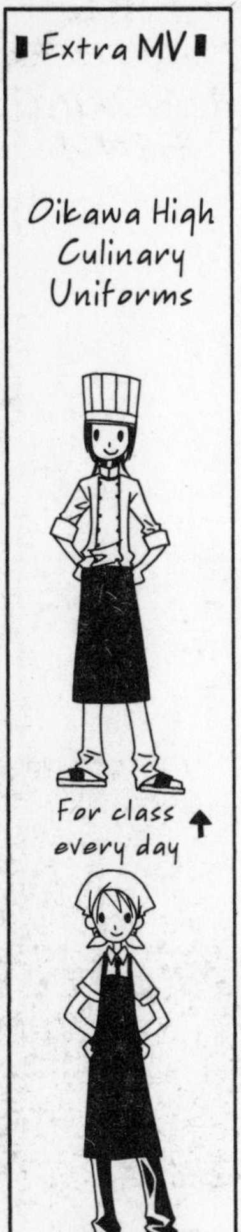
Extra MV
Oikawa High Culinary Uniforms
For class every day ↑
For dividing the ingredients ↑
Pierced earrings are okay, if appropriate.
But remove them when cooking.

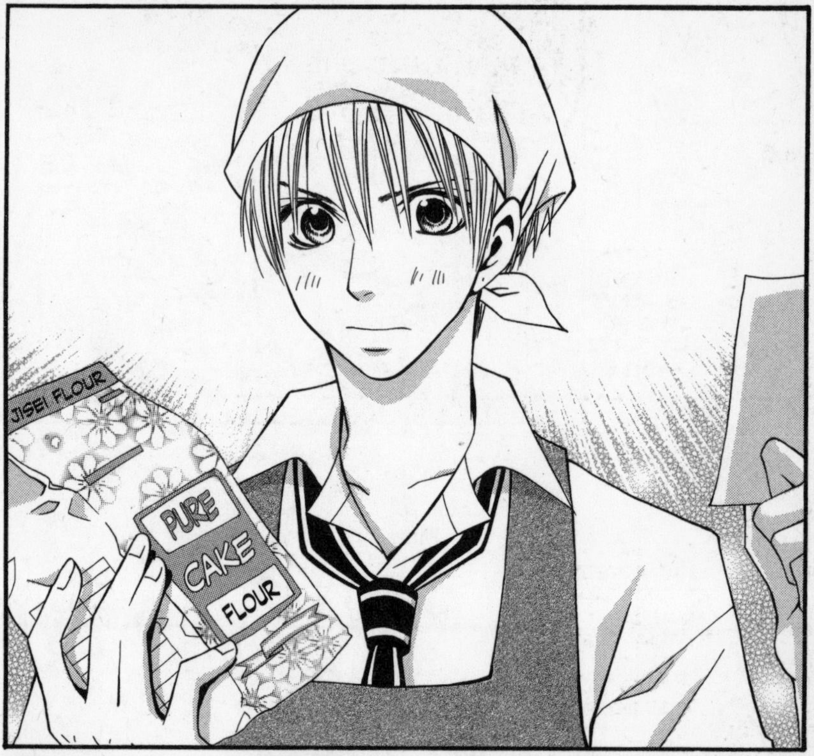
JISEI FLOUR
PURE CAKE FLOUR

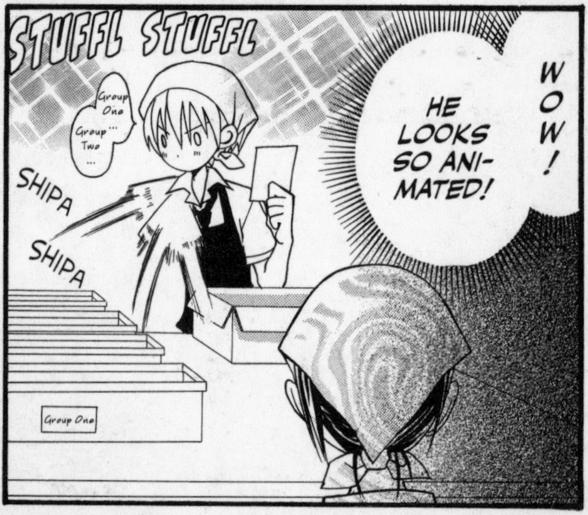
WOW!
HE LOOKS SO ANIMATED!
STUFFL STUFFL
Group One ... Group Two ...
SHIPA SHIPA
Group One

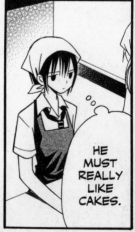

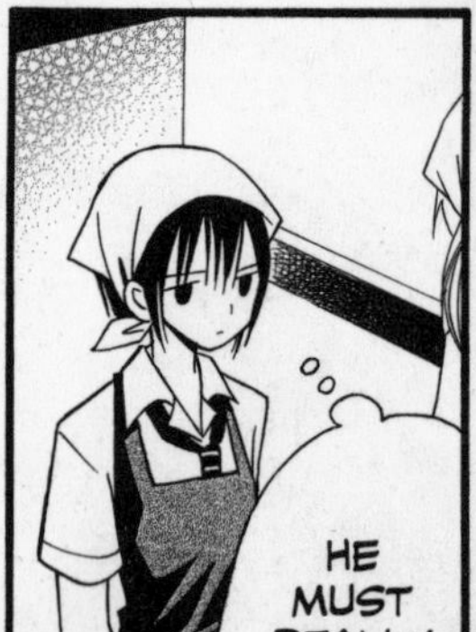
HE MUST REALLY LIKE CAKES.

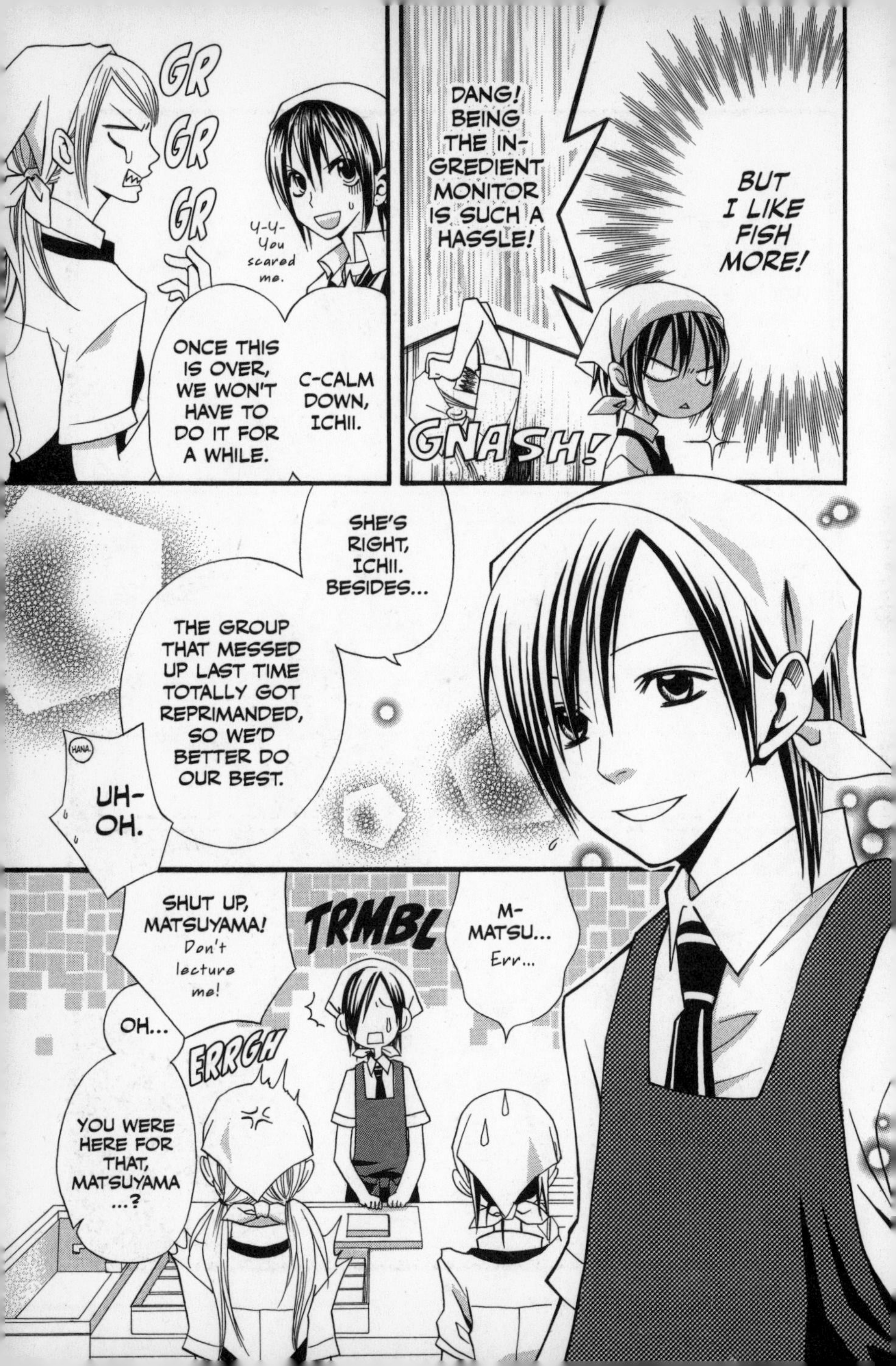
DANG! BEING THE IN-GREDIENT MONITOR IS SUCH A HASSLE!
BUT I LIKE FISH MORE!
GNASH!
GR GR GR
Y-Y-You scared me.
C-CALM DOWN, ICHII.
ONCE THIS IS OVER, WE WON'T HAVE TO DO IT FOR A WHILE.
SHE'S RIGHT, ICHII. BESIDES...
THE GROUP THAT MESSED UP LAST TIME TOTALLY GOT REPRIMANDED, SO WE'D BETTER DO OUR BEST.
HANA
UH-OH.
M-MATSU... Err...
TRMBL
SHUT UP, MATSUYAMA! Don't lecture me!
ERRGH
OH...
YOU WERE HERE FOR THAT, MATSUYAMA ...?

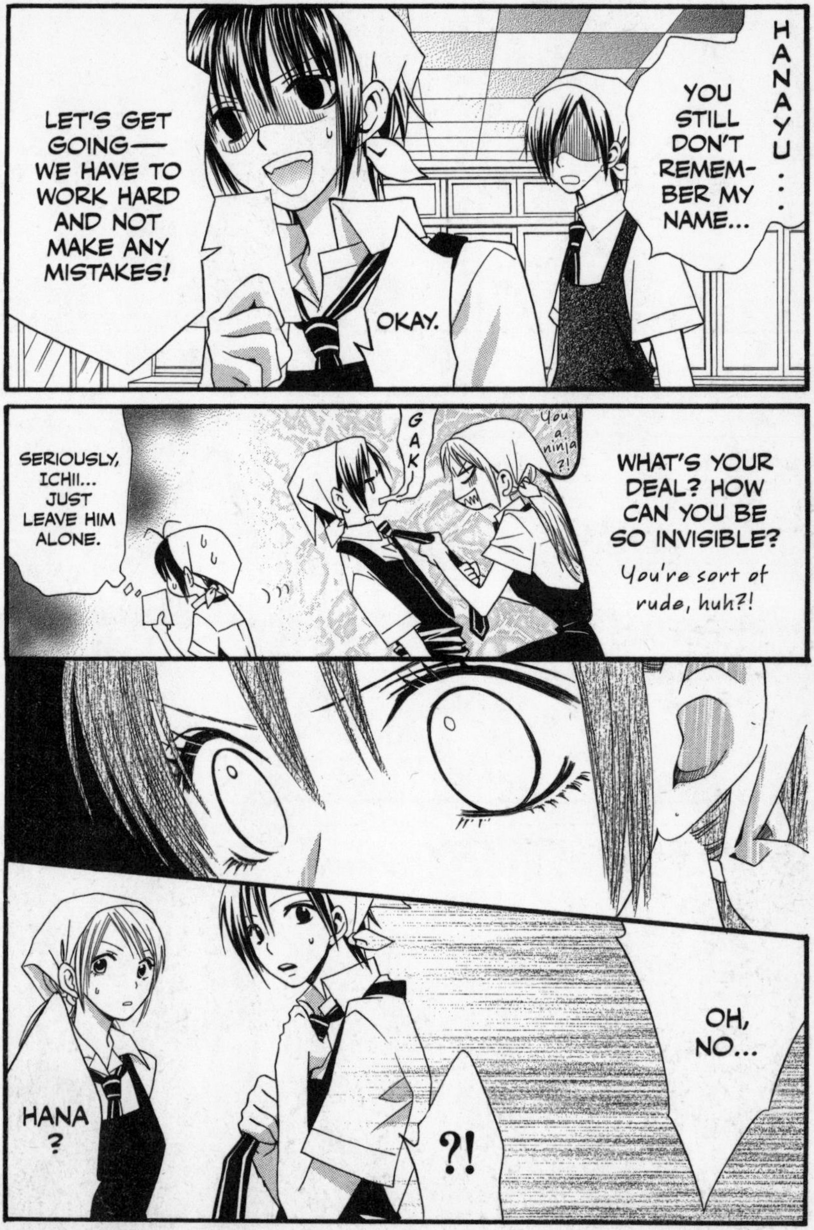
HANAYU...
YOU STILL DON'T REMEMBER MY NAME...
LET'S GET GOING—WE HAVE TO WORK HARD AND NOT MAKE ANY MISTAKES!
OKAY.
WHAT'S YOUR DEAL? HOW CAN YOU BE SO INVISIBLE?
You're sort of rude, huh?!
You a ninja?!
GAK
SERIOUSLY, ICHII... JUST LEAVE HIM ALONE.
OH, NO...
?!
HANA?

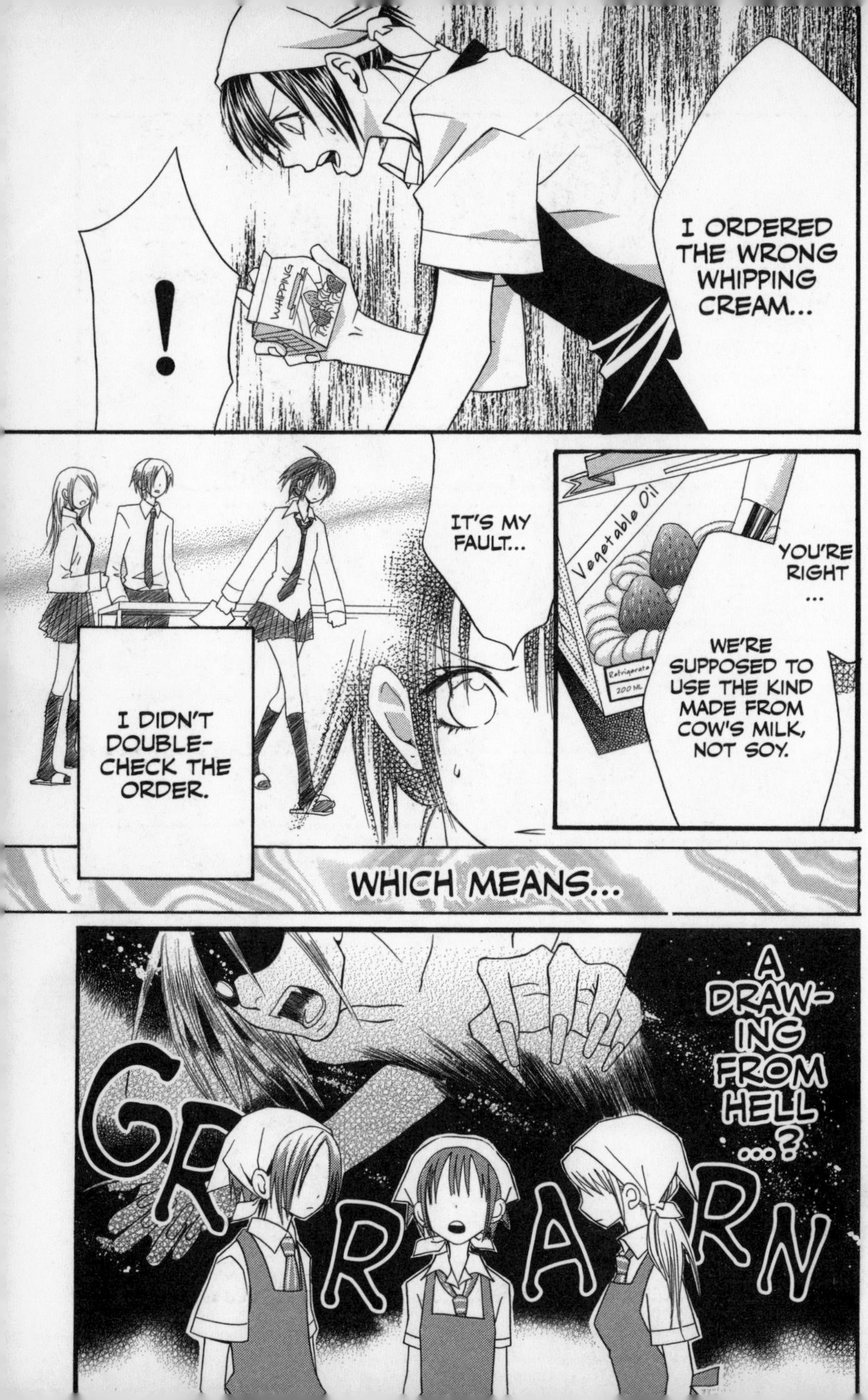
I ORDERED THE WRONG WHIPPING CREAM...
!
WHIPPING
YOU'RE RIGHT ...
WE'RE SUPPOSED TO USE THE KIND MADE FROM COW'S MILK, NOT SOY.
Vegetable Oil
200 ML
IT'S MY FAULT...
I DIDN'T DOUBLE-CHECK THE ORDER.
WHICH MEANS...
A DRAW-ING FROM HELL ...?
GRRARN

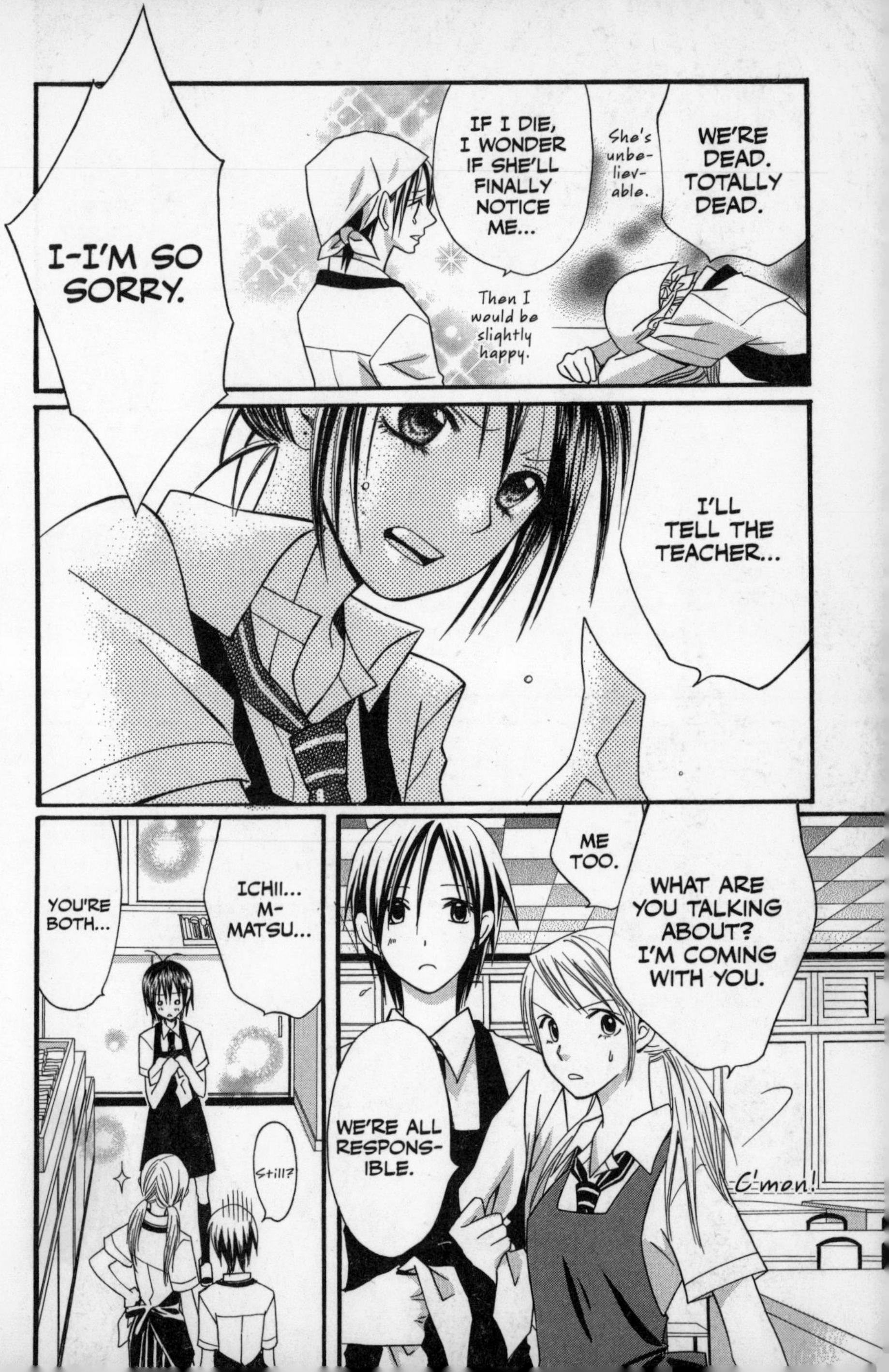
WE'RE DEAD. TOTALLY DEAD.
She's unbe-liev-able.
IF I DIE, I WONDER IF SHE'LL FINALLY NOTICE ME...
Then I would be slightly happy.
I-I'M SO SORRY.
I'LL TELL THE TEACHER...
WHAT ARE YOU TALKING ABOUT? I'M COMING WITH YOU.
ME TOO.
WE'RE ALL RESPONS-IBLE.
C'mon!
ICHII... M-MATSU...
YOU'RE BOTH...
Still?

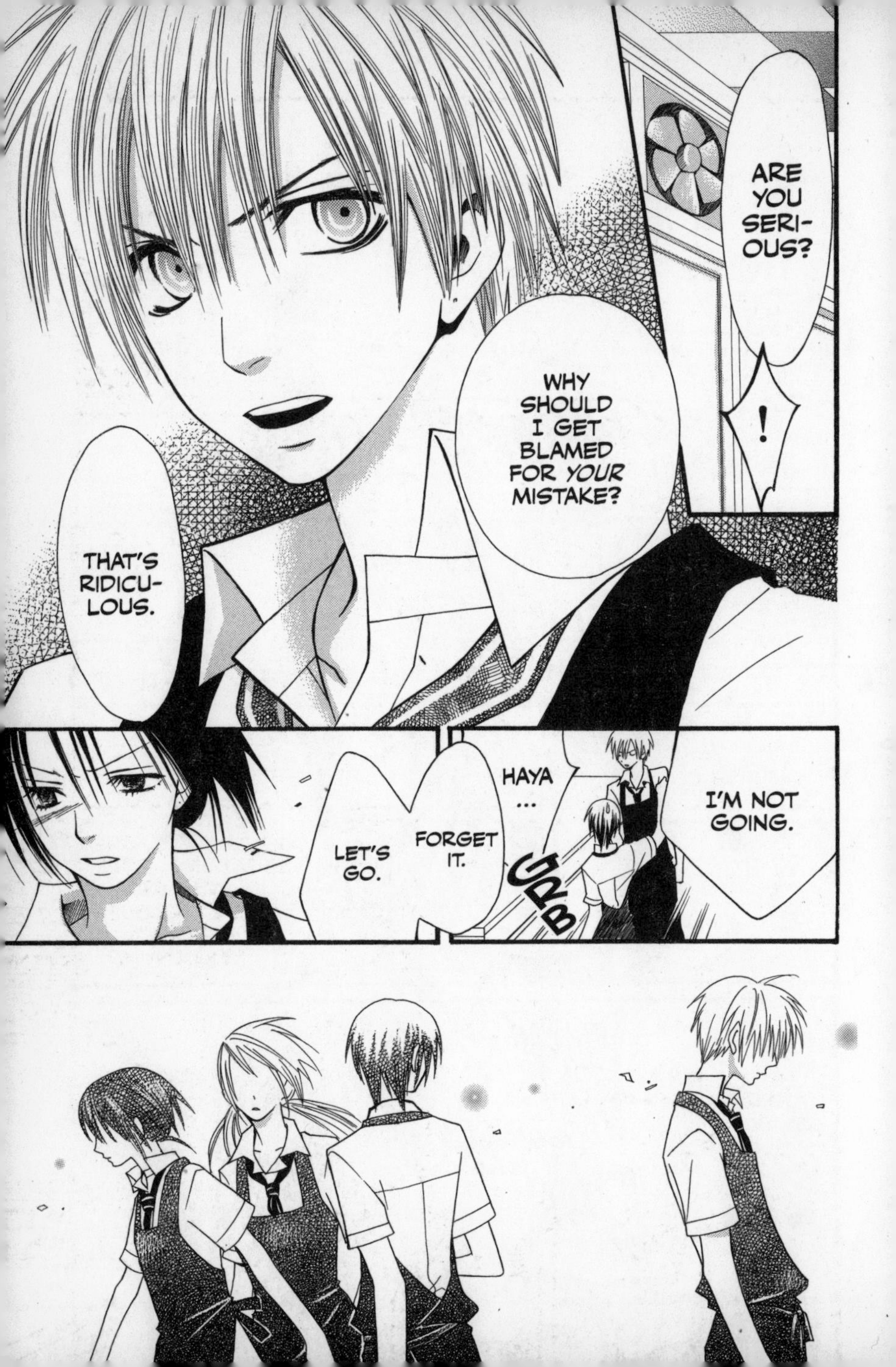
ARE YOU SERIOUS?
!
WHY SHOULD I GET BLAMED FOR *YOUR* MISTAKE?
THAT'S RIDICULOUS.
I'M NOT GOING.
HAYA...
GRAB
FORGET IT.
LET'S GO.

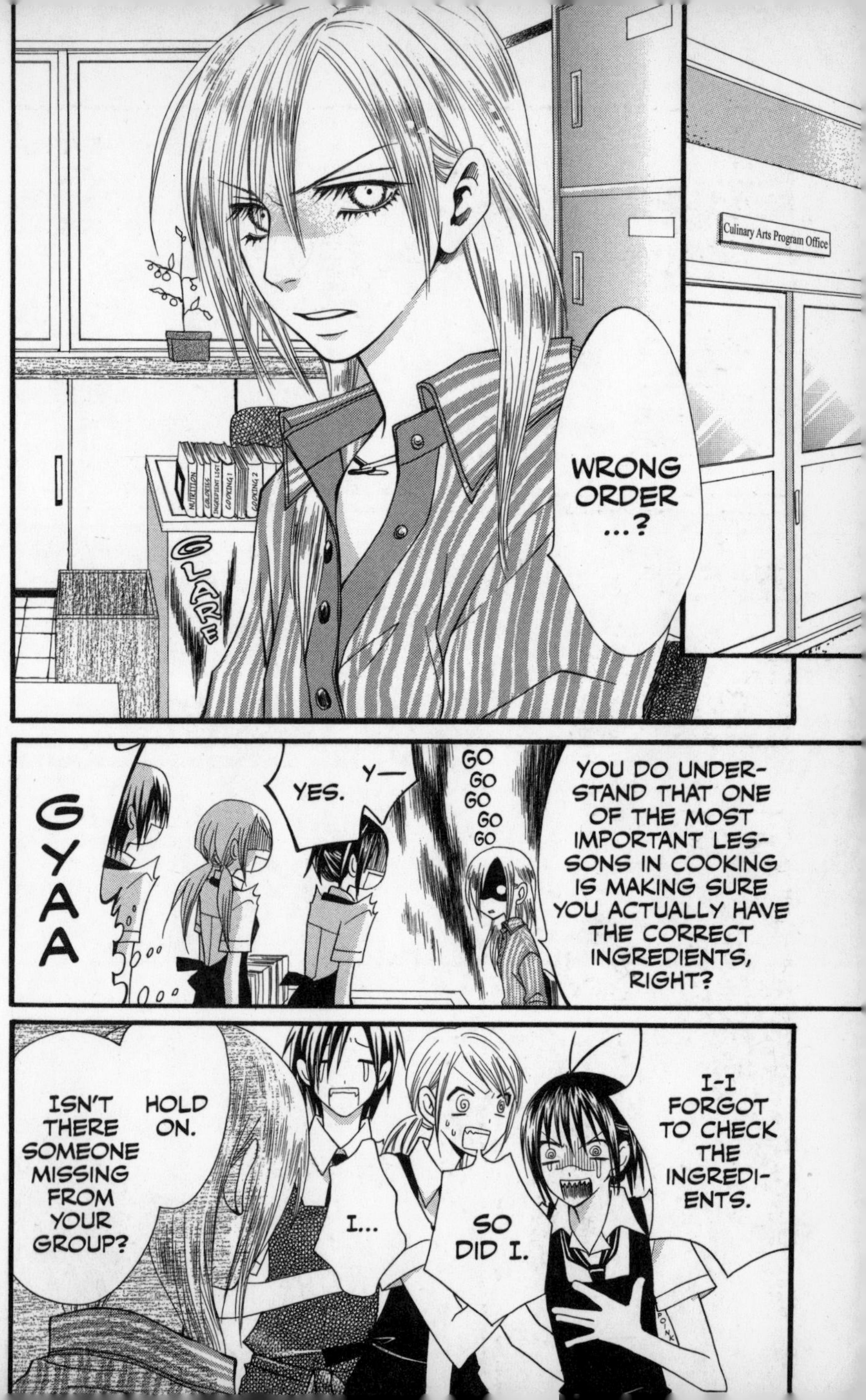
Culinary Arts Program Office
WRONG ORDER ...?
NUTRITION
CALORIES
INGREDIENT LIST
COOKING 1
COOKING 2
GLARE
YOU DO UNDER-STAND THAT ONE OF THE MOST IMPORTANT LES-SONS IN COOKING IS MAKING SURE YOU ACTUALLY HAVE THE CORRECT INGREDIENTS, RIGHT?
GO GO GO GO GO
Y— YES.
GYAA
I-I FORGOT TO CHECK THE INGREDI-ENTS.
POINK
SO DID I.
I...
HOLD ON.
ISN'T THERE SOMEONE MISSING FROM YOUR GROUP?

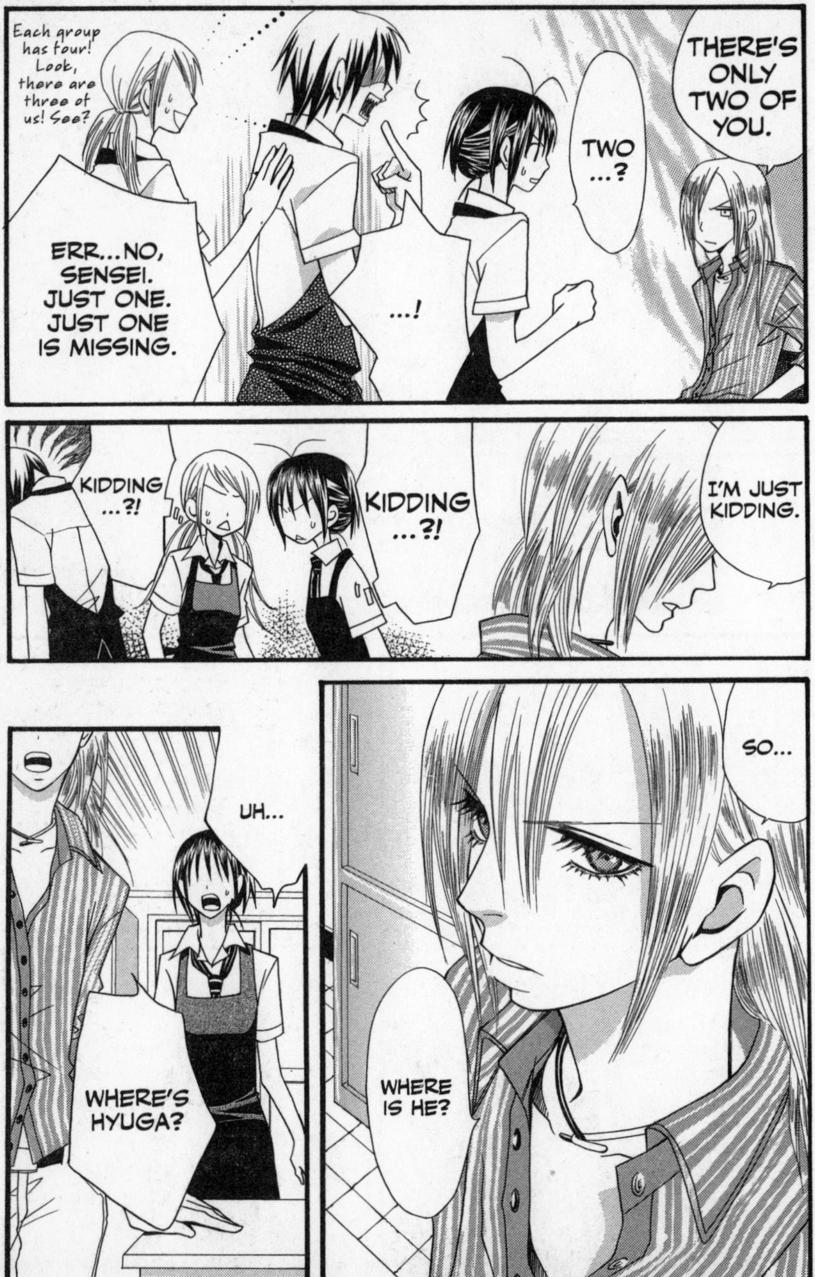
THERE'S ONLY TWO OF YOU.
TWO ...?
...!
ERR...NO, SENSEI. JUST ONE. JUST ONE IS MISSING.
Each group has four! Look, there are three of us! See?
I'M JUST KIDDING.
KIDDING ...?!
KIDDING ...?!
SO...
WHERE IS HE?
UH...
WHERE'S HYUGA?

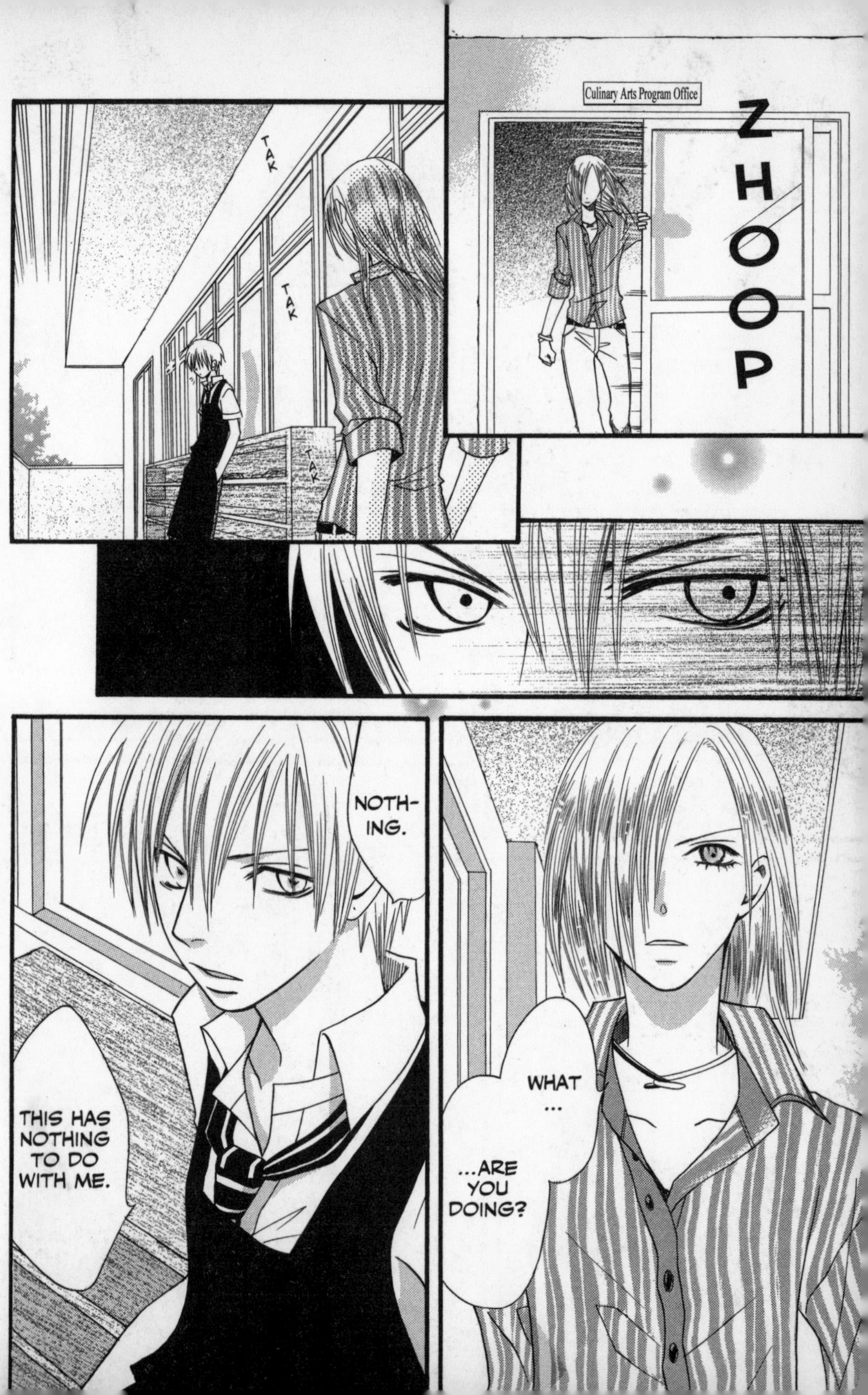
Culinary Arts Program Office
ZHOOP
TAK
TAK
TAK
WHAT ...
...ARE YOU DOING?
NOTH-ING.
THIS HAS NOTHING TO DO WITH ME.

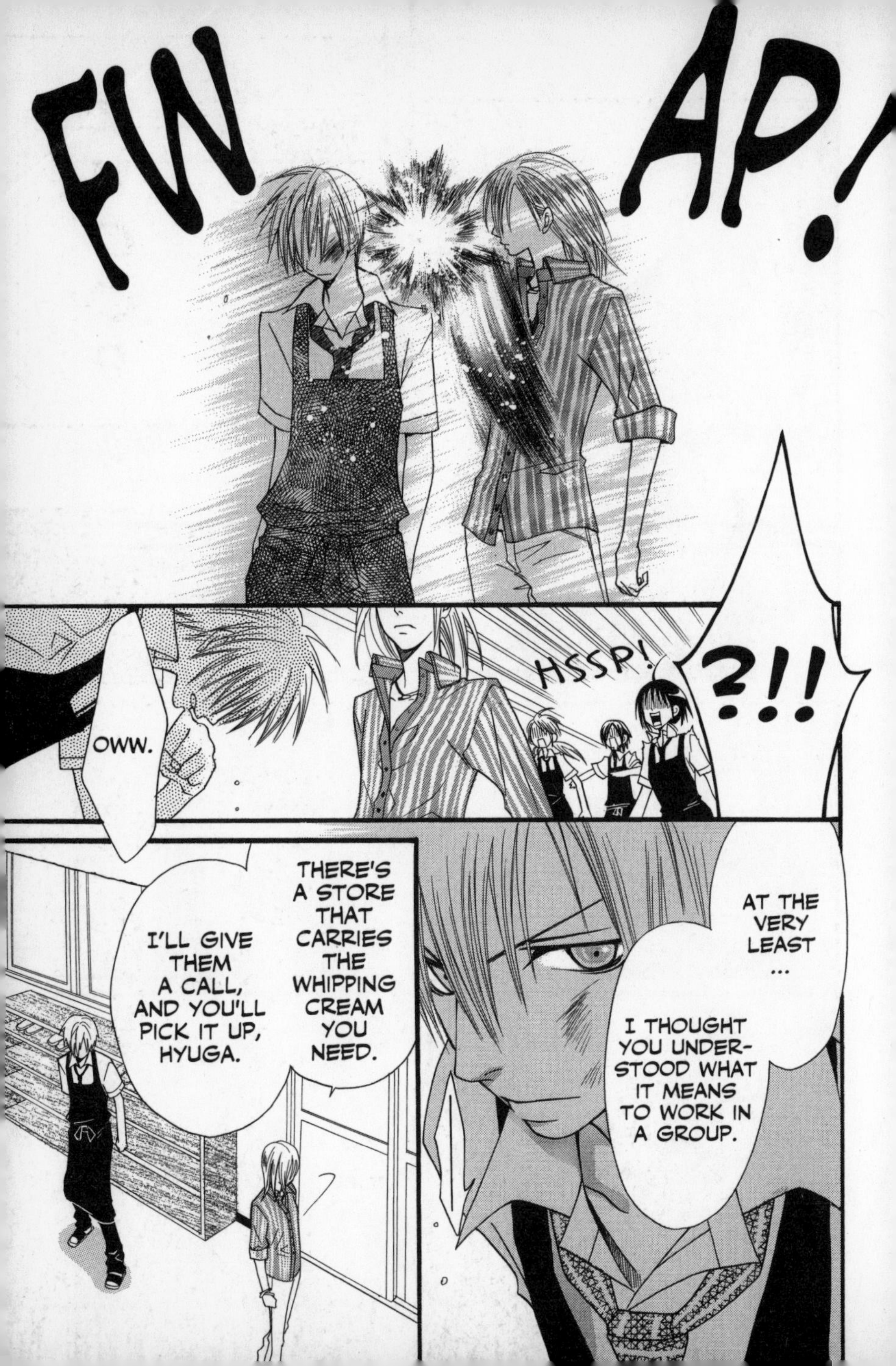
FWAP!
?!!
HSSP!
OWW.
AT THE VERY LEAST ...
I THOUGHT YOU UNDER-STOOD WHAT IT MEANS TO WORK IN A GROUP.
THERE'S A STORE THAT CARRIES THE WHIPPING CREAM YOU NEED.
I'LL GIVE THEM A CALL, AND YOU'LL PICK IT UP, HYUGA.

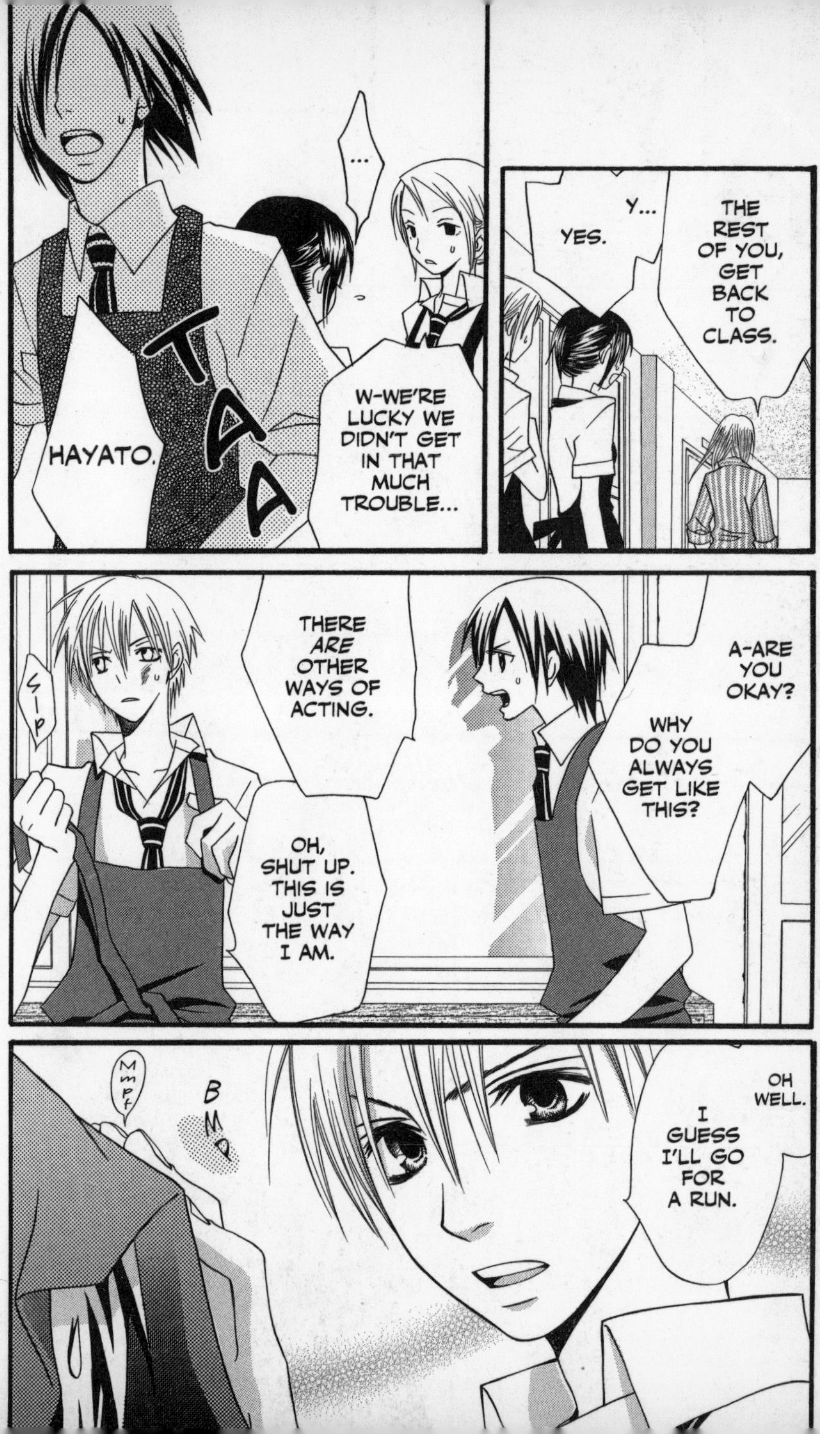
THE REST OF YOU, GET BACK TO CLASS.
Y...
YES.
...
W-WE'RE LUCKY WE DIDN'T GET IN THAT MUCH TROUBLE...
TAA
HAYATO.
A-ARE YOU OKAY?
WHY DO YOU ALWAYS GET LIKE THIS?
THERE *ARE* OTHER WAYS OF ACTING.
OH, SHUT UP. THIS IS JUST THE WAY I AM.
Slip
OH WELL.
I GUESS I'LL GO FOR A RUN.
BMP
Mmpf

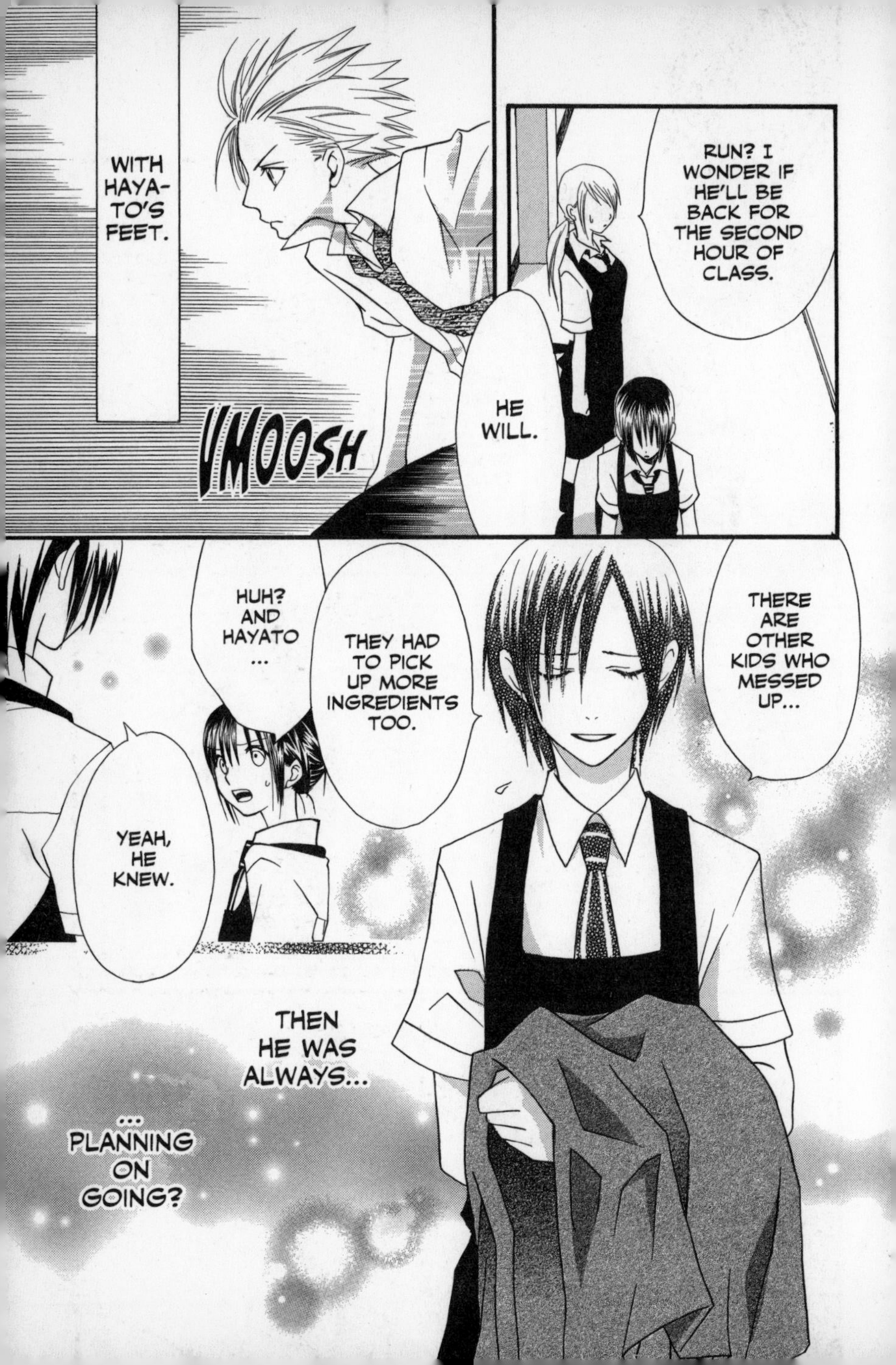
RUN? I WONDER IF HE'LL BE BACK FOR THE SECOND HOUR OF CLASS.
HE WILL.
WITH HAYA-TO'S FEET.
VMOOSH
THERE ARE OTHER KIDS WHO MESSED UP...
THEY HAD TO PICK UP MORE INGREDIENTS TOO.
HUH? AND HAYATO ...
YEAH, HE KNEW.
THEN HE WAS ALWAYS...
... PLANNING ON GOING?

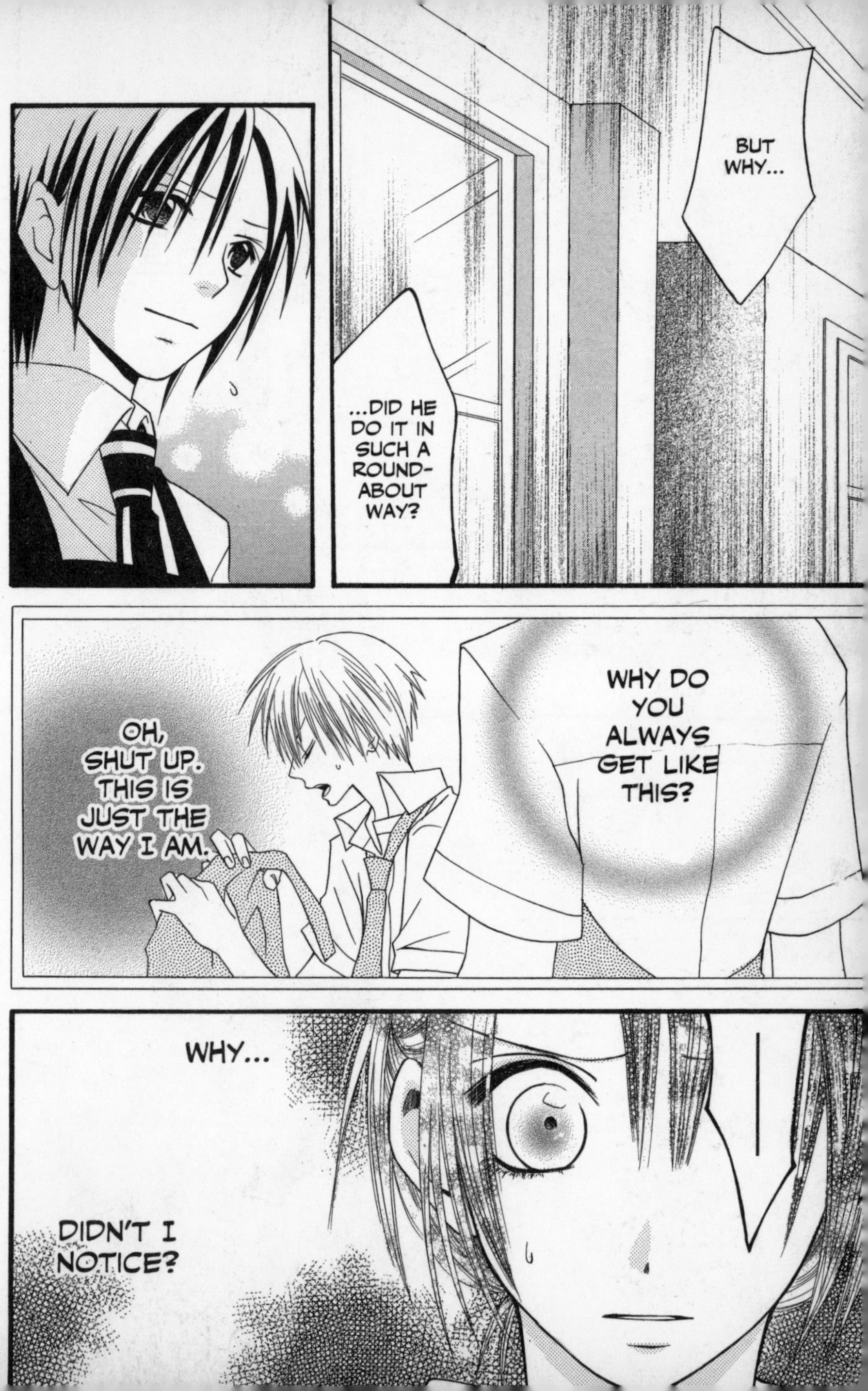
BUT WHY...
...DID HE DO IT IN SUCH A ROUND-ABOUT WAY?
WHY DO YOU ALWAYS GET LIKE THIS?
OH, SHUT UP. THIS IS JUST THE WAY I AM.
WHY...
DIDN'T I NOTICE?

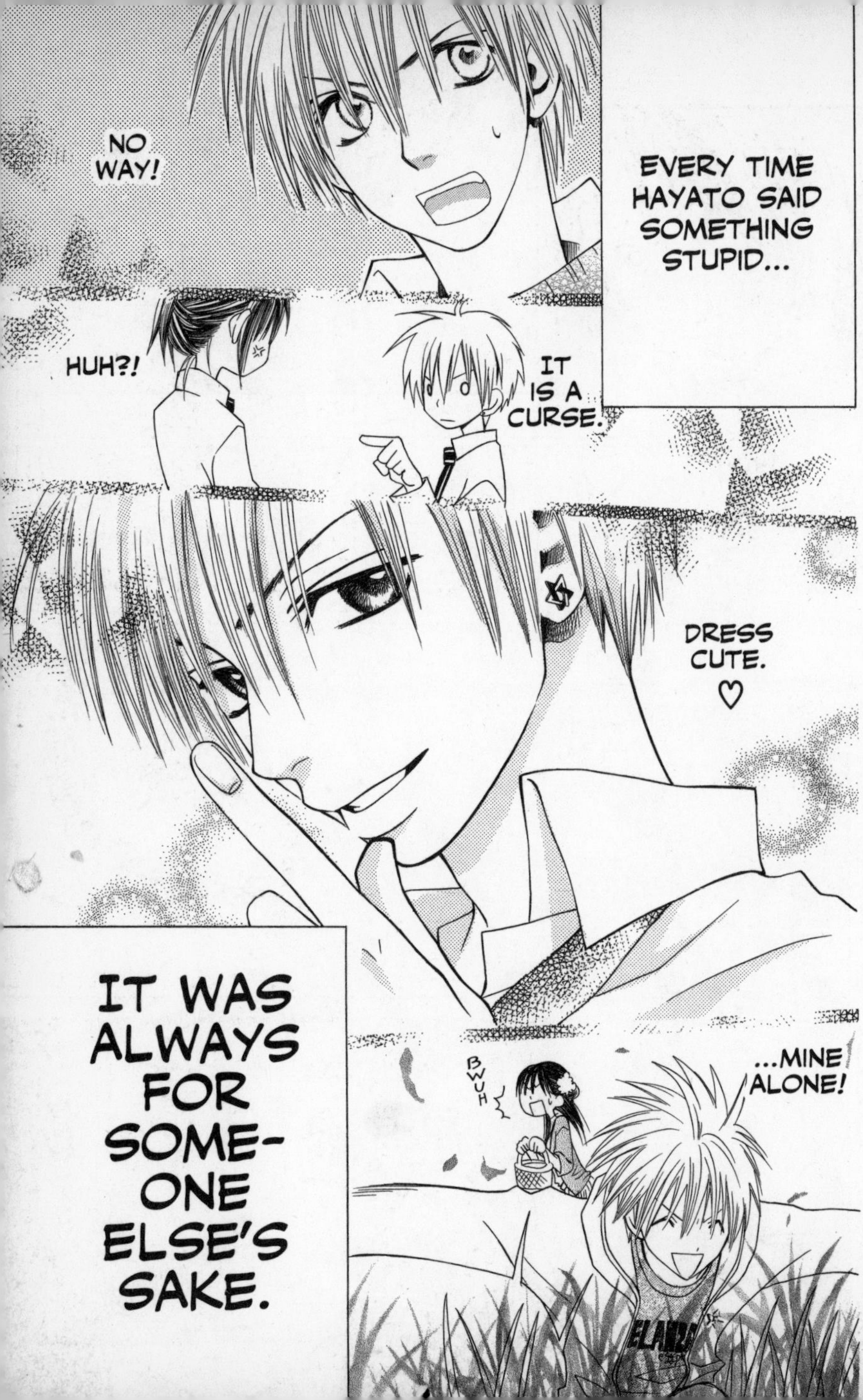
EVERY TIME HAYATO SAID SOMETHING STUPID...
NO WAY!
IT IS A CURSE.
HUH?!
DRESS CUTE. ♡
...MINE ALONE!
BWUH
IT WAS ALWAYS FOR SOME-ONE ELSE'S SAKE.

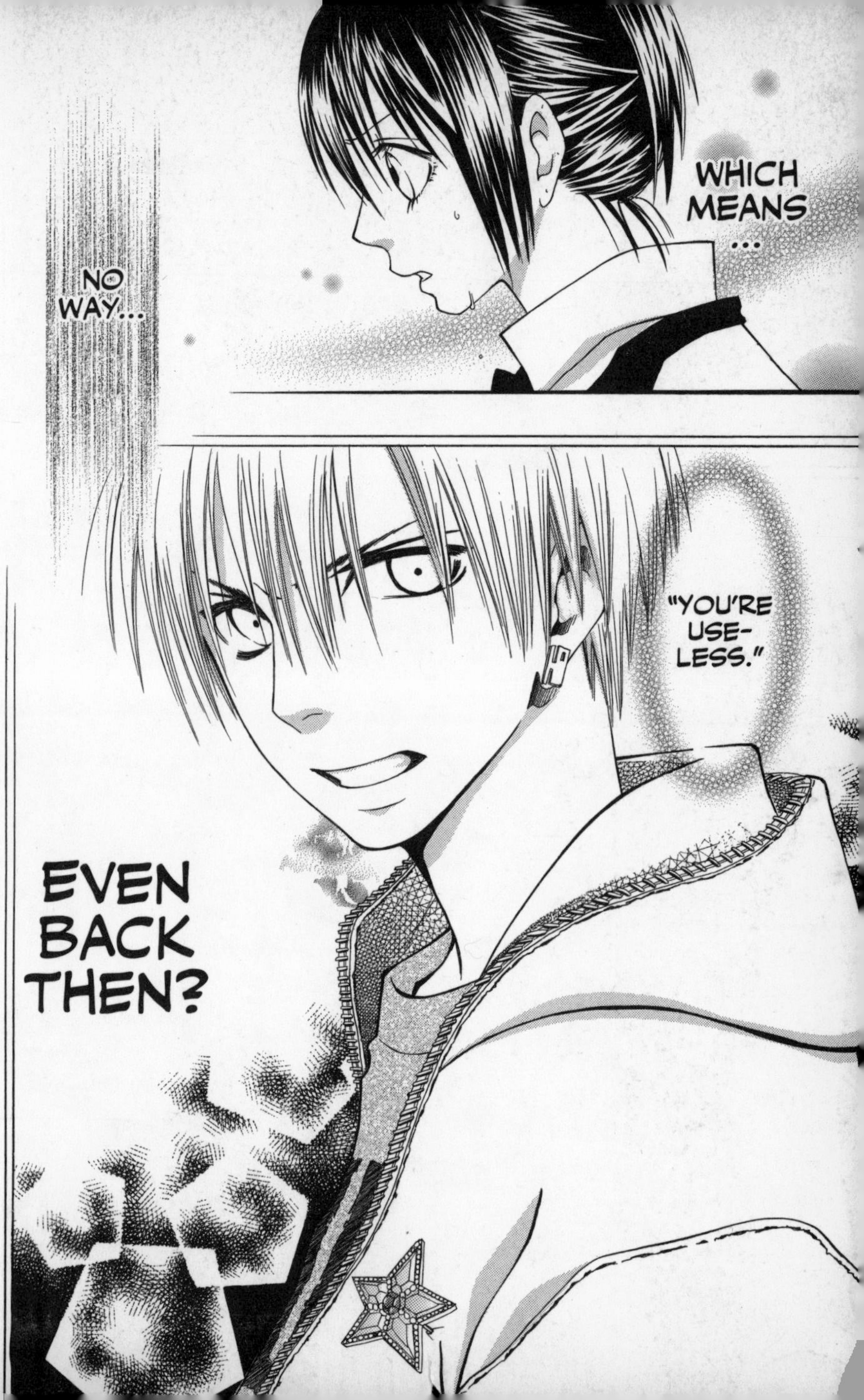
WHICH MEANS ...
NO WAY...
"YOU'RE USE-LESS."
EVEN BACK THEN?

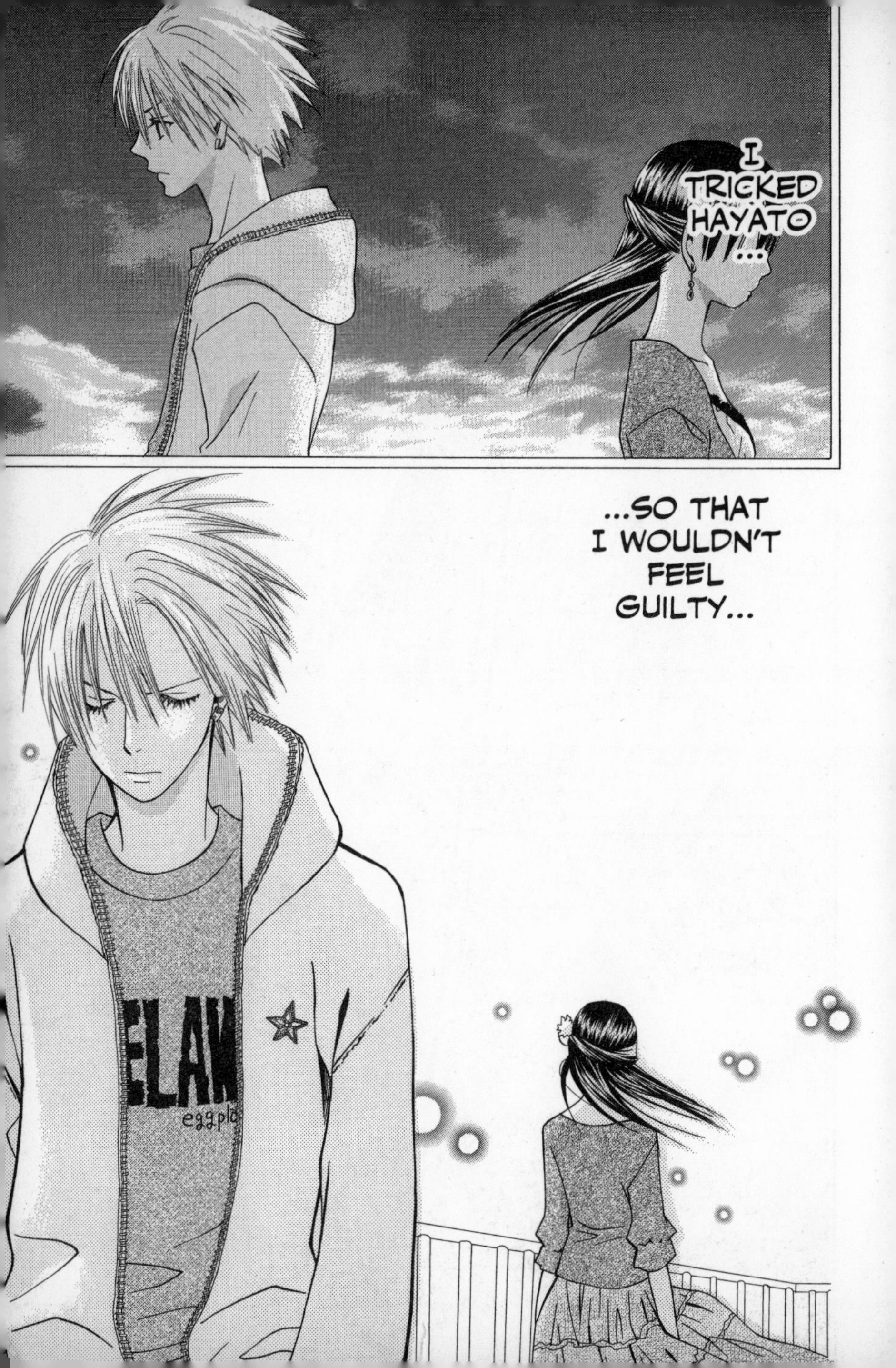
I TRICKED HAYATO ...
...SO THAT I WOULDN'T FEEL GUILTY...

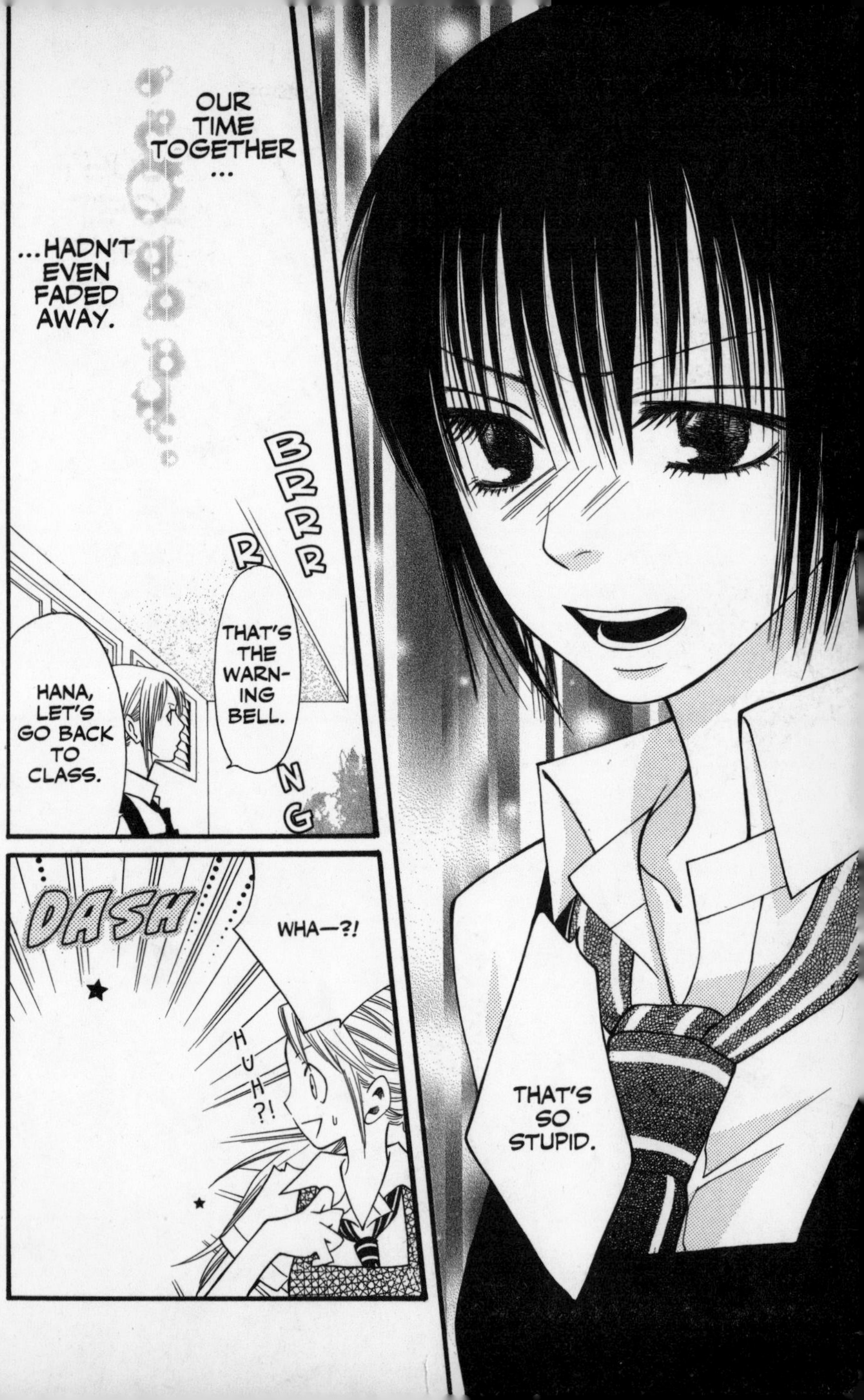
THAT'S SO STUPID.
OUR TIME TOGETHER ...
...HADN'T EVEN FADED AWAY.
BRRRRRNG
THAT'S THE WARNING BELL.
HANA, LET'S GO BACK TO CLASS.
WHA—?!
DASH
HUH?!

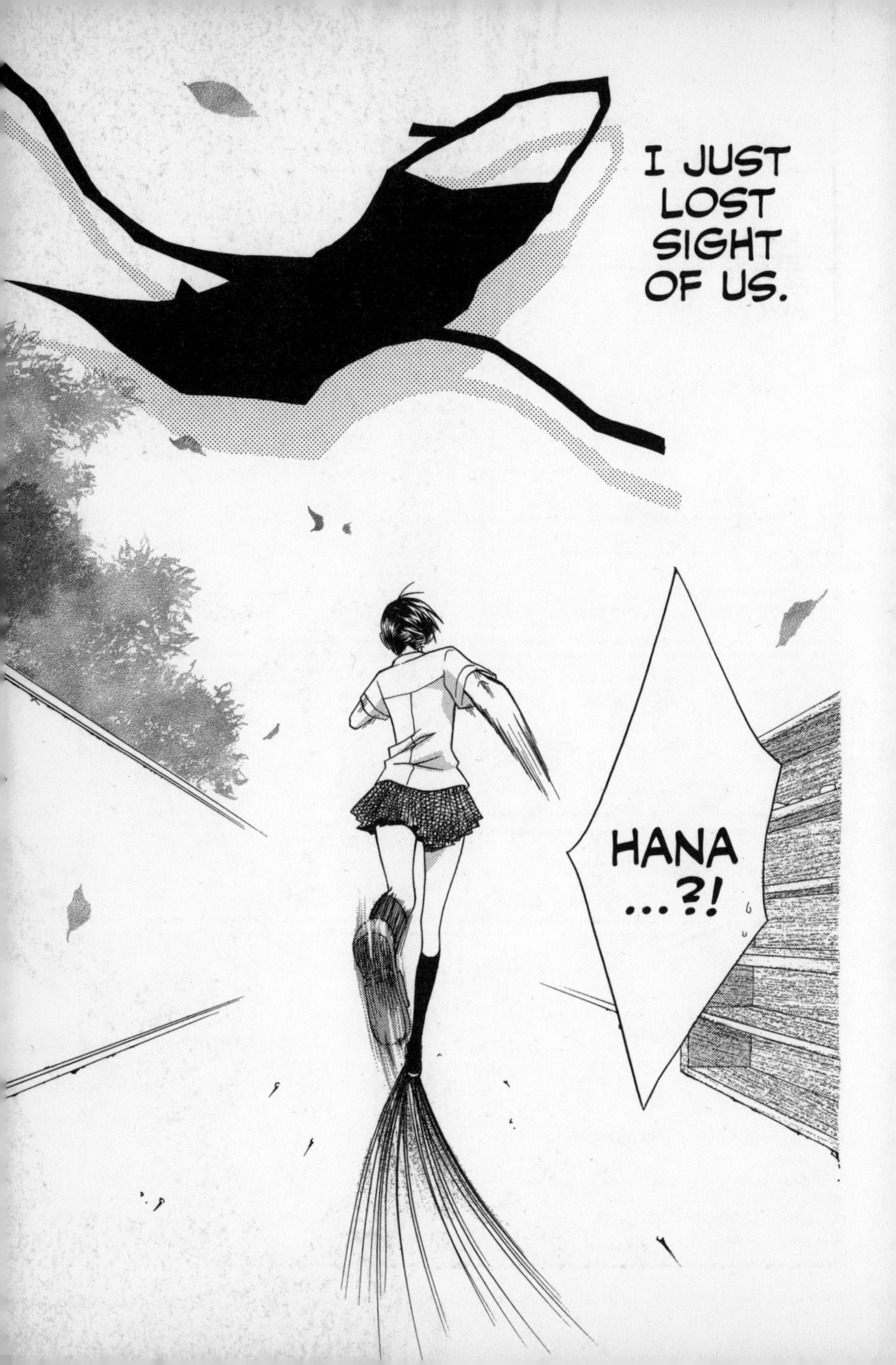
I JUST LOST SIGHT OF US.
HANA ...?!

SIDE DISH Mixed Vegetables 2

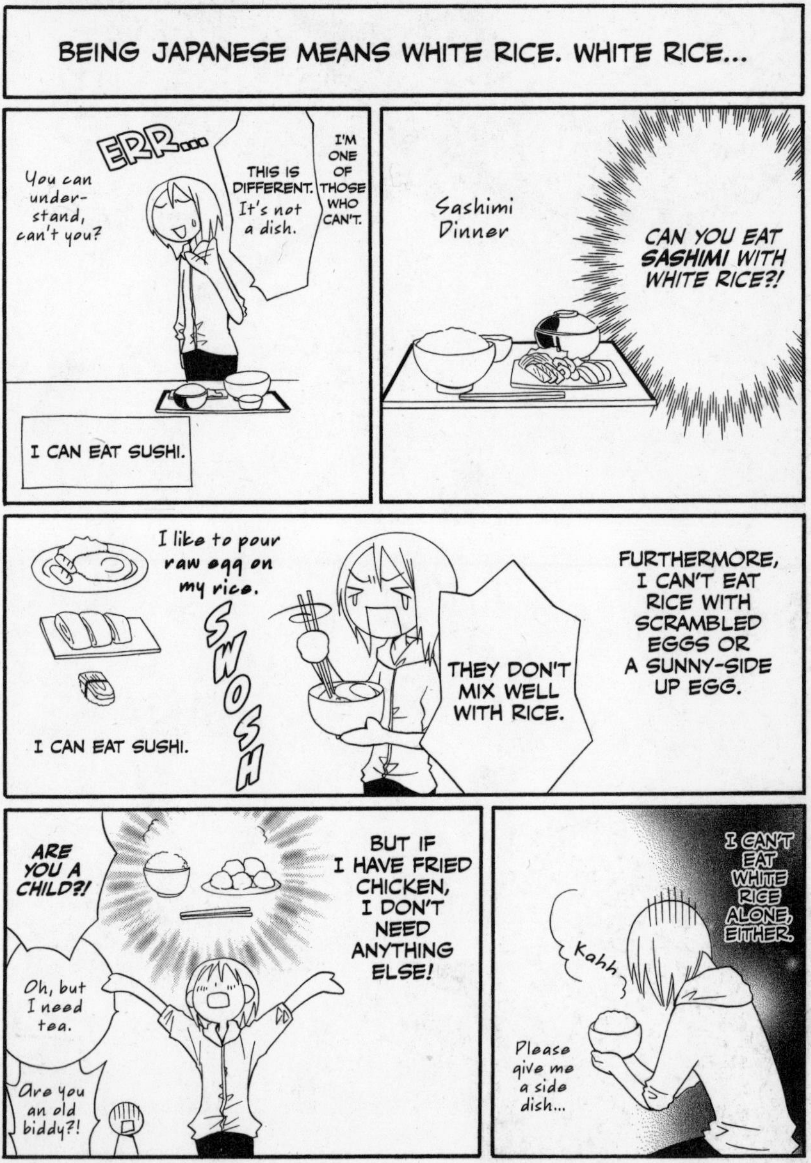
BEING JAPANESE MEANS WHITE RICE. WHITE RICE...
Sashimi Dinner
CAN YOU EAT SASHIMI WITH WHITE RICE?!
ERR...
I'M ONE OF THOSE WHO CAN'T.
THIS IS DIFFERENT. It's not a dish.
You can under-stand, can't you?
I CAN EAT SUSHI.
FURTHERMORE, I CAN'T EAT RICE WITH SCRAMBLED EGGS OR A SUNNY-SIDE UP EGG.
THEY DON'T MIX WELL WITH RICE.
SWOSH
I like to pour raw egg on my rice.
I CAN EAT SUSHI.
I CAN'T EAT WHITE RICE ALONE, EITHER.
Kahh
Please give me a side dish...
BUT IF I HAVE FRIED CHICKEN, I DON'T NEED ANYTHING ELSE!
ARE YOU A CHILD?!
Oh, but I need tea.
Are you an old biddy?!

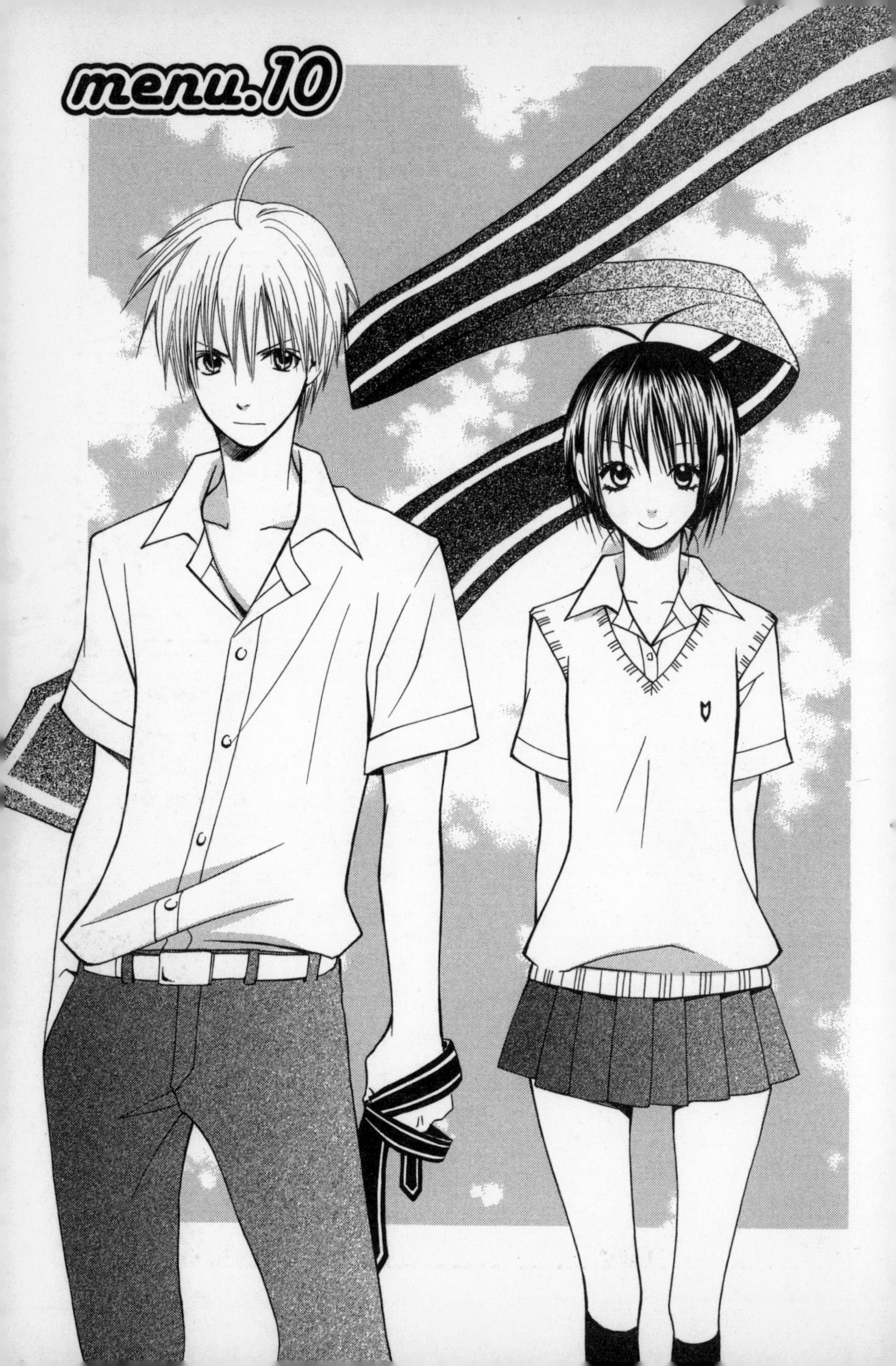
menu.10

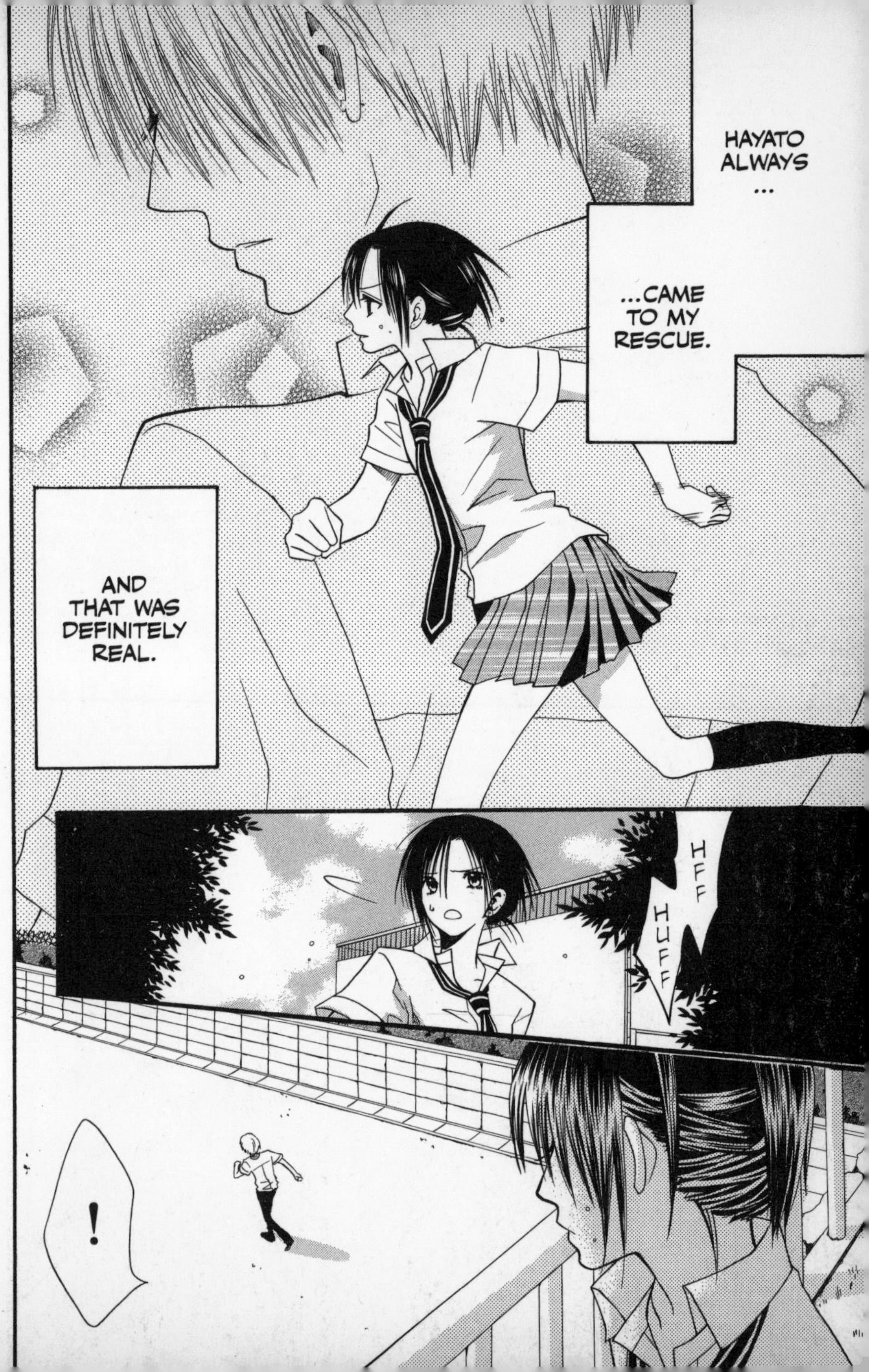
HAYATO ALWAYS ...
...CAME TO MY RESCUE.
AND THAT WAS DEFINITELY REAL.
HFF
HUFF
HUFF
!

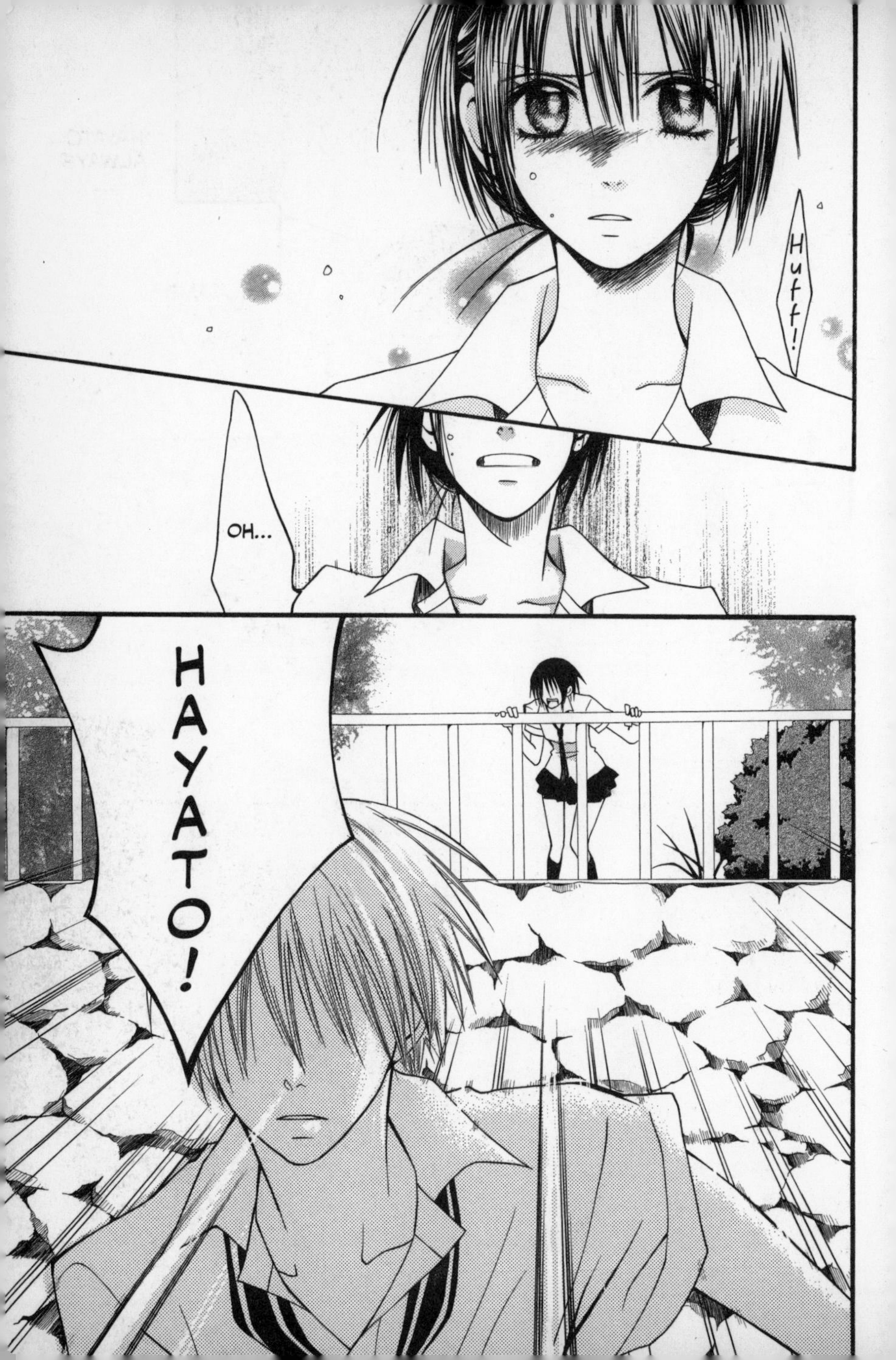
Huff!
OH...
HAYATO!

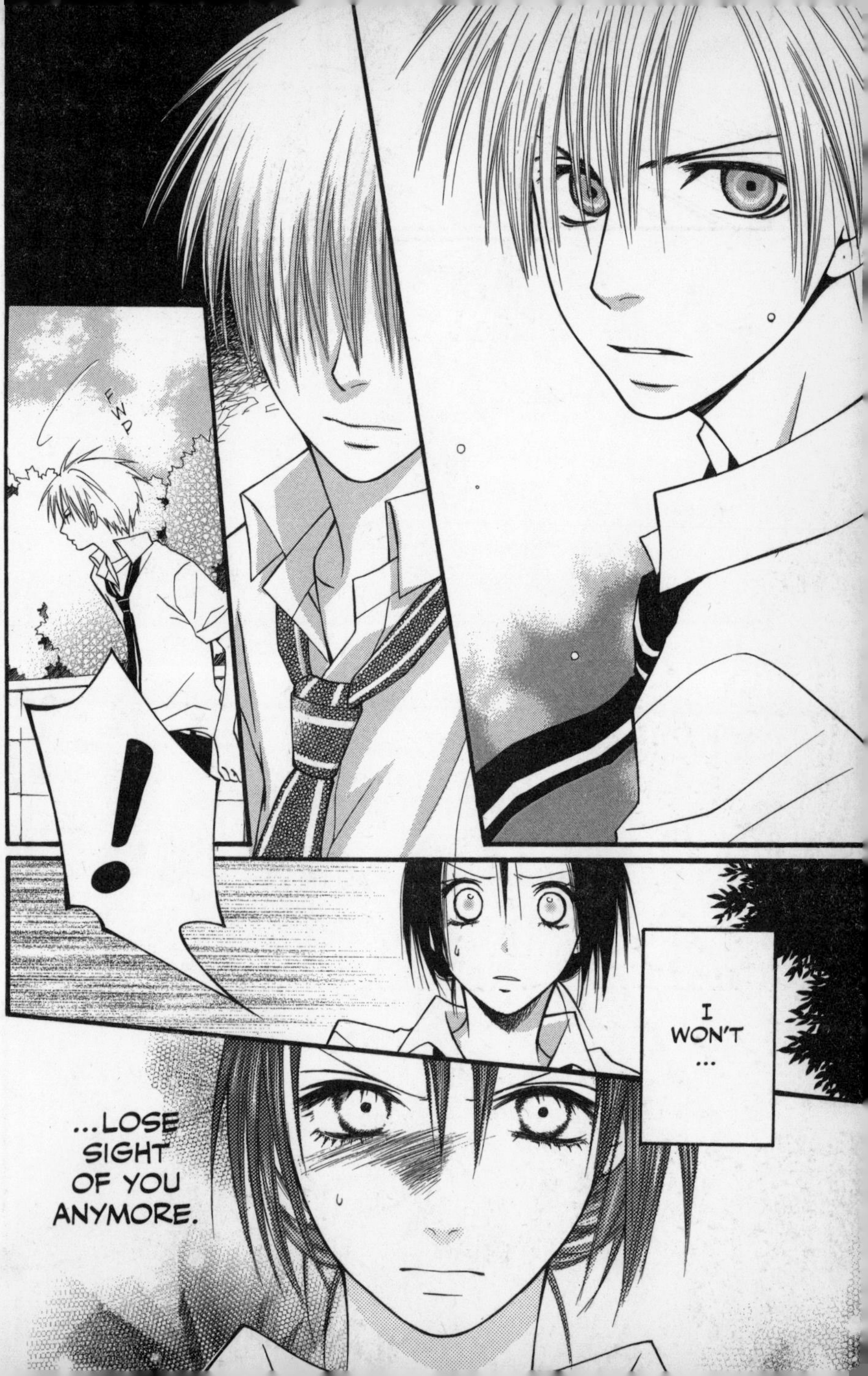
FWP
!
I WON'T ...
...LOSE SIGHT OF YOU ANYMORE.

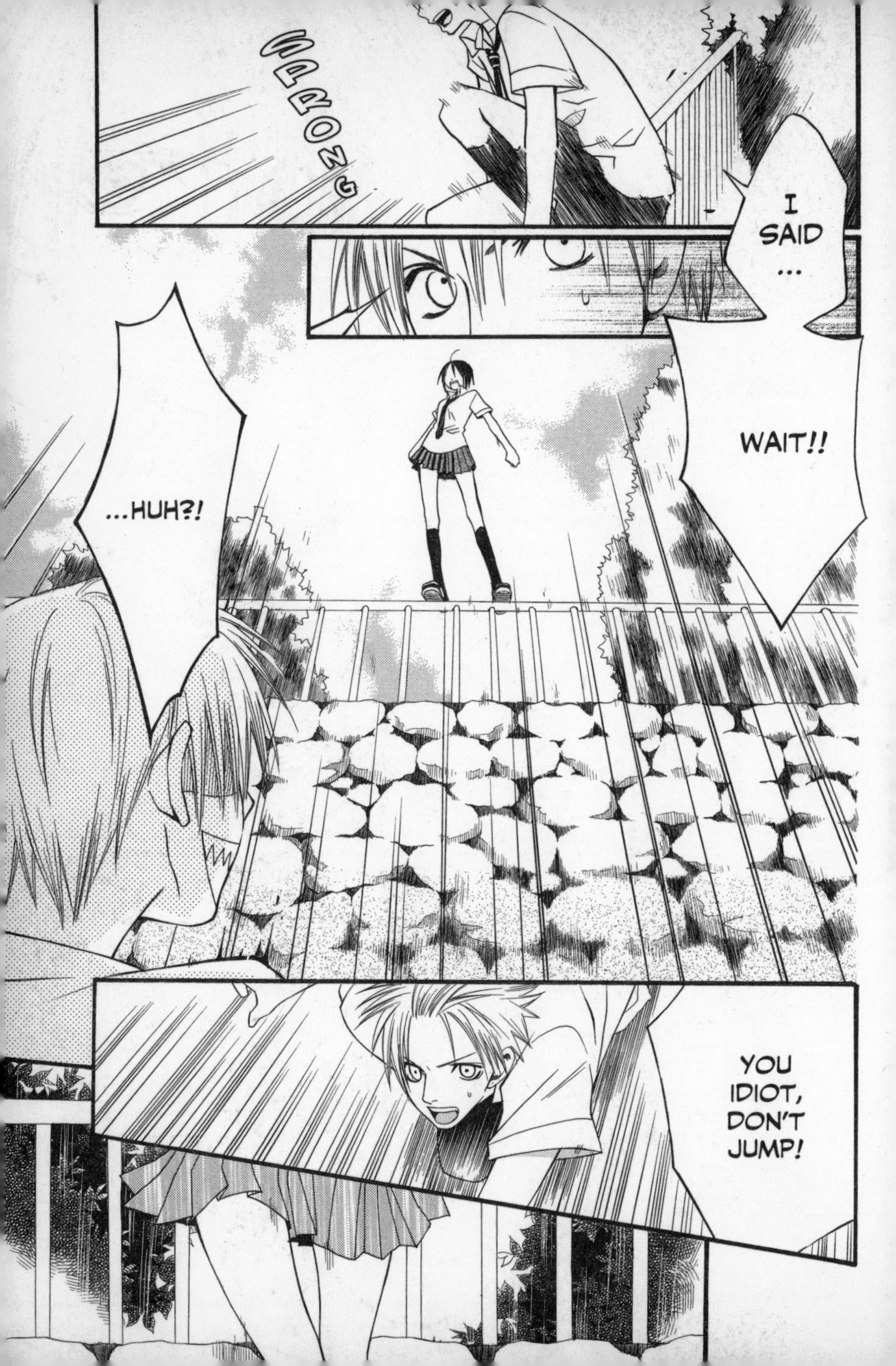
SPRONG
I SAID ...
WAIT!!
...HUH?!
YOU IDIOT, DON'T JUMP!

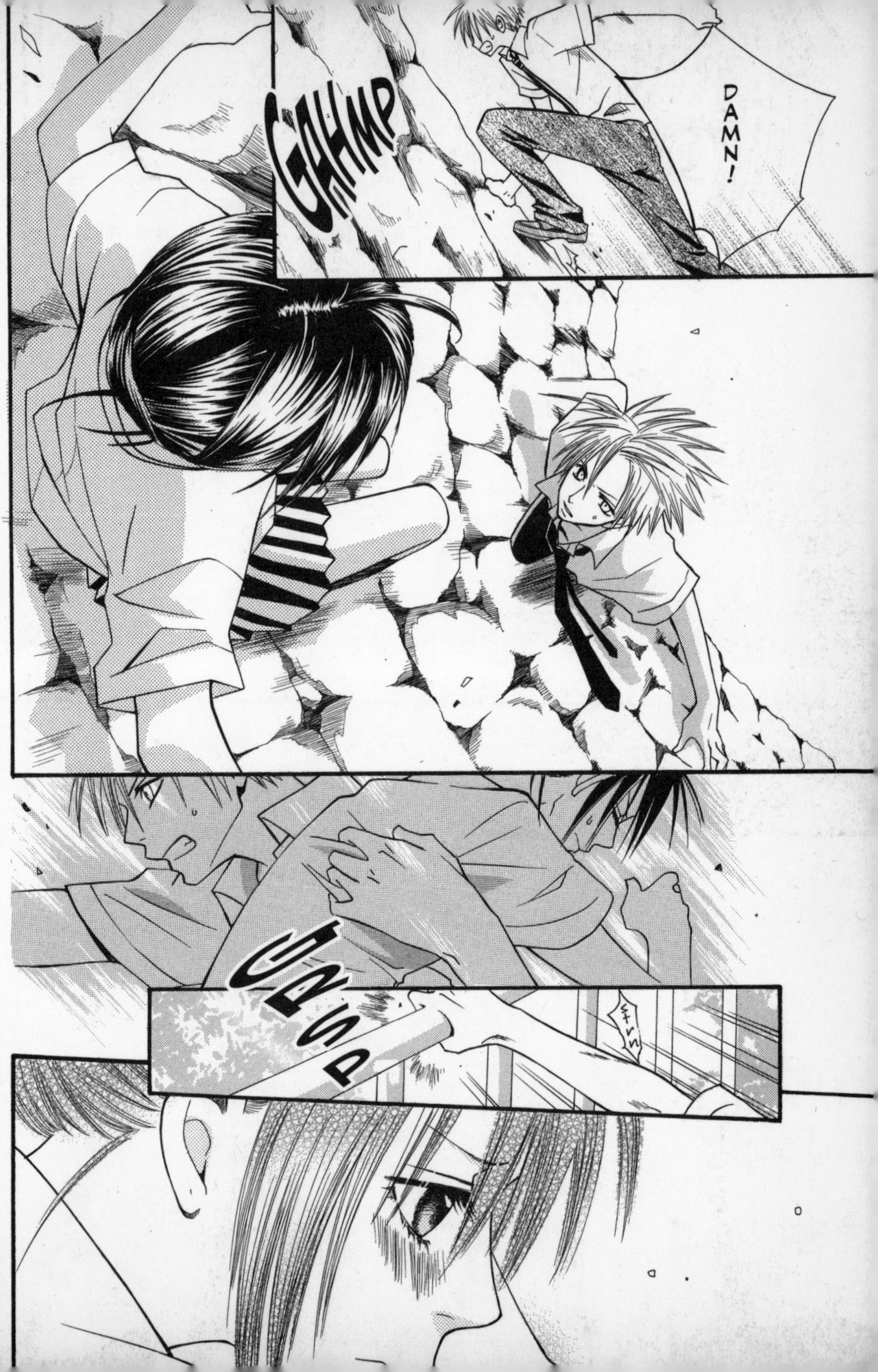
DAMN!
GAHMP
GASP
strn

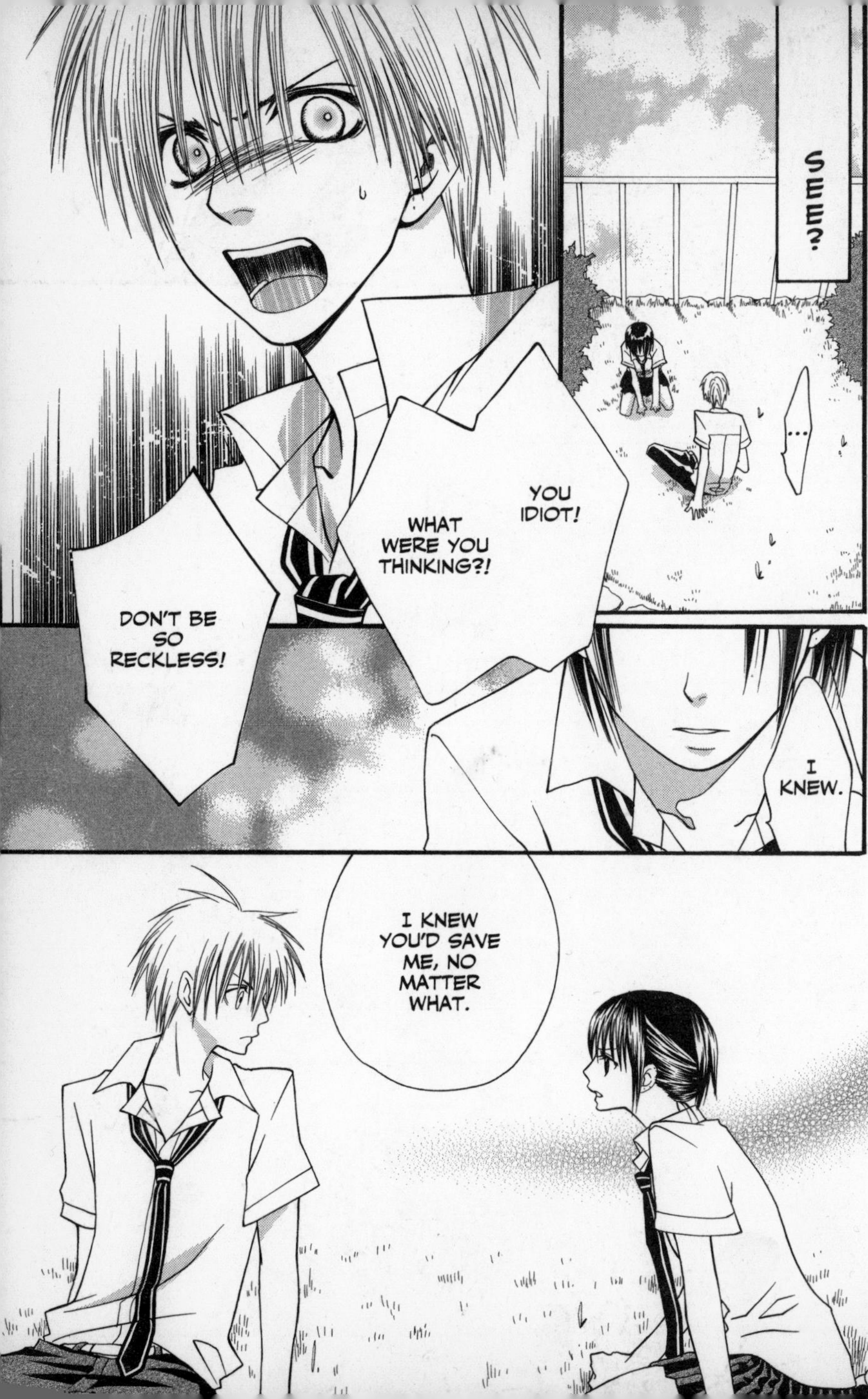
SEE?
...
YOU IDIOT!
WHAT WERE YOU THINKING?!
DON'T BE SO RECKLESS!
I KNEW.
I KNEW YOU'D SAVE ME, NO MATTER WHAT.

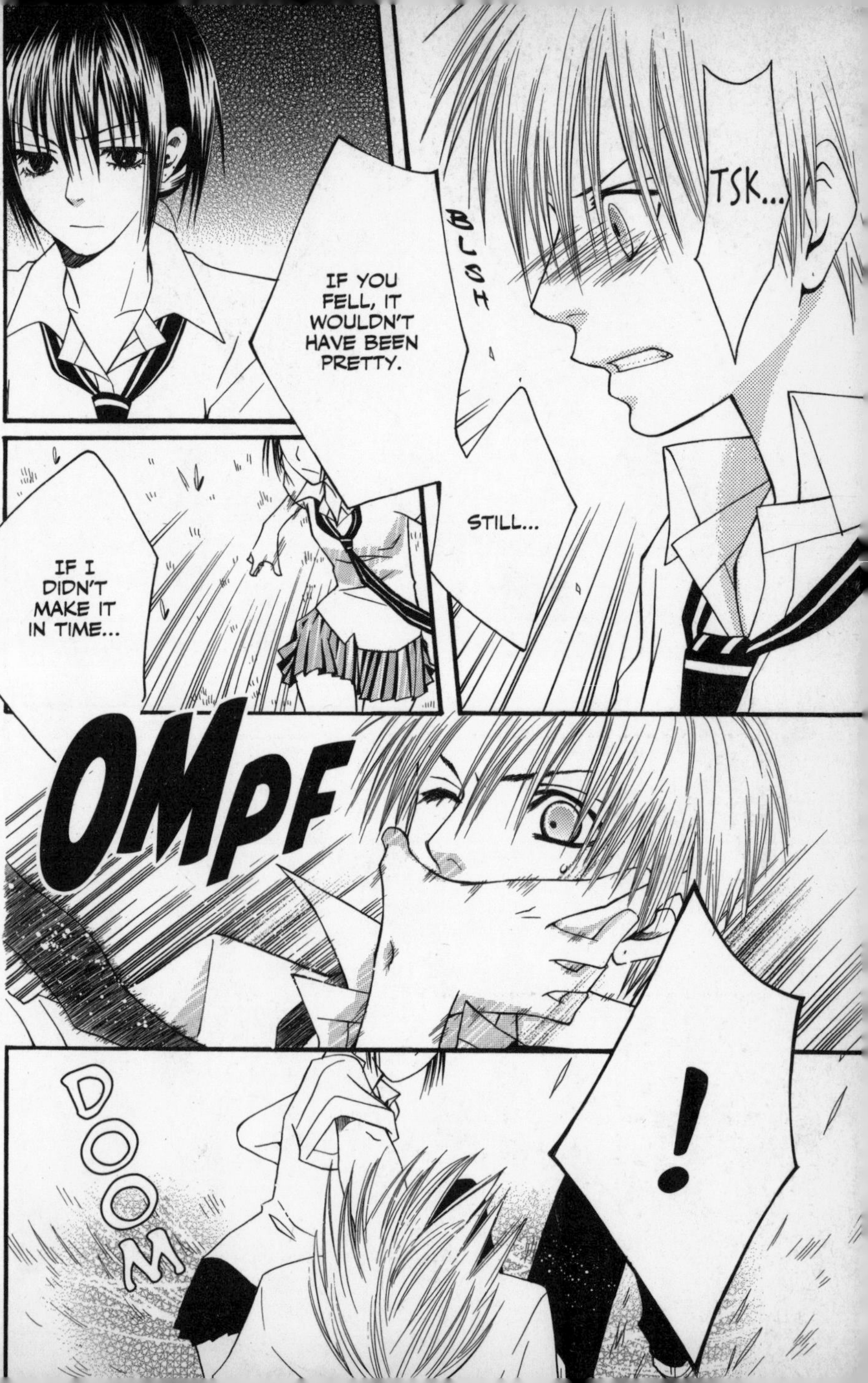
TSK...
BLSH
IF YOU FELL, IT WOULDN'T HAVE BEEN PRETTY.
STILL...
IF I DIDN'T MAKE IT IN TIME...
OMPF
!
DOOM

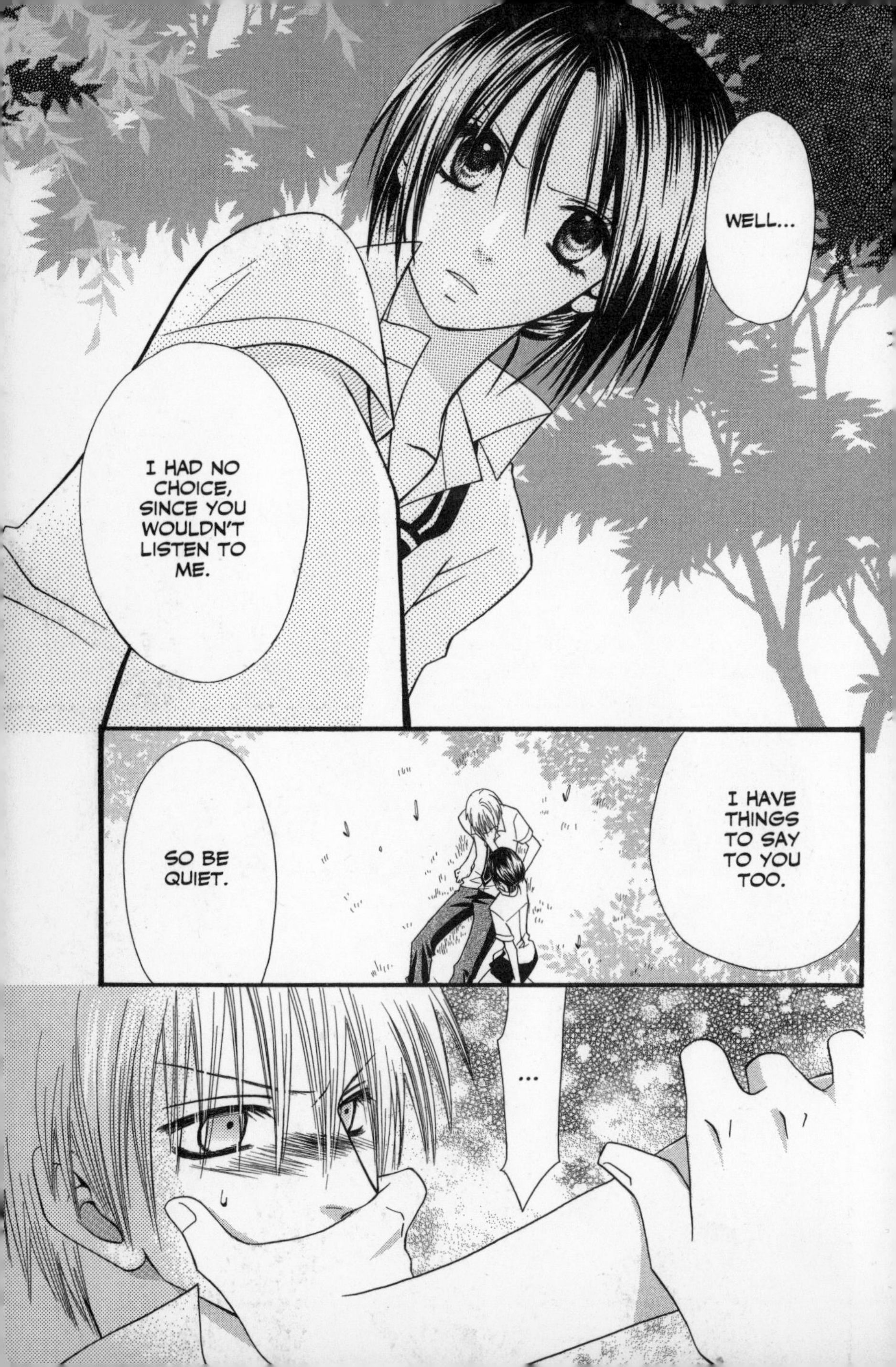
WELL...
I HAD NO CHOICE, SINCE YOU WOULDN'T LISTEN TO ME.
I HAVE THINGS TO SAY TO YOU TOO.
SO BE QUIET.
...

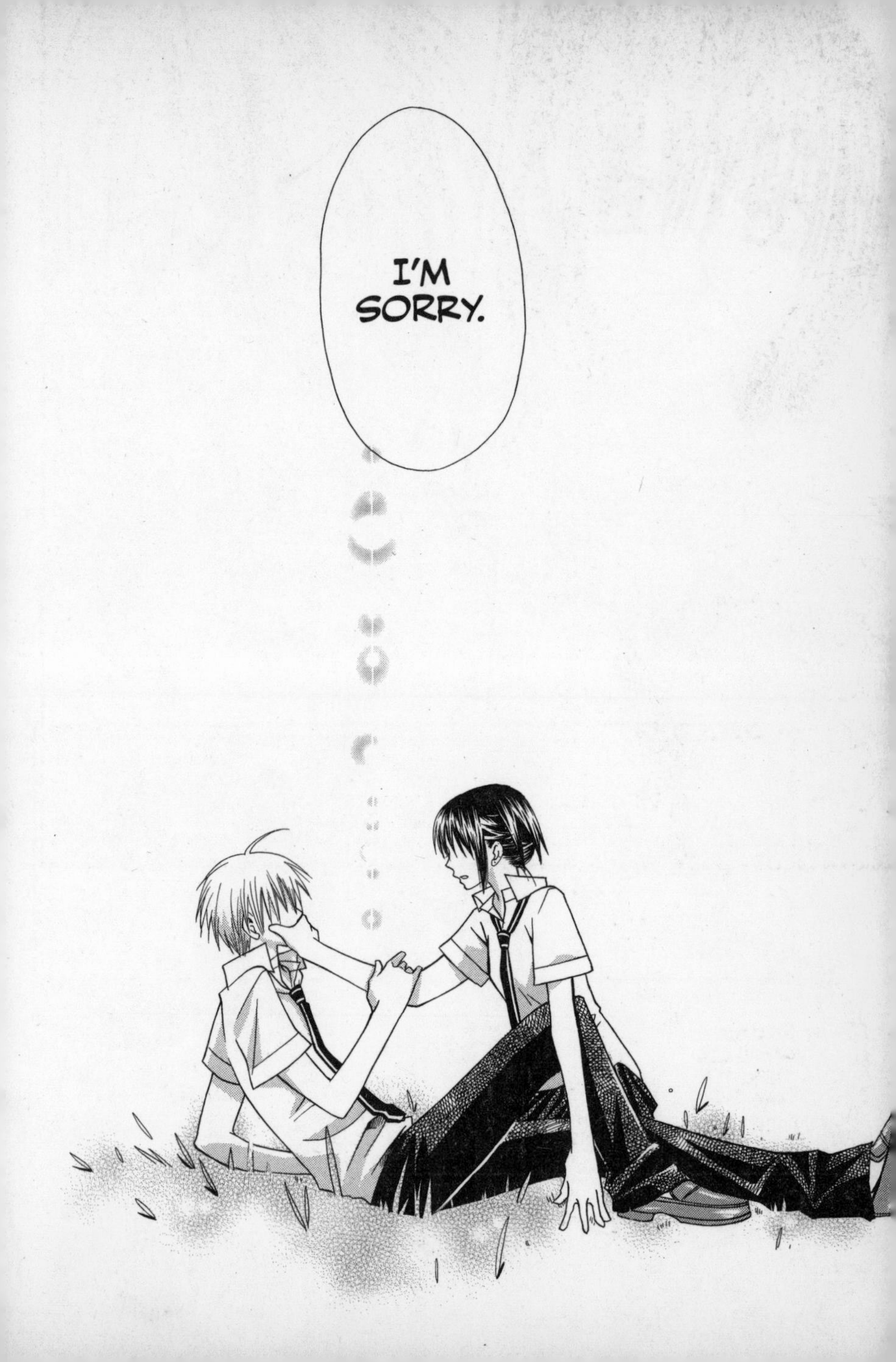
I'M SORRY.

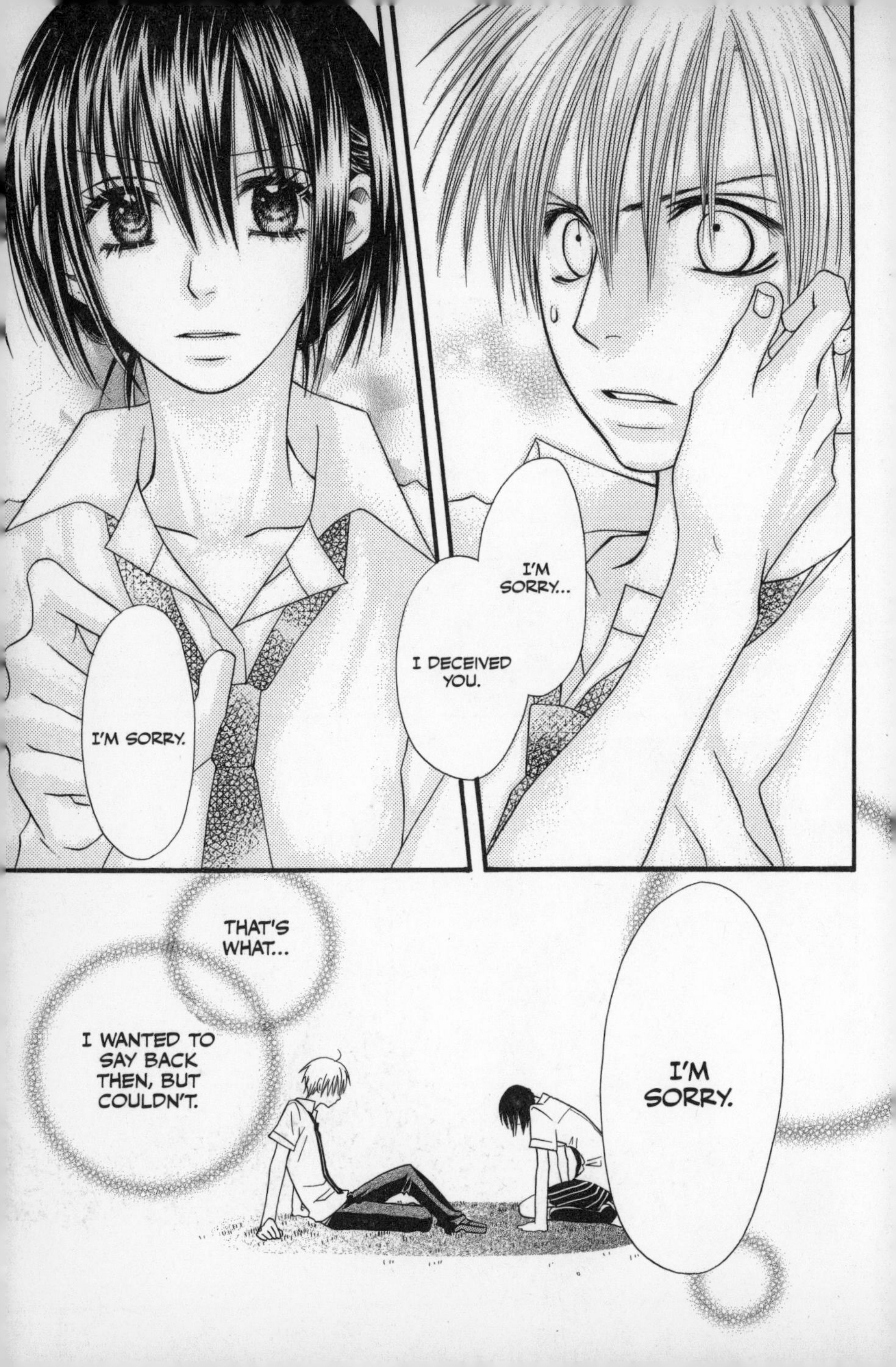
I'M SORRY... I DECEIVED YOU.
I'M SORRY.
I'M SORRY.
THAT'S WHAT...
I WANTED TO SAY BACK THEN, BUT COULDN'T.

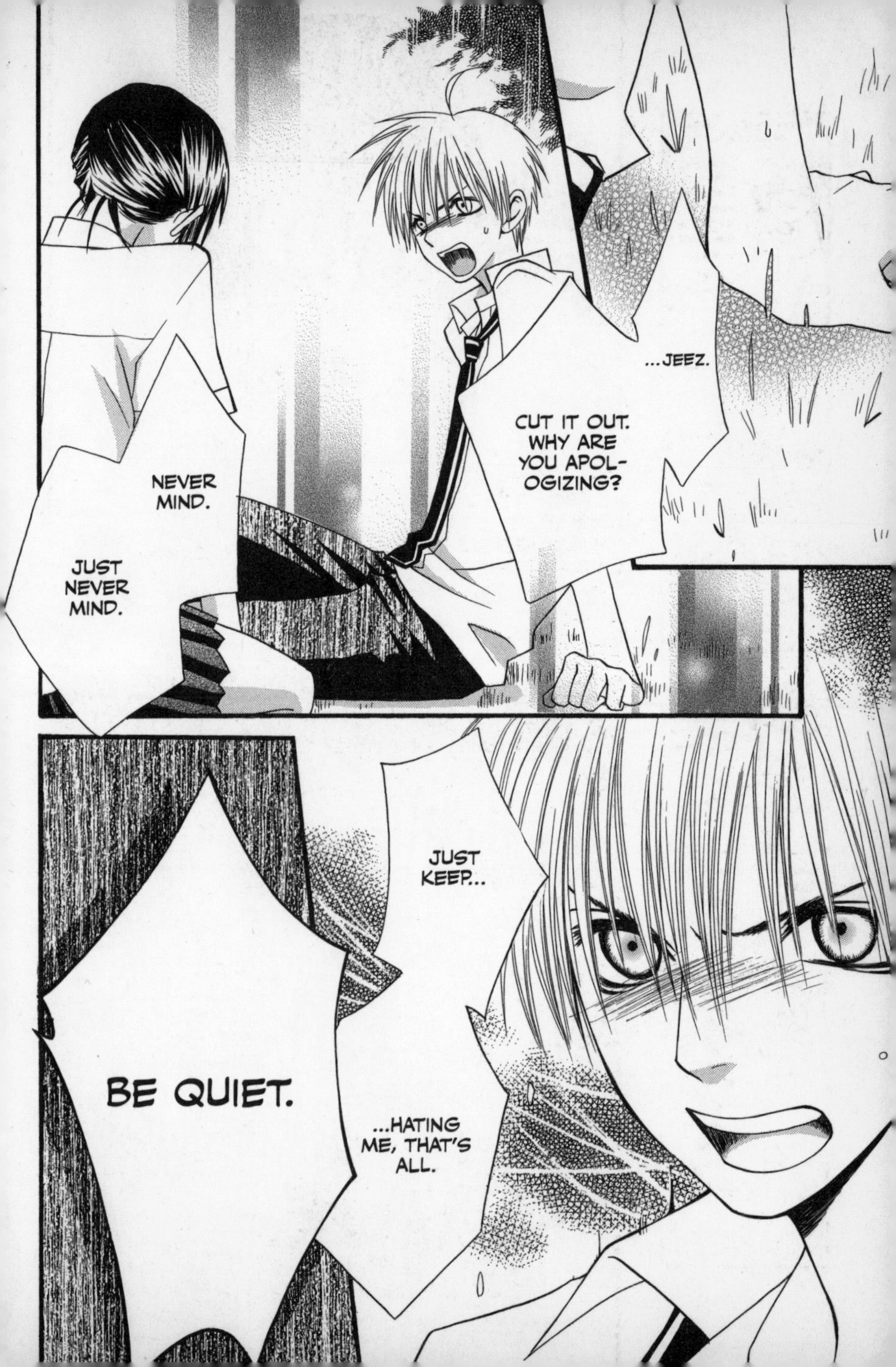
...JEEZ.
CUT IT OUT. WHY ARE YOU APOLOGIZING?
NEVER MIND.
JUST NEVER MIND.
JUST KEEP...
...HATING ME, THAT'S ALL.
BE QUIET.

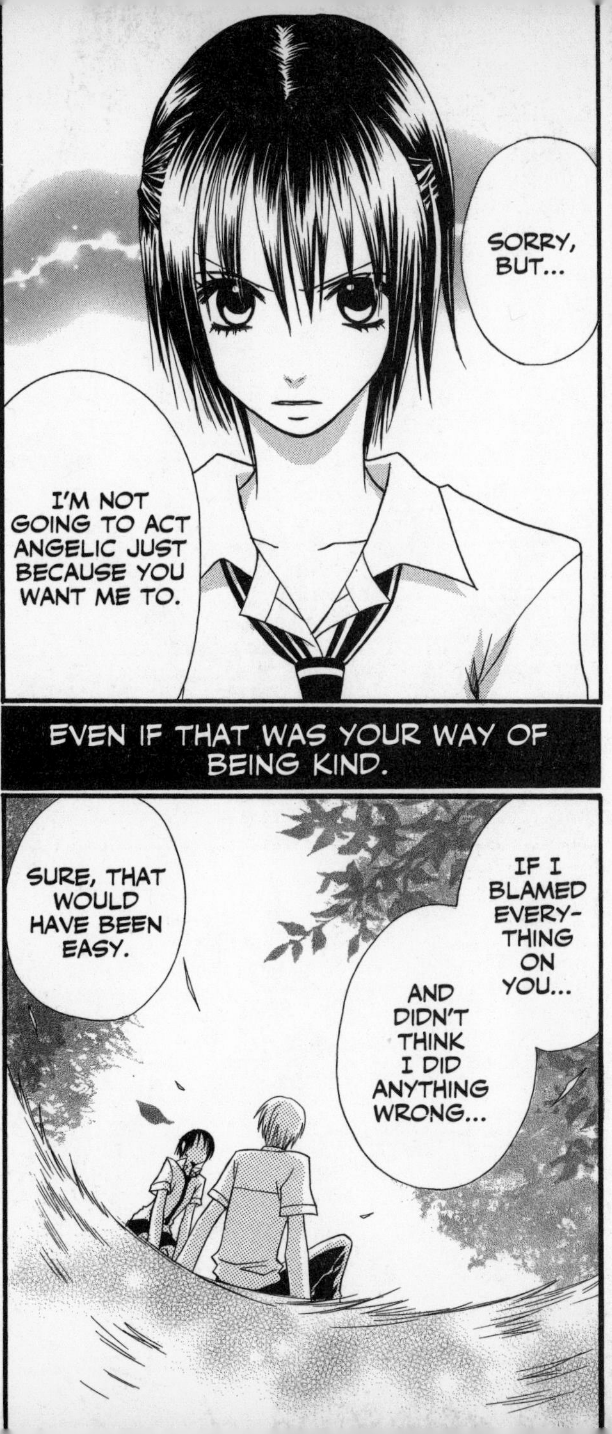
SORRY, BUT...
I'M NOT GOING TO ACT ANGELIC JUST BECAUSE YOU WANT ME TO.
EVEN IF THAT WAS YOUR WAY OF BEING KIND.
IF I BLAMED EVERYTHING ON YOU...
AND DIDN'T THINK I DID ANYTHING WRONG...
SURE, THAT WOULD HAVE BEEN EASY.

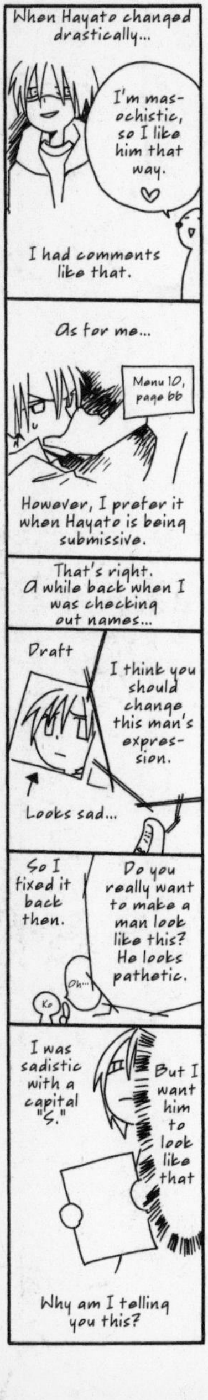
When Hayato changed drastically...
I'm masochistic, so I like him that way. ♡
I had comments like that.
As for me...
Menu 10, page 66
However, I prefer it when Hayato is being submissive.
That's right. A while back when I was checking out names...
Draft
I think you should change this man's expression.
Looks sad...
So I fixed it back then.
Do you really want to make a man look like this? He looks pathetic.
Oh...
Ko
I was sadistic with a capital "S."
But I want him to look like that
Why am I telling you this?

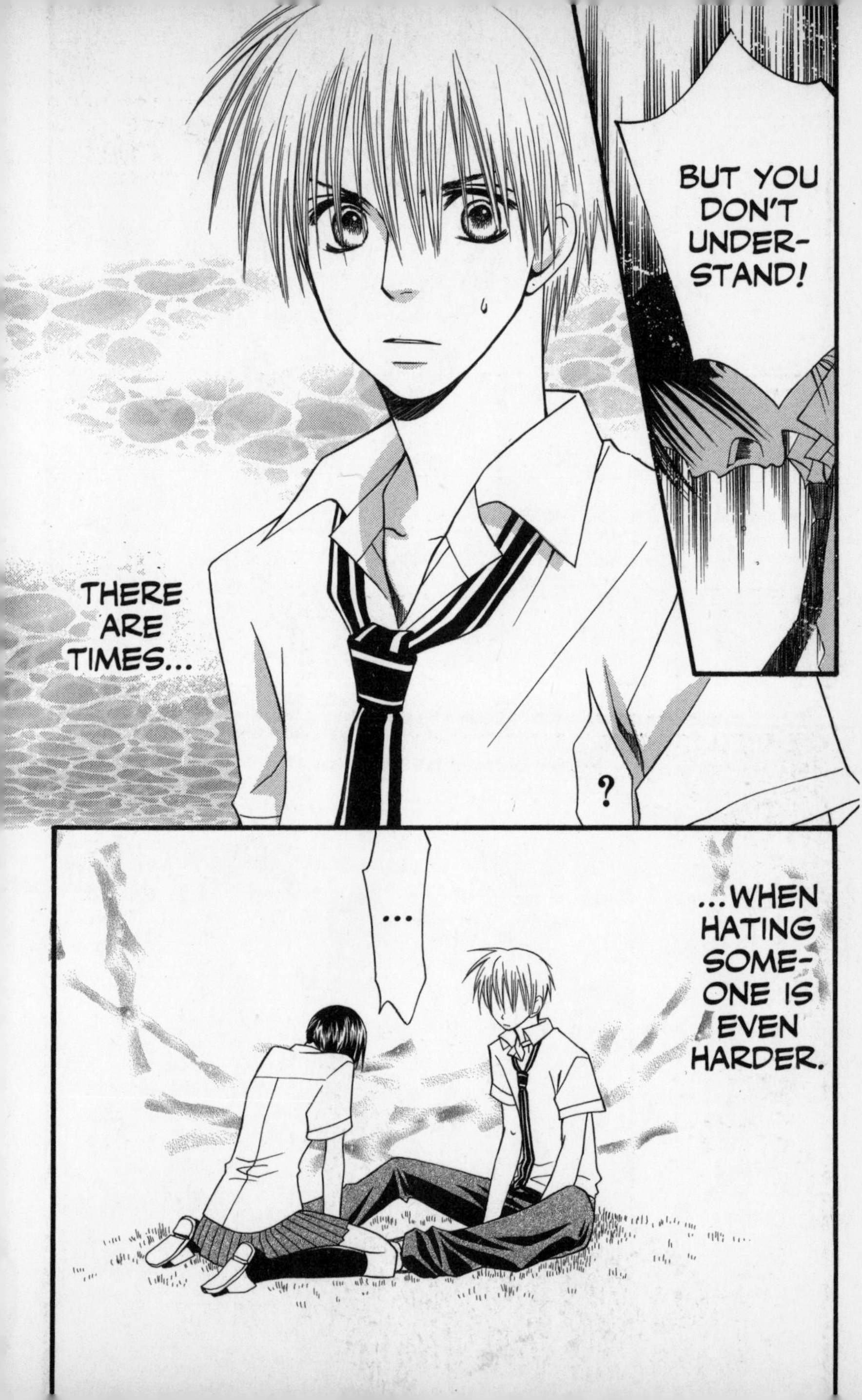
BUT YOU DON'T UNDER-STAND!
THERE ARE TIMES...
?
...WHEN HATING SOME-ONE IS EVEN HARDER.
...

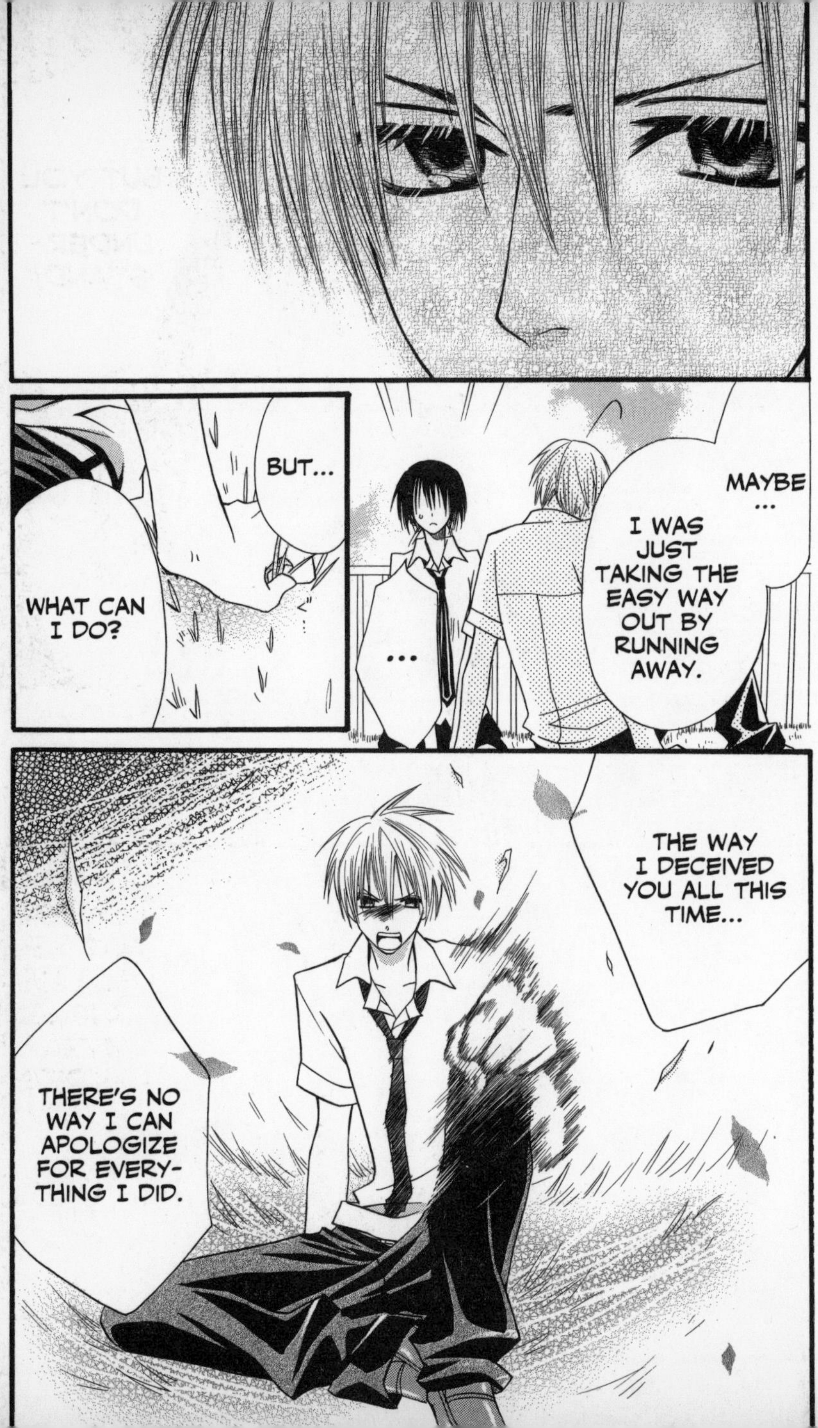
MAYBE ...
I WAS JUST TAKING THE EASY WAY OUT BY RUNNING AWAY.
...
BUT...
WHAT CAN I DO?
THE WAY I DECEIVED YOU ALL THIS TIME...
THERE'S NO WAY I CAN APOLOGIZE FOR EVERY-THING I DID.

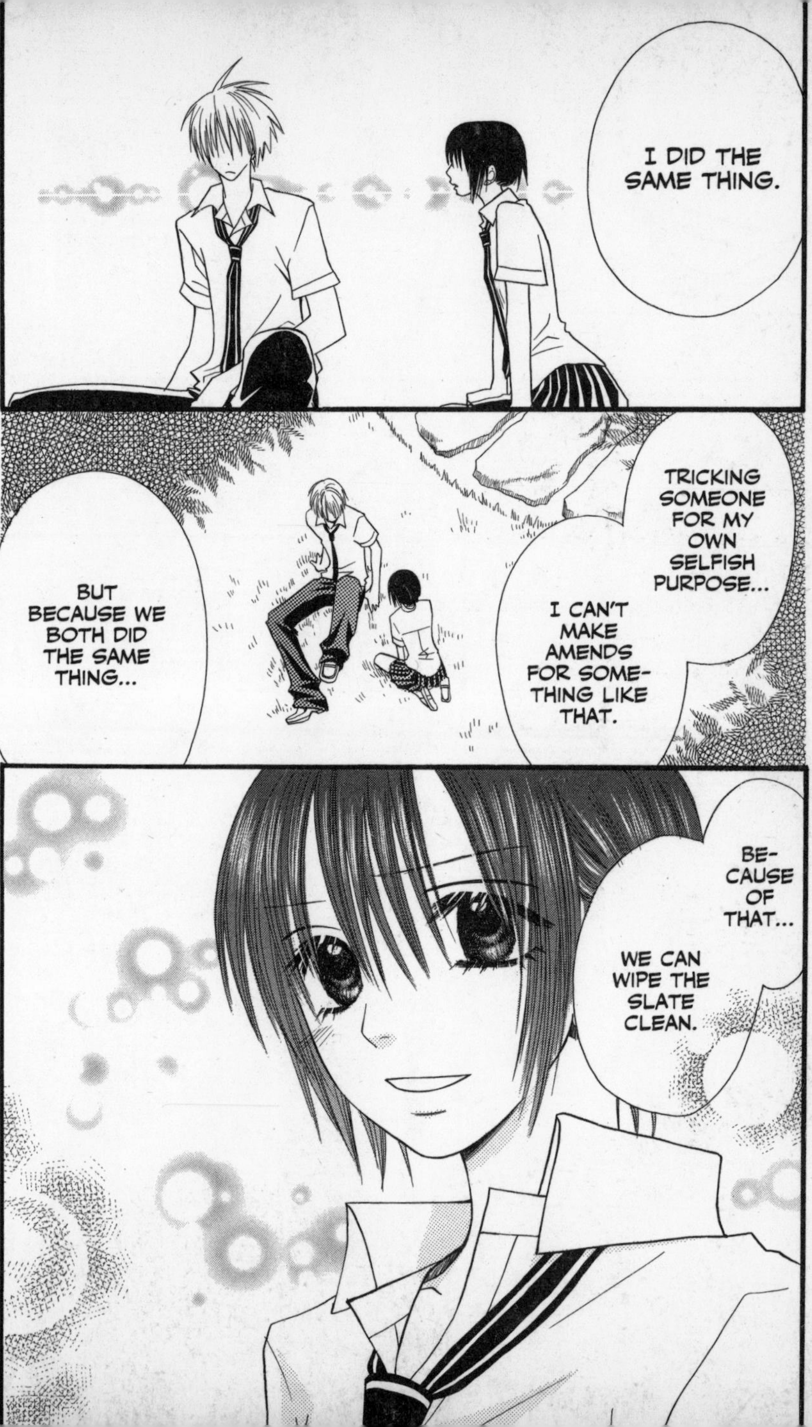
I DID THE SAME THING.
TRICKING SOMEONE FOR MY OWN SELFISH PURPOSE...
I CAN'T MAKE AMENDS FOR SOMETHING LIKE THAT.
BUT BECAUSE WE BOTH DID THE SAME THING...
BECAUSE OF THAT...
WE CAN WIPE THE SLATE CLEAN.

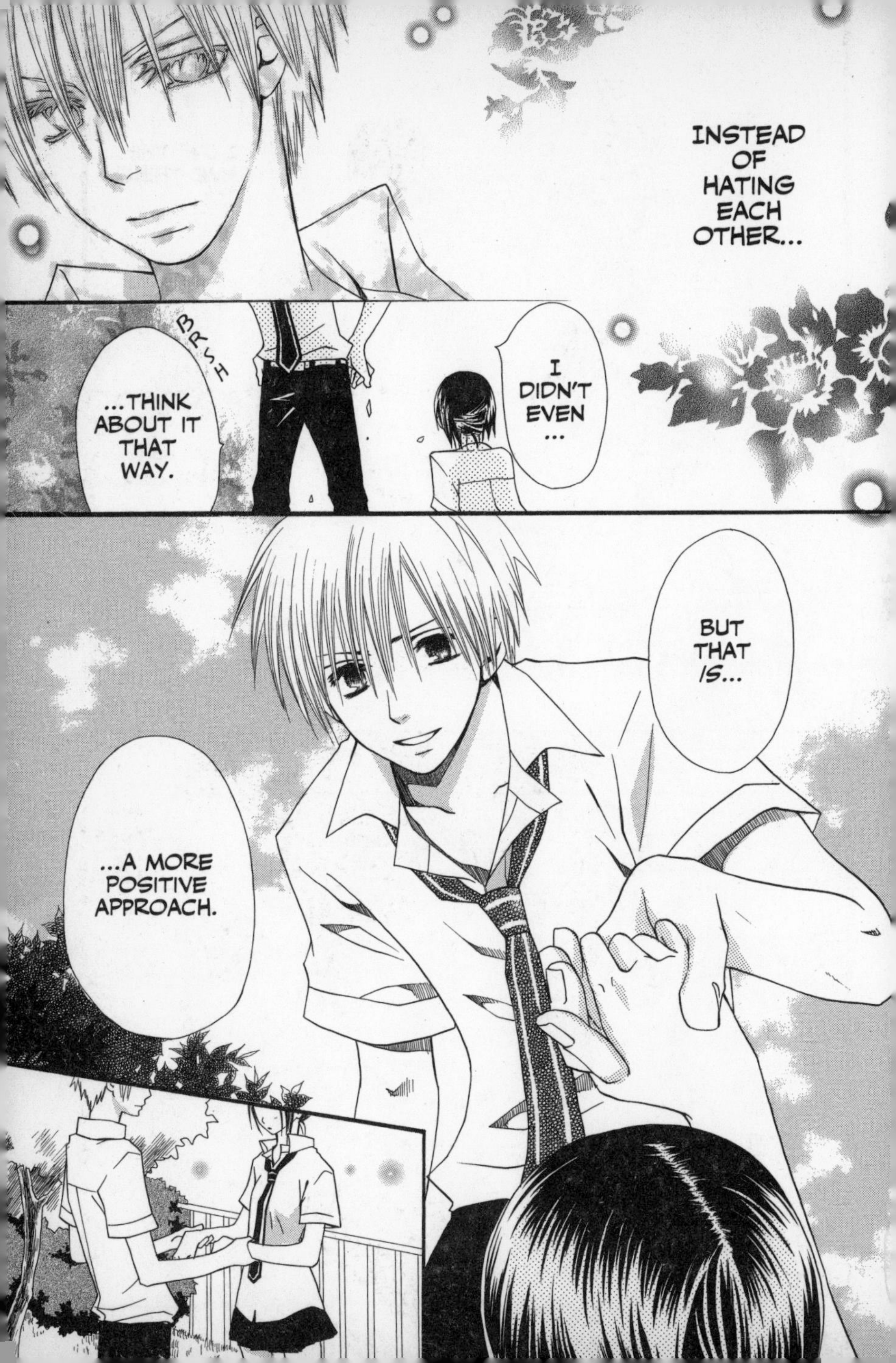
INSTEAD OF HATING EACH OTHER...
I DIDN'T EVEN ...
BRSH
...THINK ABOUT IT THAT WAY.
BUT THAT *IS*...
...A MORE POSITIVE APPROACH.

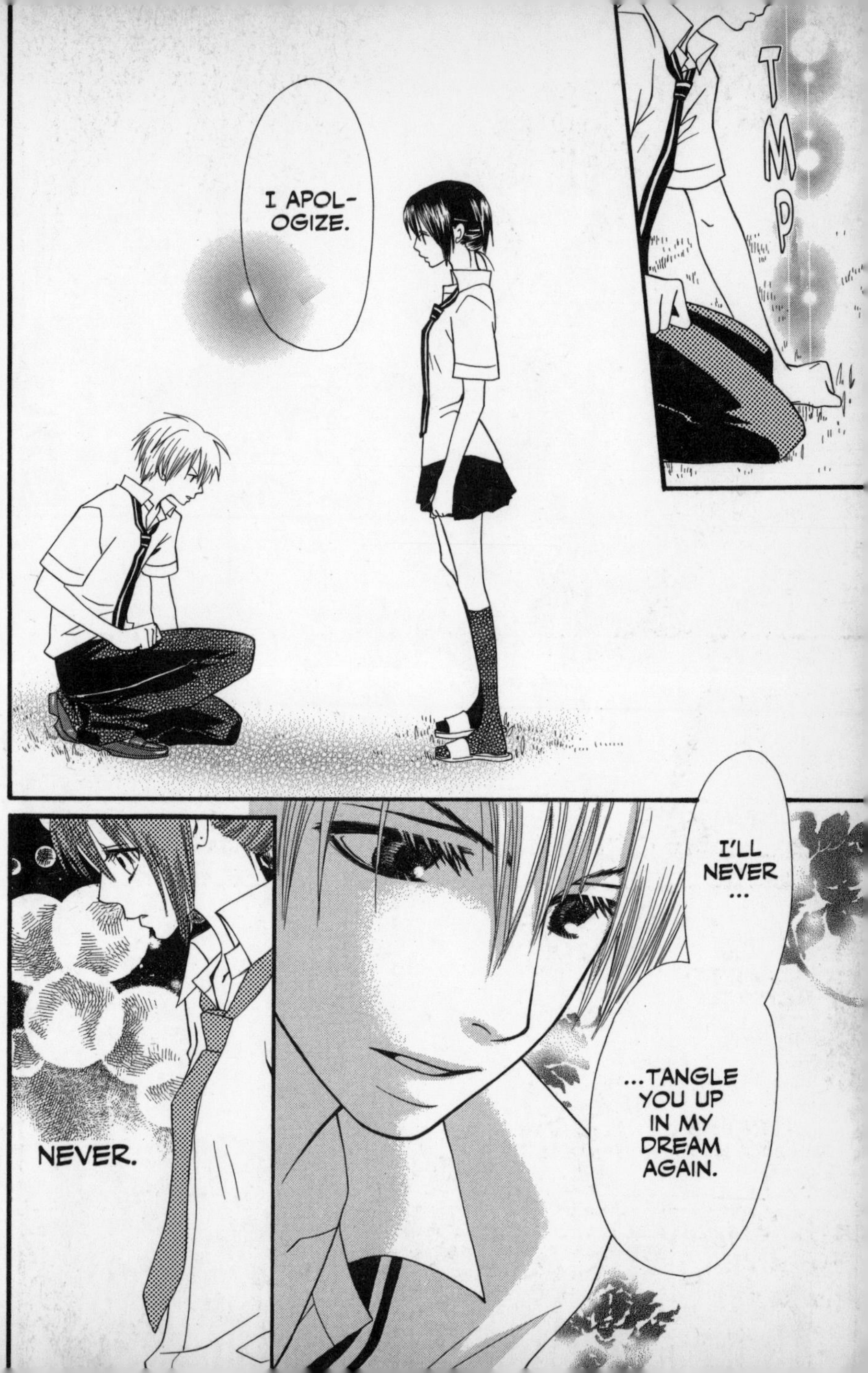
TMP
I APOLOGIZE.
I'LL NEVER ...
...TANGLE YOU UP IN MY DREAM AGAIN.
NEVER.

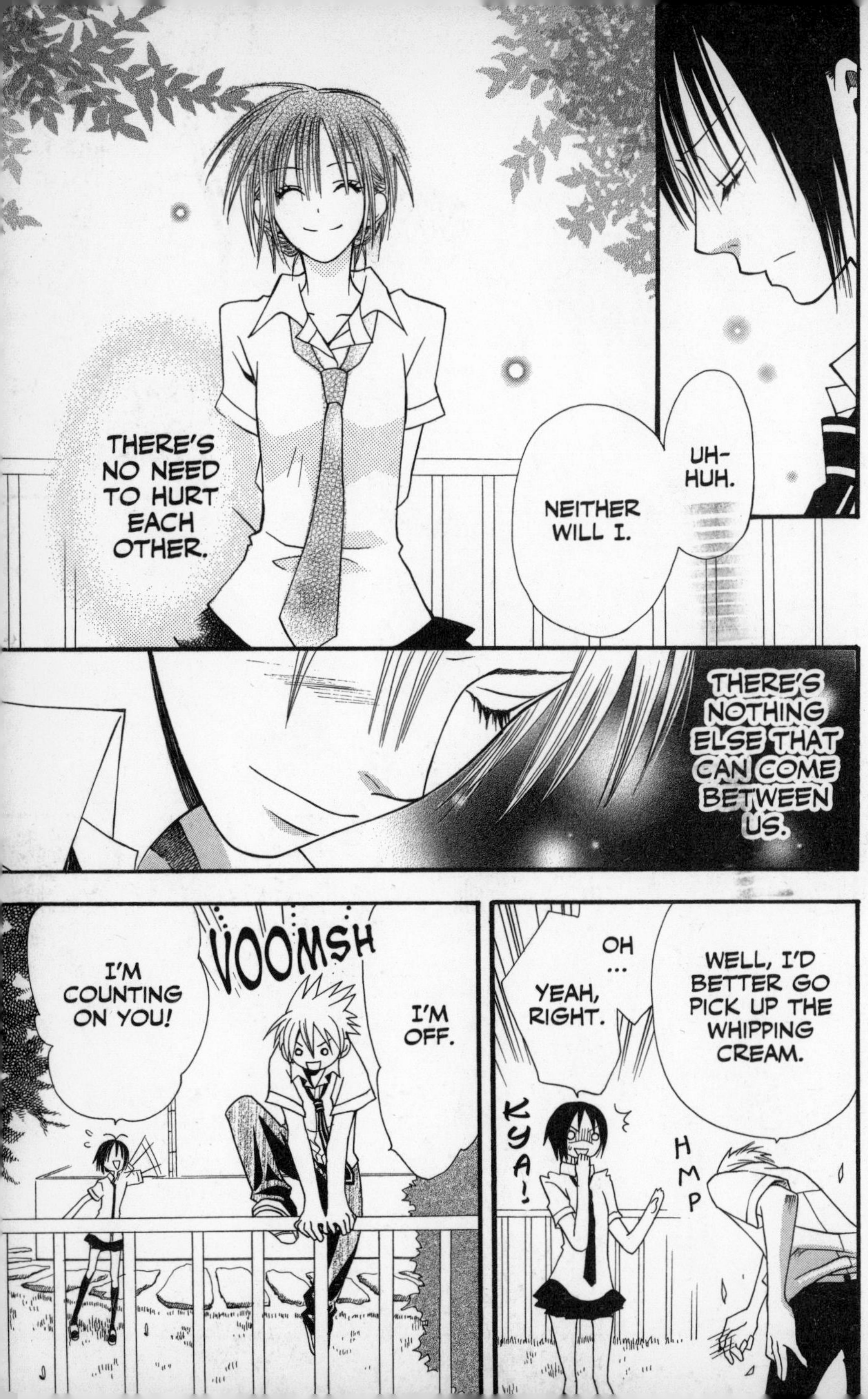

UH-HUH.
NEITHER WILL I.
THERE'S NO NEED TO HURT EACH OTHER.
THERE'S NOTHING ELSE THAT CAN COME BETWEEN US.
WELL, I'D BETTER GO PICK UP THE WHIPPING CREAM.
HMP
OH ... YEAH, RIGHT.
KYA!
VOOMSH
I'M OFF.
I'M COUNTING ON YOU!

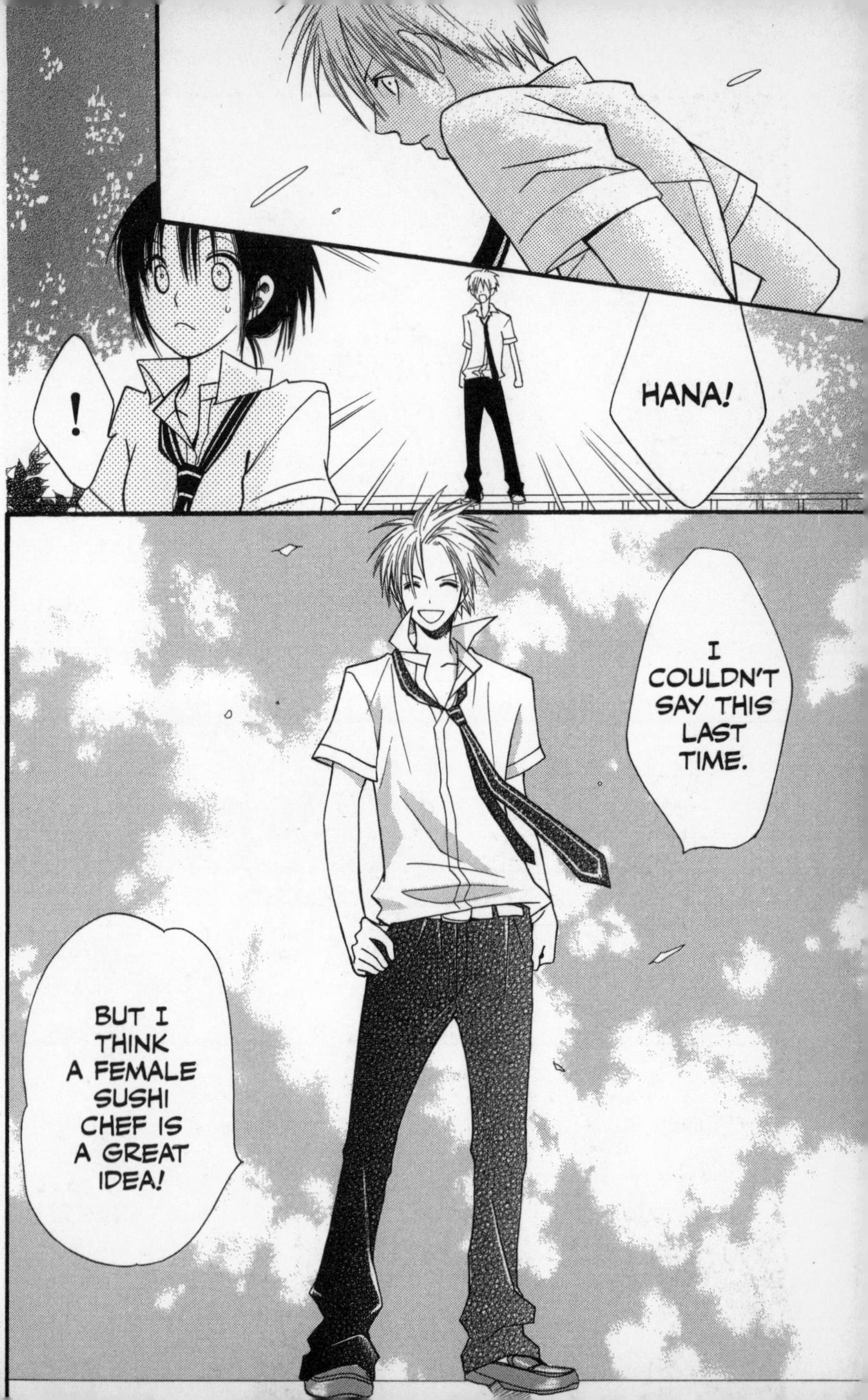
HANA!
!
I COULDN'T SAY THIS LAST TIME.
BUT I THINK A FEMALE SUSHI CHEF IS A GREAT IDEA!

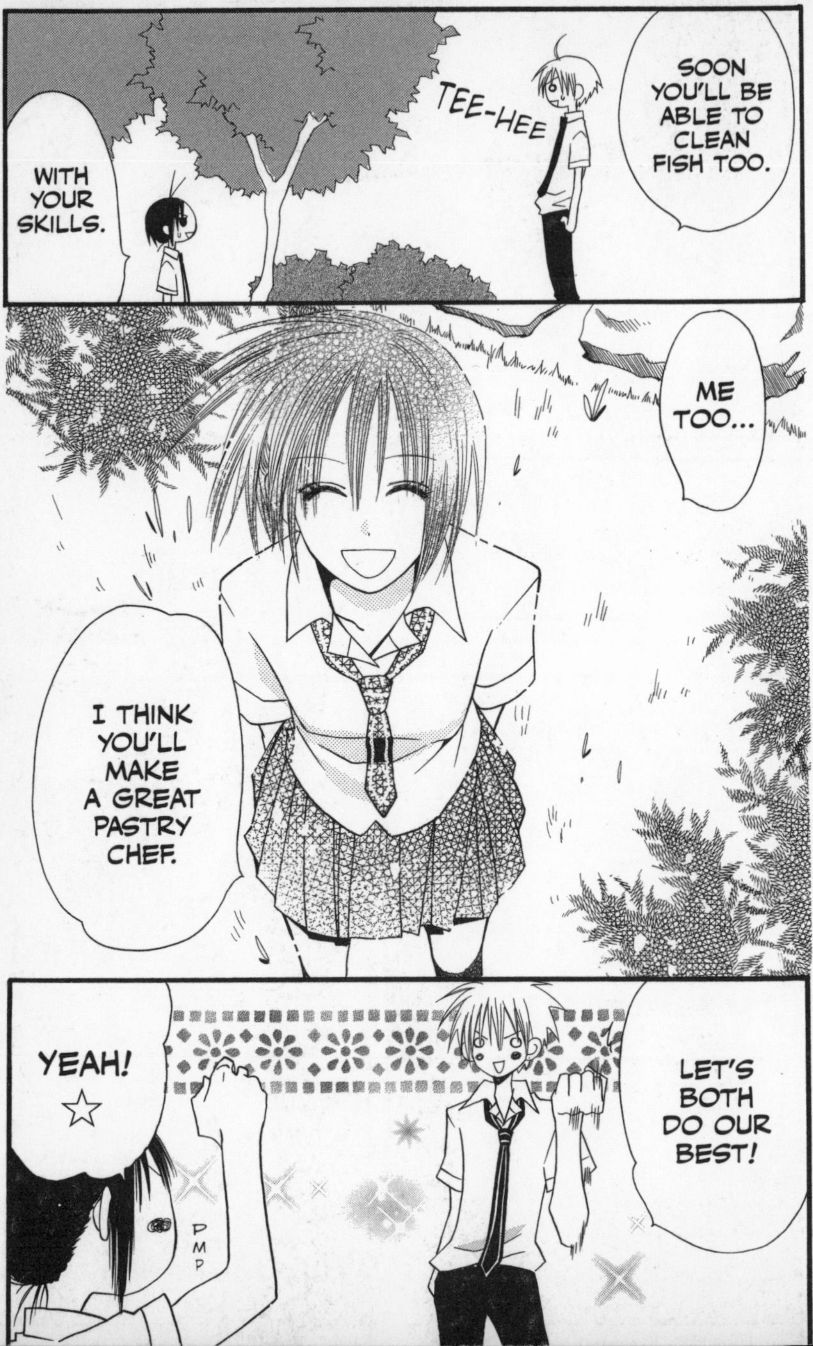
SOON YOU'LL BE ABLE TO CLEAN FISH TOO.
TEE-HEE
WITH YOUR SKILLS.
ME TOO...
I THINK YOU'LL MAKE A GREAT PASTRY CHEF.
LET'S BOTH DO OUR BEST!
YEAH! ☆
PMP

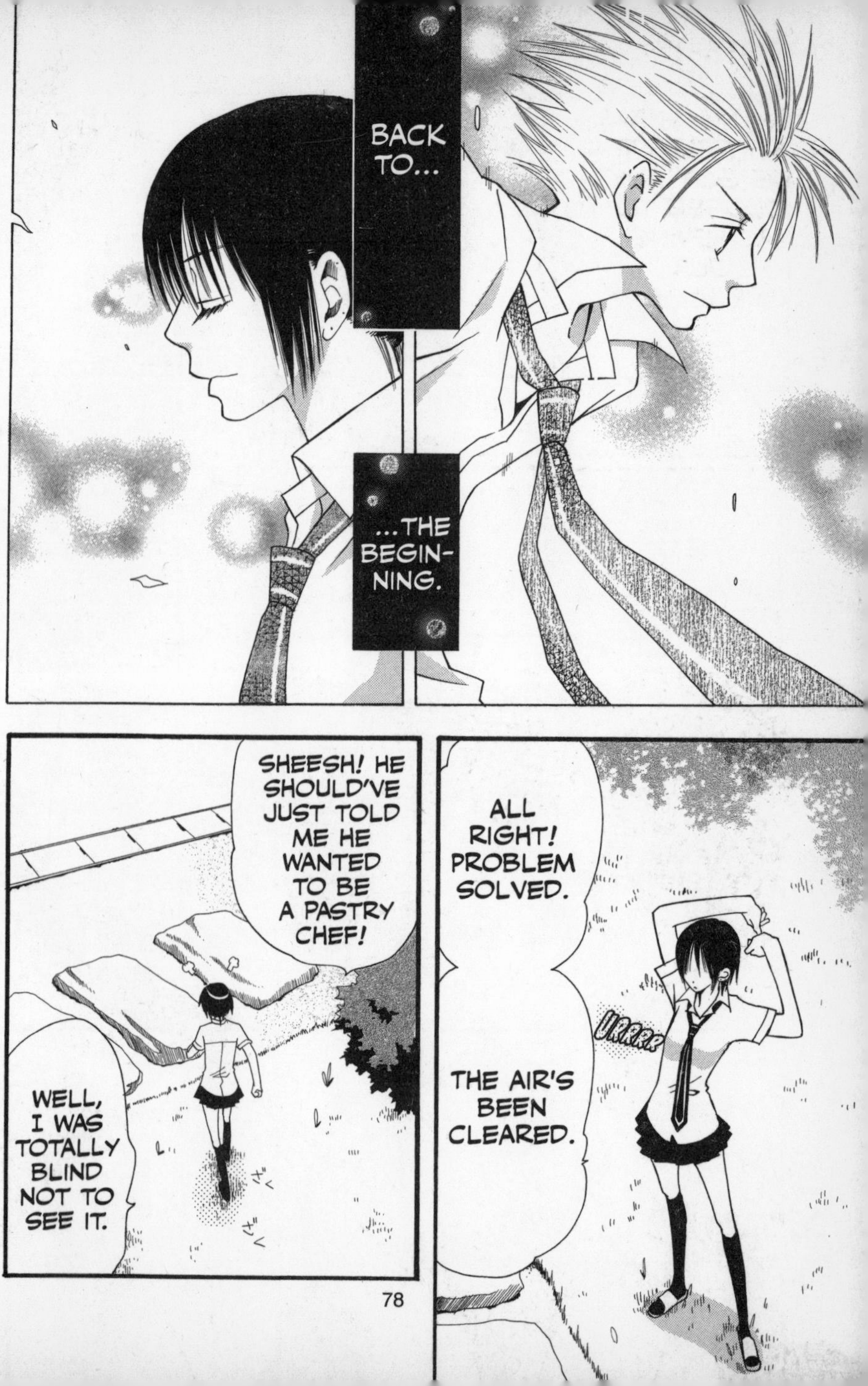
BACK TO...
...THE BEGINNING.
ALL RIGHT! PROBLEM SOLVED.
URRRR
THE AIR'S BEEN CLEARED.
SHEESH! HE SHOULD'VE JUST TOLD ME HE WANTED TO BE A PASTRY CHEF!
WELL, I WAS TOTALLY BLIND NOT TO SEE IT.

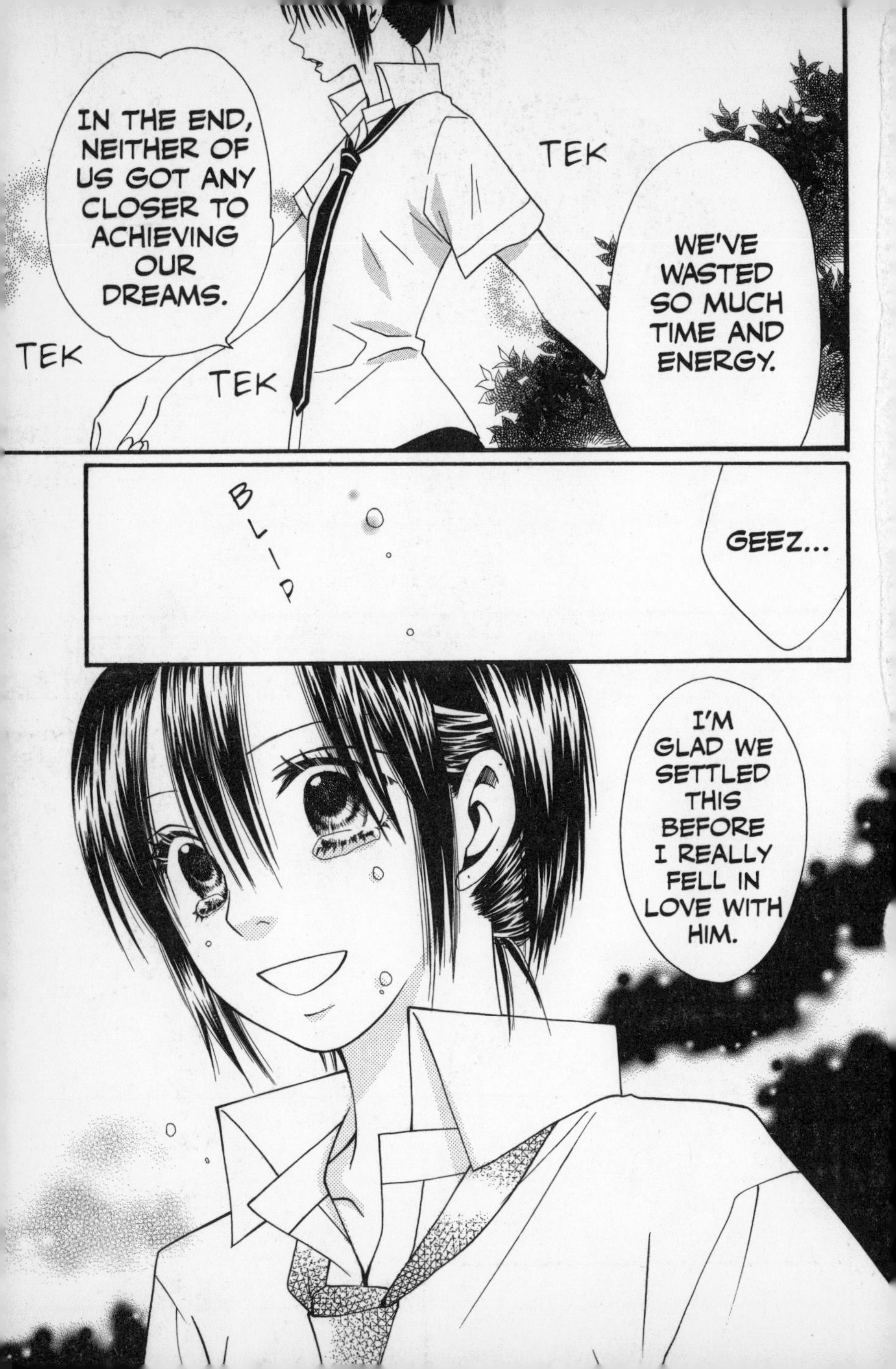
WE'VE WASTED SO MUCH TIME AND ENERGY.
TEK
IN THE END, NEITHER OF US GOT ANY CLOSER TO ACHIEVING OUR DREAMS.
TEK
TEK
GEEZ...
BLIP
I'M GLAD WE SETTLED THIS BEFORE I REALLY FELL IN LOVE WITH HIM.

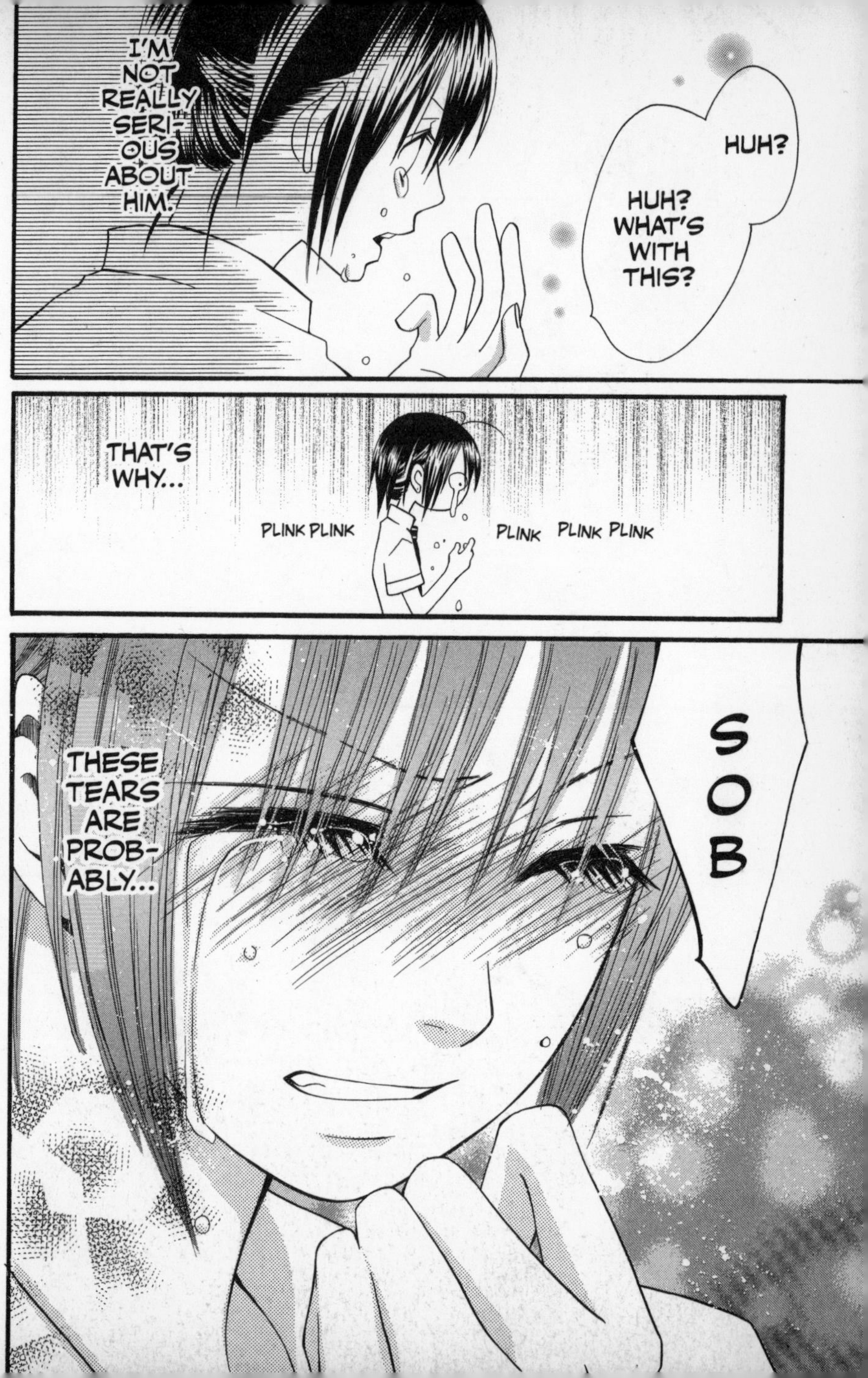
HUH?
HUH? WHAT'S WITH THIS?
I'M NOT REALLY SERIOUS ABOUT HIM.
PLINK PLINK PLINK
THAT'S WHY...
PLINK PLINK
SOB
THESE TEARS ARE PROBABLY...

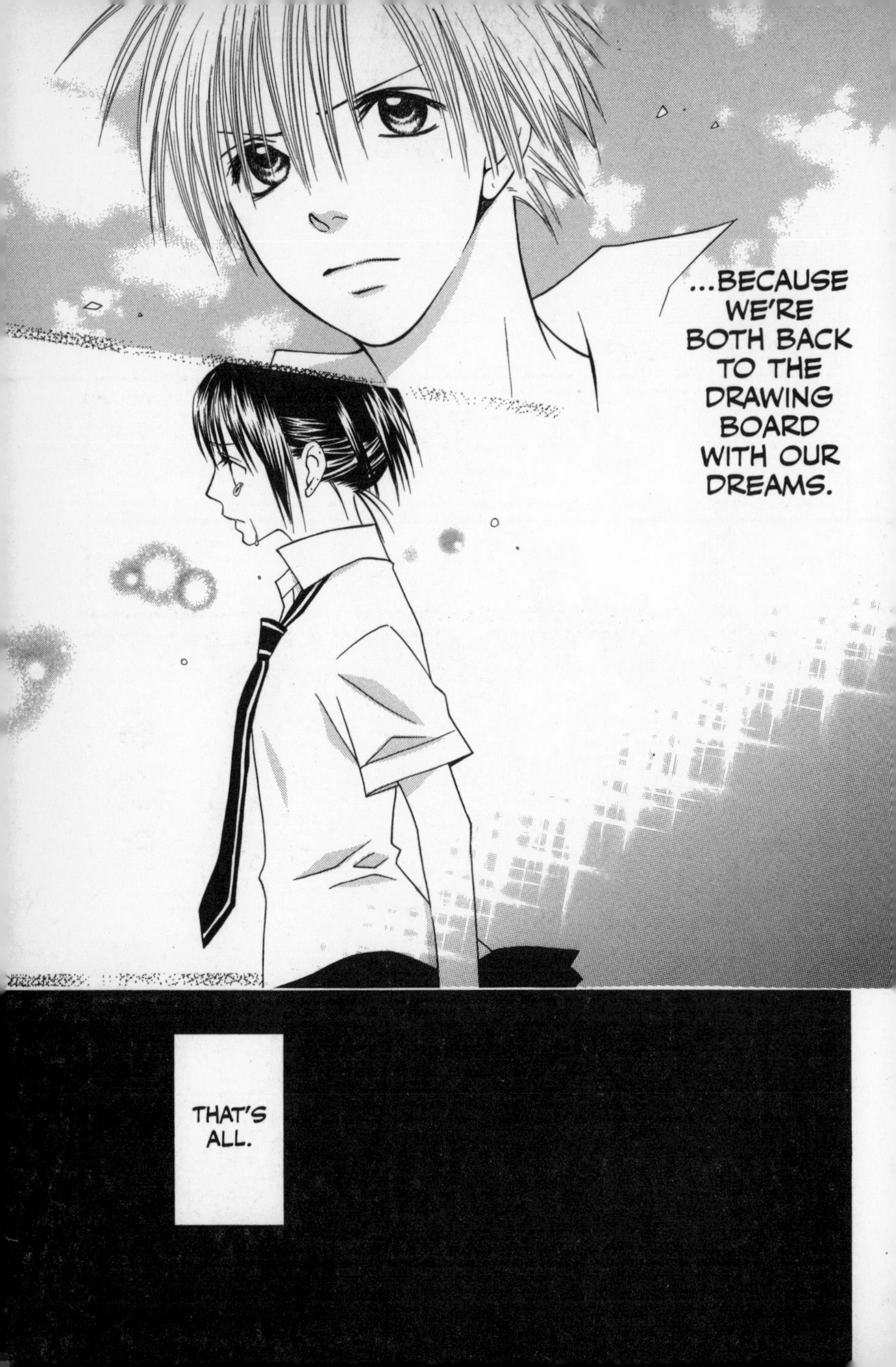
...BECAUSE WE'RE BOTH BACK TO THE DRAWING BOARD WITH OUR DREAMS.
THAT'S ALL.

SIDE DISH Mixed Vegetables 3

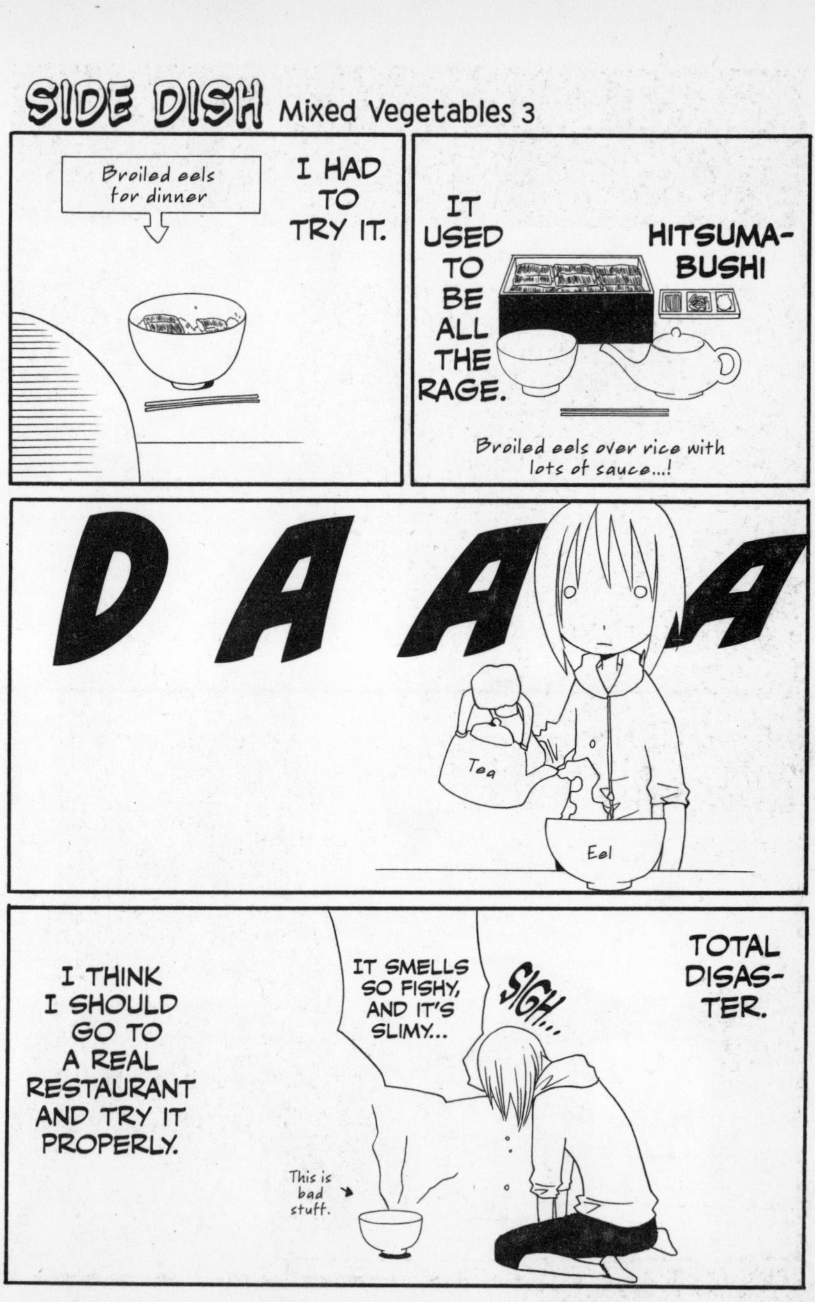
IT USED TO BE ALL THE RAGE.
HITSUMA-BUSHI
Broiled eels over rice with lots of sauce...!
I HAD TO TRY IT.
Broiled eels for dinner
DAAA
Tea
Eel
TOTAL DISASTER.
SIGH...
IT SMELLS SO FISHY, AND IT'S SLIMY...
I THINK I SHOULD GO TO A REAL RESTAURANT AND TRY IT PROPERLY.
This is bad stuff.

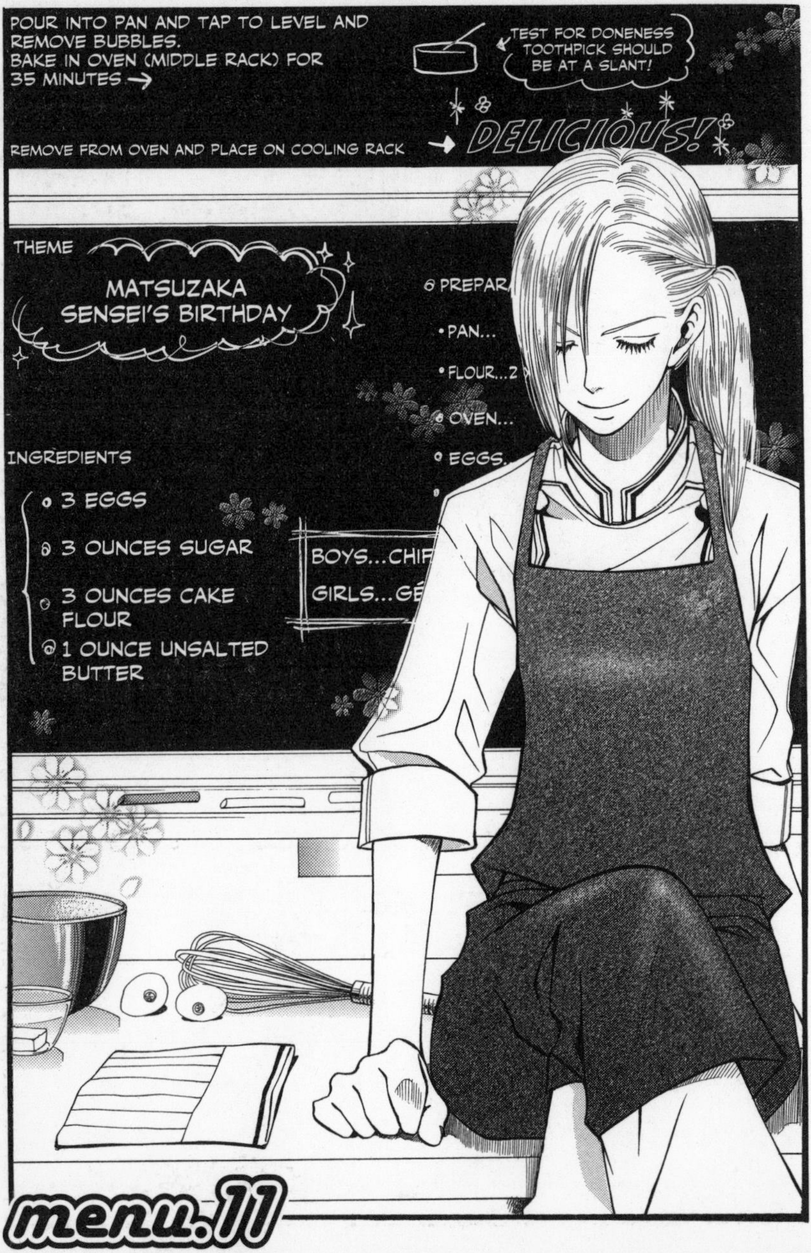
POUR INTO PAN AND TAP TO LEVEL AND REMOVE BUBBLES.
BAKE IN OVEN (MIDDLE RACK) FOR 35 MINUTES →
TEST FOR DONENESS TOOTHPICK SHOULD BE AT A SLANT!
REMOVE FROM OVEN AND PLACE ON COOLING RACK →
DELICIOUS!
THEME
MATSUZAKA SENSEI'S BIRTHDAY
PREPAR
•PAN...
•FLOUR...2
OVEN...
EGGS.
INGREDIENTS
3 EGGS
3 OUNCES SUGAR
3 OUNCES CAKE FLOUR
1 OUNCE UNSALTED BUTTER
BOYS...CHIF
GIRLS...GÉ
menu.11

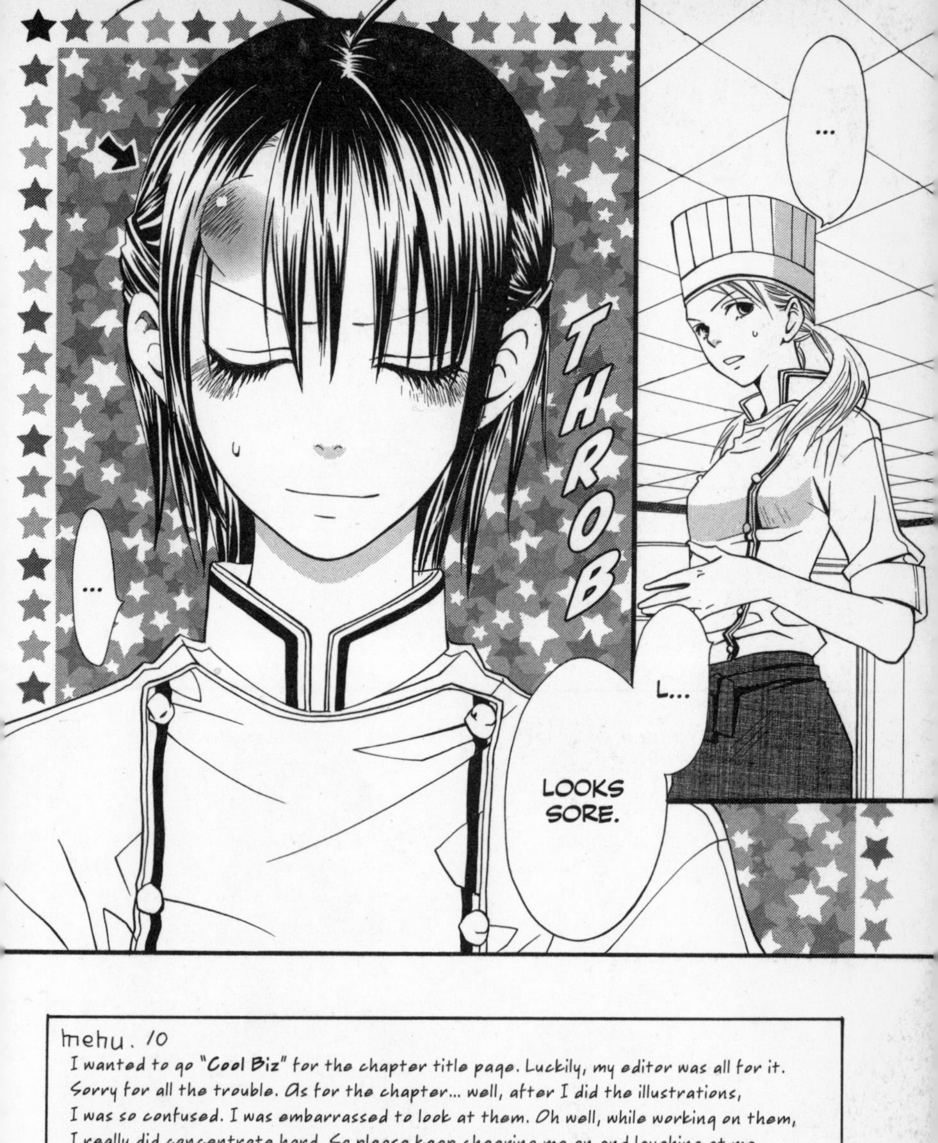
...
THROB
L...
LOOKS SORE.
...

menu. 10

I wanted to go "**Cool Biz**" for the chapter title page. Luckily, my editor was all for it. Sorry for all the trouble. As for the chapter... well, after I did the illustrations, I was so confused. I was embarrassed to look at them. Oh well, while working on them, I really did concentrate hard. So please keep cheering me on and laughing at me.

menu. 11

It's Matsuzaka Sensei's title page! An old high school friend requested the two different styles of sponge cake... I really struggled. I'm really not very good at drawing food, especially when it comes to shading. But it's getting easier to draw Hayato. Until now he was a liar, and a goody-goody, and hard to draw...

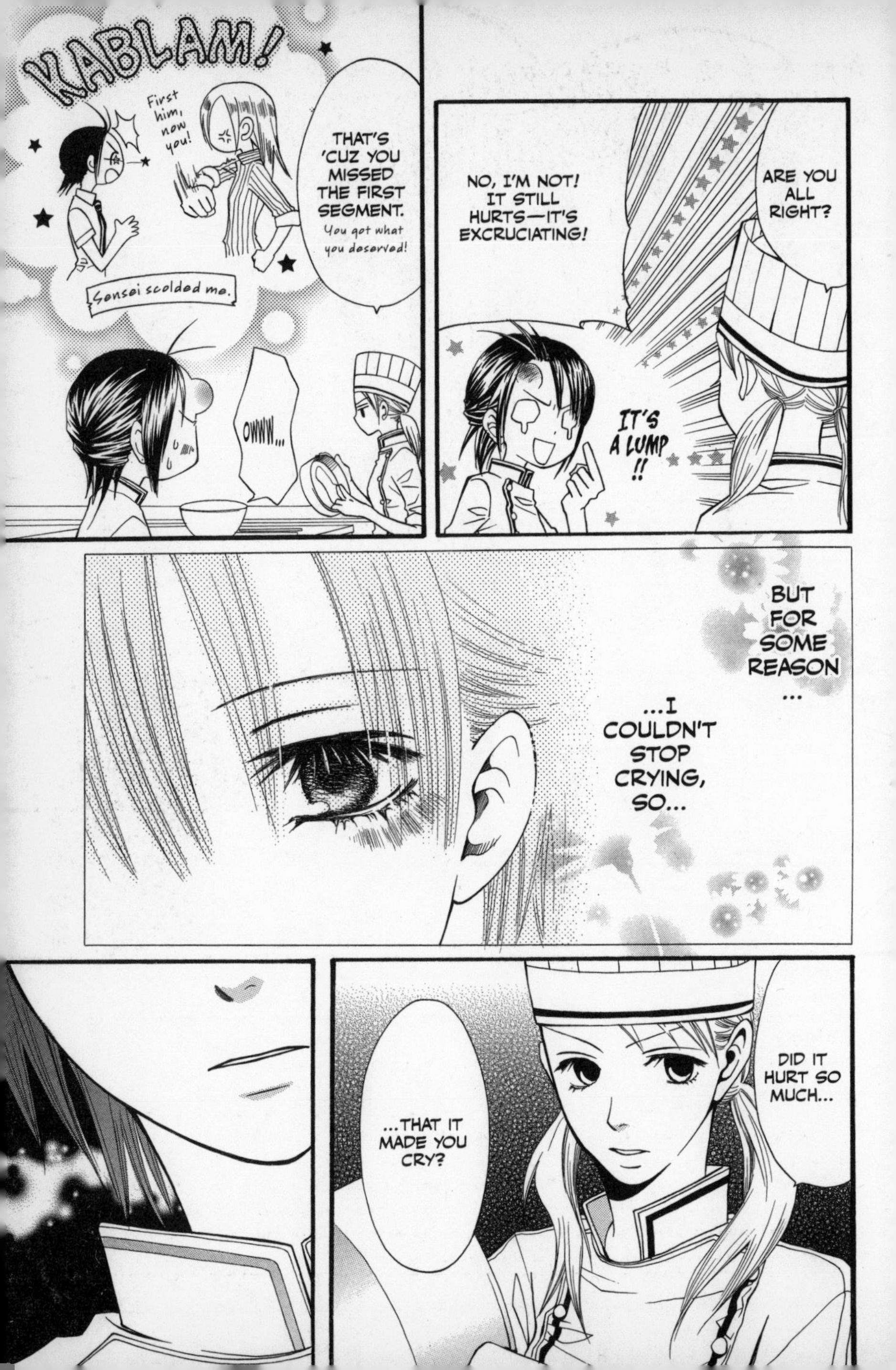
ARE YOU ALL RIGHT?
NO, I'M NOT! IT STILL HURTS—IT'S EXCRUCIATING!
IT'S A LUMP!!
THAT'S 'CUZ YOU MISSED THE FIRST SEGMENT.
You got what you deserved!
KABLAM!
First him, now you!
Sensei scolded me.
OWWW...
BUT FOR SOME REASON...
...I COULDN'T STOP CRYING, SO...
DID IT HURT SO MUCH...
...THAT IT MADE YOU CRY?

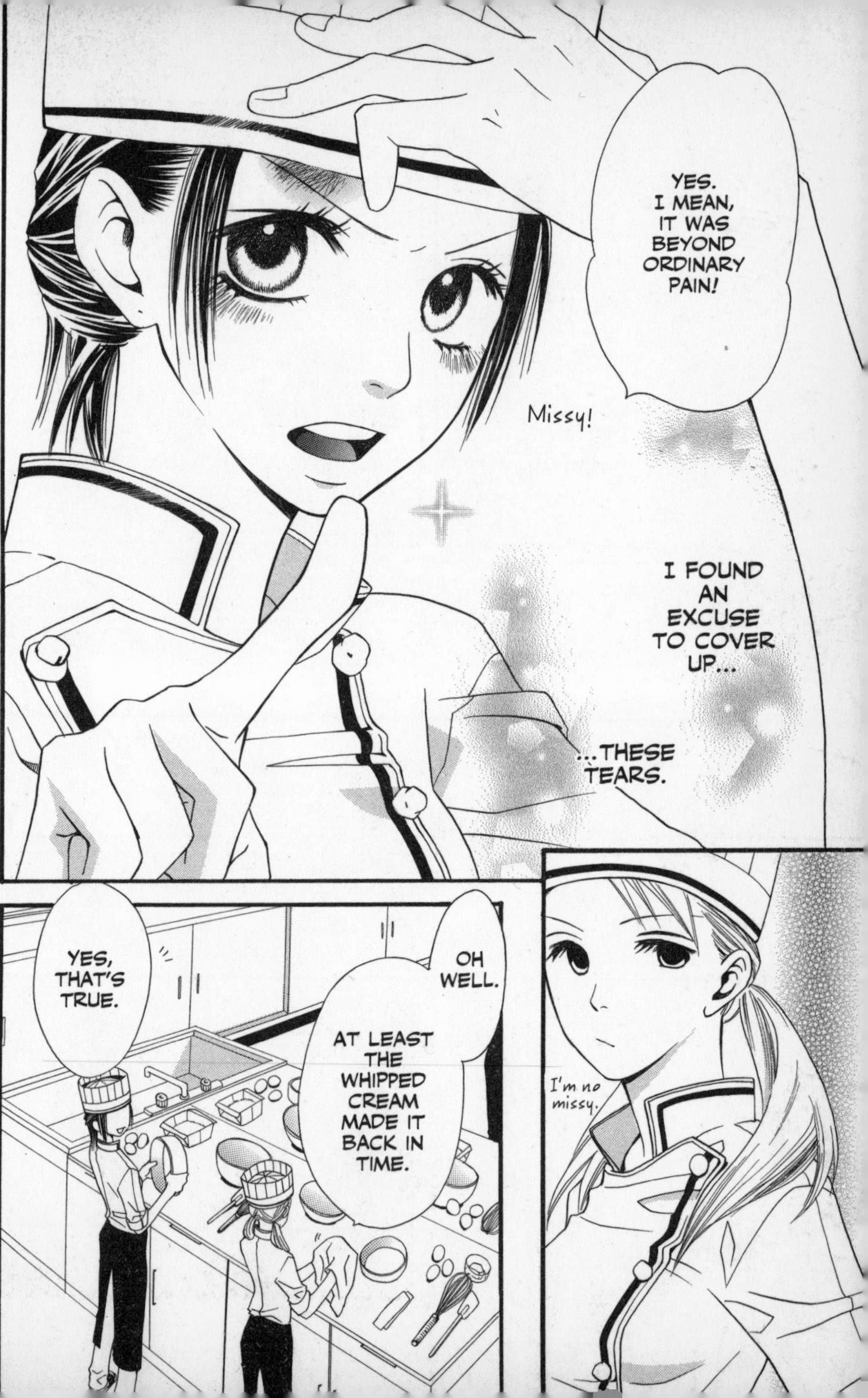
YES. I MEAN, IT WAS BEYOND ORDINARY PAIN!
Missy!
I FOUND AN EXCUSE TO COVER UP...
...THESE TEARS.
I'm no missy.
OH WELL.
AT LEAST THE WHIPPED CREAM MADE IT BACK IN TIME.
YES, THAT'S TRUE.

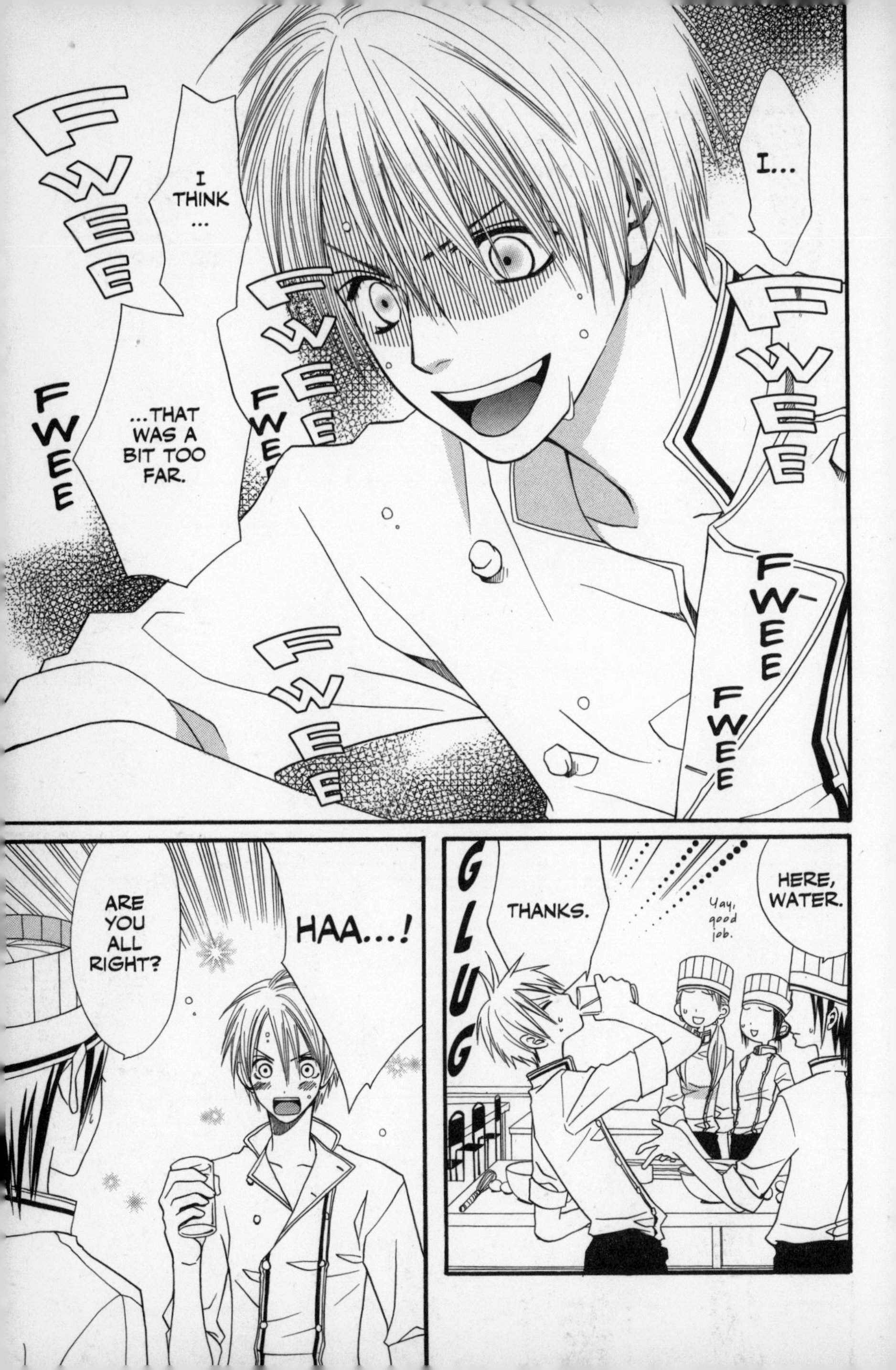
I...
FWEE
FWEE
FWEE
FWEE
FWEE
FWEE
FWEE
I THINK...
...THAT WAS A BIT TOO FAR.
HERE, WATER.
Yay, good job.
THANKS.
GLUG
HAA...!
ARE YOU ALL RIGHT?

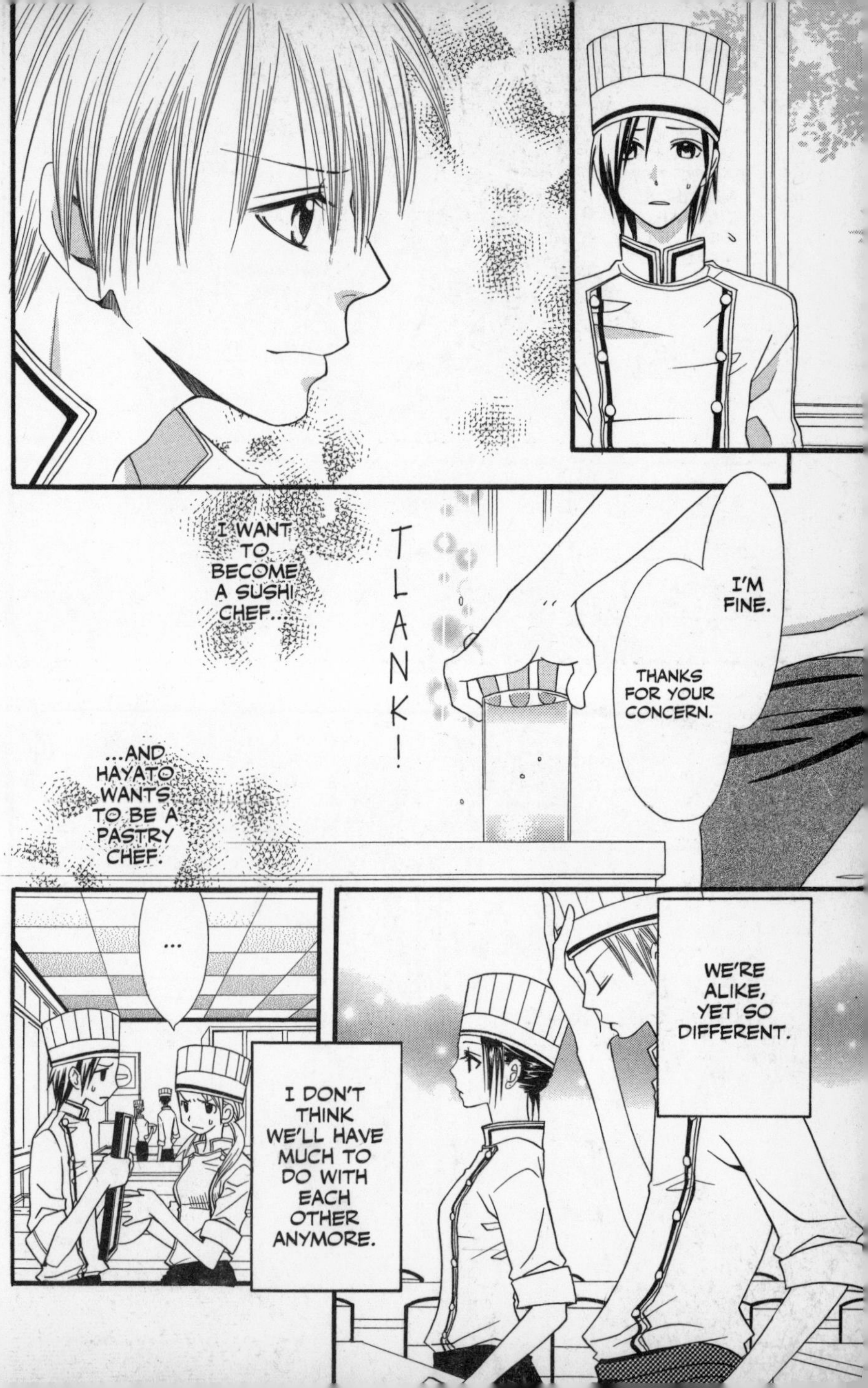
I'M FINE.
THANKS FOR YOUR CONCERN.
TLANK!
I WANT TO BECOME A SUSHI CHEF...
...AND HAYATO WANTS TO BE A PASTRY CHEF.
WE'RE ALIKE, YET SO DIFFERENT.
I DON'T THINK WE'LL HAVE MUCH TO DO WITH EACH OTHER ANYMORE.
...

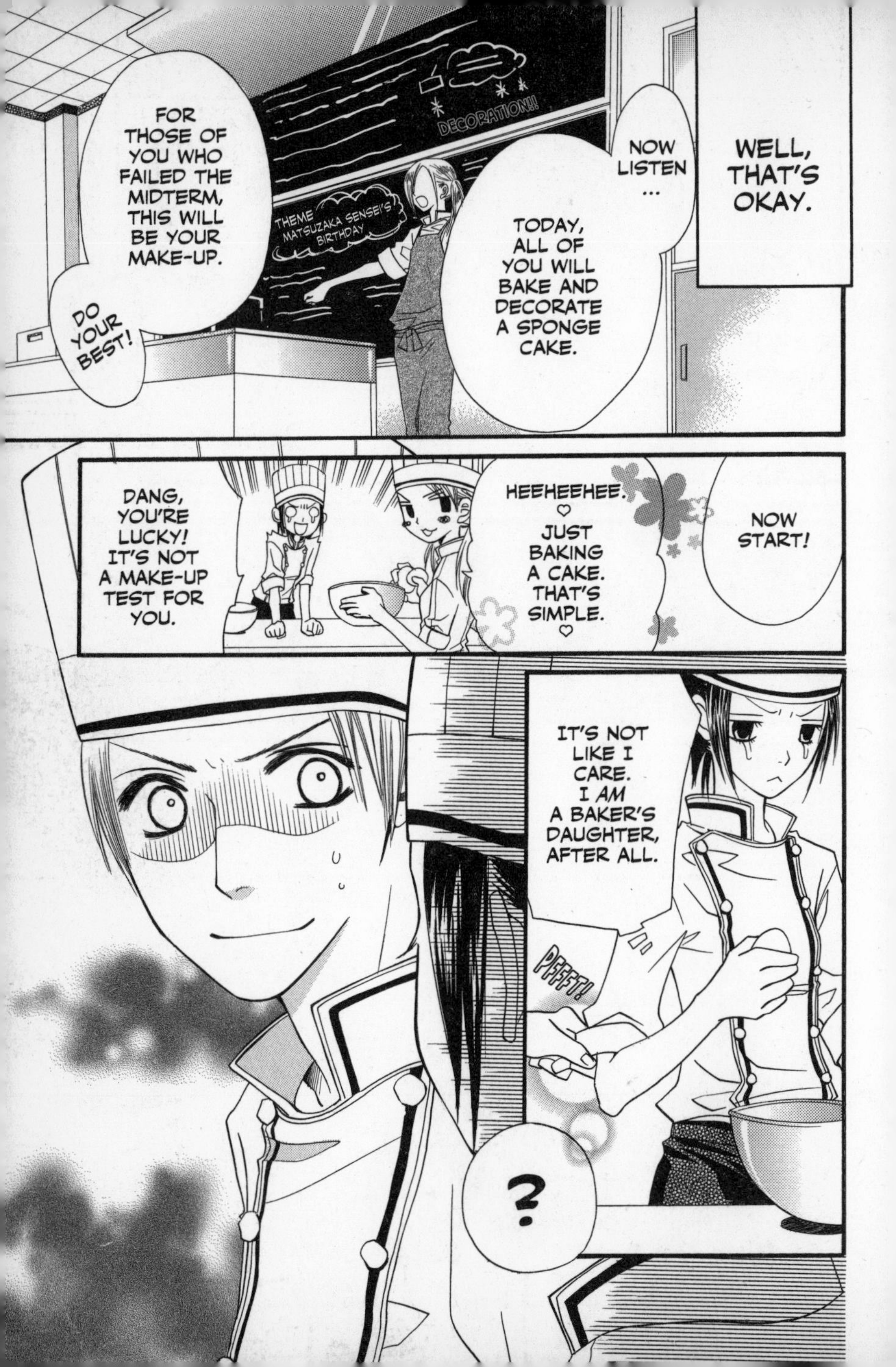
WELL, THAT'S OKAY.
NOW LISTEN ...
TODAY, ALL OF YOU WILL BAKE AND DECORATE A SPONGE CAKE.
DECORATION!!
THEME MATSUZAKA SENSEI'S BIRTHDAY
FOR THOSE OF YOU WHO FAILED THE MIDTERM, THIS WILL BE YOUR MAKE-UP.
DO YOUR BEST!
NOW START!
HEEHEEHEE. ♡ JUST BAKING A CAKE. THAT'S SIMPLE. ♡
DANG, YOU'RE LUCKY! IT'S NOT A MAKE-UP TEST FOR YOU.
IT'S NOT LIKE I CARE. I *AM* A BAKER'S DAUGHTER, AFTER ALL.
PFFFT!
?

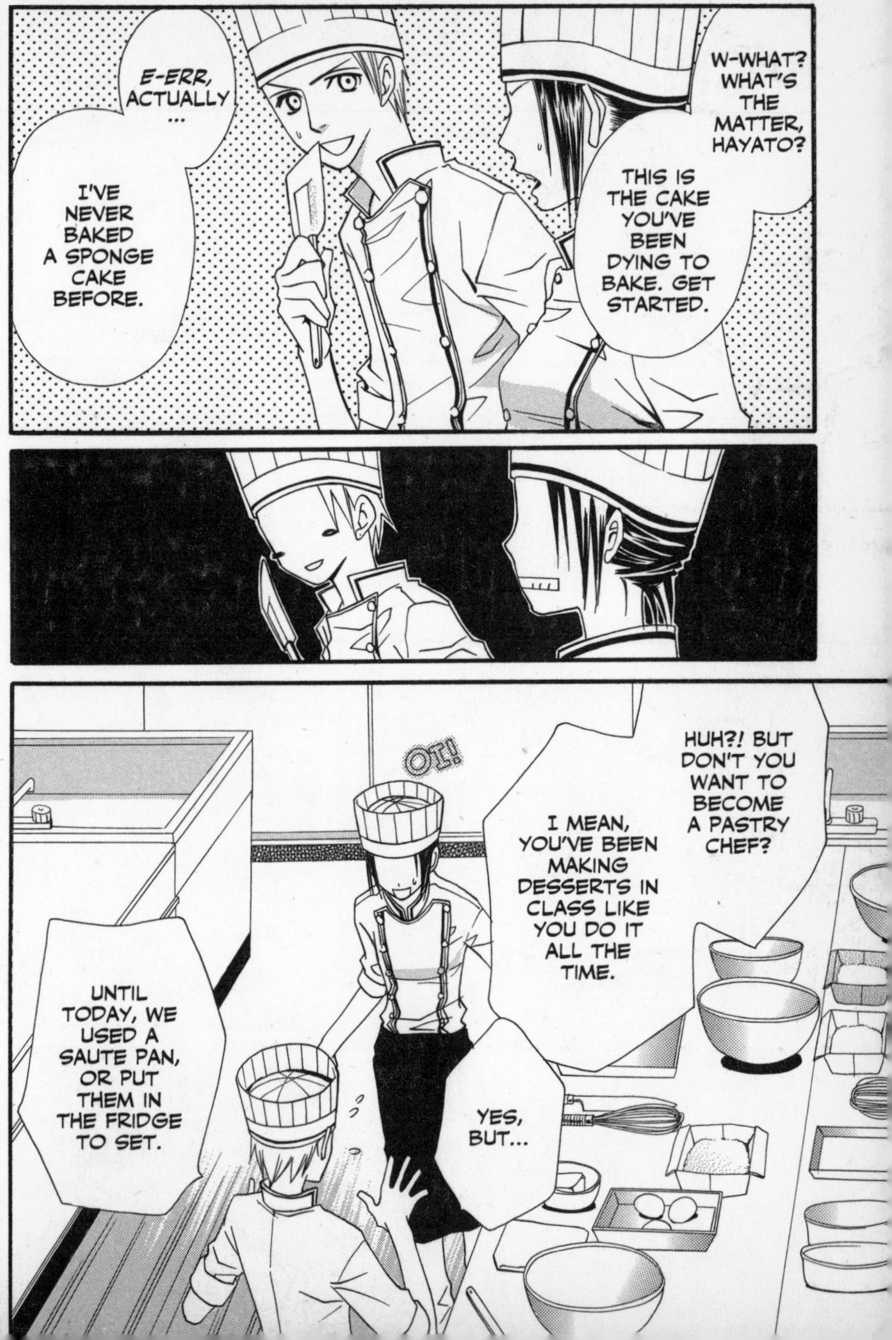
W-WHAT? WHAT'S THE MATTER, HAYATO?
THIS IS THE CAKE YOU'VE BEEN DYING TO BAKE. GET STARTED.
E-ERR, ACTUALLY ...
I'VE NEVER BAKED A SPONGE CAKE BEFORE.
HUH?! BUT DON'T YOU WANT TO BECOME A PASTRY CHEF?
I MEAN, YOU'VE BEEN MAKING DESSERTS IN CLASS LIKE YOU DO IT ALL THE TIME.
OI!
YES, BUT...
UNTIL TODAY, WE USED A SAUTE PAN, OR PUT THEM IN THE FRIDGE TO SET.

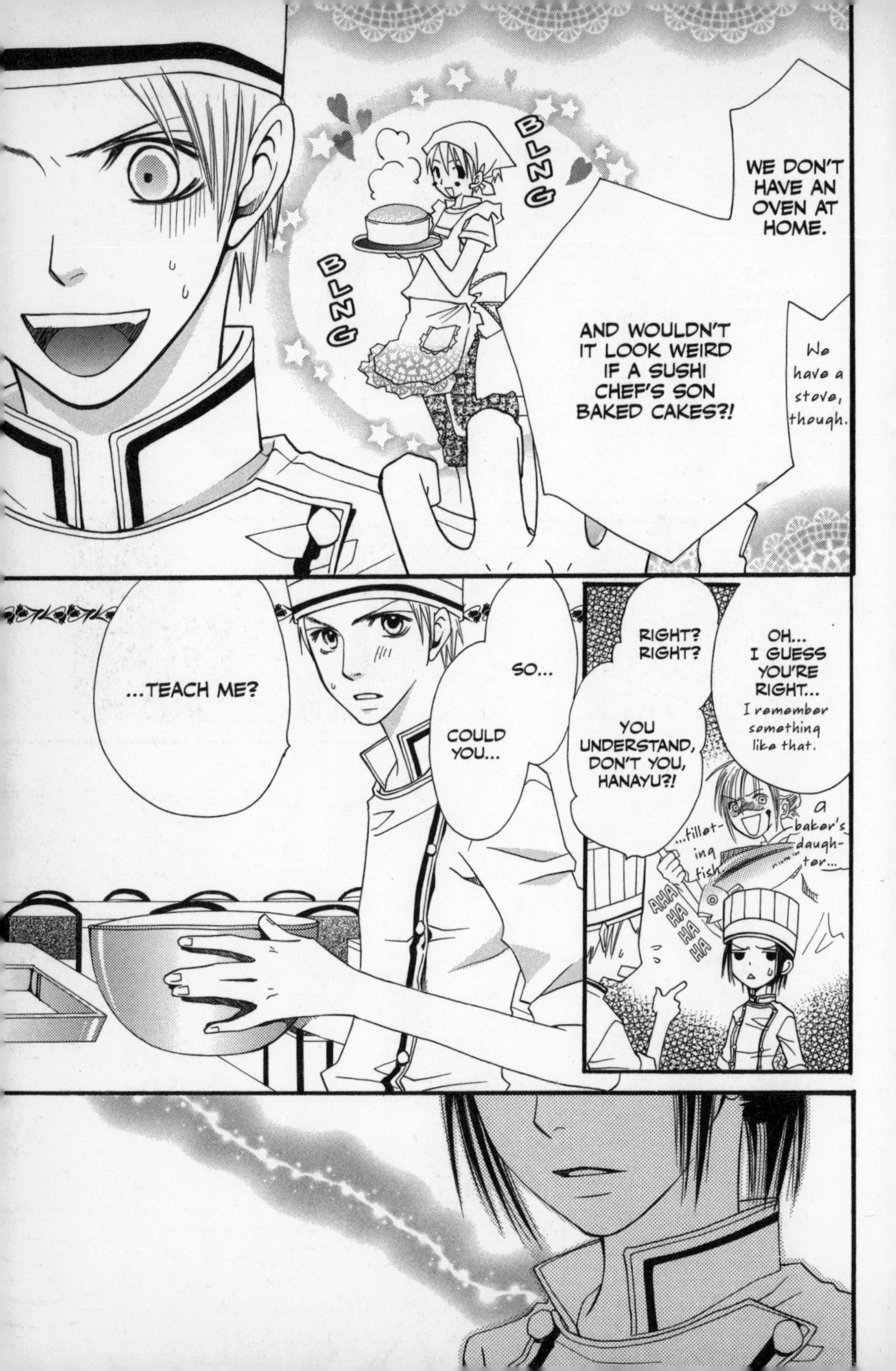
WE DON'T HAVE AN OVEN AT HOME.
We have a stove, though.
AND WOULDN'T IT LOOK WEIRD IF A SUSHI CHEF'S SON BAKED CAKES?!
BLNG
BLNG
OH... I GUESS YOU'RE RIGHT...
I remember something like that.
RIGHT? RIGHT?
YOU UNDERSTAND, DON'T YOU, HANAYU?!
a baker's daughter...
...filleting fish
AHAHAHAHA
SO...
COULD YOU...
...TEACH ME?

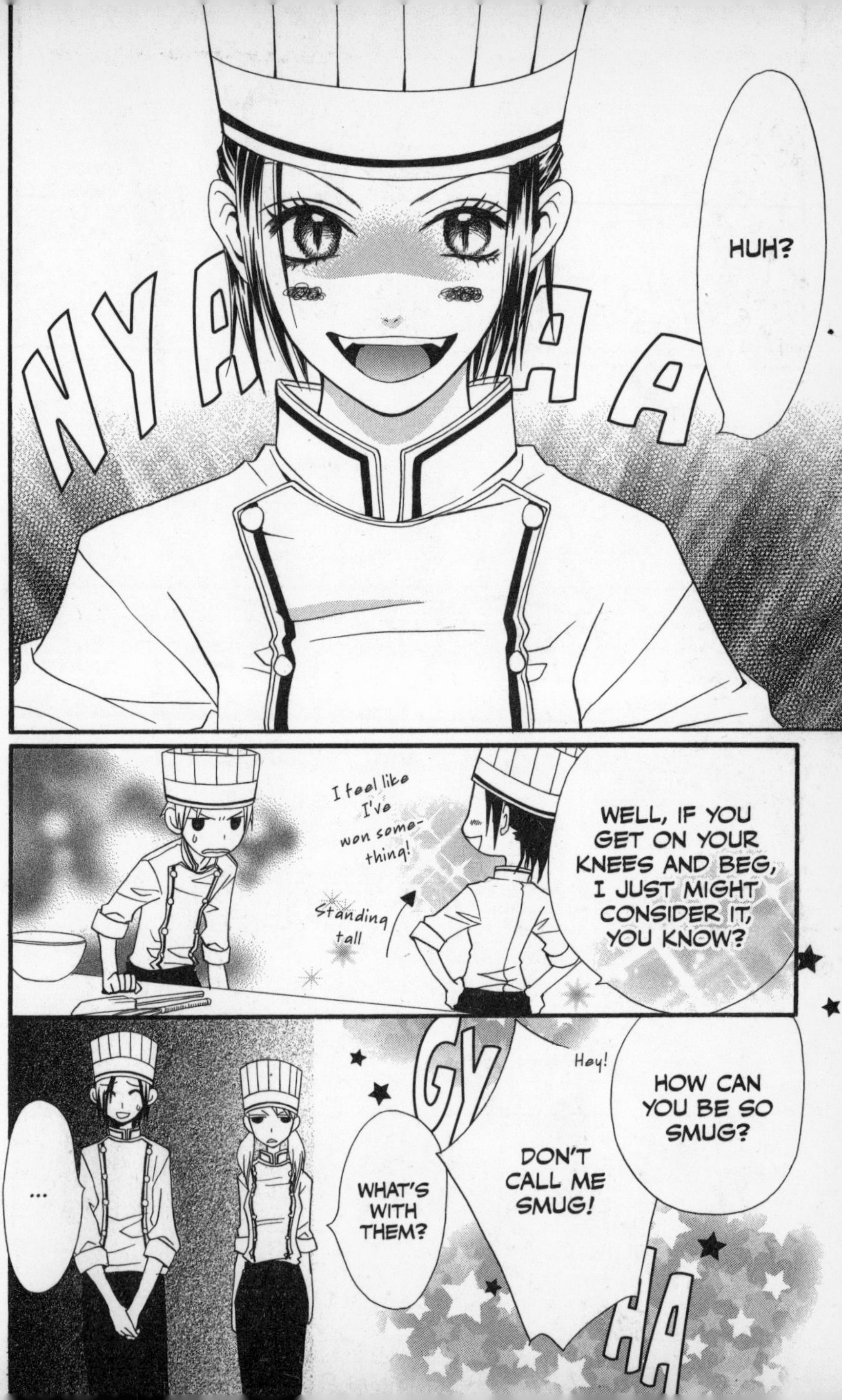
HUH?
NYAAA
WELL, IF YOU GET ON YOUR KNEES AND BEG, I JUST MIGHT CONSIDER IT, YOU KNOW?
I feel like I've won some-thing!
Standing tall
HOW CAN YOU BE SO SMUG?
Hey!
DON'T CALL ME SMUG!
GY
HA
WHAT'S WITH THEM?
...

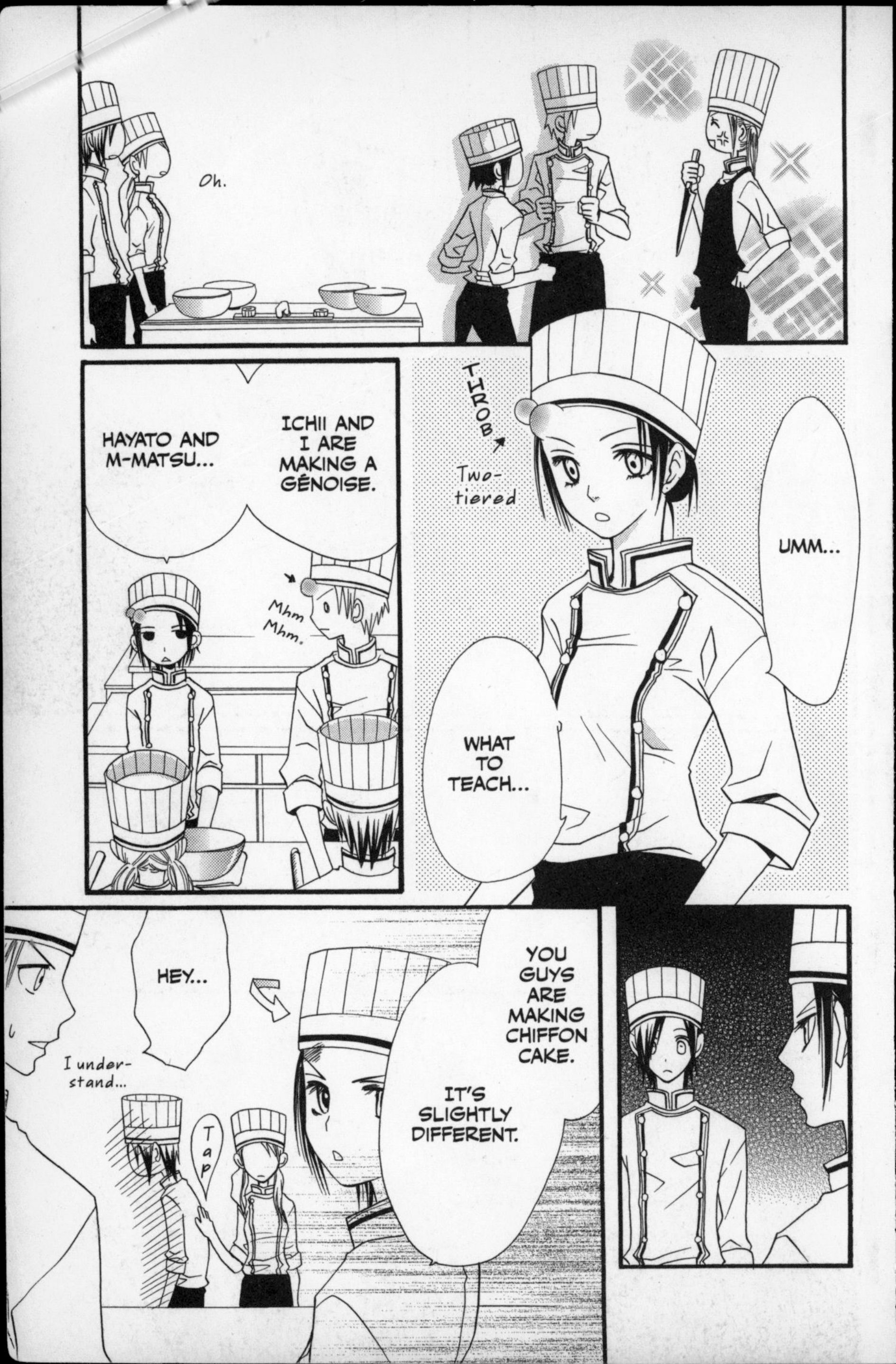
Oh.
UMM...
THROB
Two-tiered
WHAT TO TEACH...
ICHII AND I ARE MAKING A GÉNOISE.
HAYATO AND M-MATSU...
Mhm Mhm.
YOU GUYS ARE MAKING CHIFFON CAKE.
IT'S SLIGHTLY DIFFERENT.
HEY...
I under-stand...
Tap

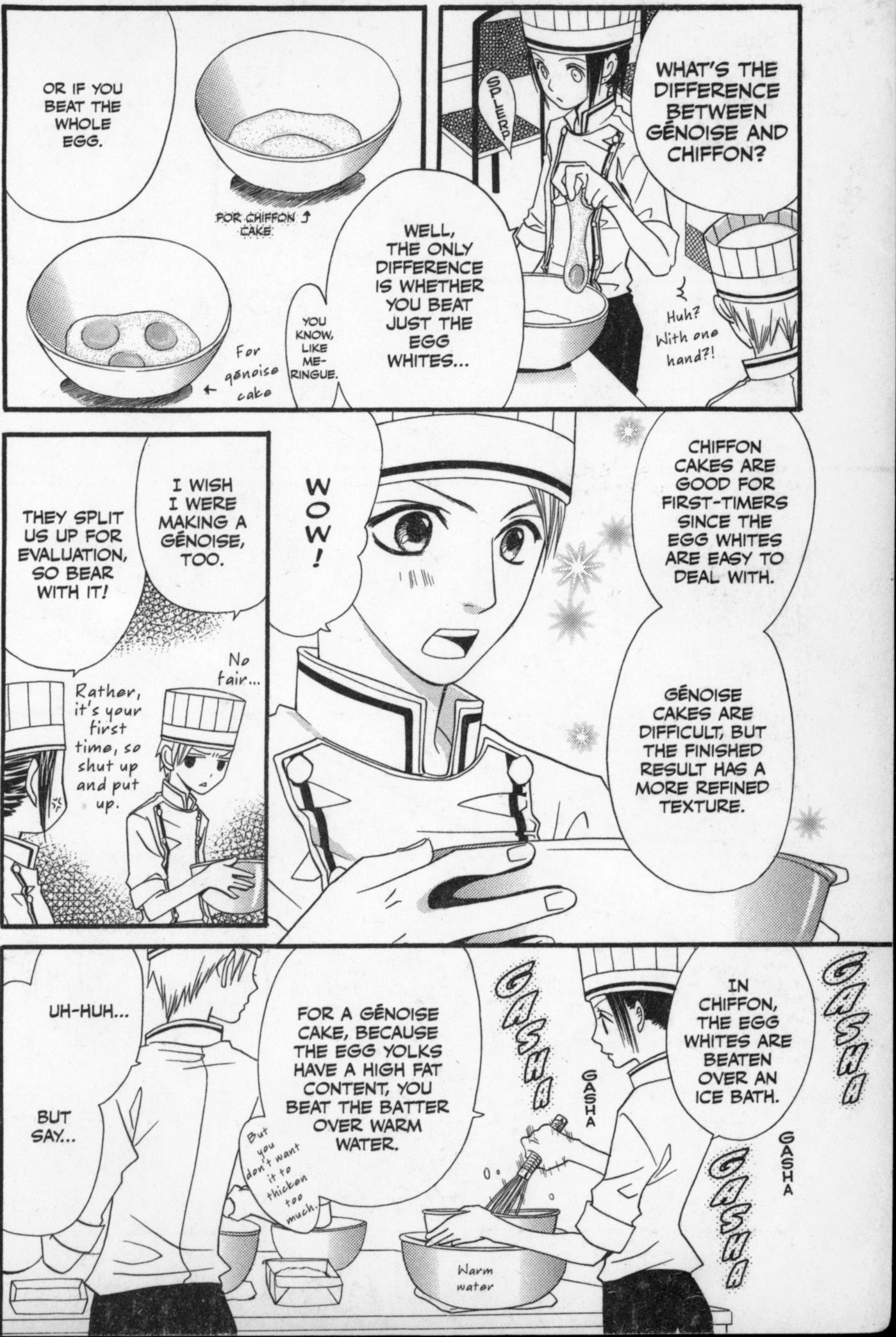
WHAT'S THE DIFFERENCE BETWEEN GÉNOISE AND CHIFFON?
SPLERP
Huh? With one hand?!
WELL, THE ONLY DIFFERENCE IS WHETHER YOU BEAT JUST THE EGG WHITES...
YOU KNOW, LIKE ME-RINGUE.
FOR CHIFFON CAKE
For génoise cake
OR IF YOU BEAT THE WHOLE EGG.
CHIFFON CAKES ARE GOOD FOR FIRST-TIMERS SINCE THE EGG WHITES ARE EASY TO DEAL WITH.
GÉNOISE CAKES ARE DIFFICULT, BUT THE FINISHED RESULT HAS A MORE REFINED TEXTURE.
WOW!
I WISH I WERE MAKING A GÉNOISE, TOO.
THEY SPLIT US UP FOR EVALUATION, SO BEAR WITH IT!
No fair...
Rather, it's your first time, so shut up and put up.
GASHA
IN CHIFFON, THE EGG WHITES ARE BEATEN OVER AN ICE BATH.
GASHA
GASHA
GASHA
GASHA
FOR A GÉNOISE CAKE, BECAUSE THE EGG YOLKS HAVE A HIGH FAT CONTENT, YOU BEAT THE BATTER OVER WARM WATER.
But you don't want it to thicken too much.
Warm water
UH-HUH...
BUT SAY...

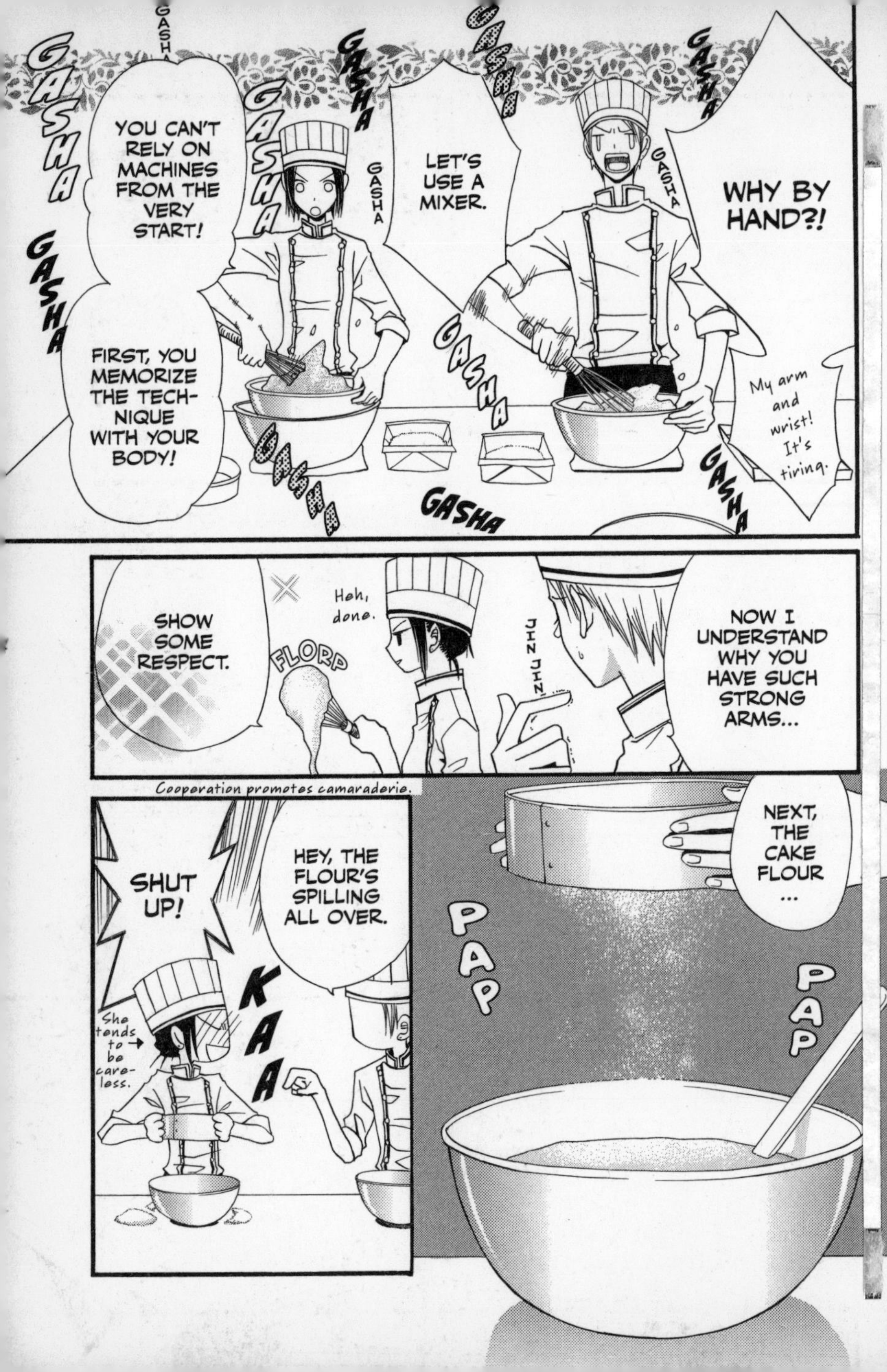
GASHA
WHY BY HAND?!
GASHA
LET'S USE A MIXER.
My arm and wrist! It's tiring.
GASHA
GASHA
GASHA
GASHA
GASHA
GASHA
YOU CAN'T RELY ON MACHINES FROM THE VERY START!
GASHA
GASHA
FIRST, YOU MEMORIZE THE TECH-NIQUE WITH YOUR BODY!
GASHA
GASHA
GASHA
NOW I UNDERSTAND WHY YOU HAVE SUCH STRONG ARMS...
JIN JIN
Heh, done.
FLORP
SHOW SOME RESPECT.
Cooperation promotes camaraderie.
NEXT, THE CAKE FLOUR ...
PAP
PAP
PAP
HEY, THE FLOUR'S SPILLING ALL OVER.
KAA
SHUT UP!
She tends to be care-less.

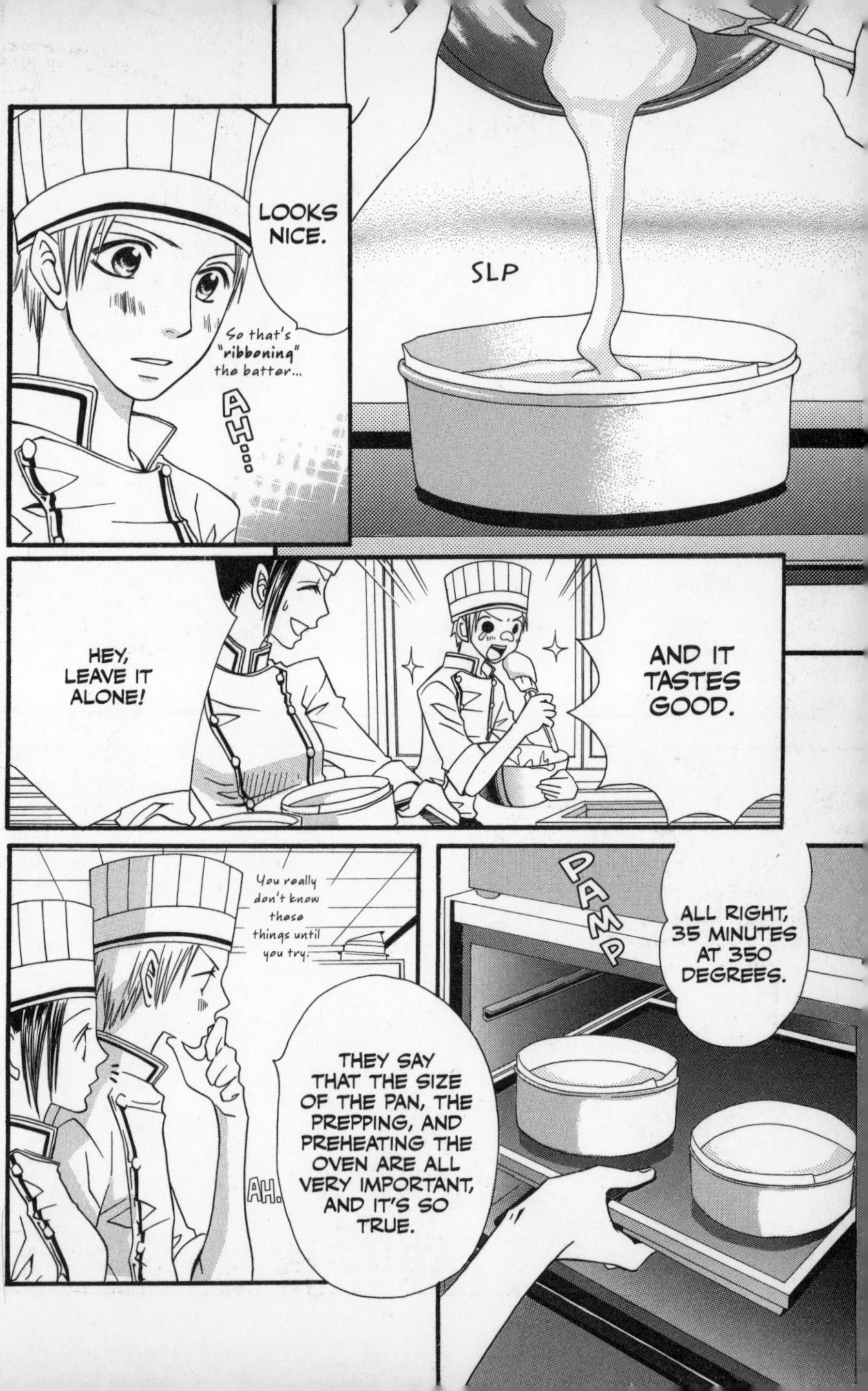
SLP
LOOKS NICE.
So that's "ribboning" the batter...
AH...
AND IT TASTES GOOD.
HEY, LEAVE IT ALONE!
PAMP
ALL RIGHT, 35 MINUTES AT 350 DEGREES.
You really don't know these things until you try.
THEY SAY THAT THE SIZE OF THE PAN, THE PREPPING, AND PREHEATING THE OVEN ARE ALL VERY IMPORTANT, AND IT'S SO TRUE.
AH.

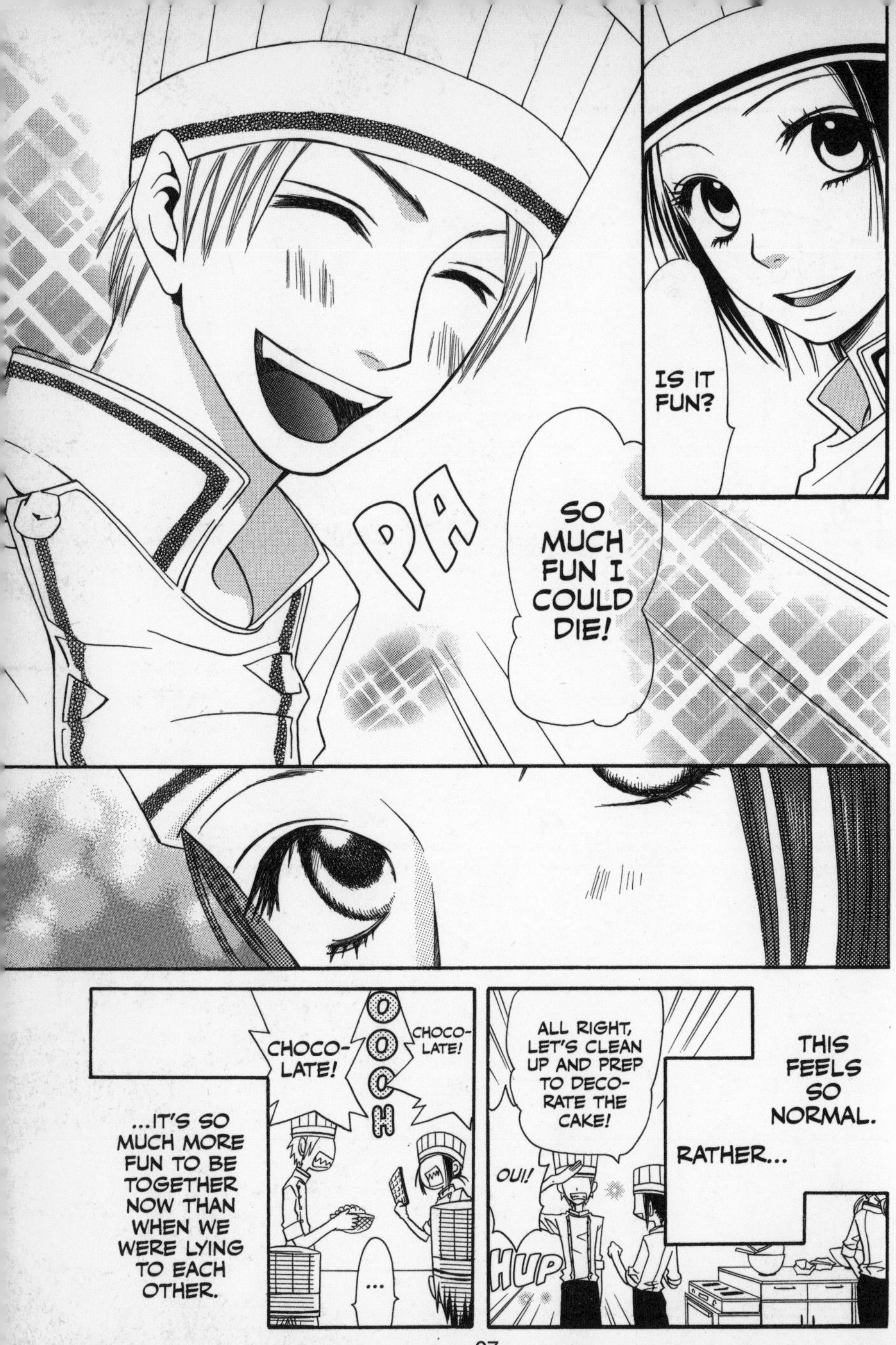
IS IT FUN?
PA
SO MUCH FUN I COULD DIE!
THIS FEELS SO NORMAL.
RATHER...
ALL RIGHT, LET'S CLEAN UP AND PREP TO DECO-RATE THE CAKE!
OUI!
HUP
...IT'S SO MUCH MORE FUN TO BE TOGETHER NOW THAN WHEN WE WERE LYING TO EACH OTHER.
CHOCO-LATE!
OOOOH
CHOCO-LATE!
...

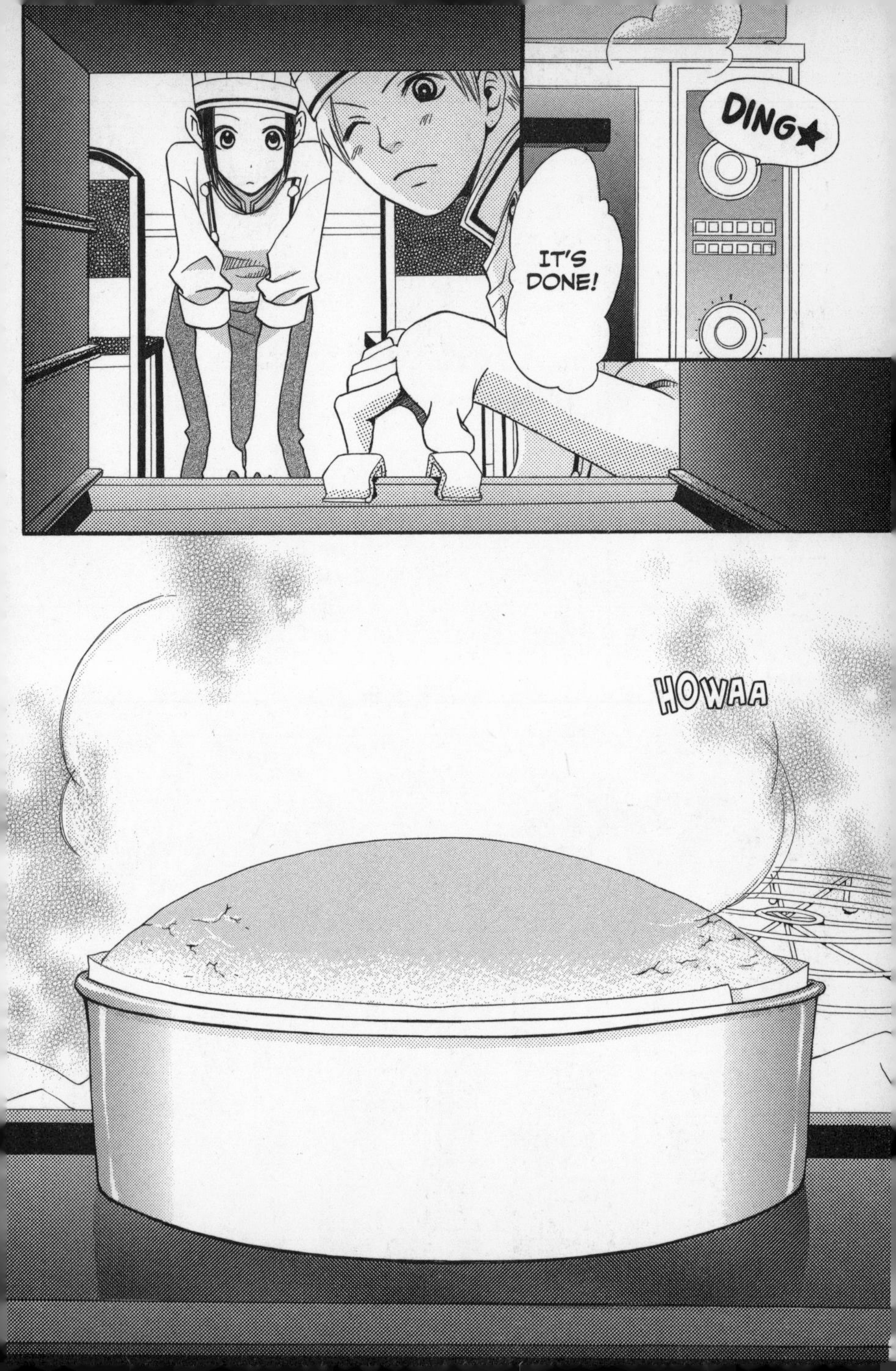
DING★
IT'S DONE!
HOWAA

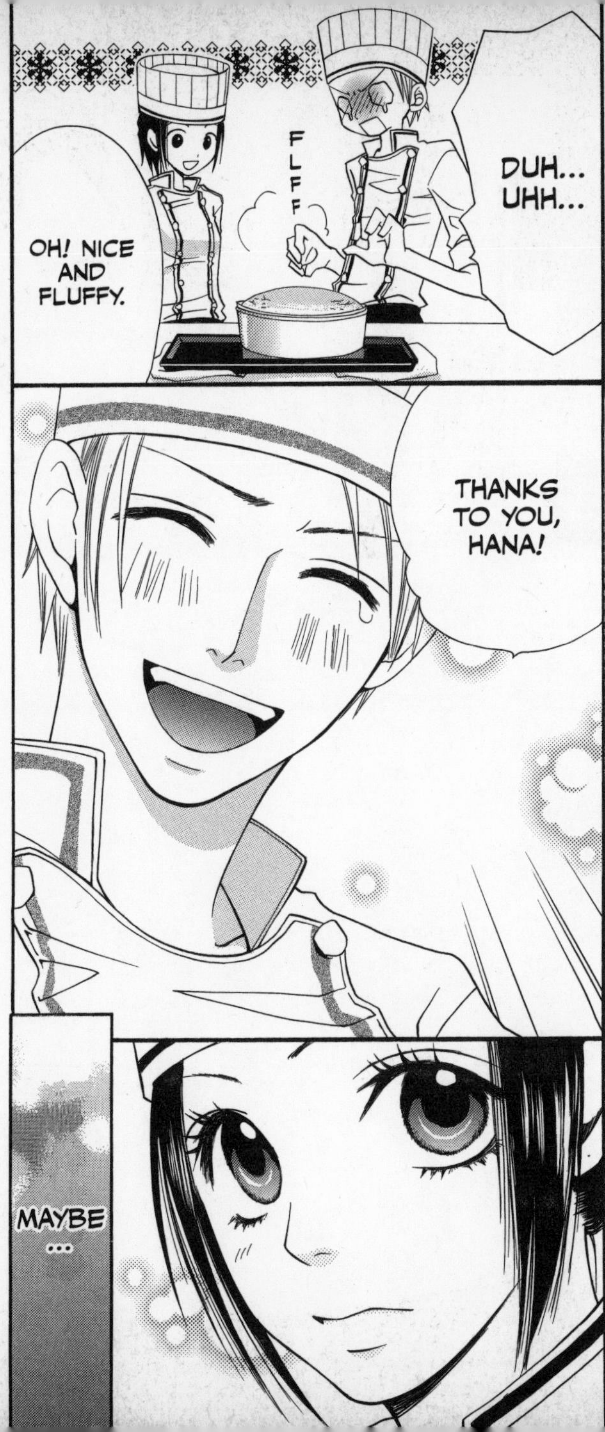
DUH... UHH...
FLFF
OH! NICE AND FLUFFY.
THANKS TO YOU, HANA!
MAYBE ...

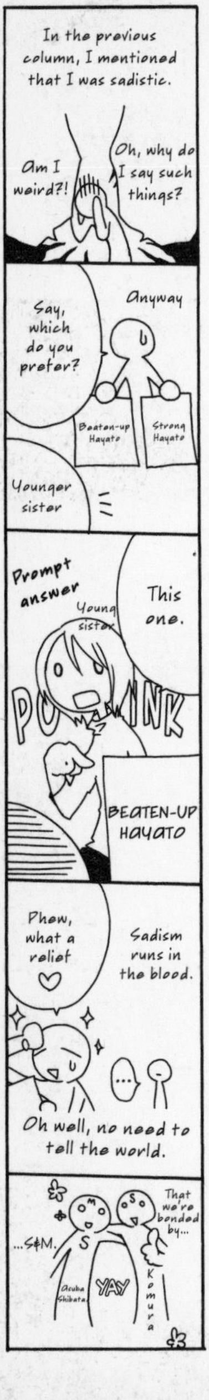
In the previous column, I mentioned that I was sadistic.
Oh, why do I say such things?
Am I weird?!
Anyway
Say, which do you prefer?
Beaten-up Hayato
Strong Hayato
Younger sister
This one.
Prompt answer
Young sister
BEATEN-UP HAYATO
Sadism runs in the blood.
Phew, what a relief ♡
...
Oh well, no need to tell the world.
That we're bonded by...
...S&M.
YAY
Komura
Asuba Shibata

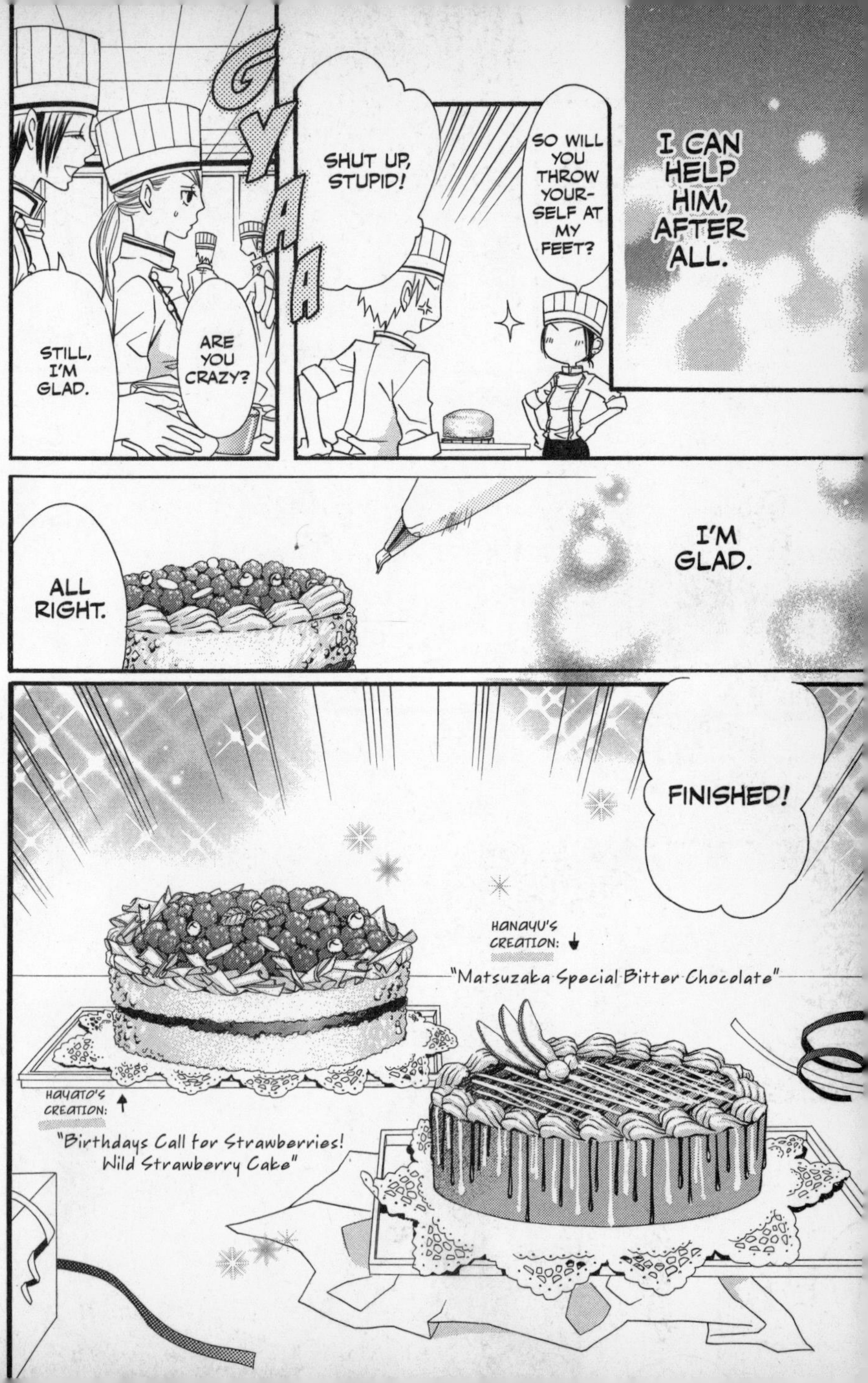
I CAN HELP HIM, AFTER ALL.
SO WILL YOU THROW YOURSELF AT MY FEET?
SHUT UP, STUPID!
GYAA
ARE YOU CRAZY?
STILL, I'M GLAD.
I'M GLAD.
ALL RIGHT.
FINISHED!
HANAYU'S CREATION:
"Matsuzaka Special Bitter Chocolate"
HAYATO'S CREATION:
"Birthdays Call for Strawberries! Wild Strawberry Cake"

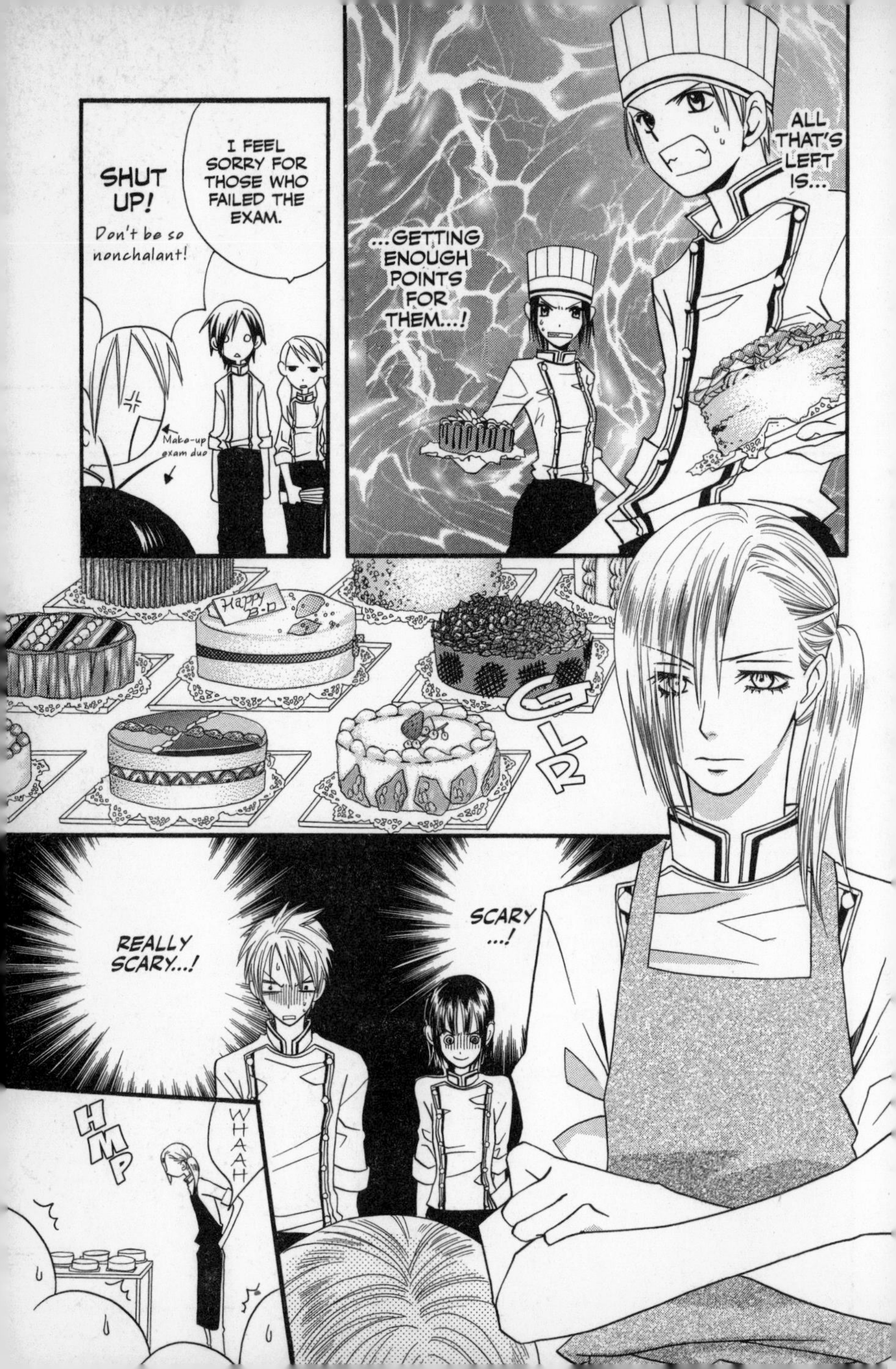
ALL THAT'S LEFT IS...
...GETTING ENOUGH POINTS FOR THEM...!
I FEEL SORRY FOR THOSE WHO FAILED THE EXAM.
SHUT UP!
Don't be so nonchalant!
Make-up exam duo
Happy B-D
GLR
SCARY ...!
REALLY SCARY...!
WHAAAH
HMP

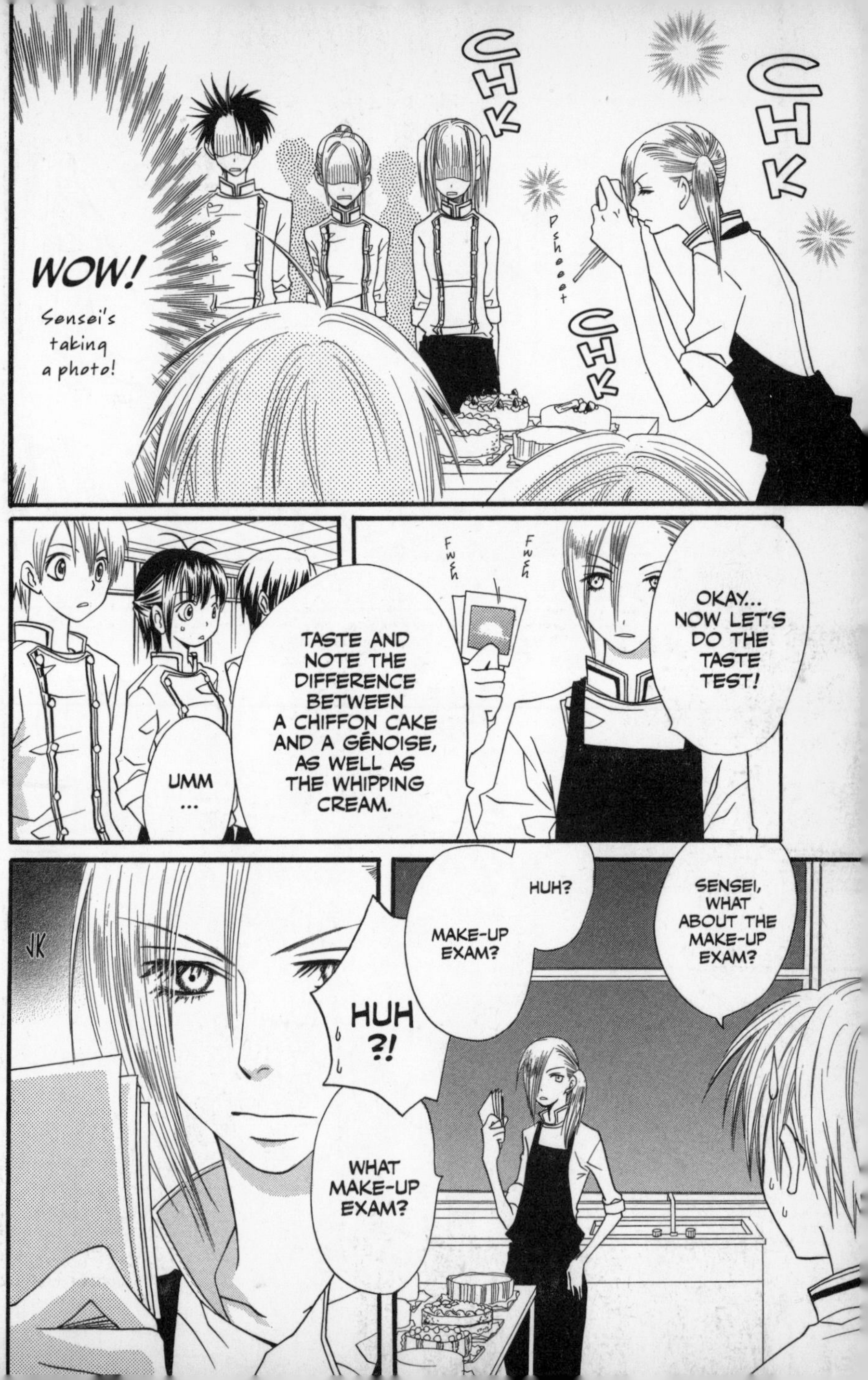
CHK
CHK
Psheeet
CHK
WOW!
Sensei's taking a photo!
Fwsh
Fwsh
OKAY... NOW LET'S DO THE TASTE TEST!
TASTE AND NOTE THE DIFFERENCE BETWEEN A CHIFFON CAKE AND A GÉNOISE, AS WELL AS THE WHIPPING CREAM.
UMM ...
SENSEI, WHAT ABOUT THE MAKE-UP EXAM?
HUH?
MAKE-UP EXAM?
JK
HUH ?!
WHAT MAKE-UP EXAM?

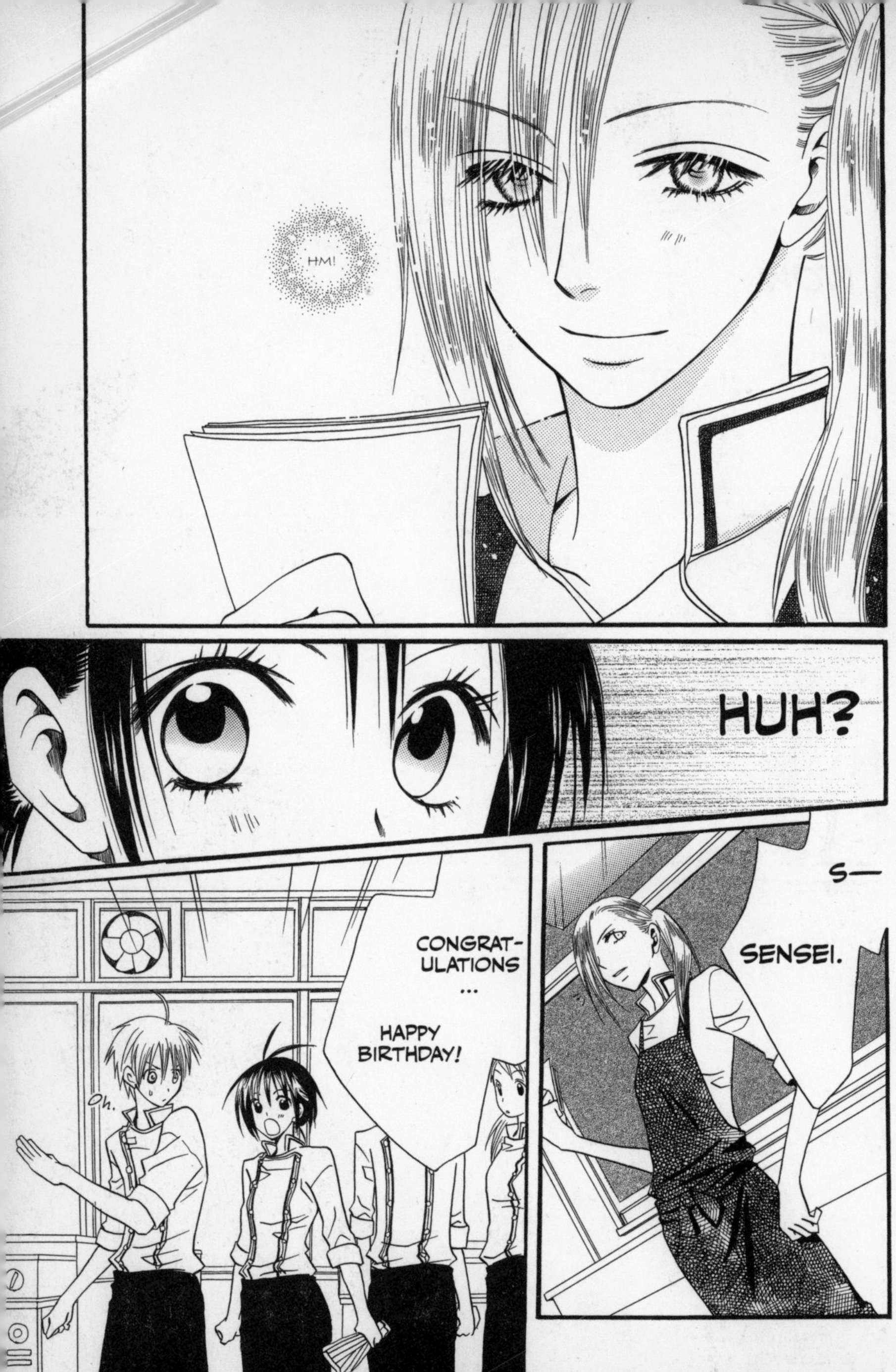
HM!
HUH?
S—
SENSEI.
CONGRAT-ULATIONS...
HAPPY BIRTHDAY!
Oh.

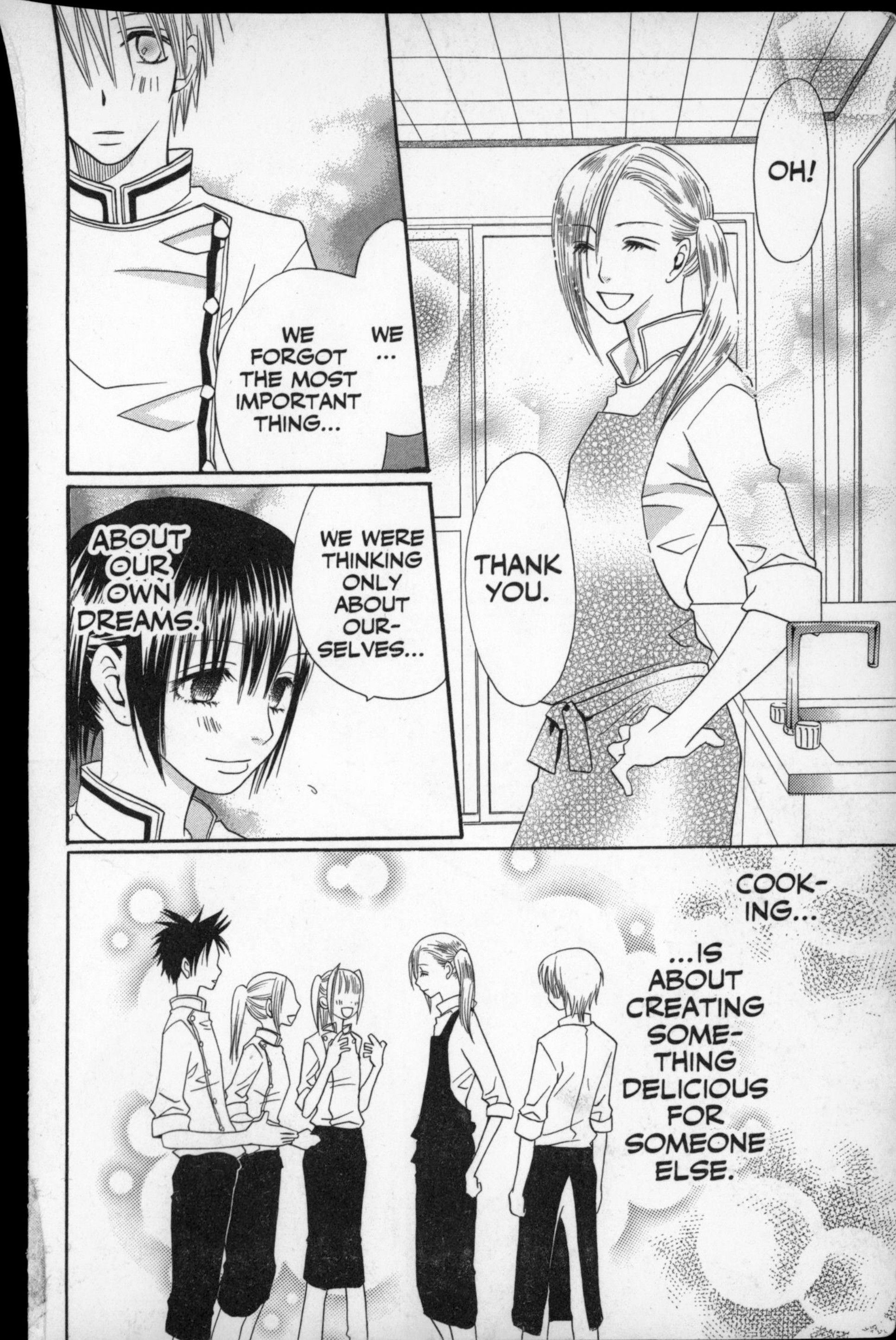
OH!
THANK YOU.
WE ...
WE FORGOT THE MOST IMPORTANT THING...
WE WERE THINKING ONLY ABOUT OUR-SELVES...
ABOUT OUR OWN DREAMS.
COOK-ING...
...IS ABOUT CREATING SOME-THING DELICIOUS FOR SOMEONE ELSE.

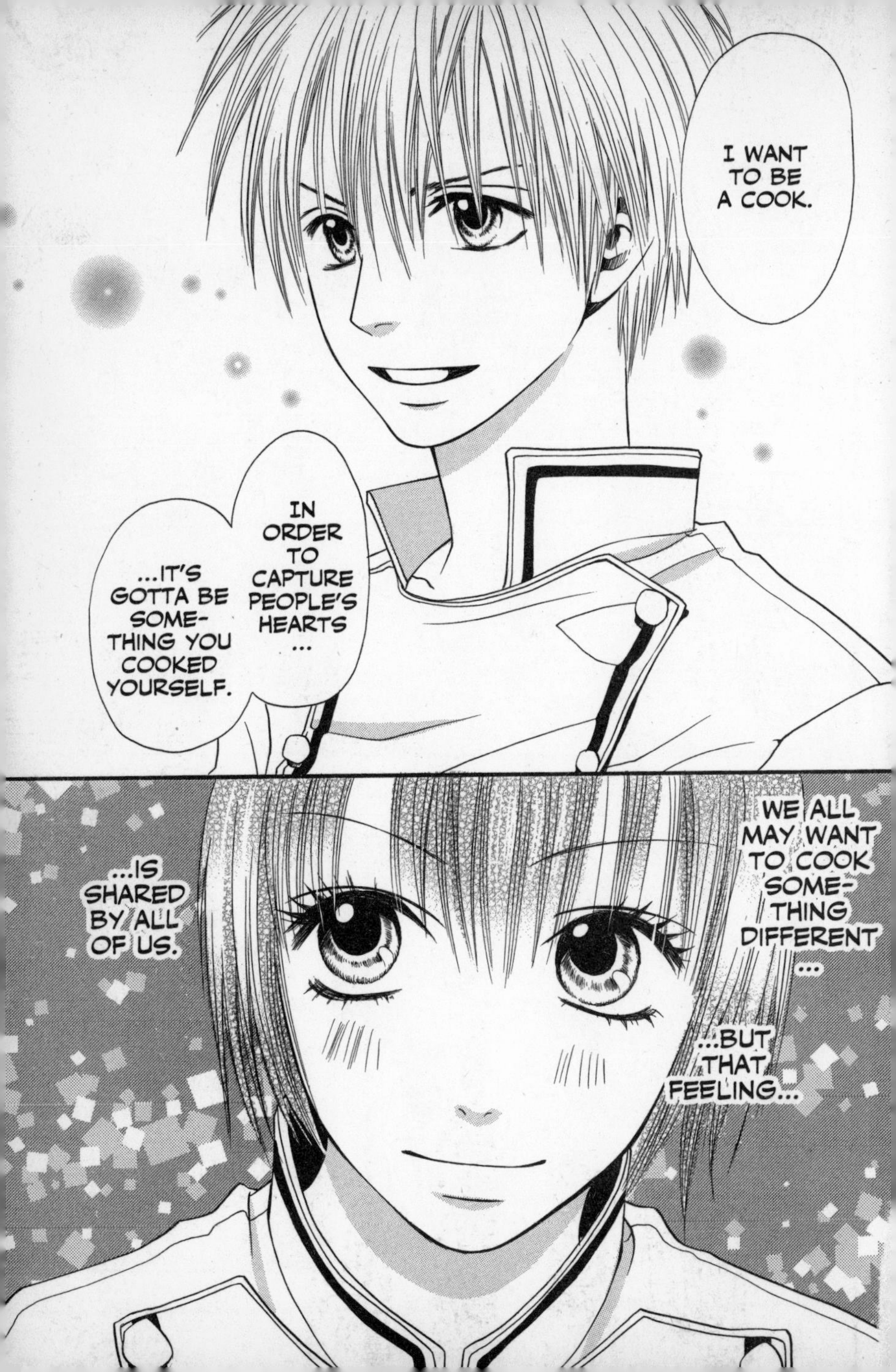
I WANT TO BE A COOK.
IN ORDER TO CAPTURE PEOPLE'S HEARTS...
...IT'S GOTTA BE SOME-THING YOU COOKED YOURSELF.
WE ALL MAY WANT TO COOK SOME-THING DIFFERENT...
...BUT THAT FEELING...
...IS SHARED BY ALL OF US.

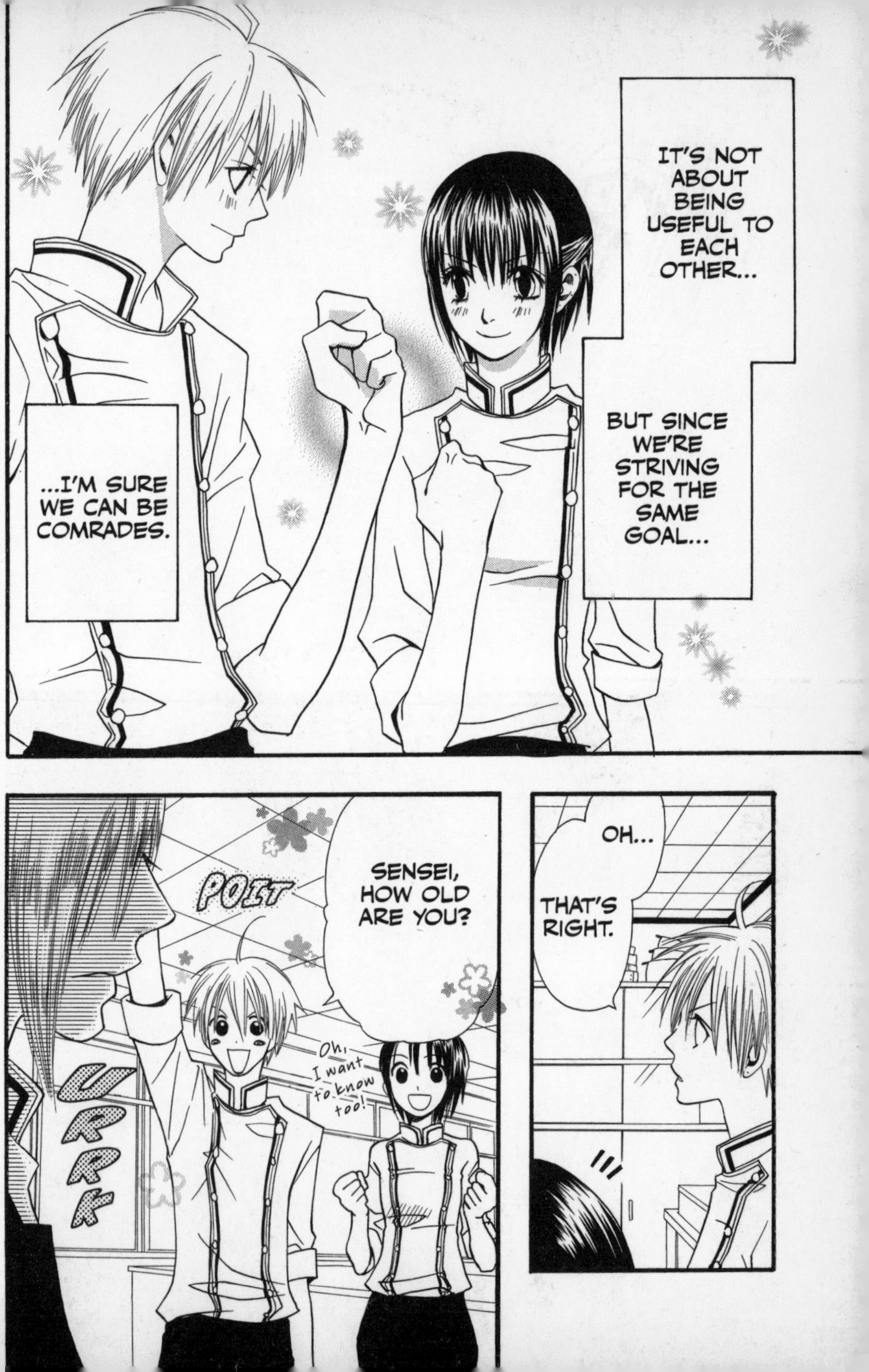
IT'S NOT ABOUT BEING USEFUL TO EACH OTHER...
BUT SINCE WE'RE STRIVING FOR THE SAME GOAL...
...I'M SURE WE CAN BE COMRADES.
OH...
THAT'S RIGHT.
SENSEI, HOW OLD ARE YOU?
POIT
Oh, I want to know too!
URRK

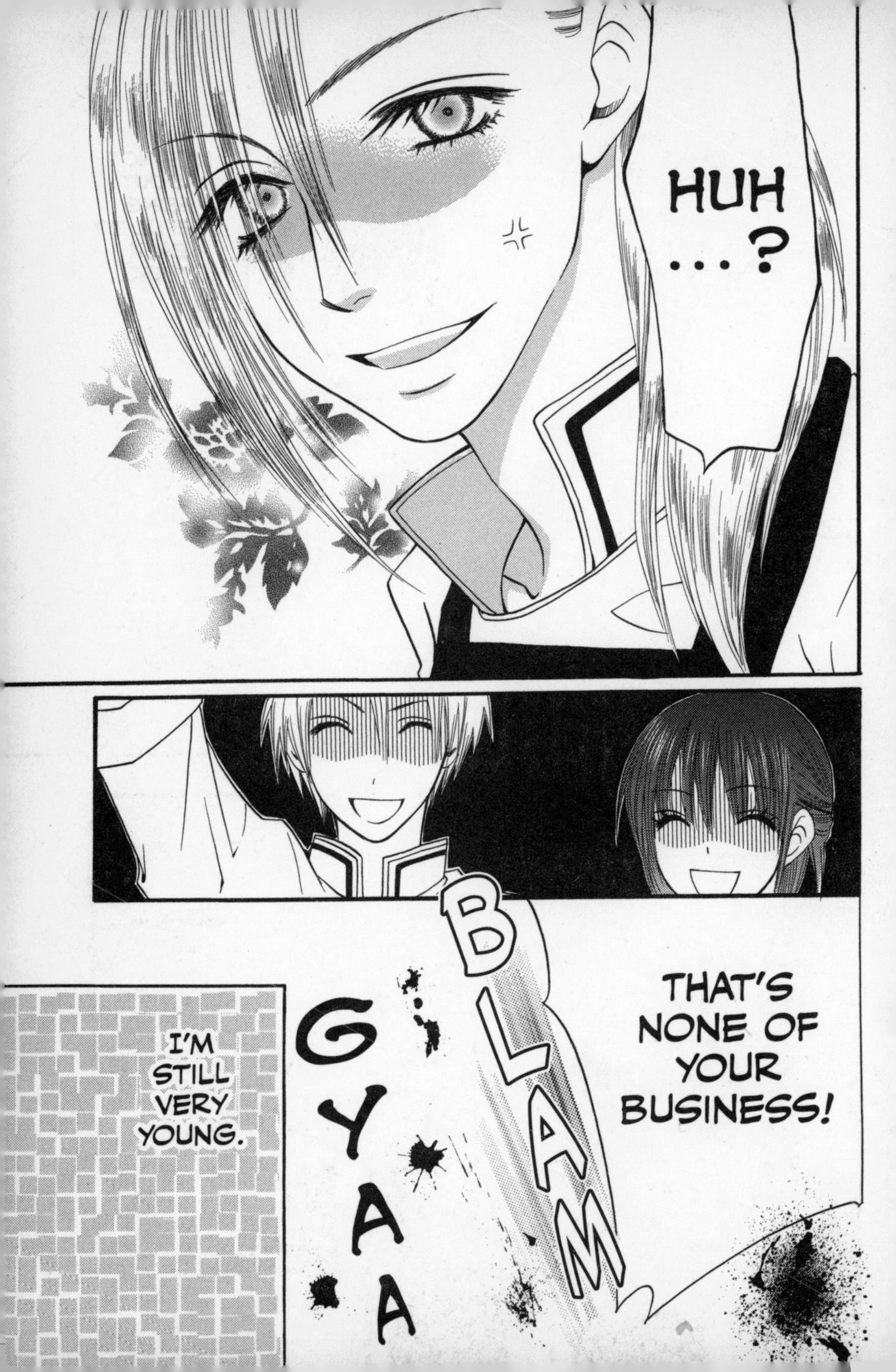
HUH ...?
THAT'S NONE OF YOUR BUSINESS!
BLAM
GYAA
I'M STILL VERY YOUNG.

SIDE DISH Mixed Vegetables 4

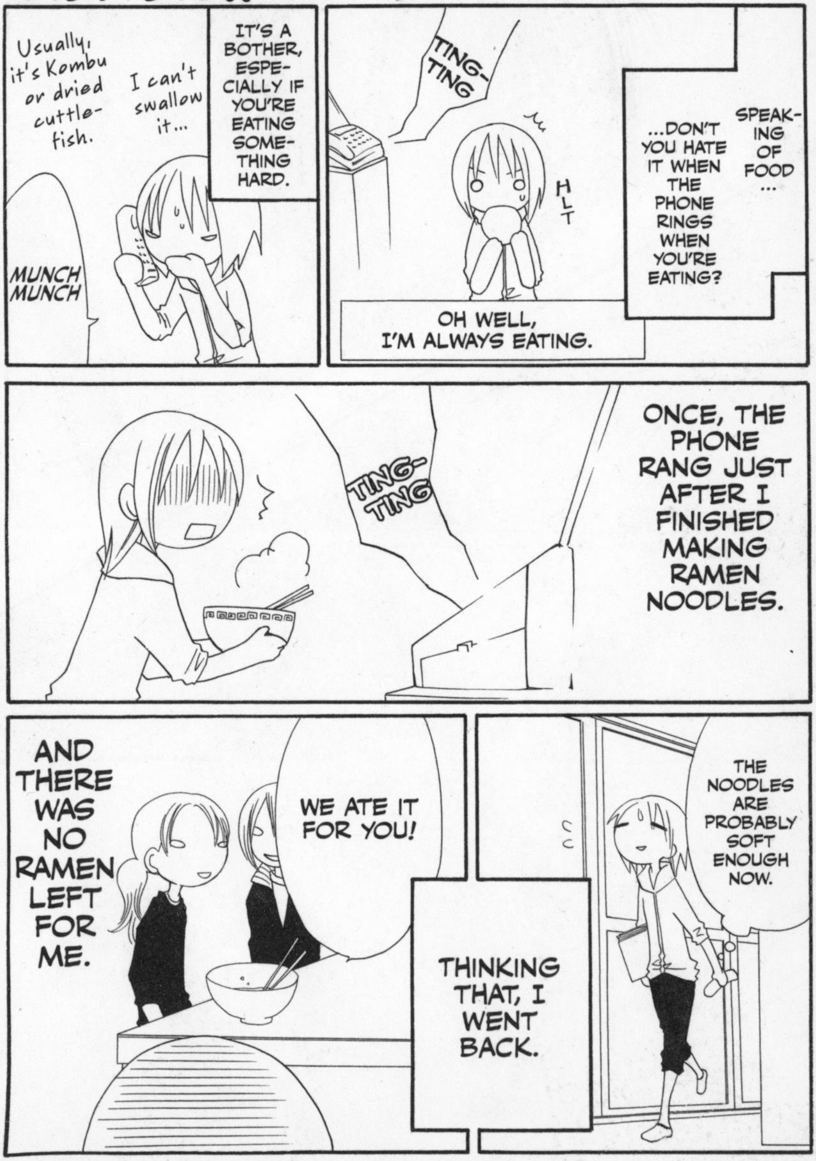
SPEAKING OF FOOD...
...DON'T YOU HATE IT WHEN THE PHONE RINGS WHEN YOU'RE EATING?
TING-TING
HLT
OH WELL, I'M ALWAYS EATING.
IT'S A BOTHER, ESPECIALLY IF YOU'RE EATING SOMETHING HARD.
I can't swallow it...
Usually, it's Kombu or dried cuttlefish.
MUNCH MUNCH
ONCE, THE PHONE RANG JUST AFTER I FINISHED MAKING RAMEN NOODLES.
TING-TING
THE NOODLES ARE PROBABLY SOFT ENOUGH NOW.
THINKING THAT, I WENT BACK.
WE ATE IT FOR YOU!
AND THERE WAS NO RAMEN LEFT FOR ME.

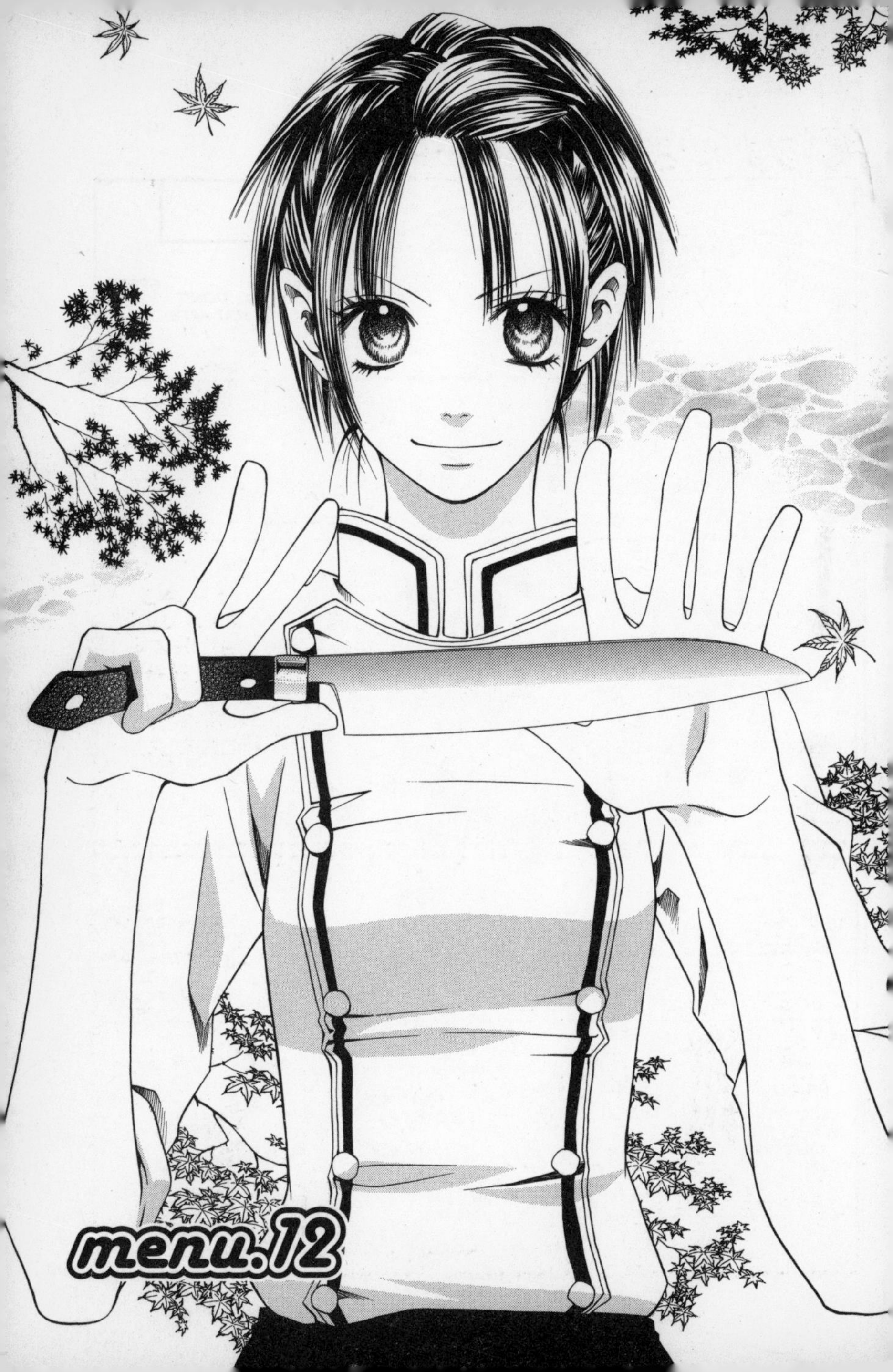
menu.12

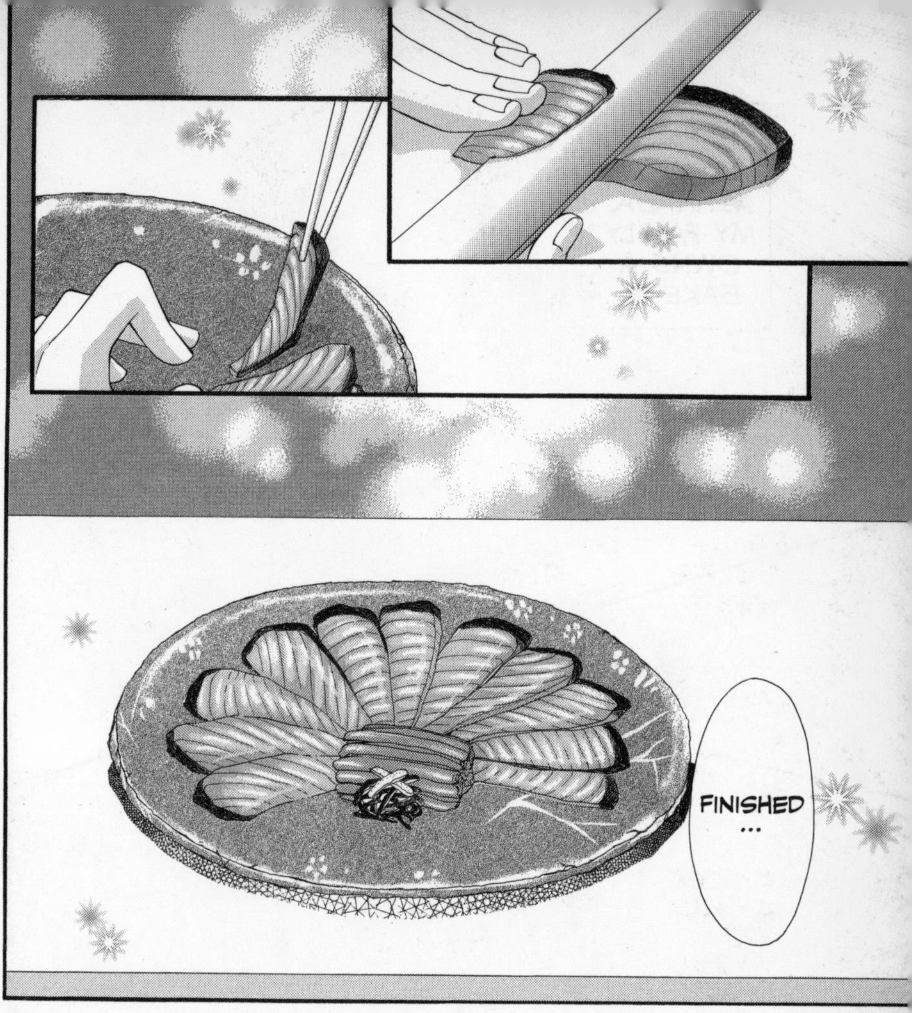
FINISHED
...

menu. 12

A new development! Or is it? In any case, Hayato is easy to draw.

Heh-heh. I made him play baseball. It was difficult, but fun!
It seems those of you who read my previous work, **Hybrid Berry** were happy, so I'm glad. ♡

Speaking of which, it's been a while since I used this. I've drawn this from time to time in the past.

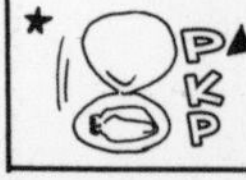
PKP

It's the "surprised scallop." I use it when a character suddenly has an idea or remembers something.

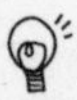

← It's the same as this. (Laugh) Try and find it.

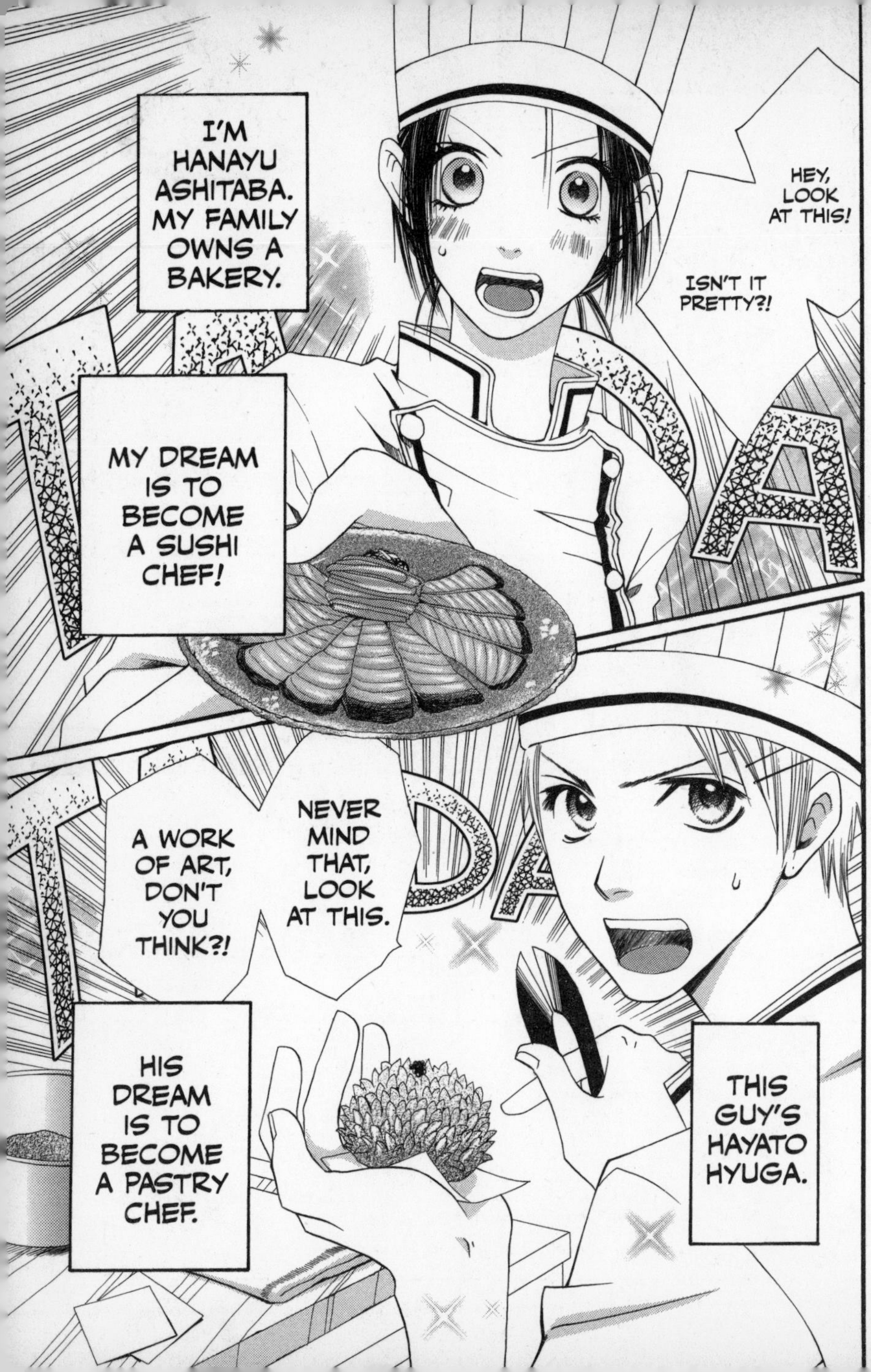
HEY, LOOK AT THIS!
ISN'T IT PRETTY?!
I'M HANAYU ASHITABA. MY FAMILY OWNS A BAKERY.
MY DREAM IS TO BECOME A SUSHI CHEF!
NEVER MIND THAT, LOOK AT THIS.
A WORK OF ART, DON'T YOU THINK?!
THIS GUY'S HAYATO HYUGA.
HIS DREAM IS TO BECOME A PASTRY CHEF.

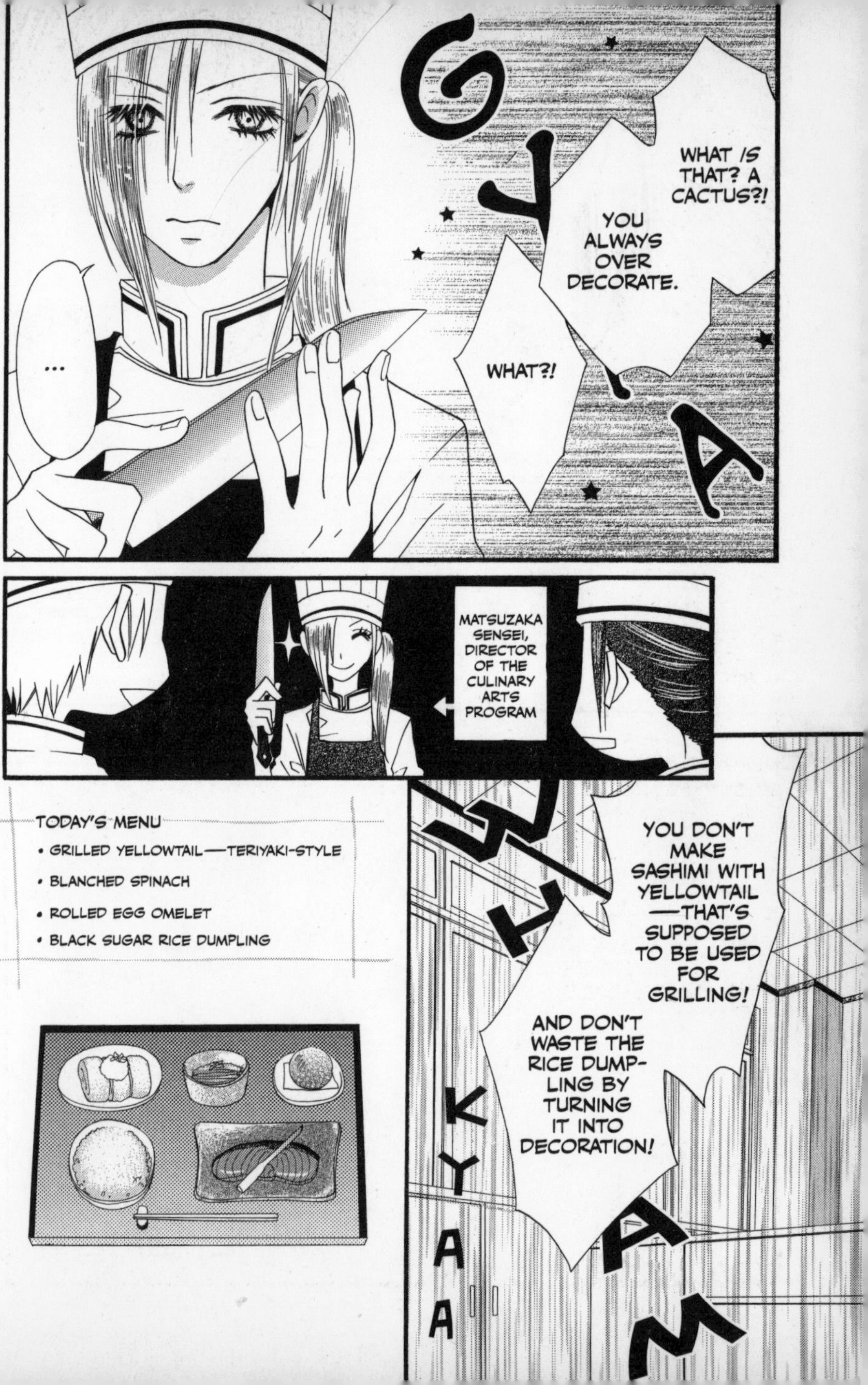

WHAT IS THAT? A CACTUS?!
YOU ALWAYS OVER DECORATE.
WHAT?!
GYA
...
MATSUZAKA SENSEI, DIRECTOR OF THE CULINARY ARTS PROGRAM
YOU DON'T MAKE SASHIMI WITH YELLOWTAIL—THAT'S SUPPOSED TO BE USED FOR GRILLING!
AND DON'T WASTE THE RICE DUMPLING BY TURNING IT INTO DECORATION!
WHAM
KYAAA
TODAY'S MENU
• GRILLED YELLOWTAIL—TERIYAKI-STYLE
• BLANCHED SPINACH
• ROLLED EGG OMELET
• BLACK SUGAR RICE DUMPLING

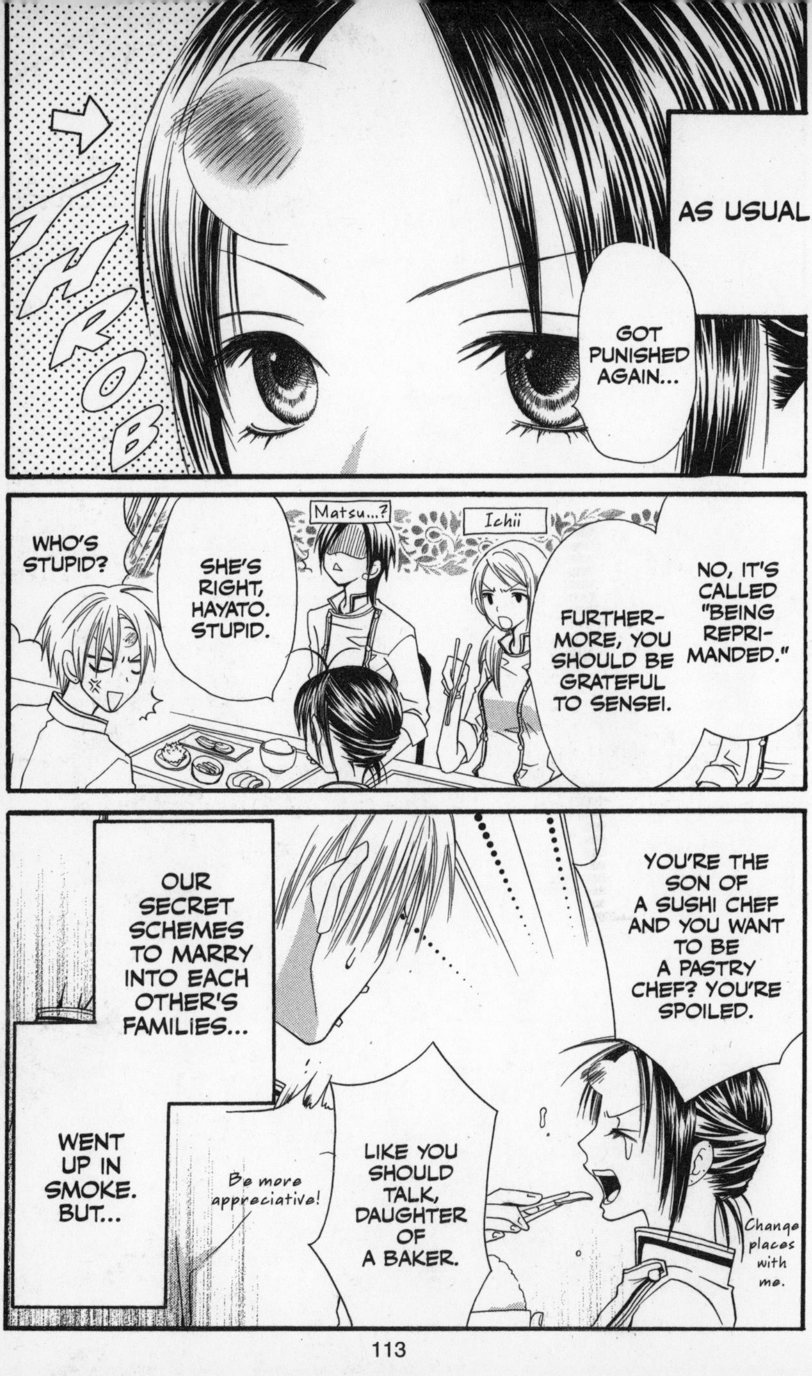
AS USUAL.
GOT PUNISHED AGAIN...
THROB
NO, IT'S CALLED "BEING REPRIMANDED."
FURTHERMORE, YOU SHOULD BE GRATEFUL TO SENSEI.
Ichii
Matsu...?
SHE'S RIGHT, HAYATO. STUPID.
WHO'S STUPID?
YOU'RE THE SON OF A SUSHI CHEF AND YOU WANT TO BE A PASTRY CHEF? YOU'RE SPOILED.
OUR SECRET SCHEMES TO MARRY INTO EACH OTHER'S FAMILIES...
Change places with me.
LIKE YOU SHOULD TALK, DAUGHTER OF A BAKER.
Be more appreciative!
WENT UP IN SMOKE. BUT...

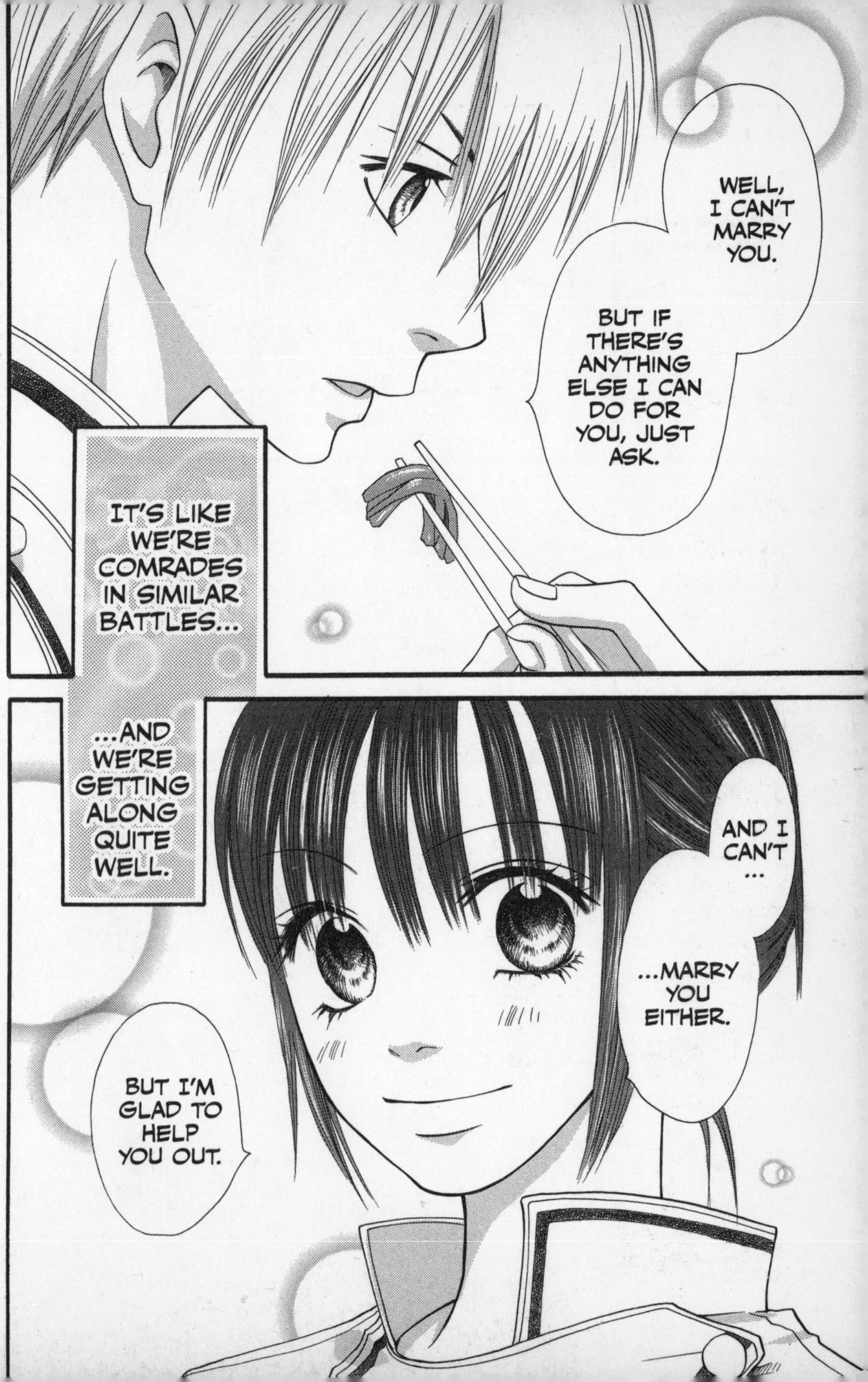
WELL, I CAN'T MARRY YOU.
BUT IF THERE'S ANYTHING ELSE I CAN DO FOR YOU, JUST ASK.
IT'S LIKE WE'RE COMRADES IN SIMILAR BATTLES...
...AND WE'RE GETTING ALONG QUITE WELL.
AND I CAN'T ...
...MARRY YOU EITHER.
BUT I'M GLAD TO HELP YOU OUT.

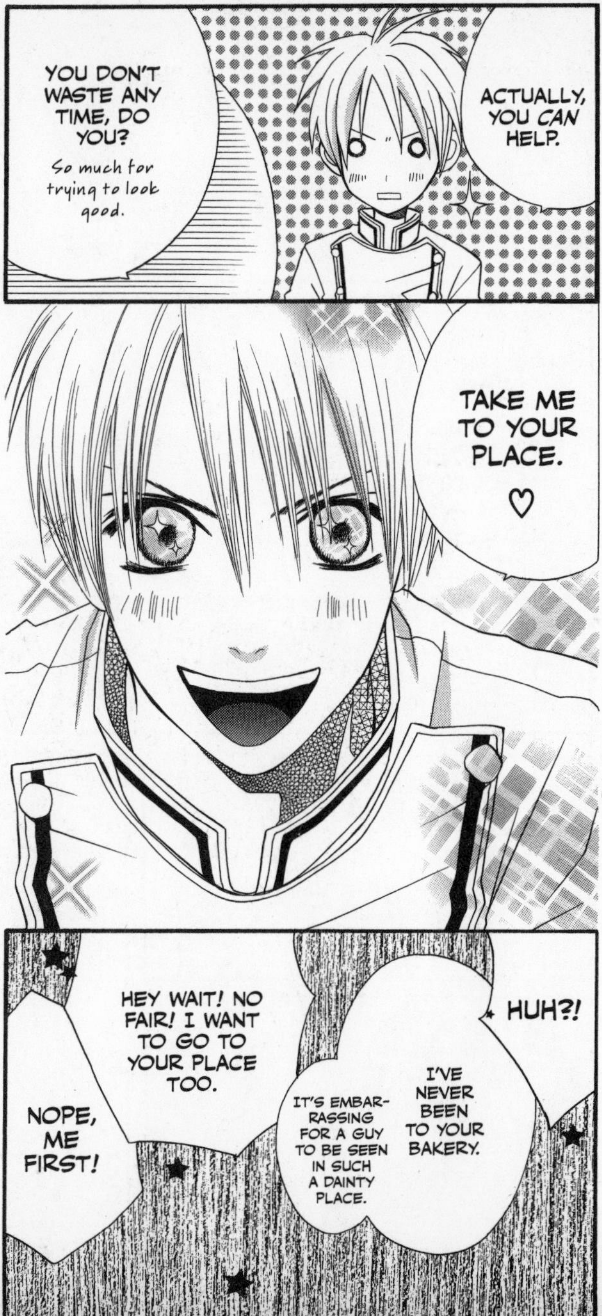
ACTUALLY, YOU CAN HELP.
YOU DON'T WASTE ANY TIME, DO YOU?
So much for trying to look good.
TAKE ME TO YOUR PLACE. ♡
HUH?!
I'VE NEVER BEEN TO YOUR BAKERY.
IT'S EMBARRASSING FOR A GUY TO BE SEEN IN SUCH A DAINTY PLACE.
HEY WAIT! NO FAIR! I WANT TO GO TO YOUR PLACE TOO.
NOPE, ME FIRST!
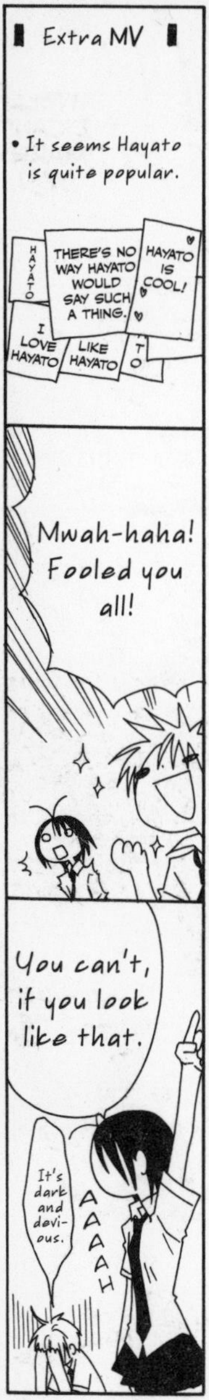
Extra MV
• It seems Hayato is quite popular.
HAYATO IS COOL!
THERE'S NO WAY HAYATO WOULD SAY SUCH A THING.
HAYATO
I LOVE HAYATO
LIKE HAYATO
Mwah-haha! Fooled you all!
You can't, if you look like that.
It's dark and devious.
AAAAAH

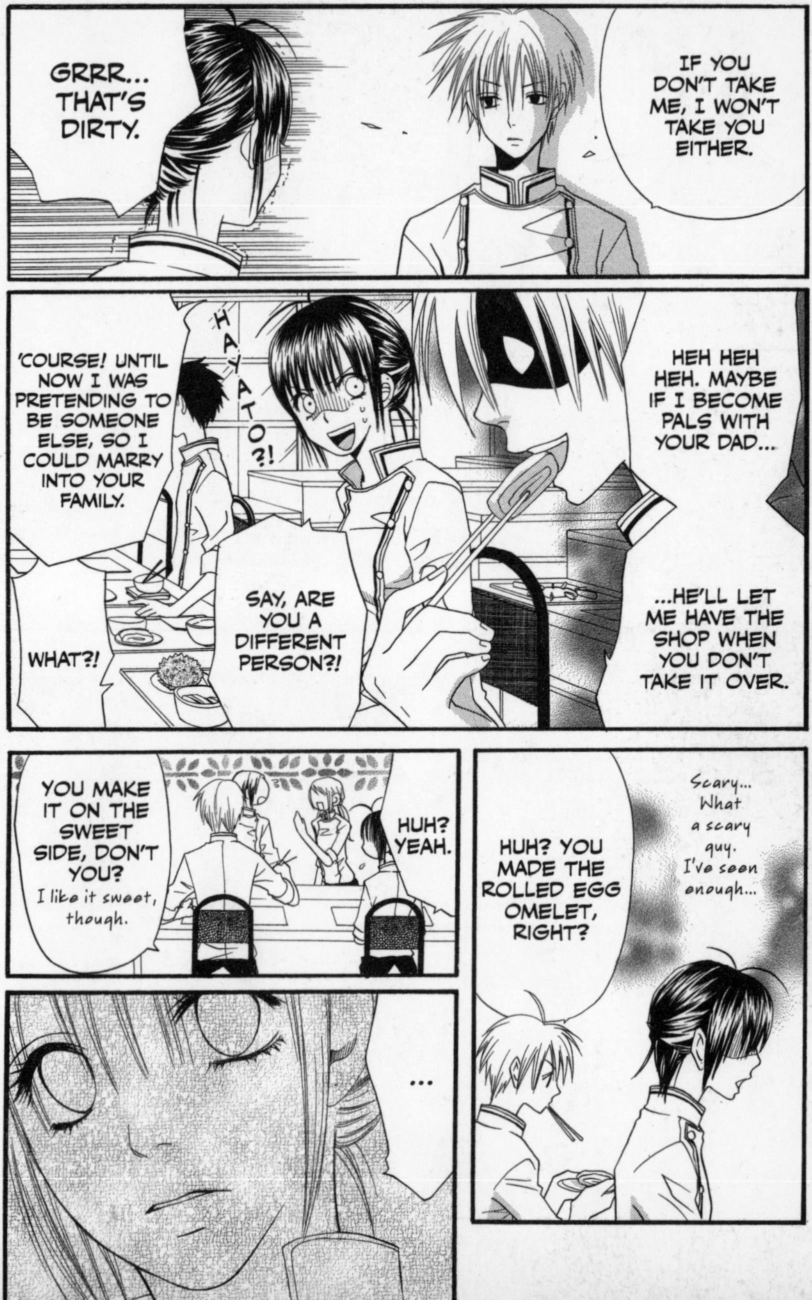
IF YOU DON'T TAKE ME, I WON'T TAKE YOU EITHER.
GRRR... THAT'S DIRTY.
HEH HEH HEH. MAYBE IF I BECOME PALS WITH YOUR DAD...
...HE'LL LET ME HAVE THE SHOP WHEN YOU DON'T TAKE IT OVER.
HAYATO?!
SAY, ARE YOU A DIFFERENT PERSON?!
'COURSE! UNTIL NOW I WAS PRETENDING TO BE SOMEONE ELSE, SO I COULD MARRY INTO YOUR FAMILY.
WHAT?!
Scary... What a scary guy. I've seen enough...
HUH? YOU MADE THE ROLLED EGG OMELET, RIGHT?
HUH? YEAH.
YOU MAKE IT ON THE SWEET SIDE, DON'T YOU?
I like it sweet, though.
...

BAM

THAT...

?!

WHAT'S THE MATTER, SENSEI?

OH, GOOD. YOU ALL SEEM TO BE FREE.

PASS THIS OUT FOR ME.

SHf

SHf

She scared me.

QUESTION-NAIRE?!

Future Plans Questionnaire

Cooking Class	Student Number	Name	

*Education (College – Junior college – Vocational school)

First choice

Second choice

d choice

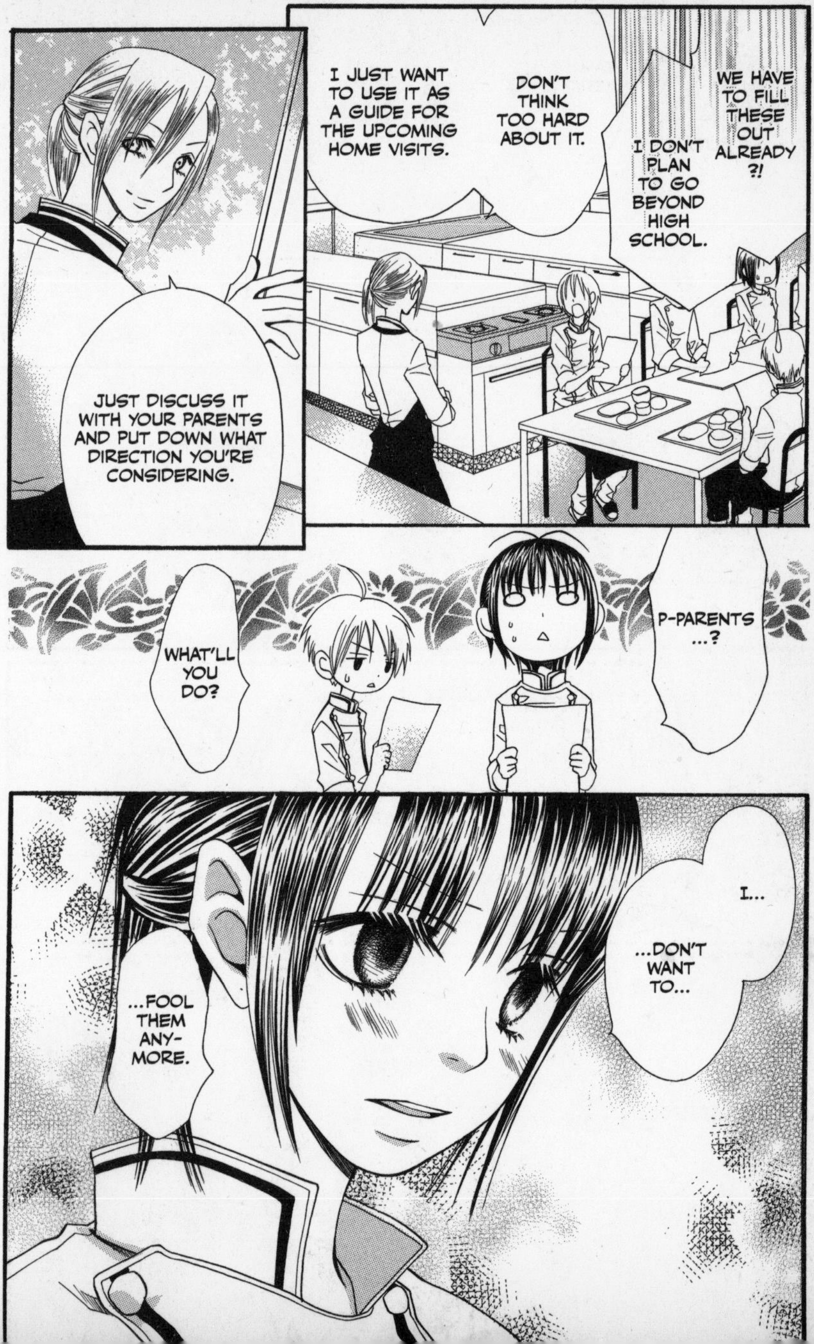
WE HAVE TO FILL THESE OUT ALREADY ?!
I DON'T PLAN TO GO BEYOND HIGH SCHOOL.
DON'T THINK TOO HARD ABOUT IT.
I JUST WANT TO USE IT AS A GUIDE FOR THE UPCOMING HOME VISITS.
JUST DISCUSS IT WITH YOUR PARENTS AND PUT DOWN WHAT DIRECTION YOU'RE CONSIDERING.
P-PARENTS ...?
WHAT'LL YOU DO?
I...
...DON'T WANT TO...
...FOOL THEM ANY-MORE.

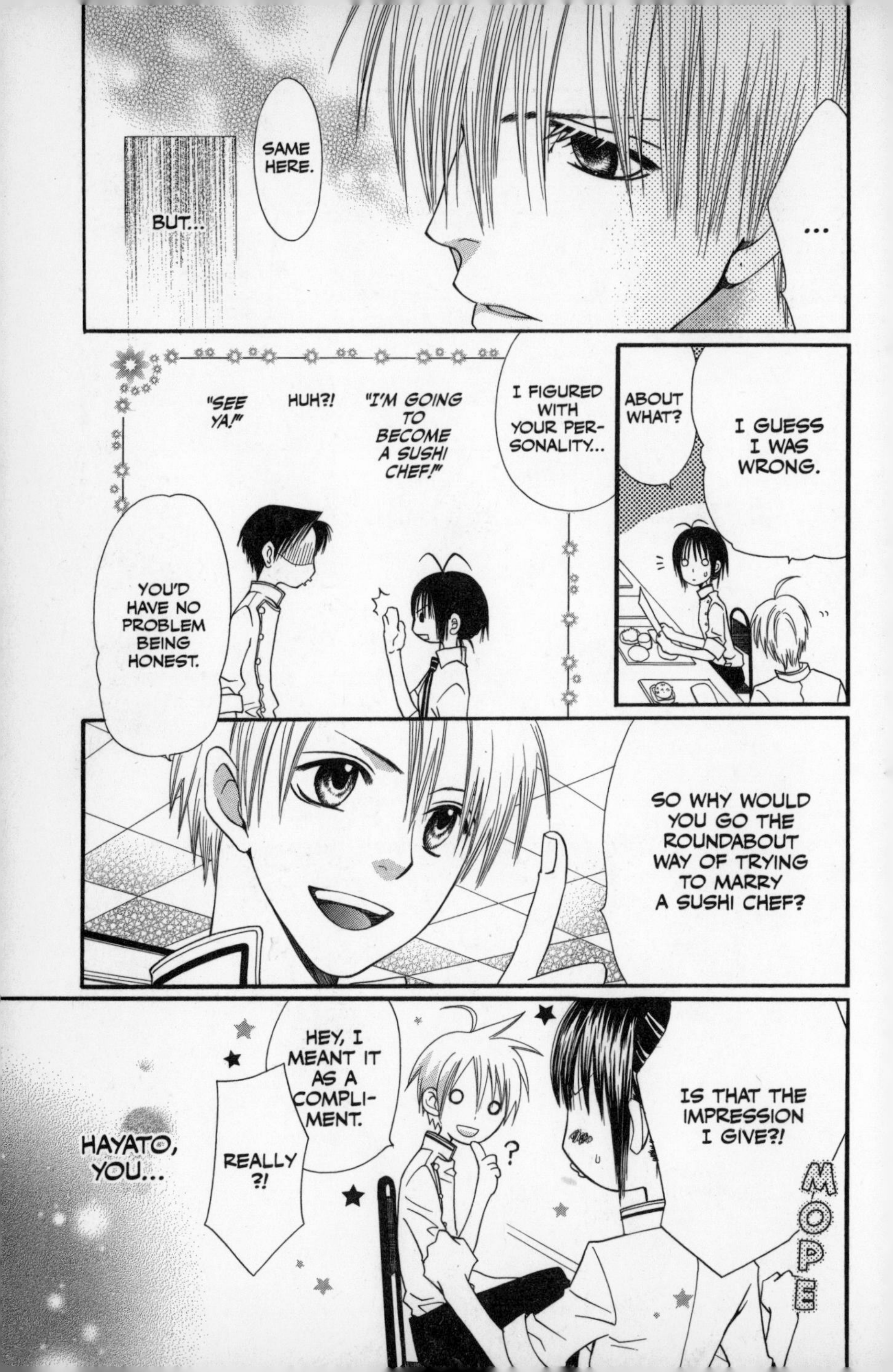
...
SAME HERE.
BUT...
I GUESS I WAS WRONG.
ABOUT WHAT?
I FIGURED WITH YOUR PER-SONALITY...
"I'M GOING TO BECOME A SUSHI CHEF!"
HUH?!
"SEE YA!"
YOU'D HAVE NO PROBLEM BEING HONEST.
SO WHY WOULD YOU GO THE ROUNDABOUT WAY OF TRYING TO MARRY A SUSHI CHEF?
MOPE
IS THAT THE IMPRESSION I GIVE?!
HEY, I MEANT IT AS A COMPLI-MENT.
REALLY?!
HAYATO, YOU...

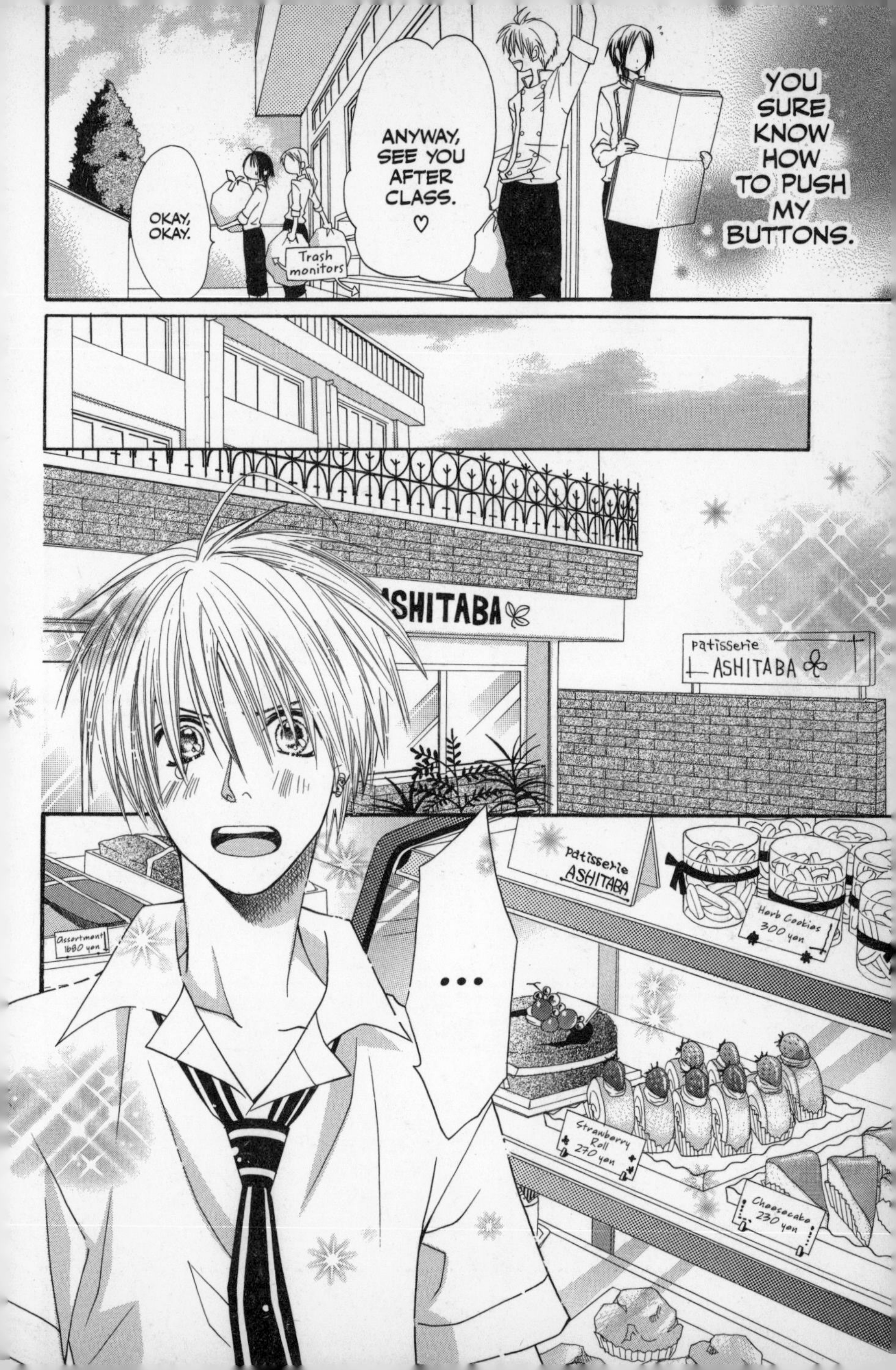
YOU SURE KNOW HOW TO PUSH MY BUTTONS.
ANYWAY, SEE YOU AFTER CLASS. ♡
Trash monitors
OKAY, OKAY.
ASHITABA
patisserie ASHITABA
patisserie ASHITABA
Herb Cookies 300 yen
Assortment 1680 yen
...
Strawberry Roll 270 yen
Cheesecake 230 yen

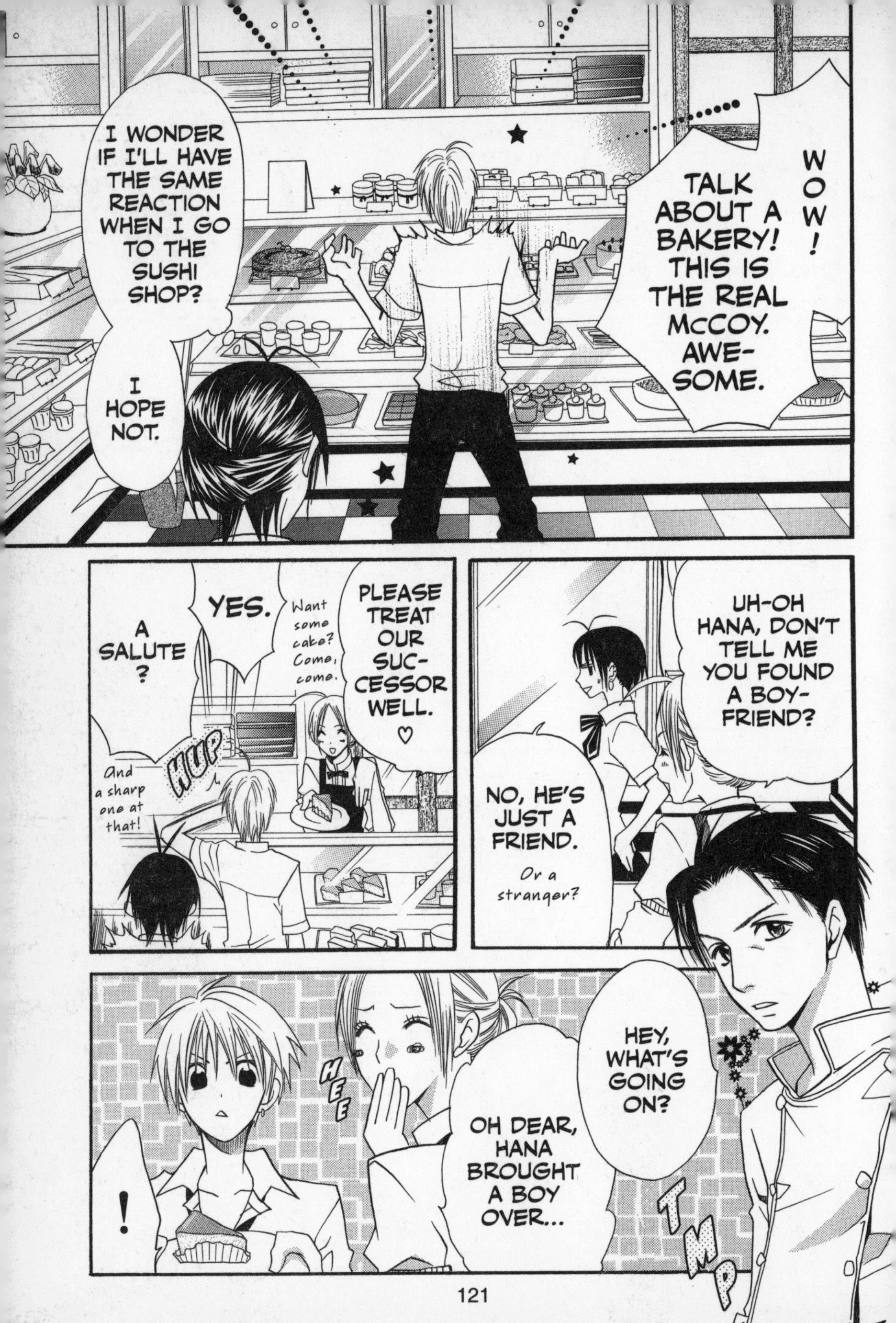
WOW!
TALK ABOUT A BAKERY! THIS IS THE REAL McCOY. AWESOME.
I WONDER IF I'LL HAVE THE SAME REACTION WHEN I GO TO THE SUSHI SHOP?
I HOPE NOT.
UH-OH HANA, DON'T TELL ME YOU FOUND A BOYFRIEND?
NO, HE'S JUST A FRIEND.
Or a stranger?
PLEASE TREAT OUR SUCCESSOR WELL. ♡
Want some cake? Come, come.
YES.
A SALUTE?
HUP
And a sharp one at that!
HEY, WHAT'S GOING ON?
TMP
OH DEAR, HANA BROUGHT A BOY OVER...
HEE
!

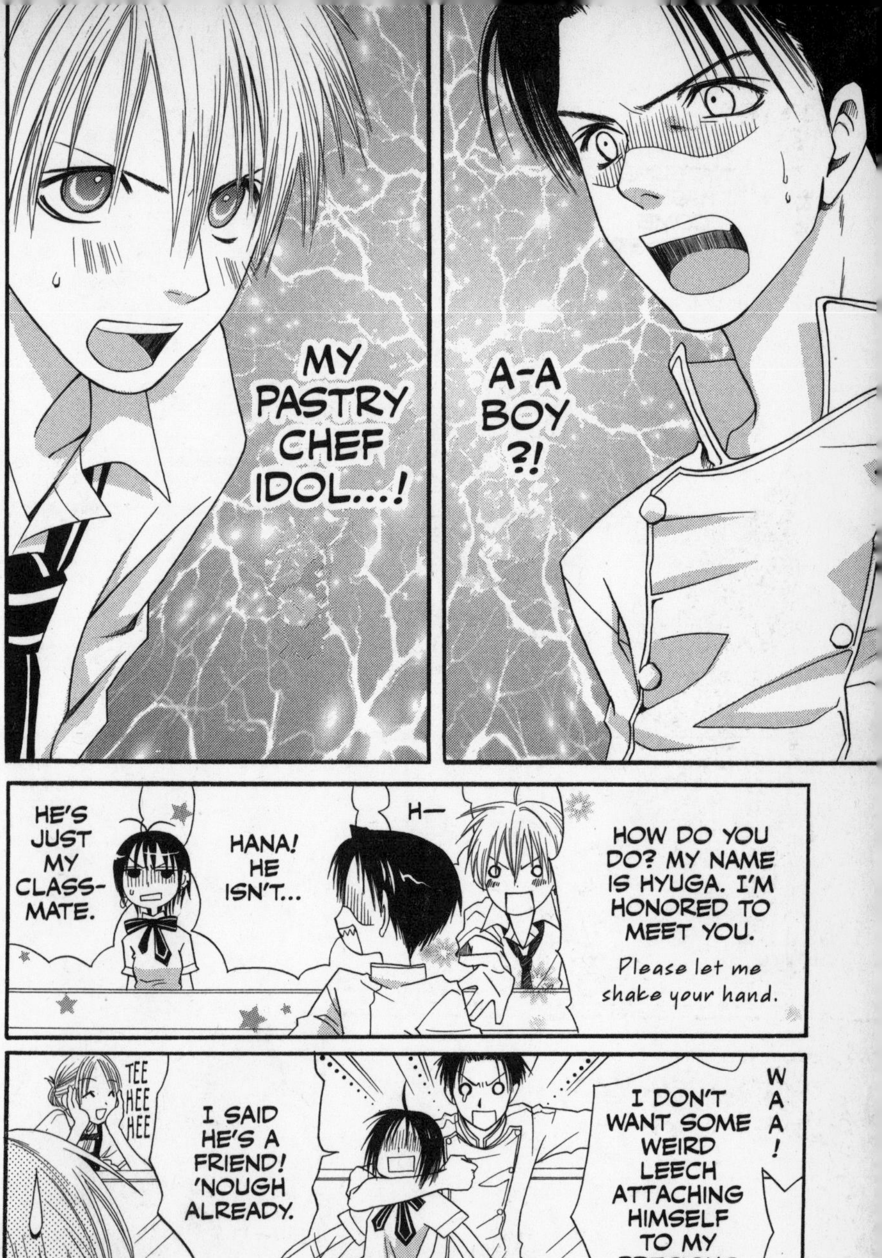
A-A BOY ?!
MY PASTRY CHEF IDOL...!
HOW DO YOU DO? MY NAME IS HYUGA. I'M HONORED TO MEET YOU.
Please let me shake your hand.
H—
HANA! HE ISN'T...
HE'S JUST MY CLASS-MATE.
WAA!
I DON'T WANT SOME WEIRD LEECH ATTACHING HIMSELF TO MY PRECIOUS DAUGHTER!
I SAID HE'S A FRIEND! 'NOUGH ALREADY.
TEE HEE HEE

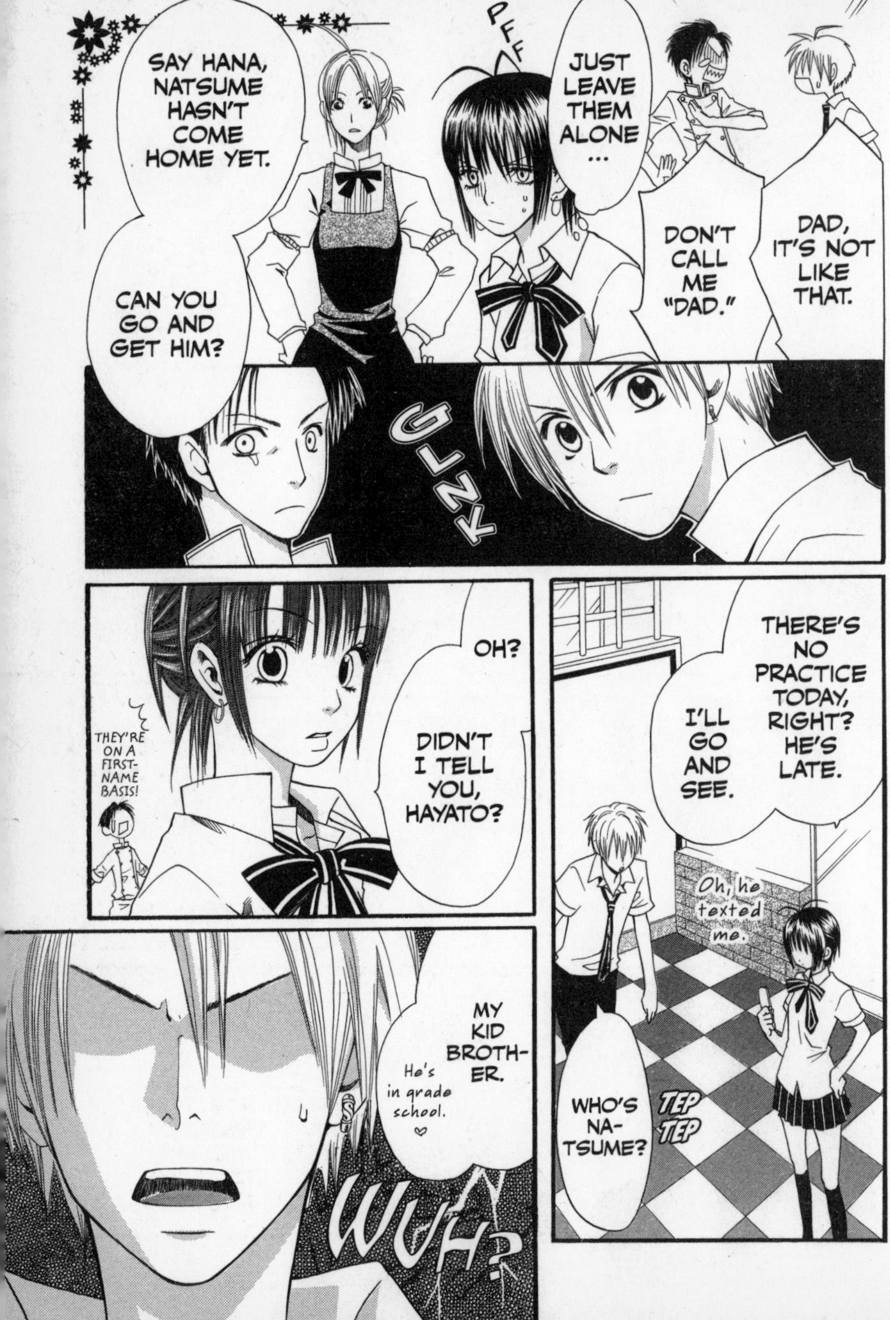
DAD, IT'S NOT LIKE THAT.
DON'T CALL ME "DAD."
PFF
JUST LEAVE THEM ALONE ...
SAY HANA, NATSUME HASN'T COME HOME YET.
CAN YOU GO AND GET HIM?
GLNK
THERE'S NO PRACTICE TODAY, RIGHT? HE'S LATE.
I'LL GO AND SEE.
Oh, he texted me.
WHO'S NA-TSUME?
TEP TEP
OH?
DIDN'T I TELL YOU, HAYATO?
THEY'RE ON A FIRST-NAME BASIS!
MY KID BROTH-ER.
He's in grade school.
WUH?

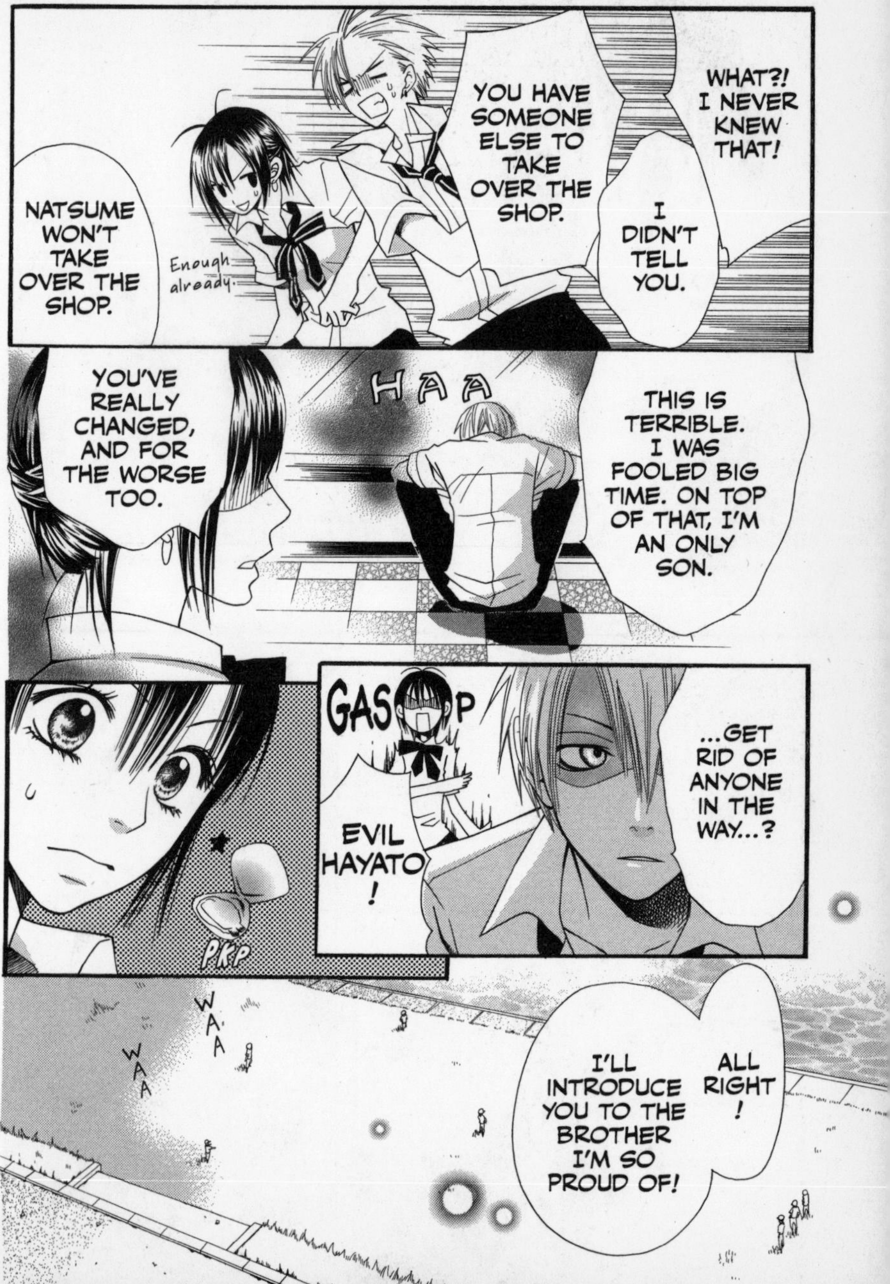
WHAT?! I NEVER KNEW THAT!
YOU HAVE SOMEONE ELSE TO TAKE OVER THE SHOP.
I DIDN'T TELL YOU.
NATSUME WON'T TAKE OVER THE SHOP.
Enough already.
THIS IS TERRIBLE. I WAS FOOLED BIG TIME. ON TOP OF THAT, I'M AN ONLY SON.
HAA
YOU'VE REALLY CHANGED, AND FOR THE WORSE TOO.
...GET RID OF ANYONE IN THE WAY...?
GASP
EVIL HAYATO!
PKP
ALL RIGHT!
I'LL INTRODUCE YOU TO THE BROTHER I'M SO PROUD OF!
WAA
WAA

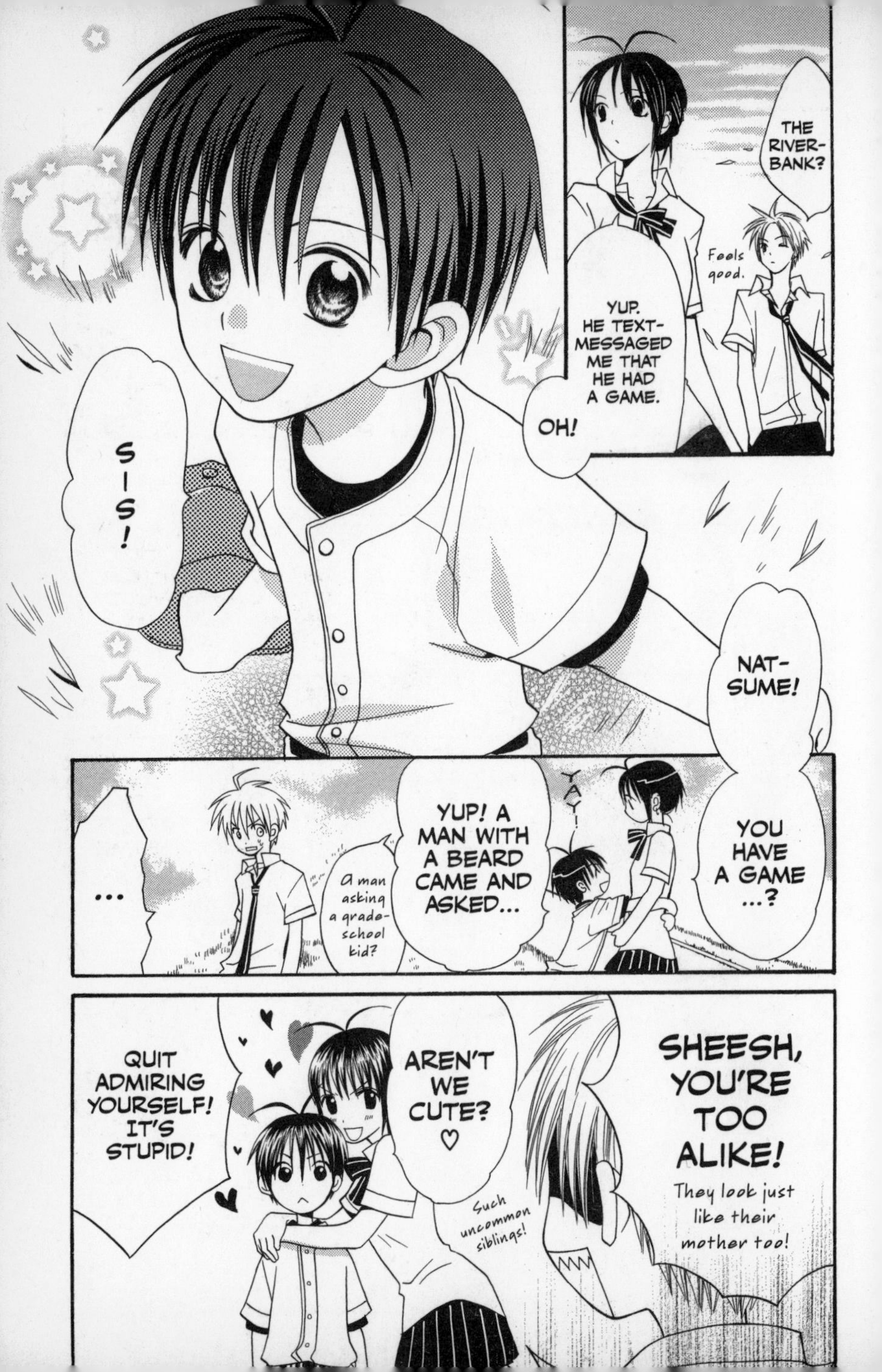
THE RIVER-BANK?
Feels good.
YUP. HE TEXT-MESSAGED ME THAT HE HAD A GAME.
OH!
NAT-SUME!
SIS!
YOU HAVE A GAME ...?
YAY!
YUP! A MAN WITH A BEARD CAME AND ASKED...
A man asking a grade-school kid?
...
SHEESH, YOU'RE TOO ALIKE!
They look just like their mother too!
Such uncommon siblings!
AREN'T WE CUTE? ♡
QUIT ADMIRING YOURSELF! IT'S STUPID!

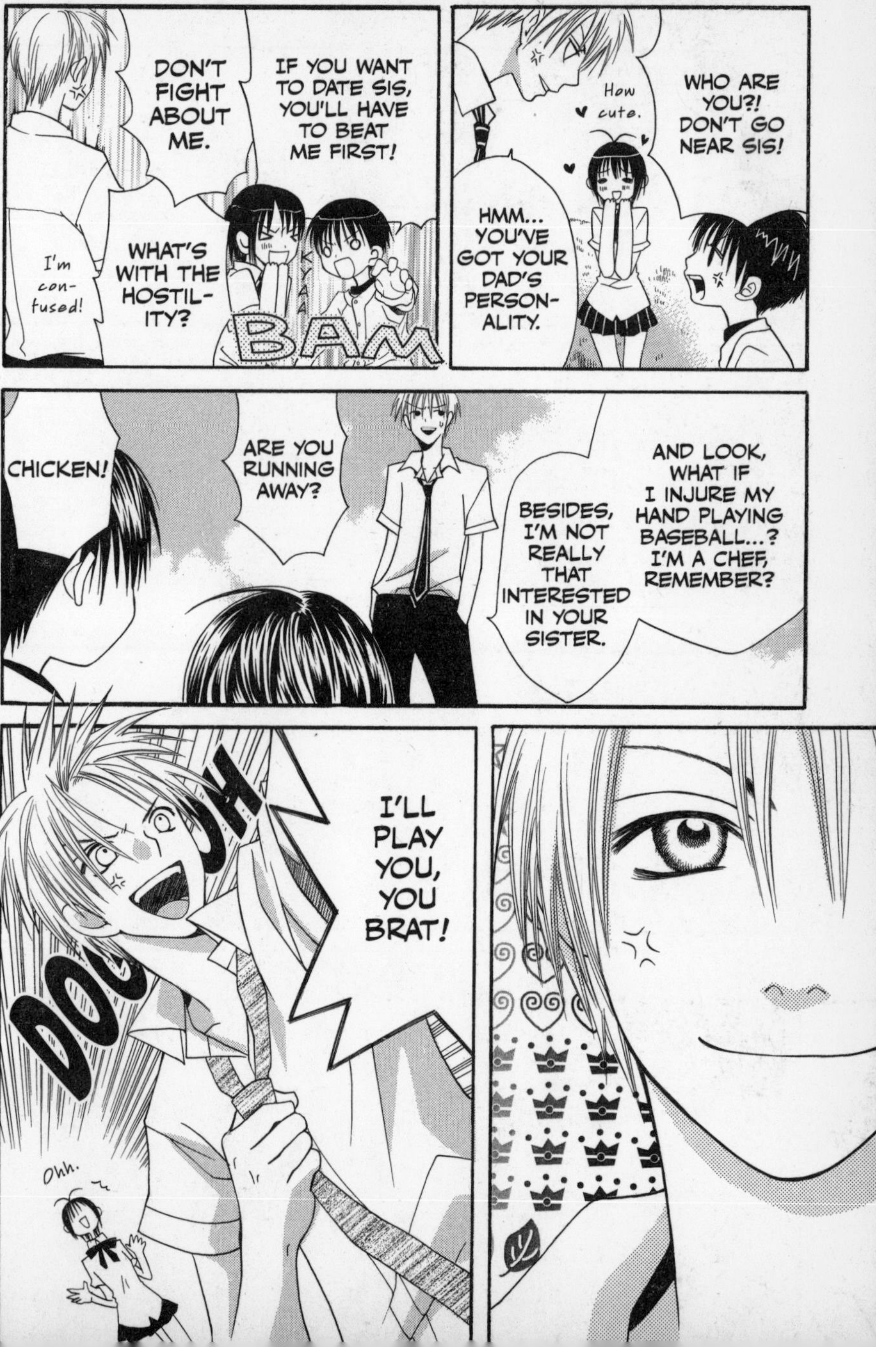
WHO ARE YOU?! DON'T GO NEAR SIS!
How cute.
HMM... YOU'VE GOT YOUR DAD'S PERSON-ALITY.
IF YOU WANT TO DATE SIS, YOU'LL HAVE TO BEAT ME FIRST!
DON'T FIGHT ABOUT ME.
BAM
WHAT'S WITH THE HOSTIL-ITY?
I'm con-fused!
AND LOOK, WHAT IF I INJURE MY HAND PLAYING BASEBALL...? I'M A CHEF, REMEMBER?
BESIDES, I'M NOT REALLY THAT INTERESTED IN YOUR SISTER.
ARE YOU RUNNING AWAY?
CHICKEN!
I'LL PLAY YOU, YOU BRAT!
Ohh.

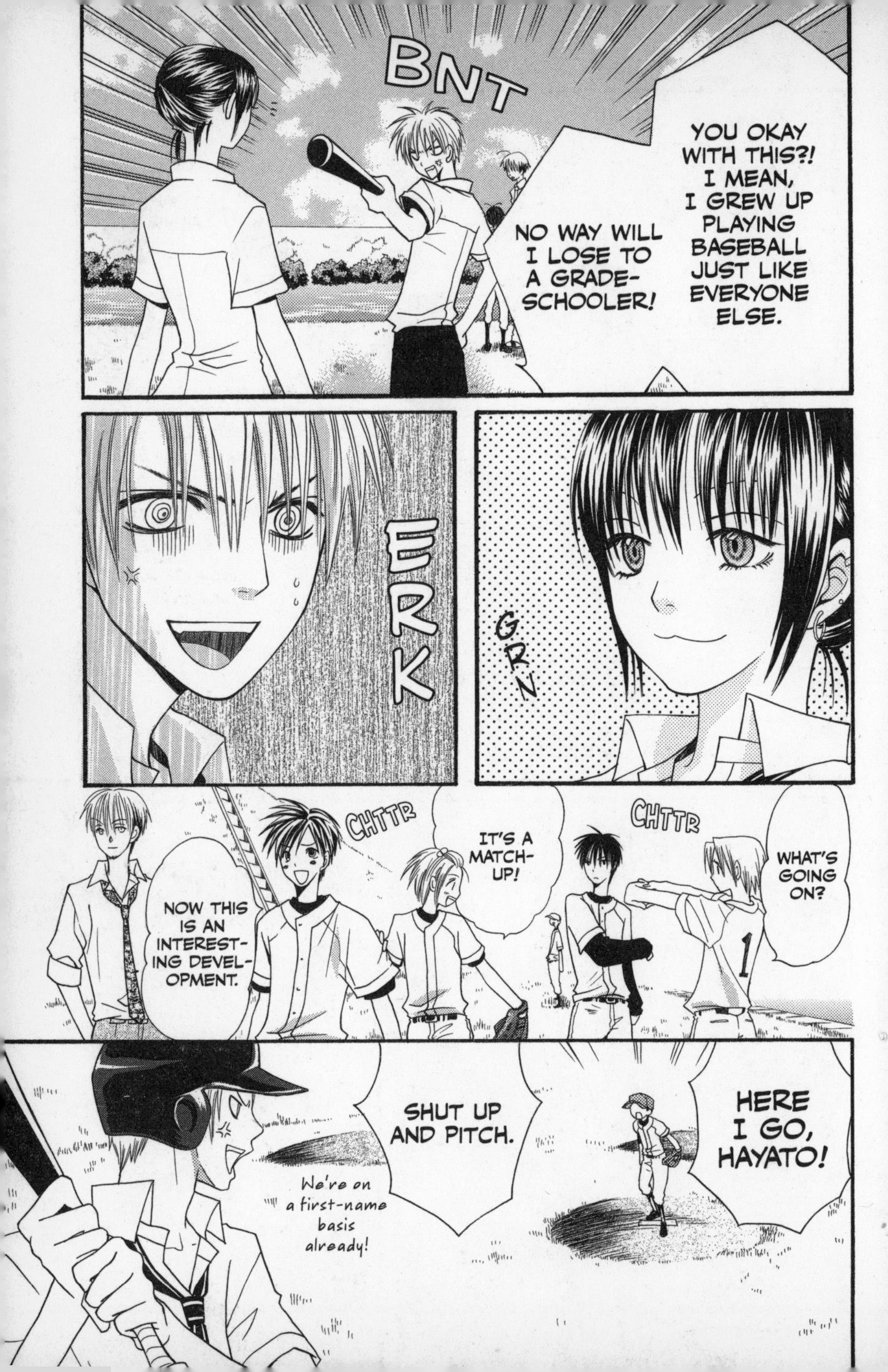
BNT
YOU OKAY WITH THIS?! I MEAN, I GREW UP PLAYING BASEBALL JUST LIKE EVERYONE ELSE.
NO WAY WILL I LOSE TO A GRADE-SCHOOLER!
GRN
ERK
CHTTR
WHAT'S GOING ON?
CHTTR
IT'S A MATCH-UP!
NOW THIS IS AN INTERESTING DEVELOPMENT.
HERE I GO, HAYATO!
SHUT UP AND PITCH.
We're on a first-name basis already!

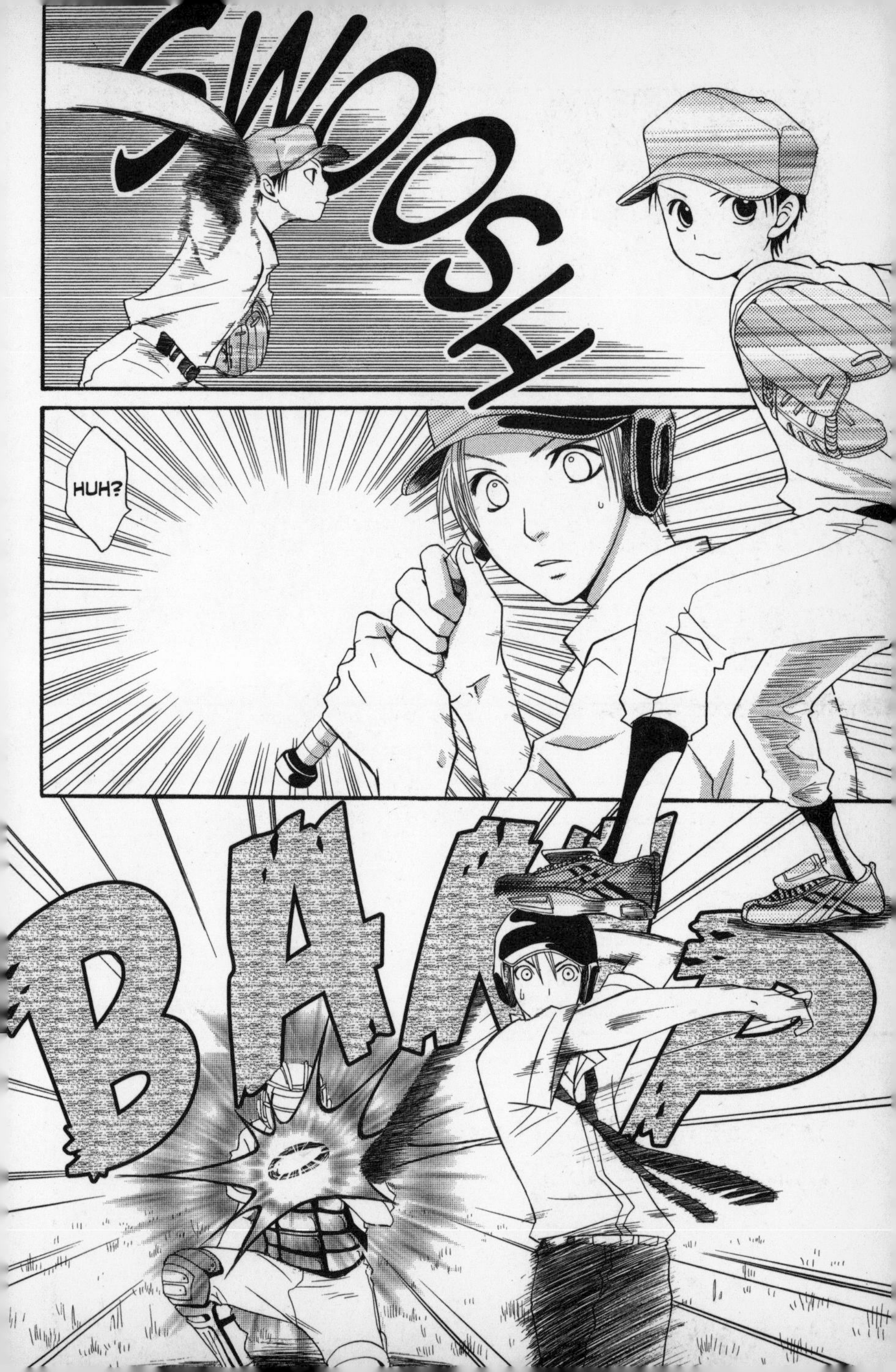
SWOOSH
HUH?
BAM

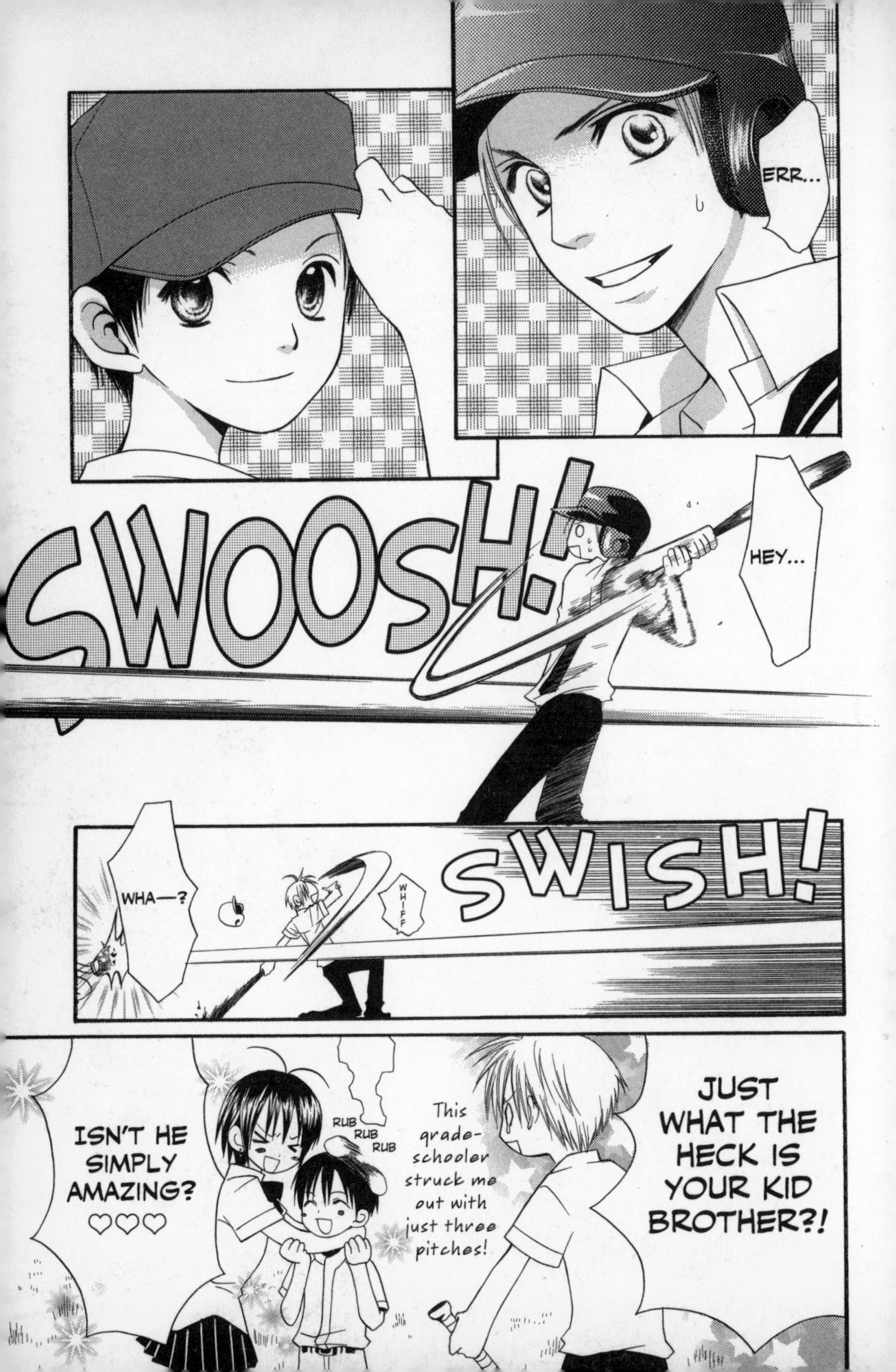
ERR...
HEY...
SWOOSH!
SWISH!
WHIFF
WHA—?
JUST WHAT THE HECK IS YOUR KID BROTHER?!
This grade-schooler struck me out with just three pitches!
RUB RUB RUB
ISN'T HE SIMPLY AMAZING? ♡♡♡

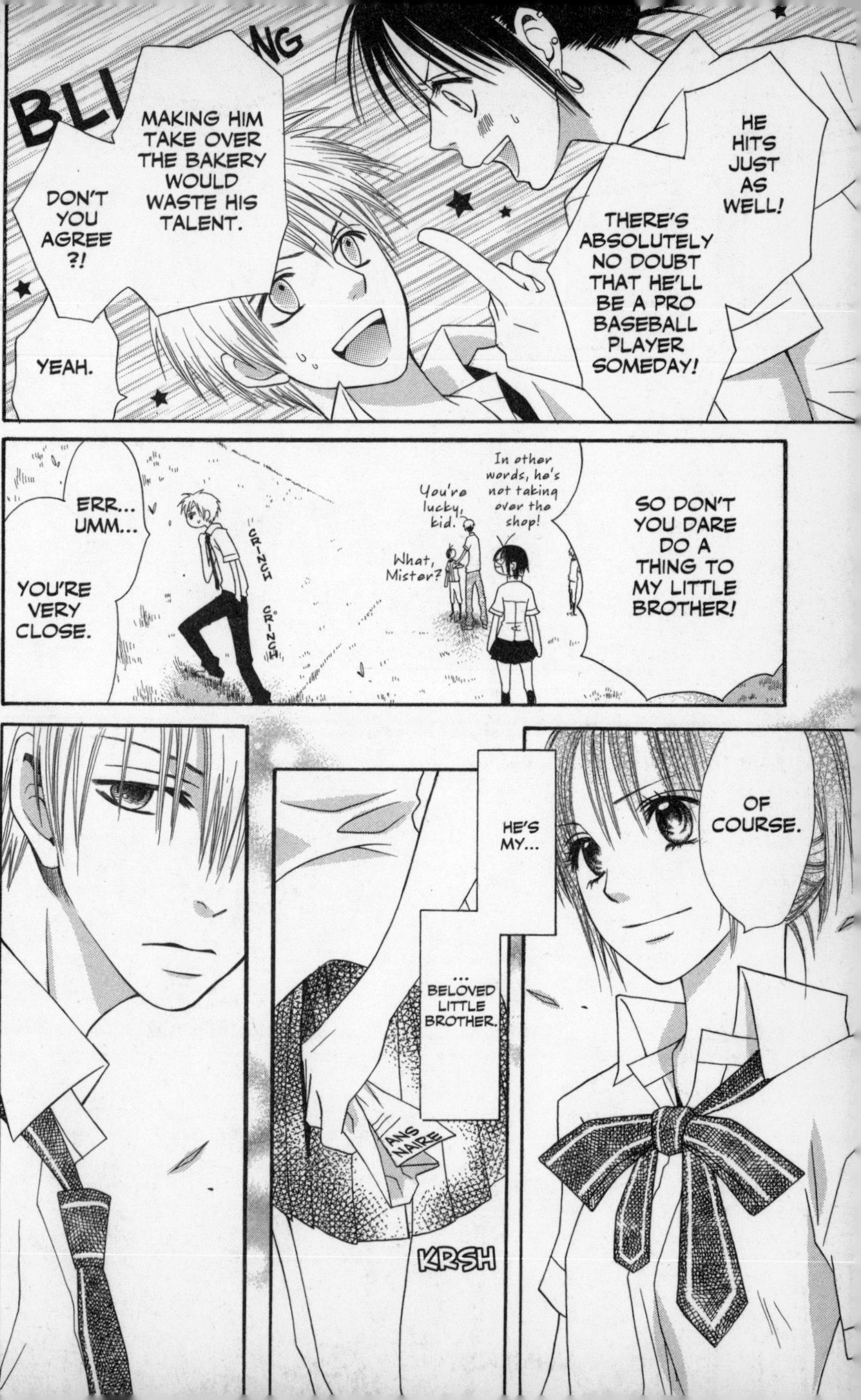
HE HITS JUST AS WELL!
THERE'S ABSOLUTELY NO DOUBT THAT HE'LL BE A PRO BASEBALL PLAYER SOMEDAY!
BLING
MAKING HIM TAKE OVER THE BAKERY WOULD WASTE HIS TALENT.
DON'T YOU AGREE?!
YEAH.
SO DON'T YOU DARE DO A THING TO MY LITTLE BROTHER!
In other words, he's not taking over the shop!
You're lucky, kid.
What, Mister?
CRINCH
CRINCH
ERR... UMM...
YOU'RE VERY CLOSE.
OF COURSE.
HE'S MY...
...BELOVED LITTLE BROTHER.
ANS NAIRE
KRSH

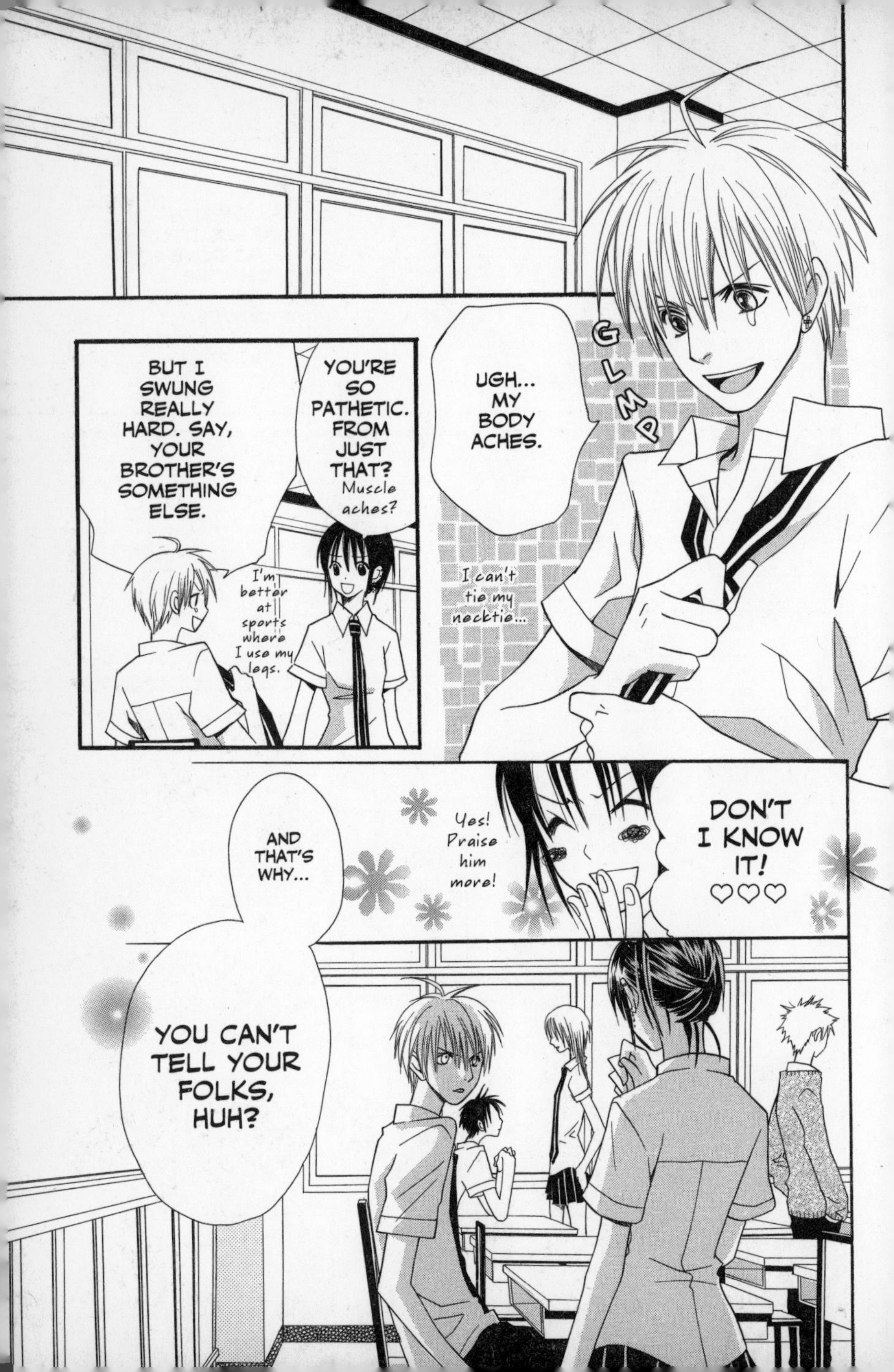

GLMP
UGH... MY BODY ACHES.
I can't tie my necktie...
YOU'RE SO PATHETIC. FROM JUST THAT?
Muscle aches?
BUT I SWUNG REALLY HARD. SAY, YOUR BROTHER'S SOMETHING ELSE.
I'm better at sports where I use my legs.
DON'T I KNOW IT! ♡♡♡
Yes! Praise him more!
AND THAT'S WHY...
YOU CAN'T TELL YOUR FOLKS, HUH?

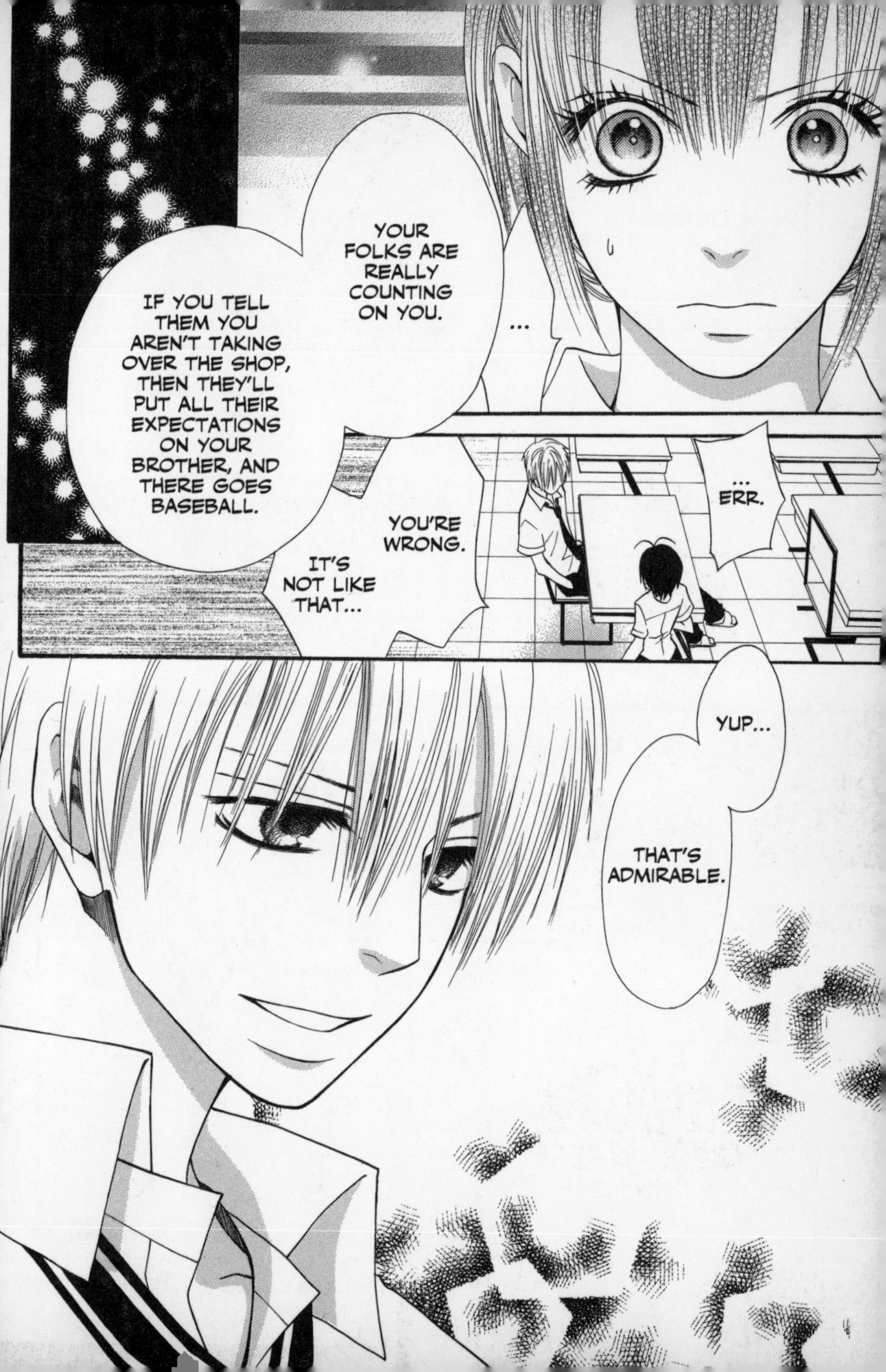
YOUR FOLKS ARE REALLY COUNTING ON YOU.
IF YOU TELL THEM YOU AREN'T TAKING OVER THE SHOP, THEN THEY'LL PUT ALL THEIR EXPECTATIONS ON YOUR BROTHER, AND THERE GOES BASEBALL.
...
... ERR.
YOU'RE WRONG.
IT'S NOT LIKE THAT...
YUP...
THAT'S ADMIRABLE.

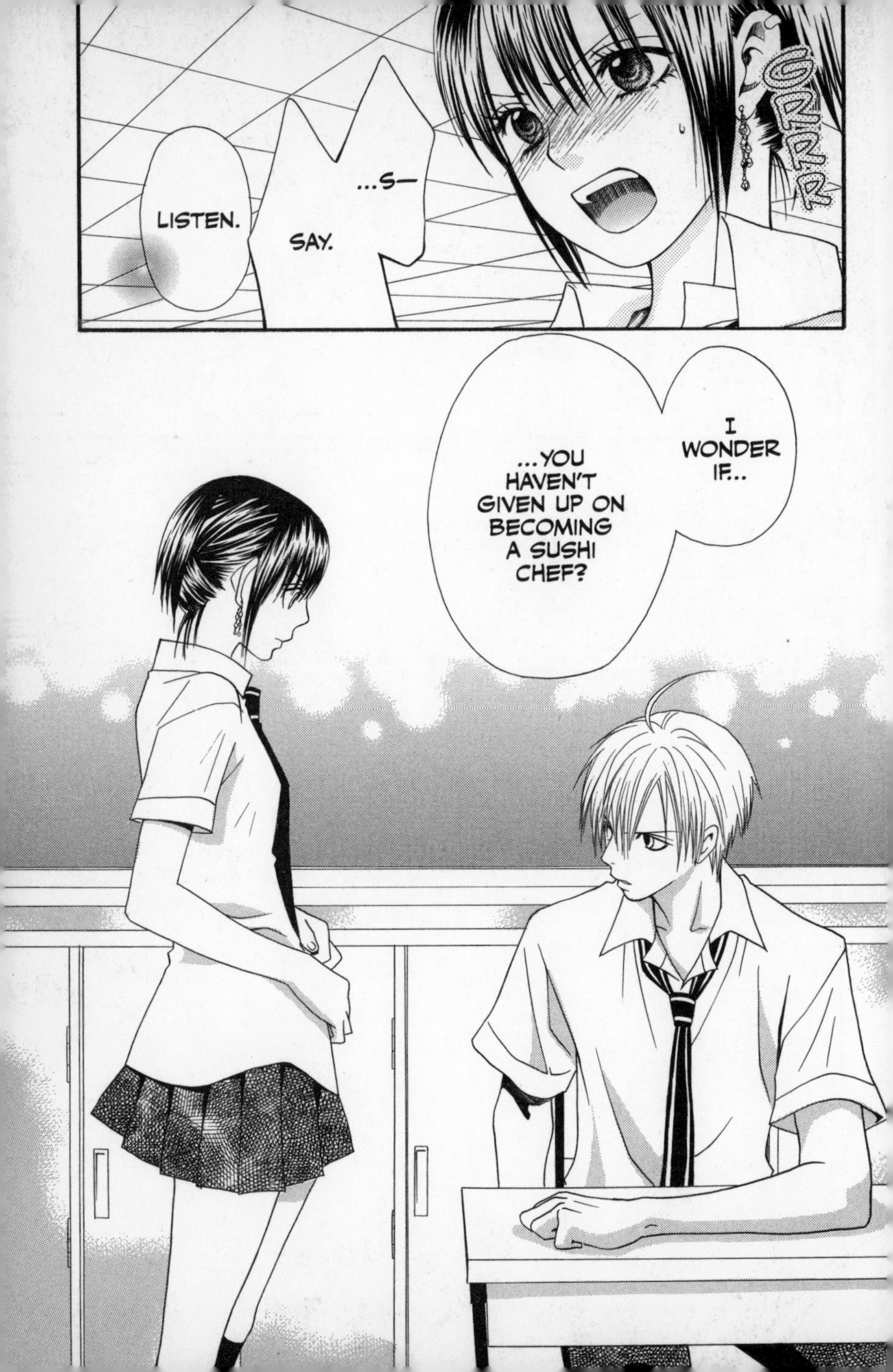
GRRR
...S— SAY.
LISTEN.
I WONDER IF...
...YOU HAVEN'T GIVEN UP ON BECOMING A SUSHI CHEF?

SIDE DISH Mixed Vegetables 5

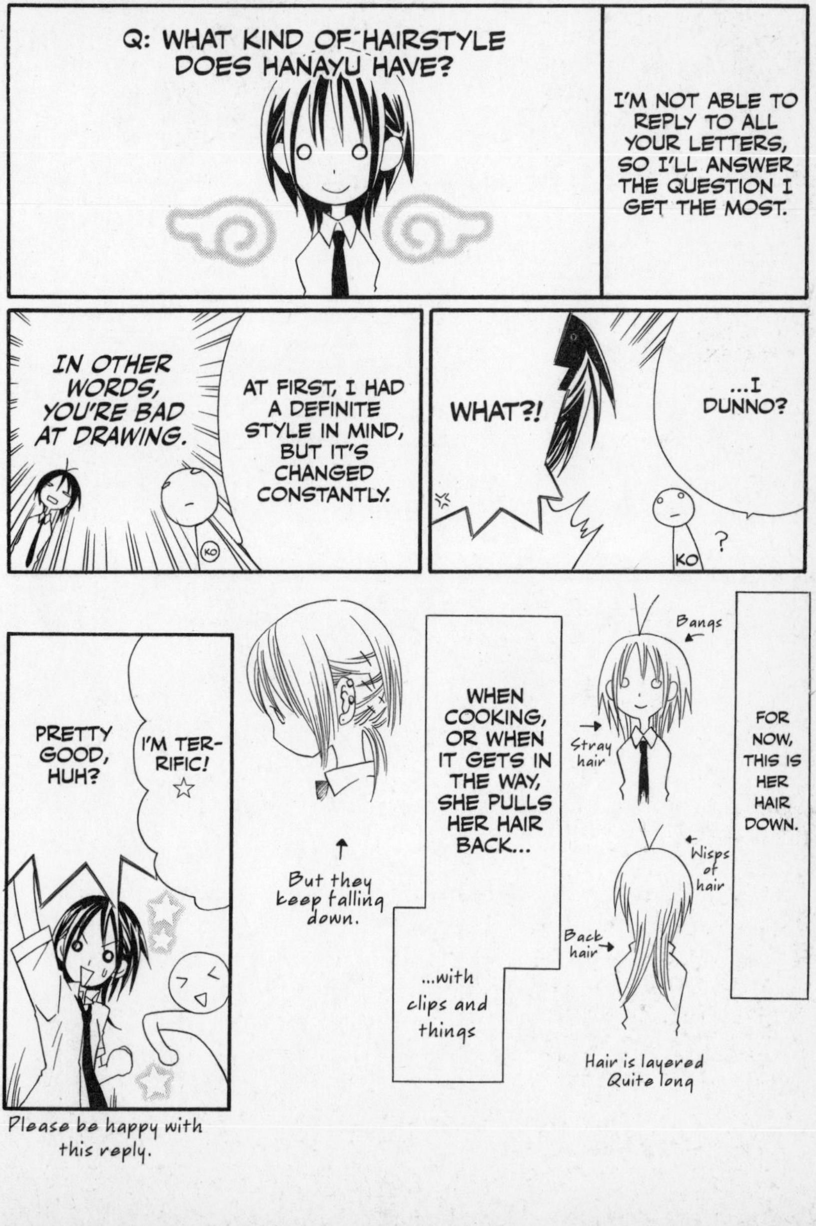
I'M NOT ABLE TO REPLY TO ALL YOUR LETTERS, SO I'LL ANSWER THE QUESTION I GET THE MOST.
Q: WHAT KIND OF HAIRSTYLE DOES HANAYU HAVE?
...I DUNNO?
WHAT?!
KO
?
AT FIRST, I HAD A DEFINITE STYLE IN MIND, BUT IT'S CHANGED CONSTANTLY.
IN OTHER WORDS, YOU'RE BAD AT DRAWING.
KO
FOR NOW, THIS IS HER HAIR DOWN.
Bangs
Stray hair
Wisps of hair
Back hair
Hair is layered
Quite long
WHEN COOKING, OR WHEN IT GETS IN THE WAY, SHE PULLS HER HAIR BACK...
...with clips and things
But they keep falling down.
I'M TERRIFIC!
PRETTY GOOD, HUH?
Please be happy with this reply.

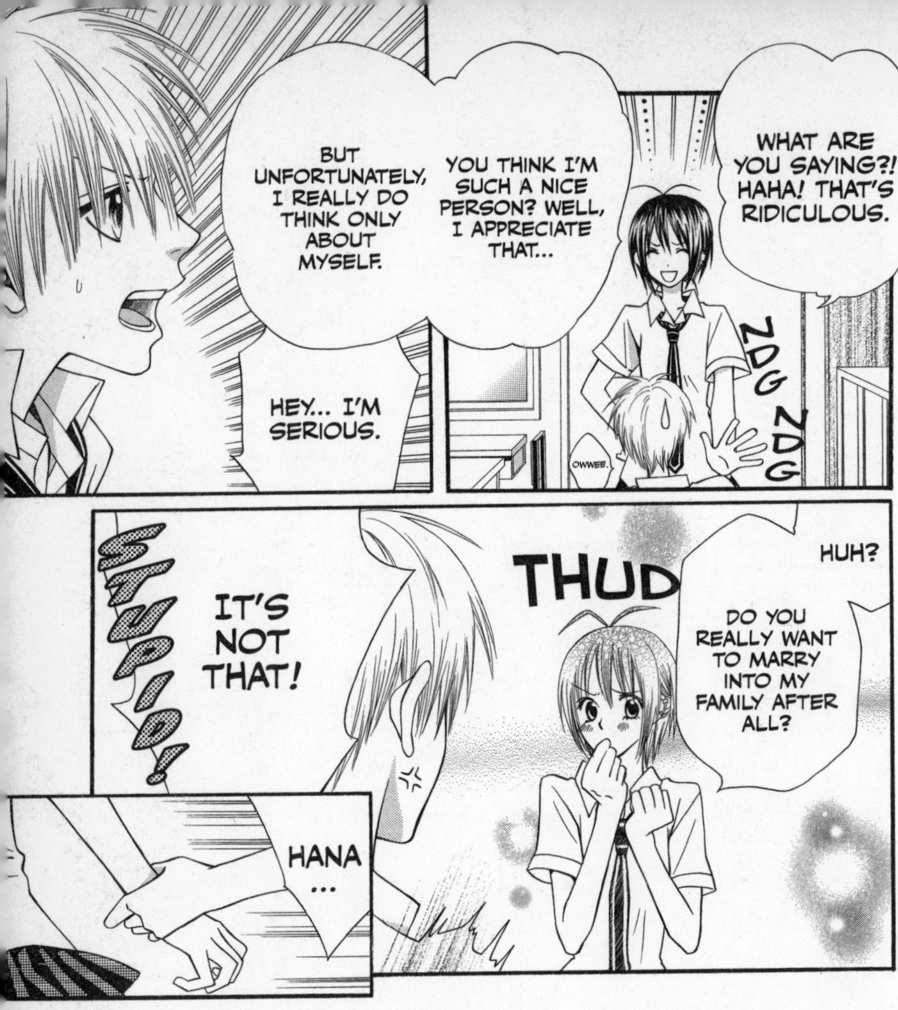
WHAT ARE YOU SAYING?! HAHA! THAT'S RIDICULOUS.
ZDG ZDG
OWWEE.
YOU THINK I'M SUCH A NICE PERSON? WELL, I APPRECIATE THAT...
BUT UNFORTUNATELY, I REALLY DO THINK ONLY ABOUT MYSELF.
HEY... I'M SERIOUS.
HUH?
DO YOU REALLY WANT TO MARRY INTO MY FAMILY AFTER ALL?
THUD
IT'S NOT THAT!
STUPID!
HANA...

menu. 13

After evaluating the colors on the previous illustration (Menu 8), I limited the contents of this one (to only eggs). Hanayu's hair seems a bit short... The main chapter...I did it to my heart's content.
I wasn't sure about it, but I enjoy it.
By the way, a character named Kitamikado from my first manga shows up here. If you get a chance, please look for him.

Maguro maguro maguro! ...What is your magic word?
(Any nice expressions?)

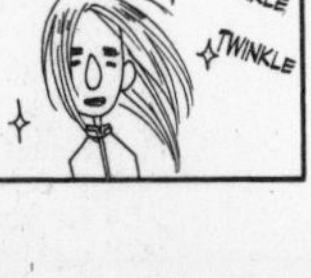
TWINKLE
TWINKLE

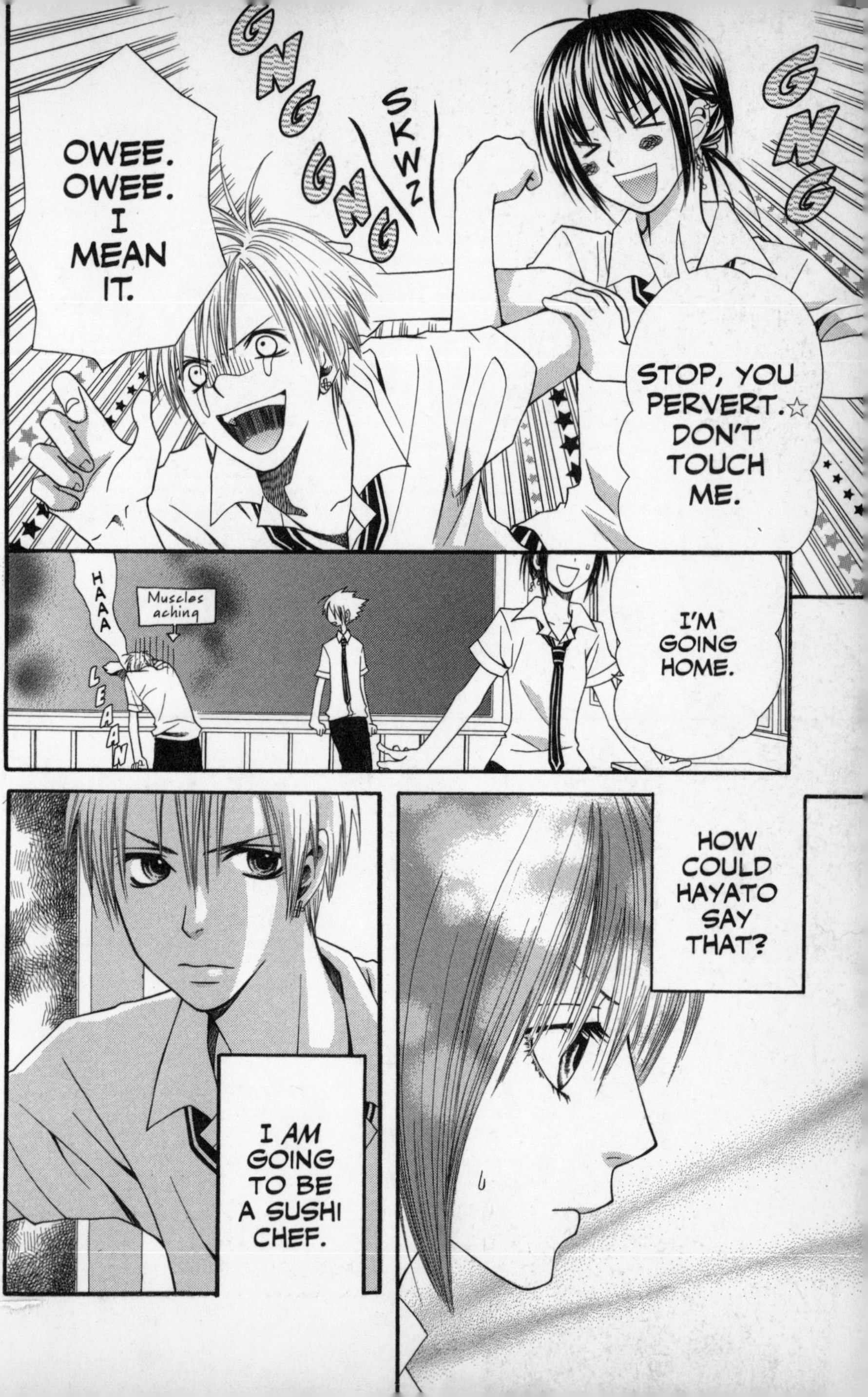
GNG
STOP, YOU PERVERT.☆ DON'T TOUCH ME.
SKWZ
GNG GNG
OWEE. OWEE. I MEAN IT.
I'M GOING HOME.
Muscles aching
HAAA
LEAAN
HOW COULD HAYATO SAY THAT?
I AM GOING TO BE A SUSHI CHEF.

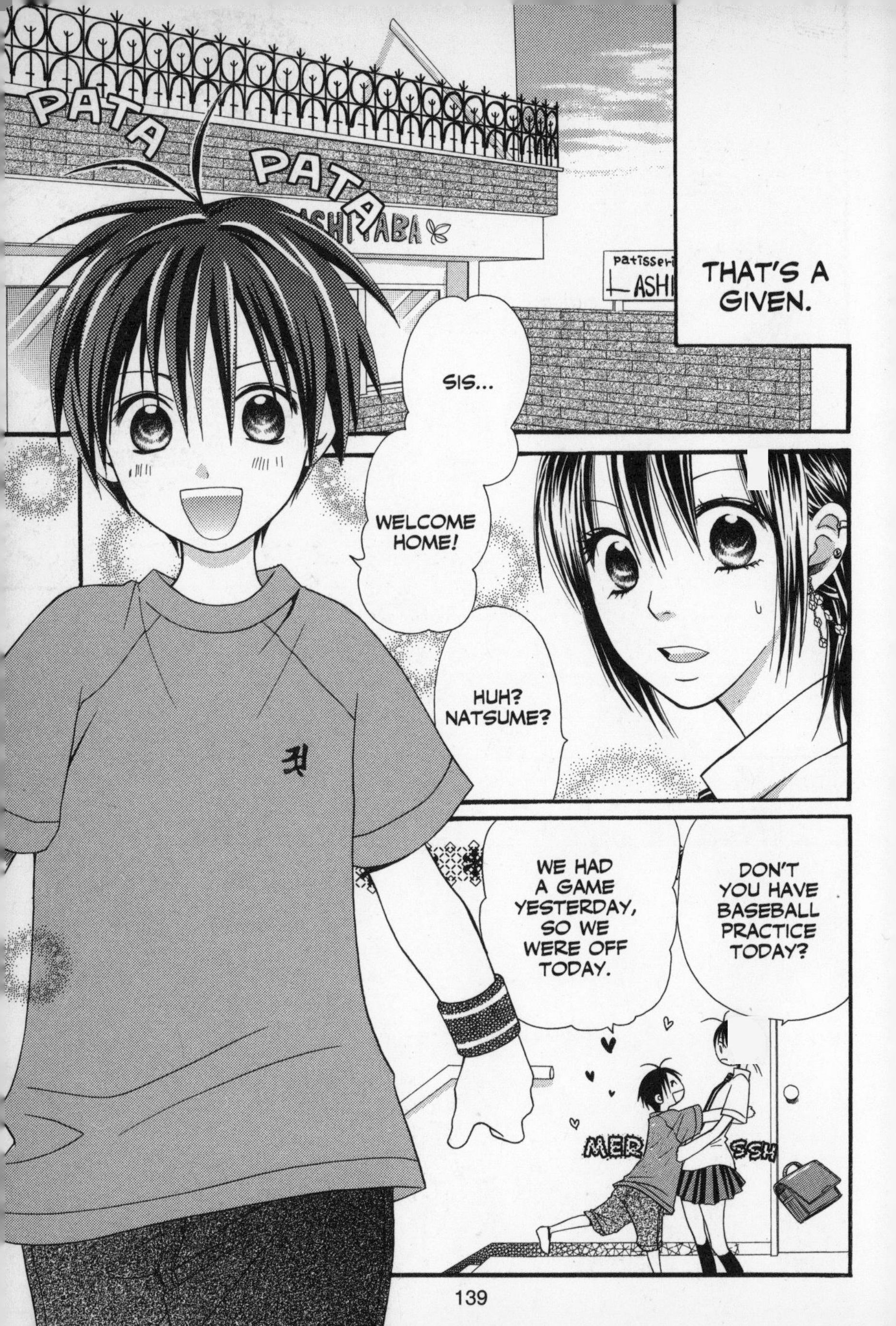
THAT'S A GIVEN.
PATA PATA
SIS...
WELCOME HOME!
HUH? NATSUME?
DON'T YOU HAVE BASEBALL PRACTICE TODAY?
WE HAD A GAME YESTERDAY, SO WE WERE OFF TODAY.
MER SSH

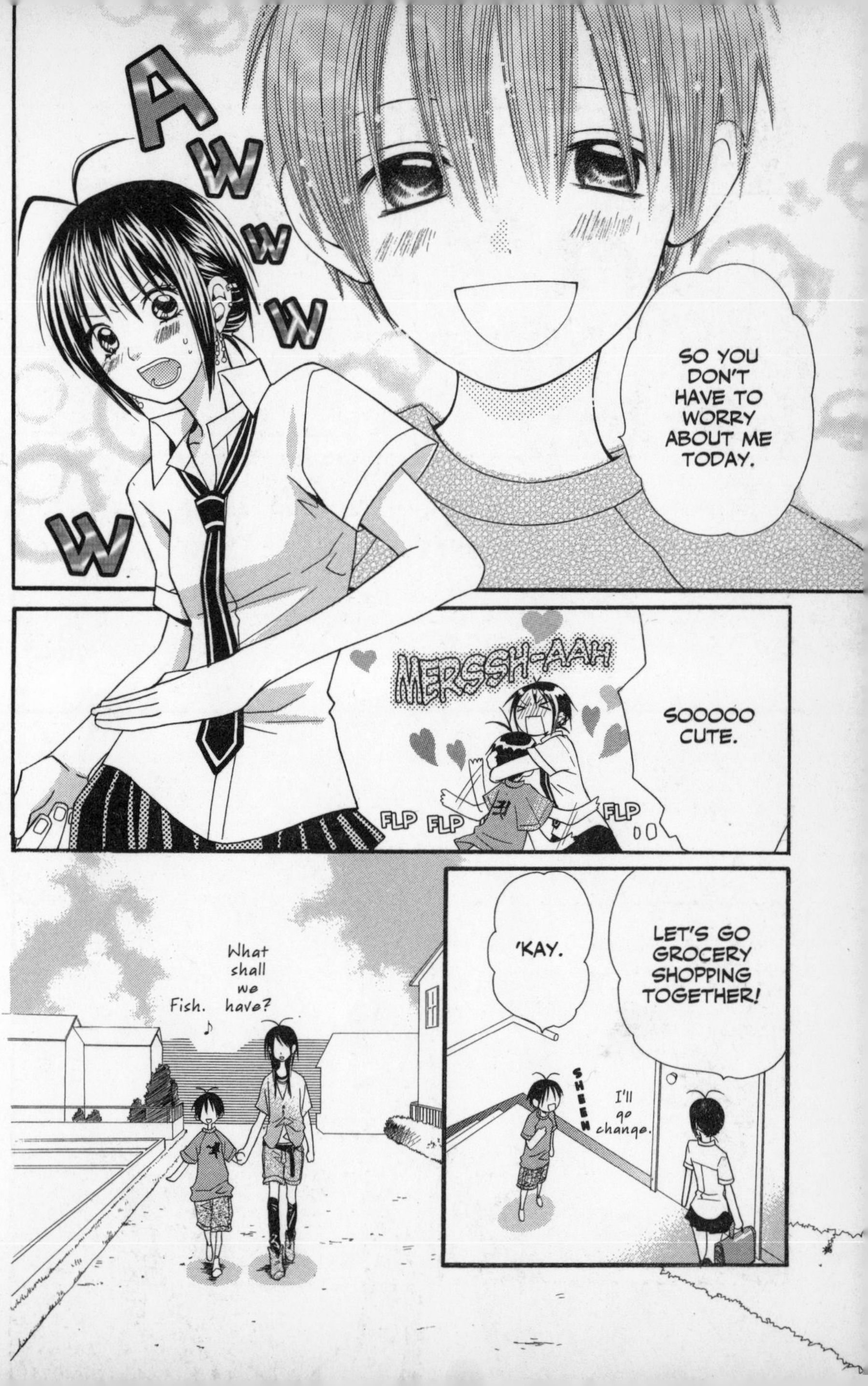
SO YOU DON'T HAVE TO WORRY ABOUT ME TODAY.
AWWWWW
SOOOOO CUTE.
MERSSH-AAH
FLP FLP FLP
LET'S GO GROCERY SHOPPING TOGETHER!
'KAY.
SHEEN
I'll go change.
What shall we have?
Fish. ♪

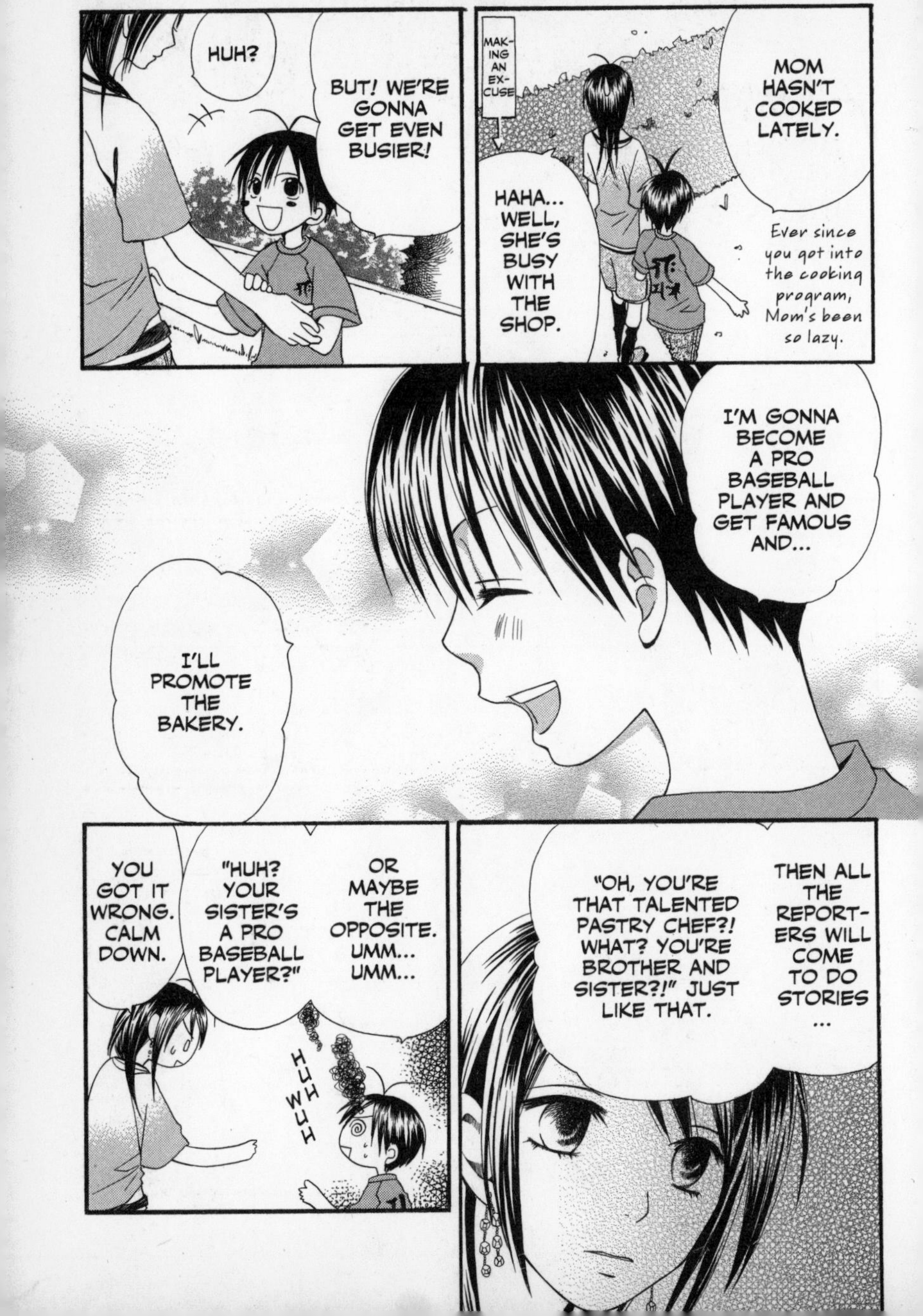
MOM HASN'T COOKED LATELY.
Ever since you got into the cooking program, Mom's been so lazy.
MAKING AN EXCUSE
HAHA... WELL, SHE'S BUSY WITH THE SHOP.
BUT! WE'RE GONNA GET EVEN BUSIER!
HUH?
I'M GONNA BECOME A PRO BASEBALL PLAYER AND GET FAMOUS AND...
I'LL PROMOTE THE BAKERY.
THEN ALL THE REPORTERS WILL COME TO DO STORIES ...
"OH, YOU'RE THAT TALENTED PASTRY CHEF?! WHAT? YOU'RE BROTHER AND SISTER?!" JUST LIKE THAT.
OR MAYBE THE OPPOSITE. UMM... UMM...
"HUH? YOUR SISTER'S A PRO BASEBALL PLAYER?"
YOU GOT IT WRONG. CALM DOWN.
HUH WUH

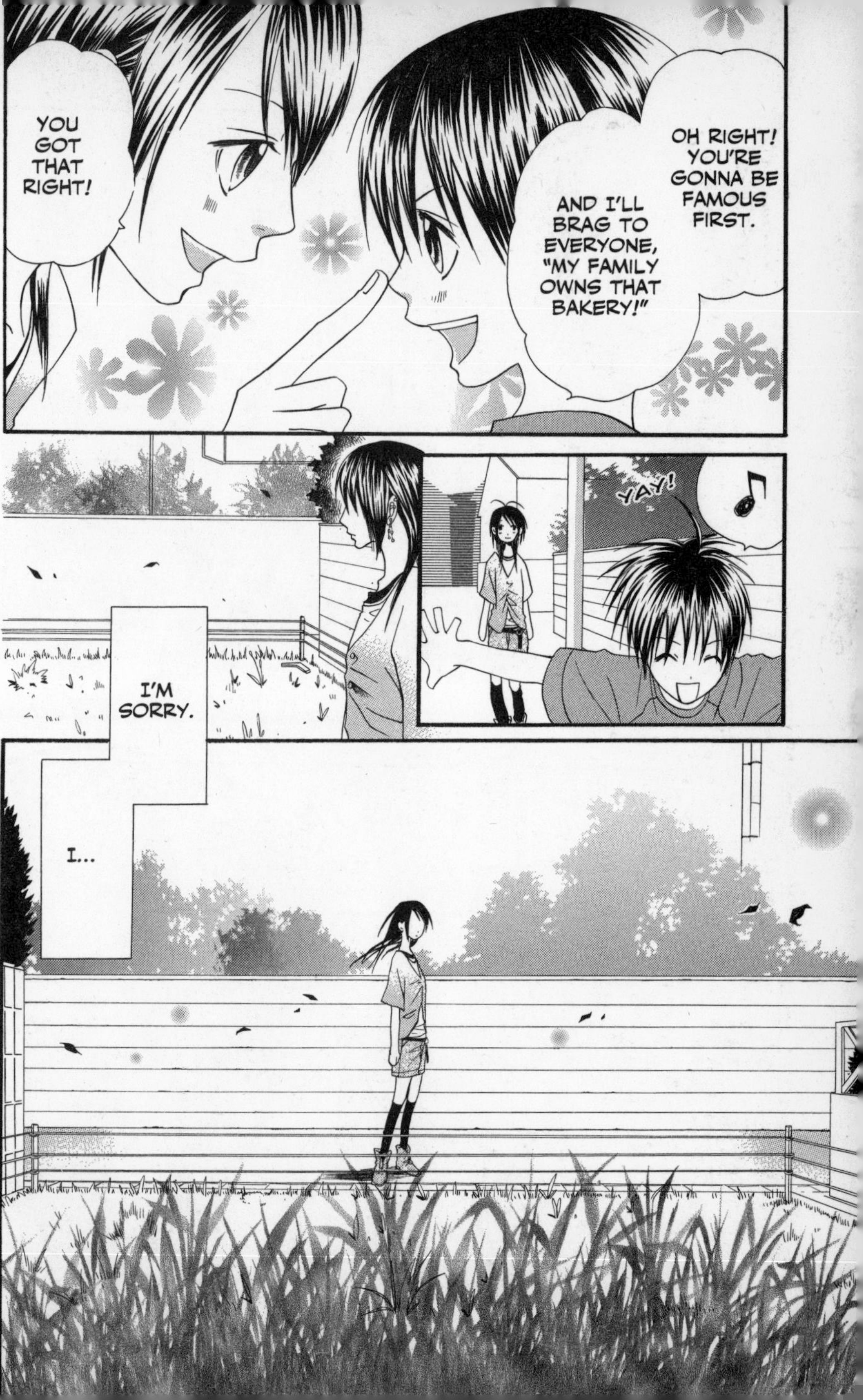
OH RIGHT! YOU'RE GONNA BE FAMOUS FIRST.
AND I'LL BRAG TO EVERYONE, "MY FAMILY OWNS THAT BAKERY!"
YOU GOT THAT RIGHT!
YAY!
I'M SORRY.
I...

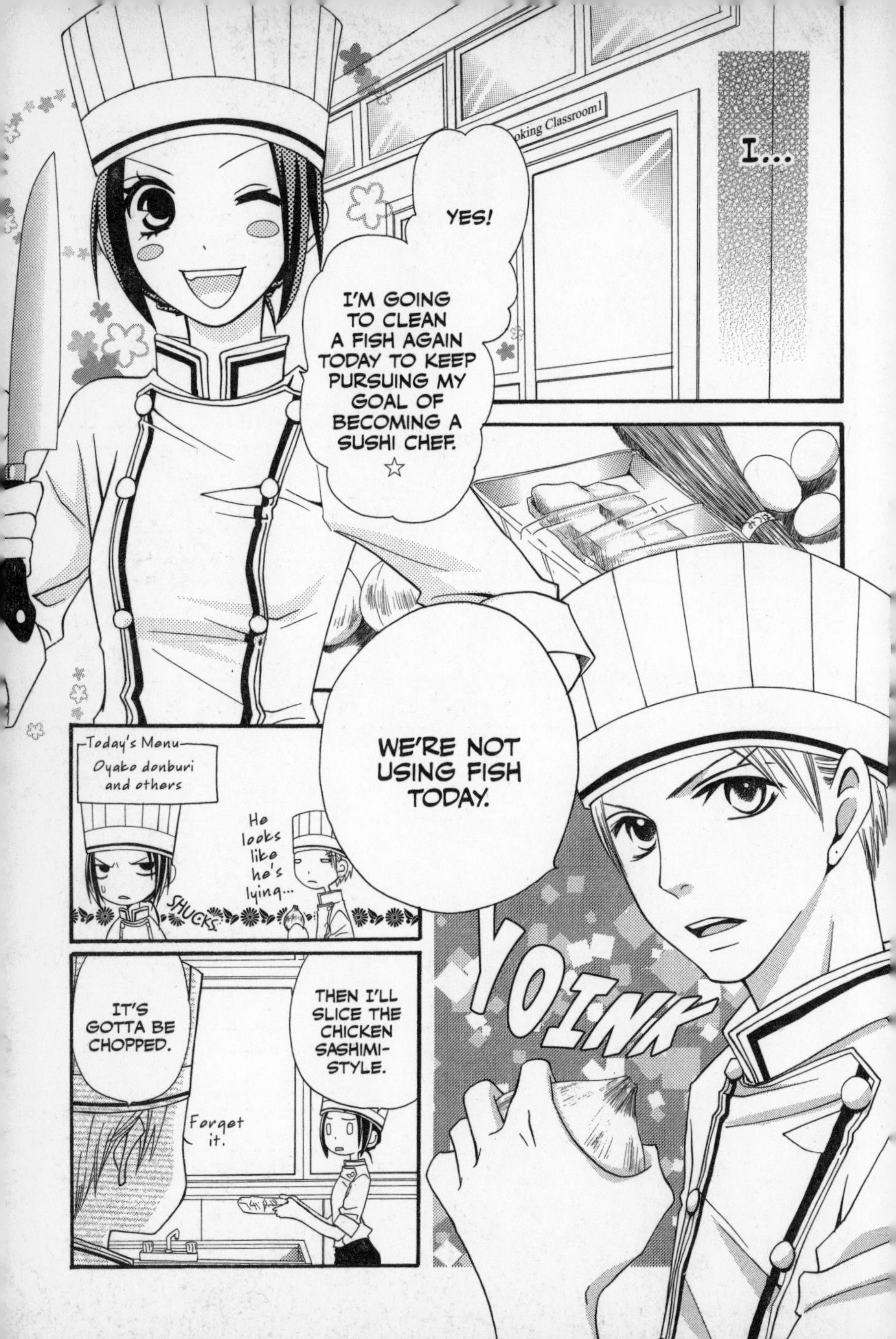
I...
YES!
I'M GOING TO CLEAN A FISH AGAIN TODAY TO KEEP PURSUING MY GOAL OF BECOMING A SUSHI CHEF. ☆
WE'RE NOT USING FISH TODAY.
YOINK
Today's Menu
Oyako donburi and others
He looks like he's lying...
SHUCKS
THEN I'LL SLICE THE CHICKEN SASHIMI-STYLE.
IT'S GOTTA BE CHOPPED.
Forget it.

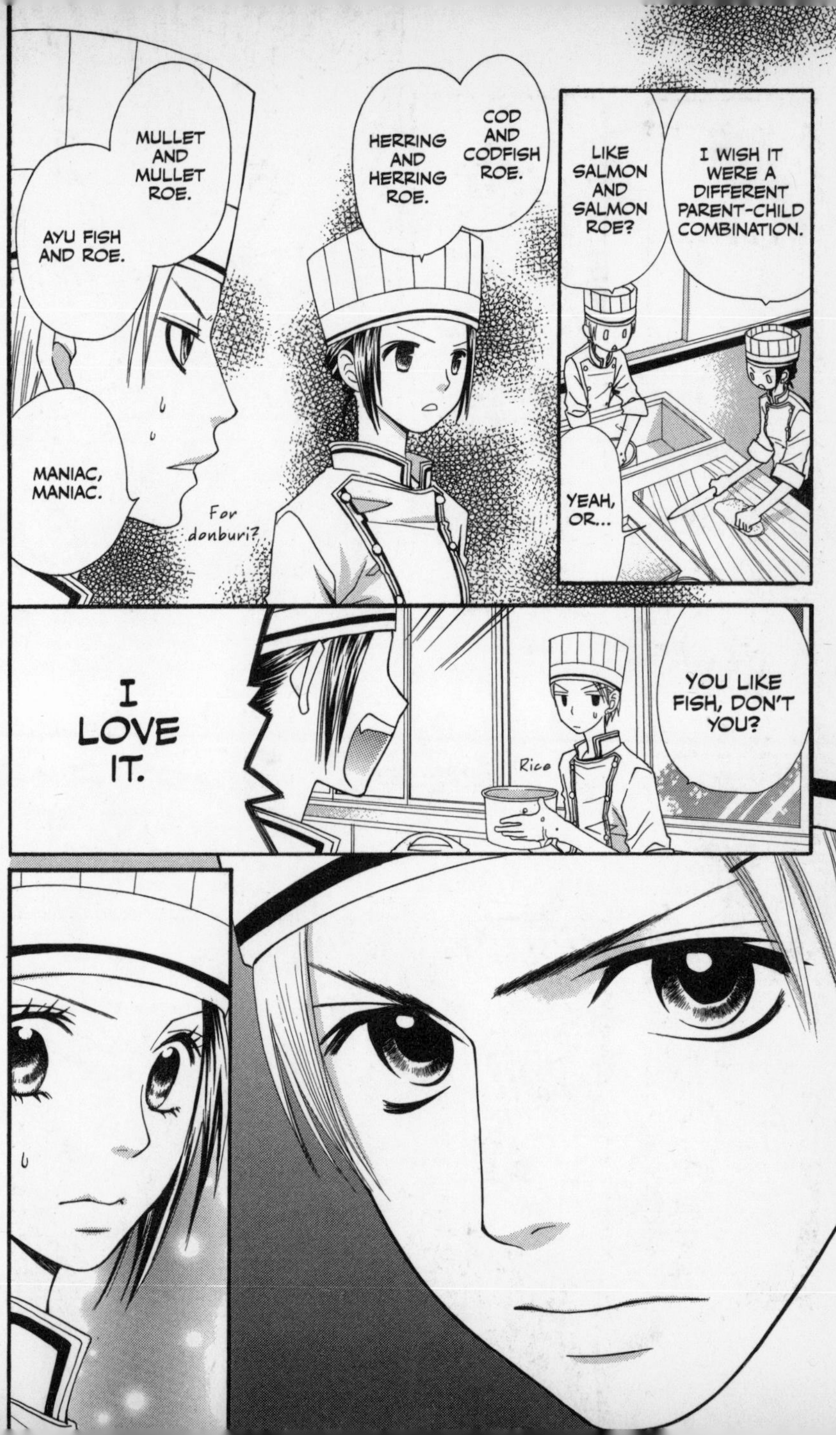
I WISH IT WERE A DIFFERENT PARENT-CHILD COMBINATION.
LIKE SALMON AND SALMON ROE?
YEAH, OR...
COD AND CODFISH ROE.
HERRING AND HERRING ROE.
MULLET AND MULLET ROE.
AYU FISH AND ROE.
For donburi?
MANIAC, MANIAC.
YOU LIKE FISH, DON'T YOU?
Rice
I LOVE IT.

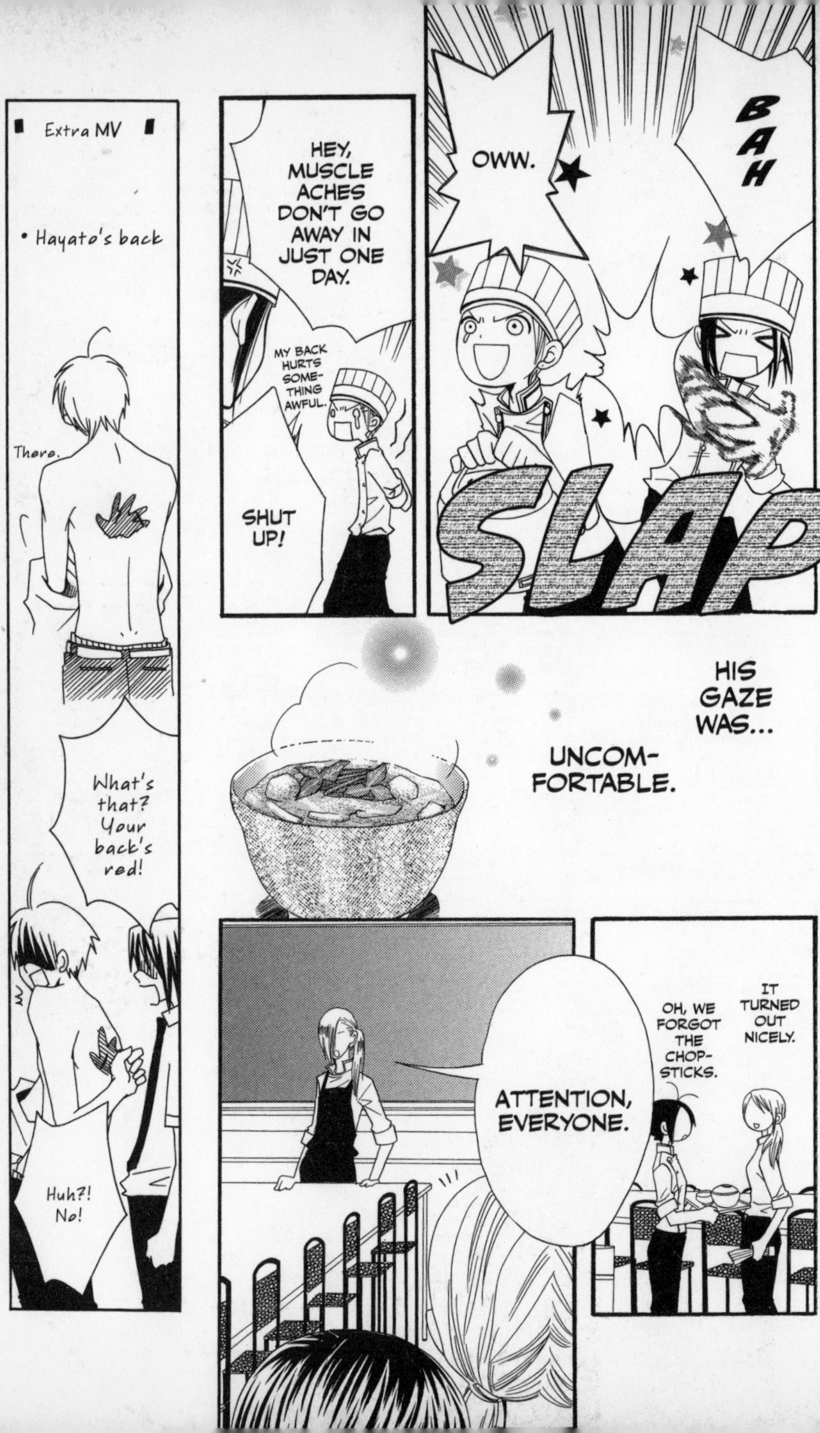
BAH
OWW.
SLAP
HEY, MUSCLE ACHES DON'T GO AWAY IN JUST ONE DAY.
MY BACK HURTS SOMETHING AWFUL.
SHUT UP!
HIS GAZE WAS...
UNCOMFORTABLE.
IT TURNED OUT NICELY.
OH, WE FORGOT THE CHOPSTICKS.
ATTENTION, EVERYONE.
Extra MV
• Hayato's back
There.
What's that? Your back's red!
Huh?! No!

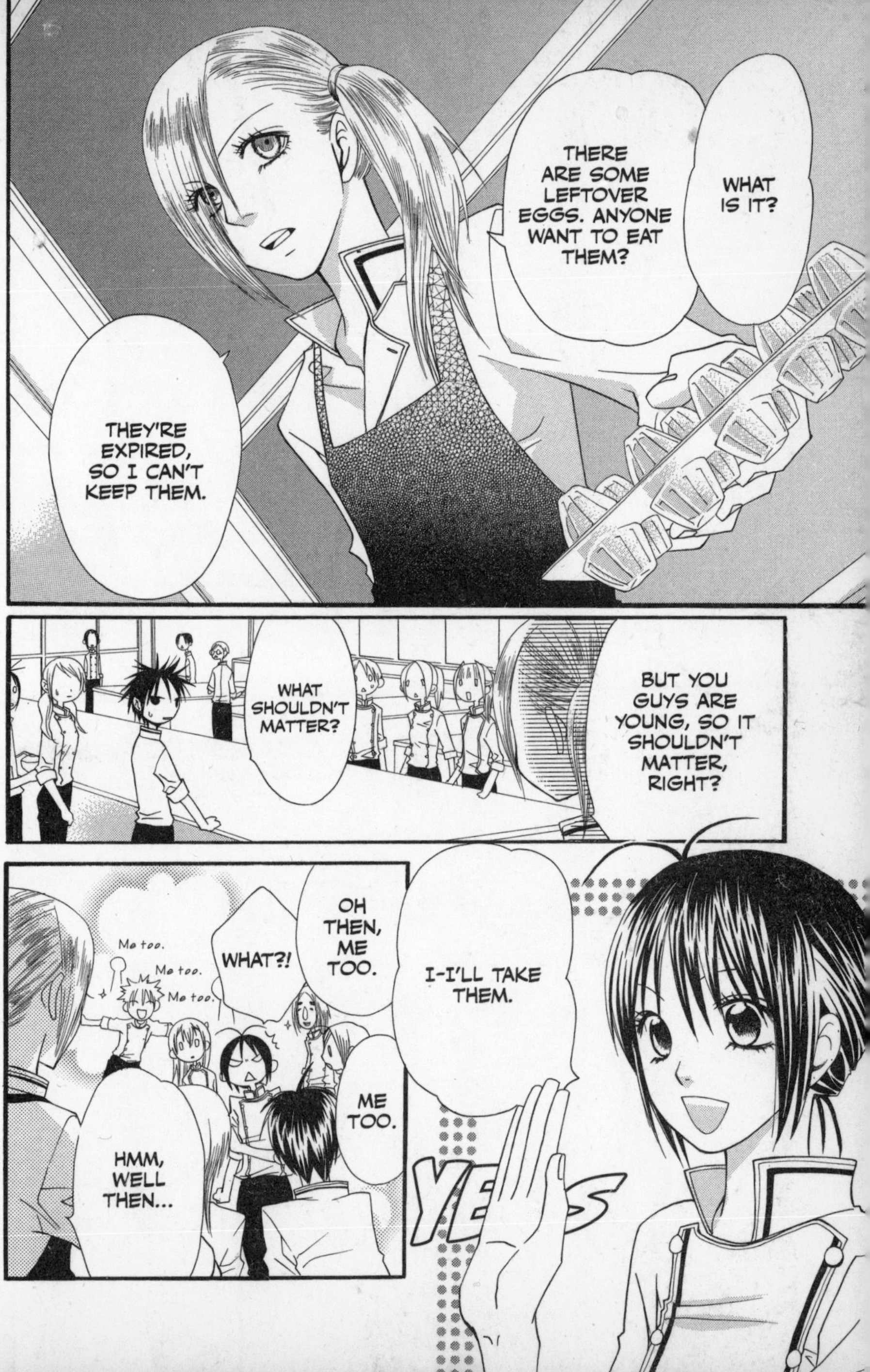
WHAT IS IT?
THERE ARE SOME LEFTOVER EGGS. ANYONE WANT TO EAT THEM?
THEY'RE EXPIRED, SO I CAN'T KEEP THEM.
BUT YOU GUYS ARE YOUNG, SO IT SHOULDN'T MATTER, RIGHT?
WHAT SHOULDN'T MATTER?
I-I'LL TAKE THEM.
OH THEN, ME TOO.
WHAT?!
Me too.
Me too.
Me too.
ME TOO.
HMM, WELL THEN...

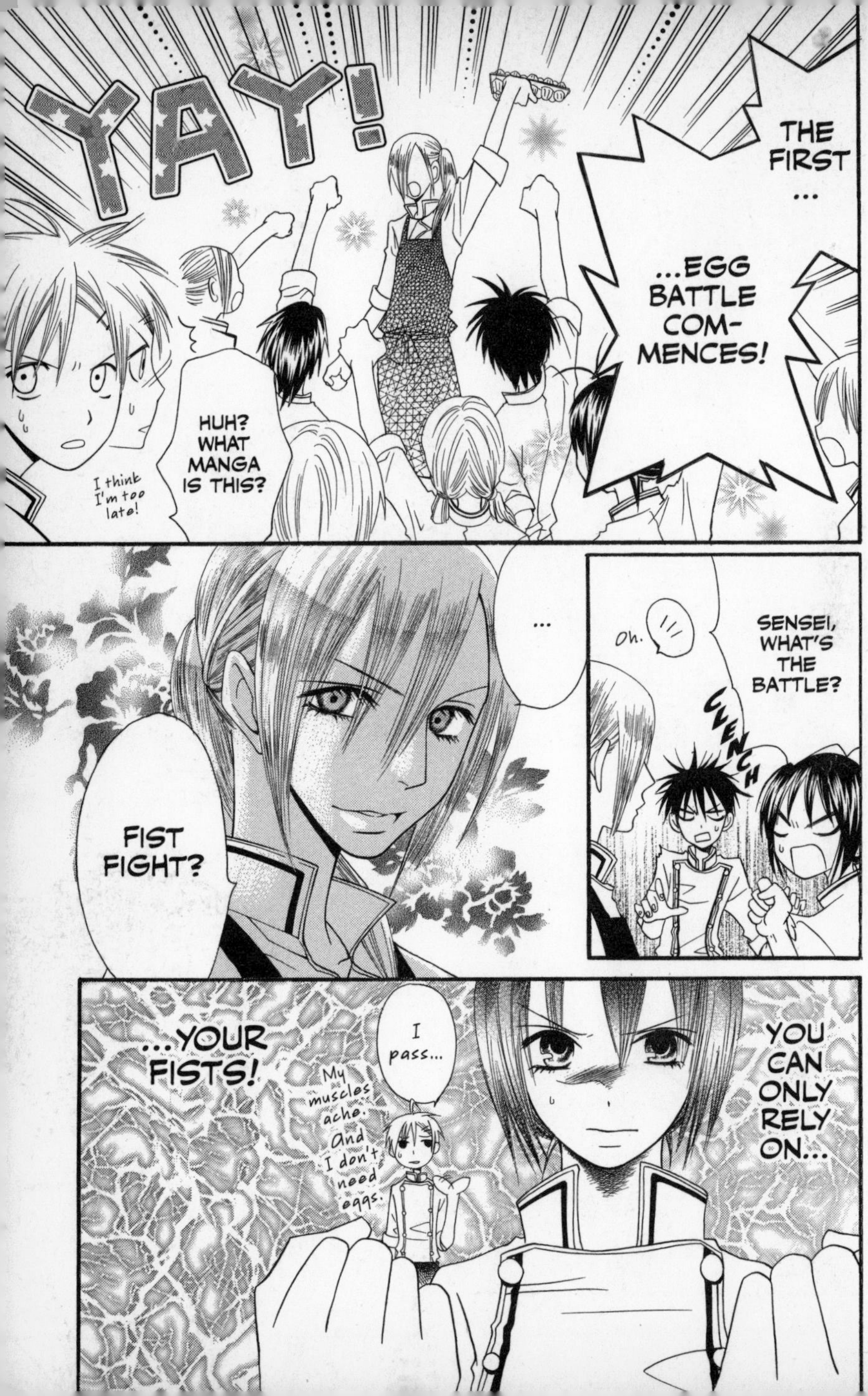
THE FIRST ...
...EGG BATTLE COM-MENCES!
YAY!
HUH? WHAT MANGA IS THIS?
I think I'm too late!
SENSEI, WHAT'S THE BATTLE?
Oh.
CLENCH
...
FIST FIGHT?
YOU CAN ONLY RELY ON...
...YOUR FISTS!
I pass...
My muscles ache. And I don't need eggs.

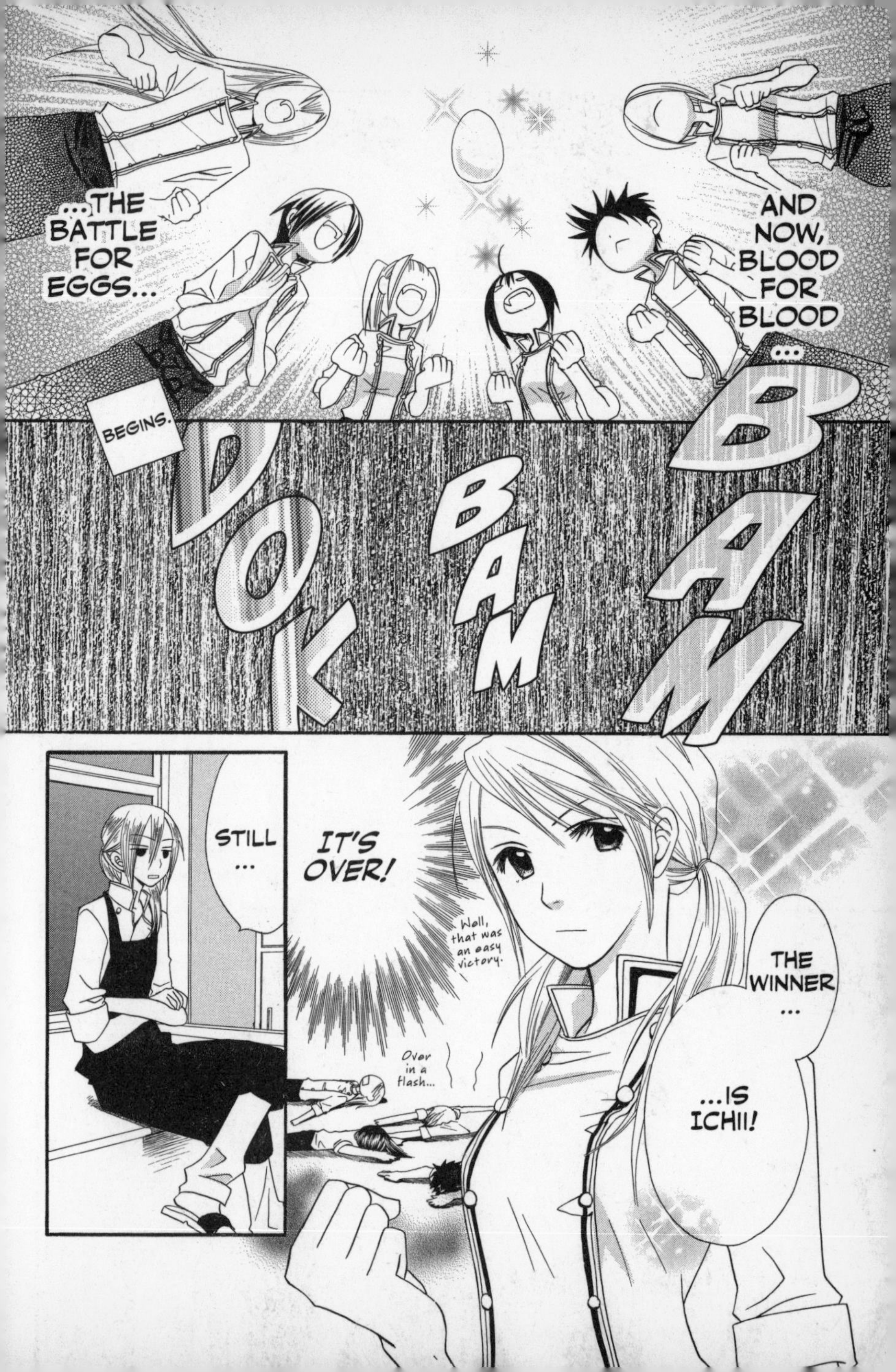
AND NOW, BLOOD FOR BLOOD...
...THE BATTLE FOR EGGS...
BEGINS.
BAM
BAM
DOK
THE WINNER...
...IS ICHII!
Well, that was an easy victory.
IT'S OVER!
Over in a flash...
STILL...

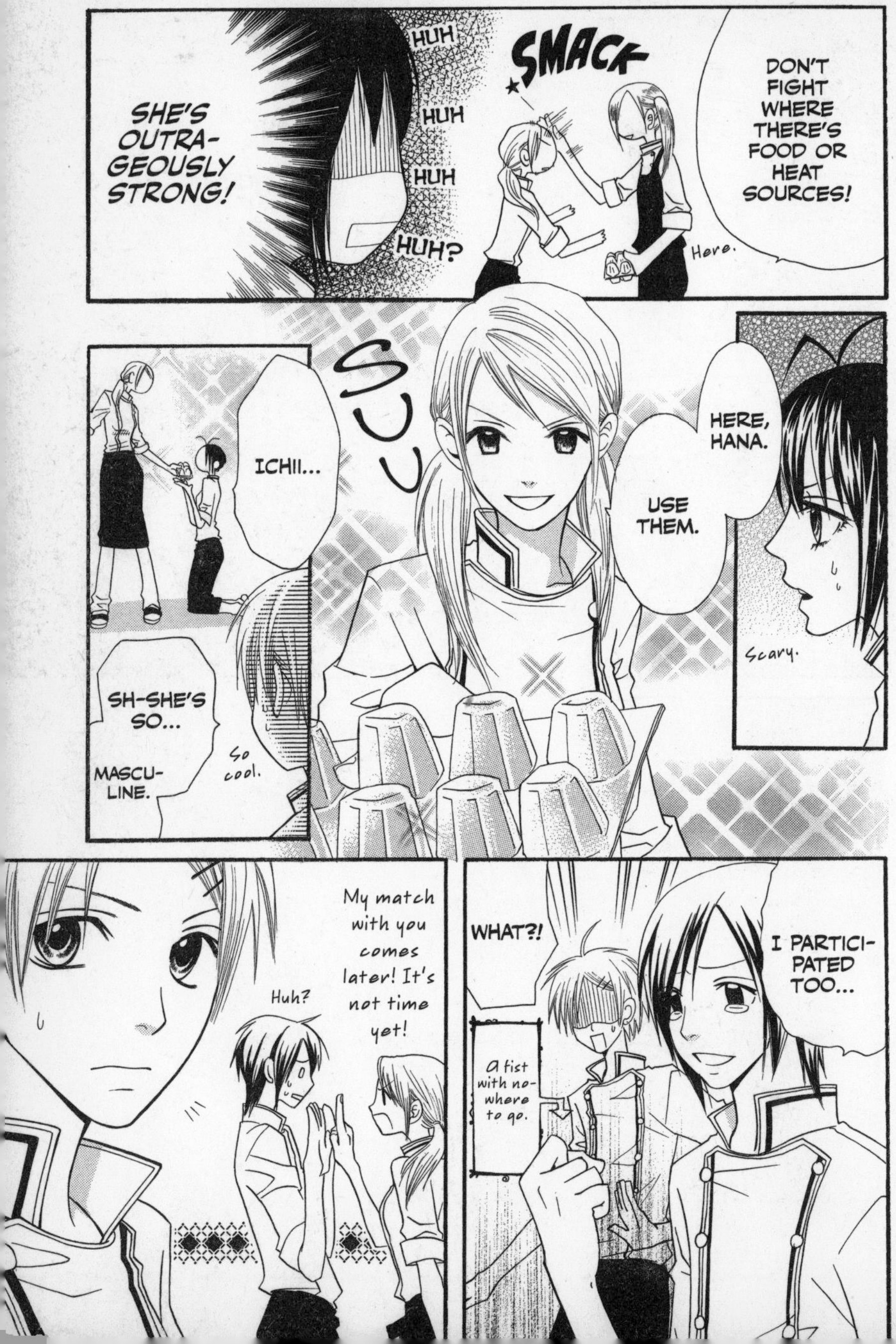
DON'T FIGHT WHERE THERE'S FOOD OR HEAT SOURCES!
SMACK
Here.
HUH
HUH
HUH
HUH?
SHE'S OUTRA-GEOUSLY STRONG!
HERE, HANA.
USE THEM.
Scary.
SUU
ICHII...
SH-SHE'S SO...
MASCU-LINE.
So cool.
I PARTICI-PATED TOO...
WHAT?!
A fist with no-where to go.
My match with you comes later! It's not time yet!
Huh?

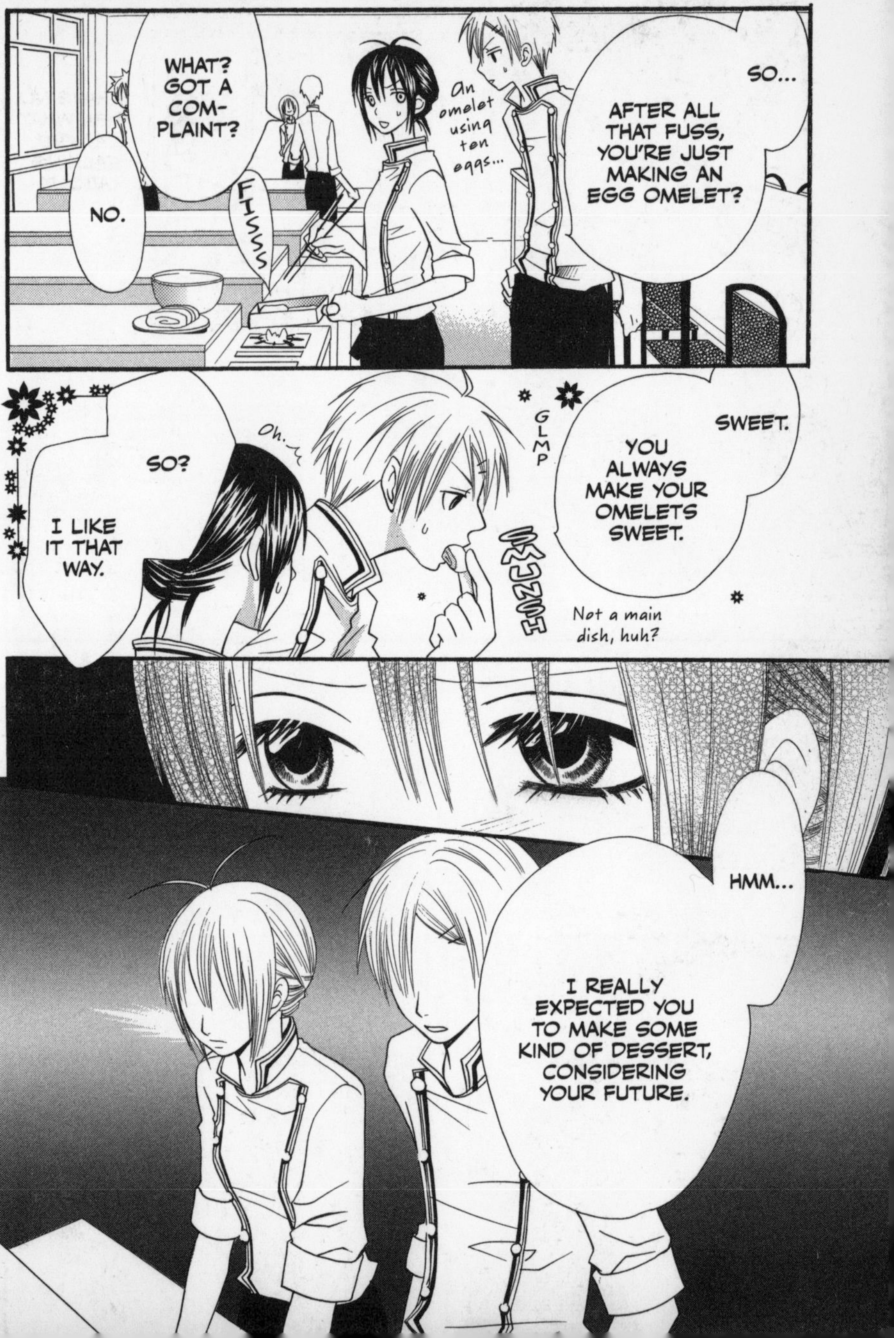
SO...
AFTER ALL THAT FUSS, YOU'RE JUST MAKING AN EGG OMELET?
An omelet using ten eggs...
WHAT? GOT A COM-PLAINT?
FISSS
NO.
SWEET.
YOU ALWAYS MAKE YOUR OMELETS SWEET.
GLMP
Oh...
SO?
I LIKE IT THAT WAY.
MUNCH
Not a main dish, huh?
HMM...
I REALLY EXPECTED YOU TO MAKE SOME KIND OF DESSERT, CONSIDERING YOUR FUTURE.

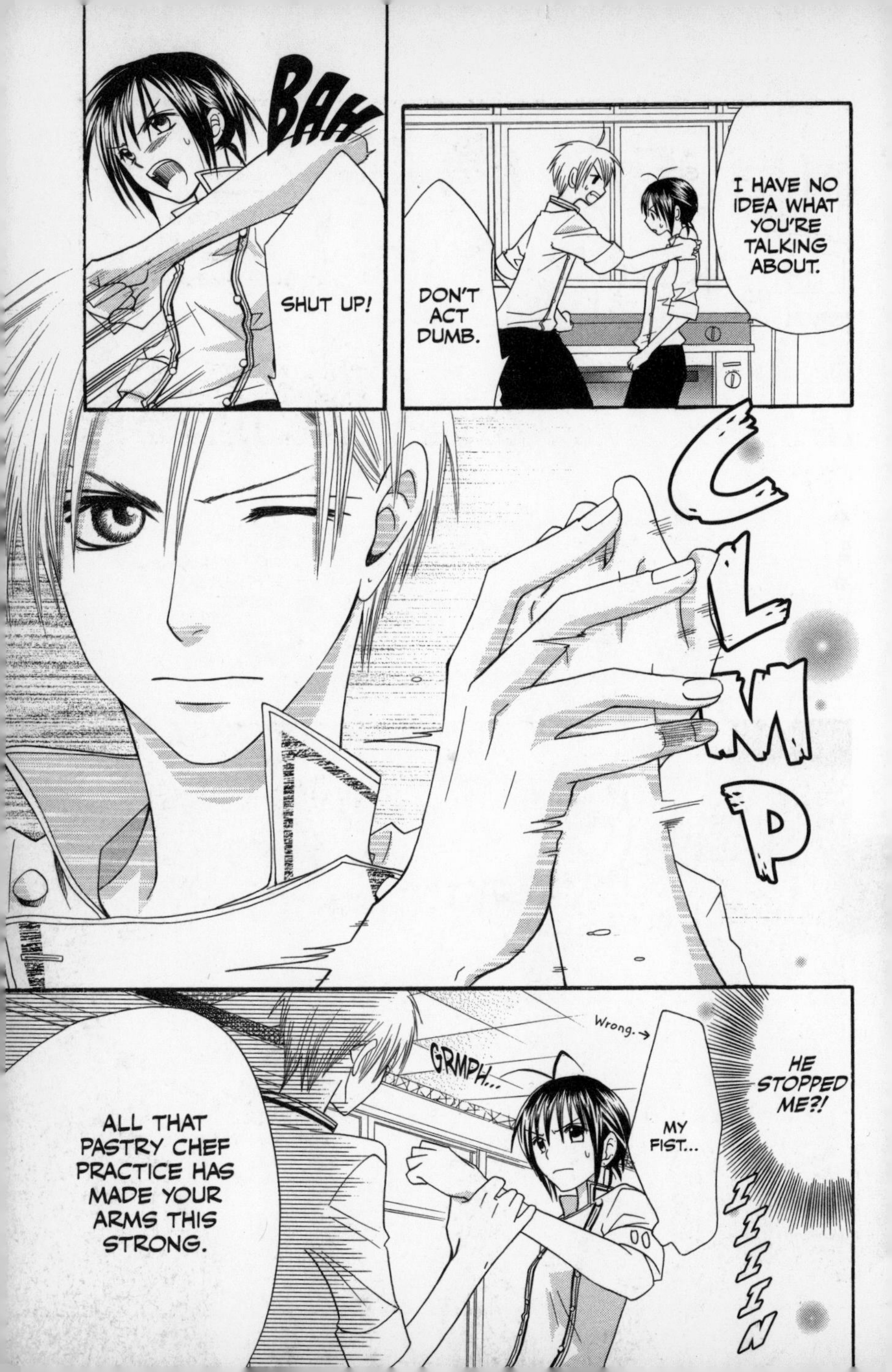
I HAVE NO IDEA WHAT YOU'RE TALKING ABOUT.
DON'T ACT DUMB.
BAH
SHUT UP!
CLMP
HE STOPPED ME?!
MY FIST...
Wrong. →
GRMPH...
ALL THAT PASTRY CHEF PRACTICE HAS MADE YOUR ARMS THIS STRONG.

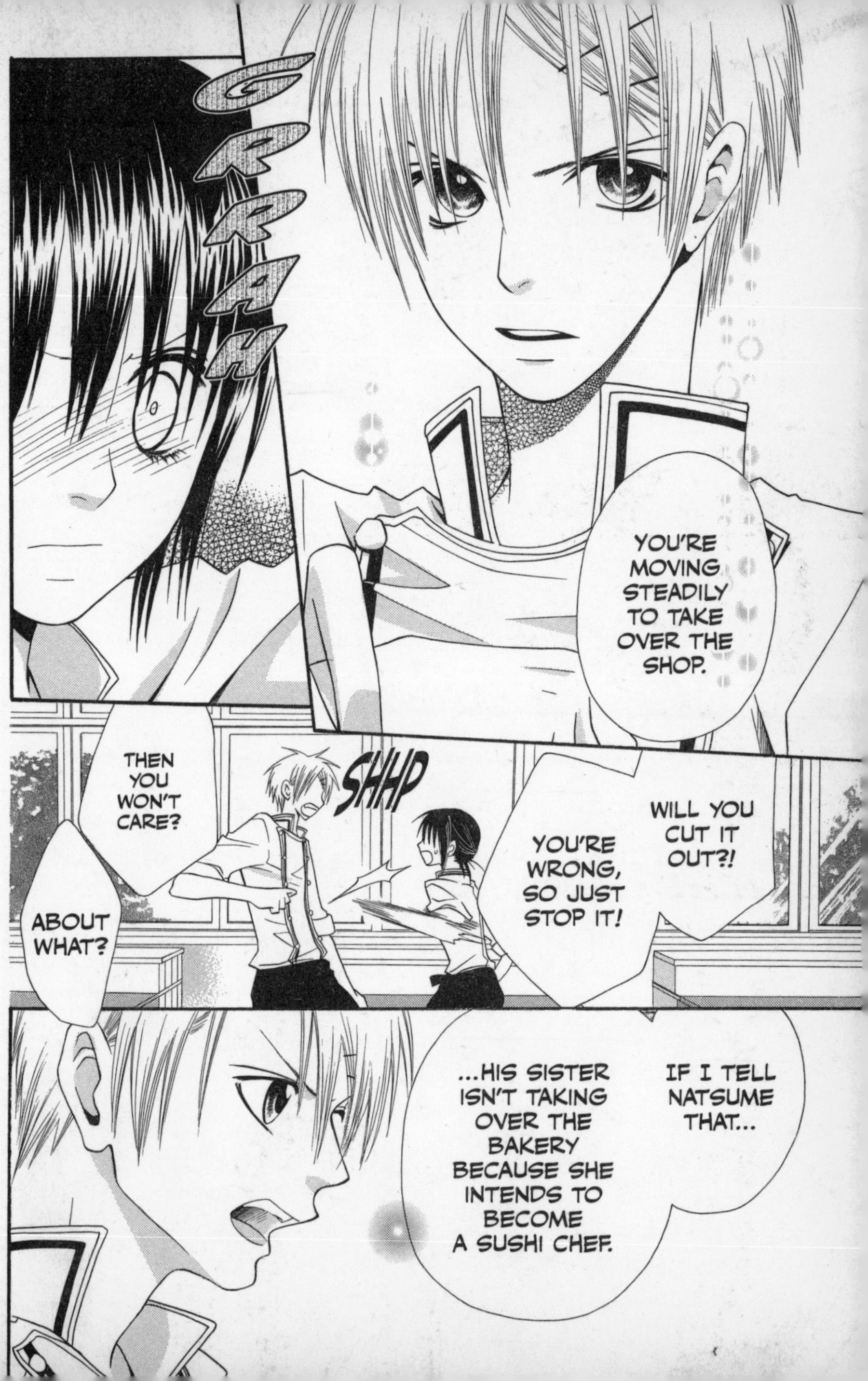
GRRAH
YOU'RE MOVING STEADILY TO TAKE OVER THE SHOP.
WILL YOU CUT IT OUT?!
YOU'RE WRONG, SO JUST STOP IT!
SHHP
THEN YOU WON'T CARE?
ABOUT WHAT?
IF I TELL NATSUME THAT...
...HIS SISTER ISN'T TAKING OVER THE BAKERY BECAUSE SHE INTENDS TO BECOME A SUSHI CHEF.

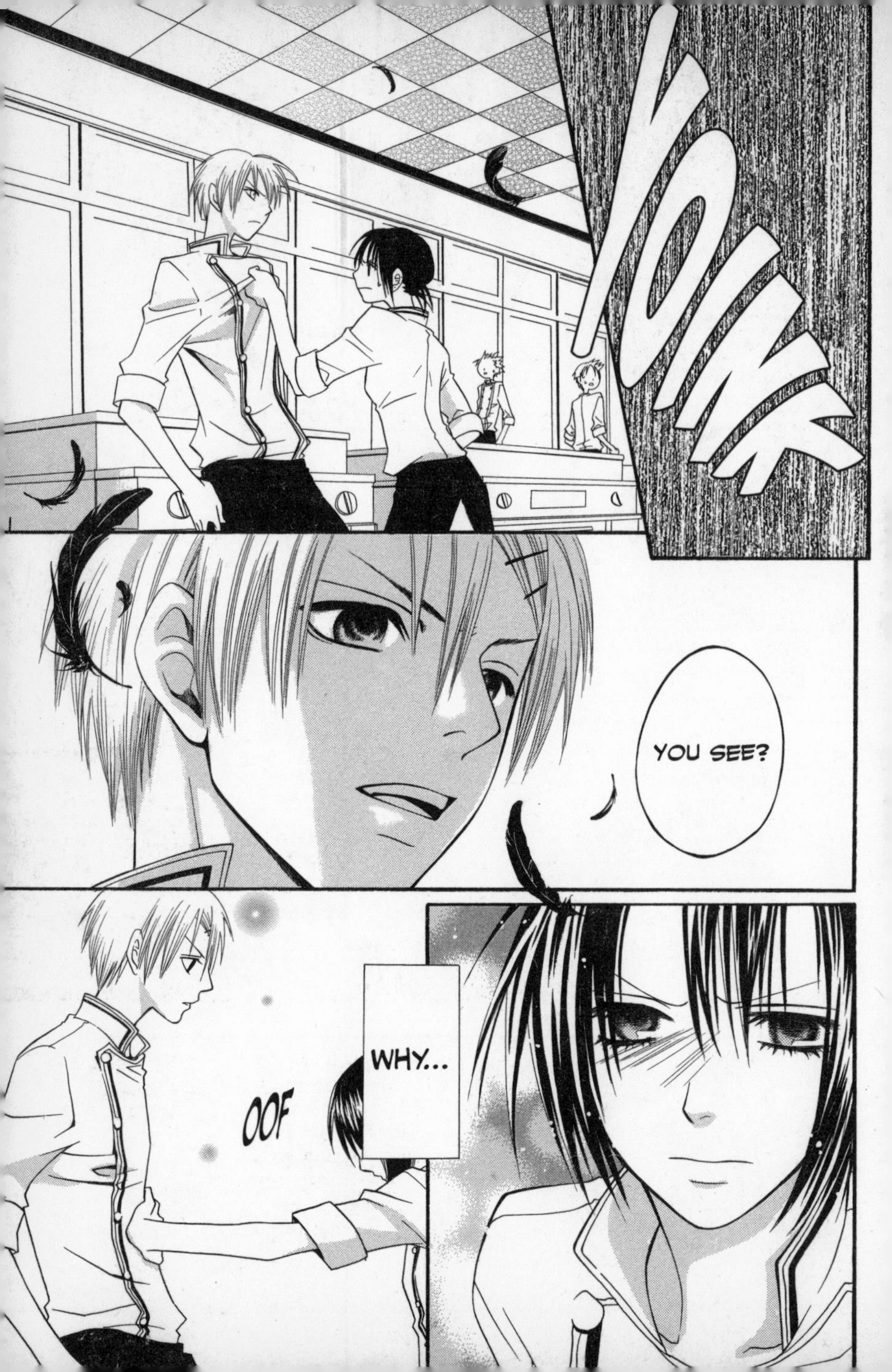
YOINK
YOU SEE?
WHY...
OOF

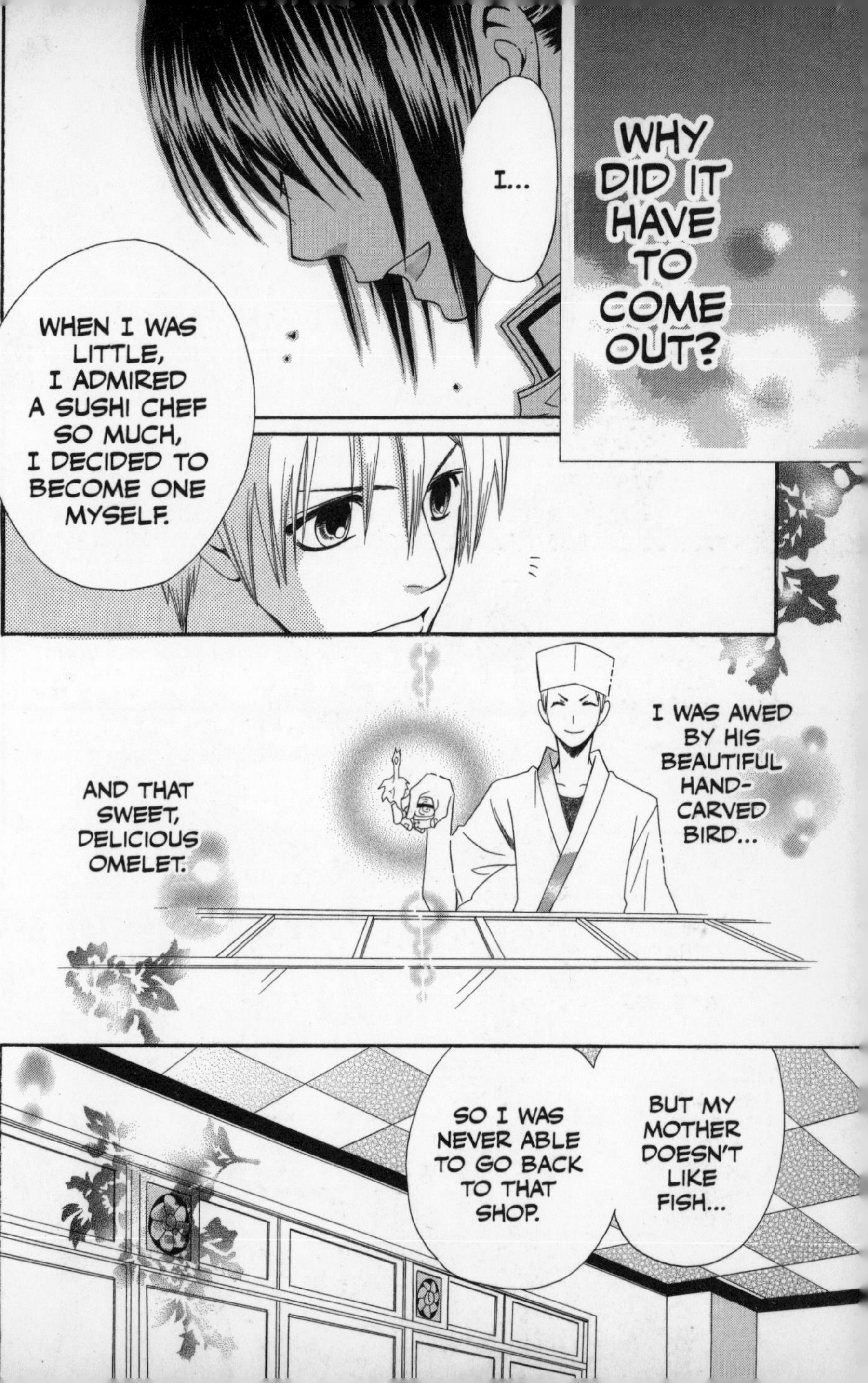
WHY DID IT HAVE TO COME OUT?
I...
WHEN I WAS LITTLE, I ADMIRED A SUSHI CHEF SO MUCH, I DECIDED TO BECOME ONE MYSELF.
I WAS AWED BY HIS BEAUTIFUL HAND-CARVED BIRD...
AND THAT SWEET, DELICIOUS OMELET.
BUT MY MOTHER DOESN'T LIKE FISH...
SO I WAS NEVER ABLE TO GO BACK TO THAT SHOP.

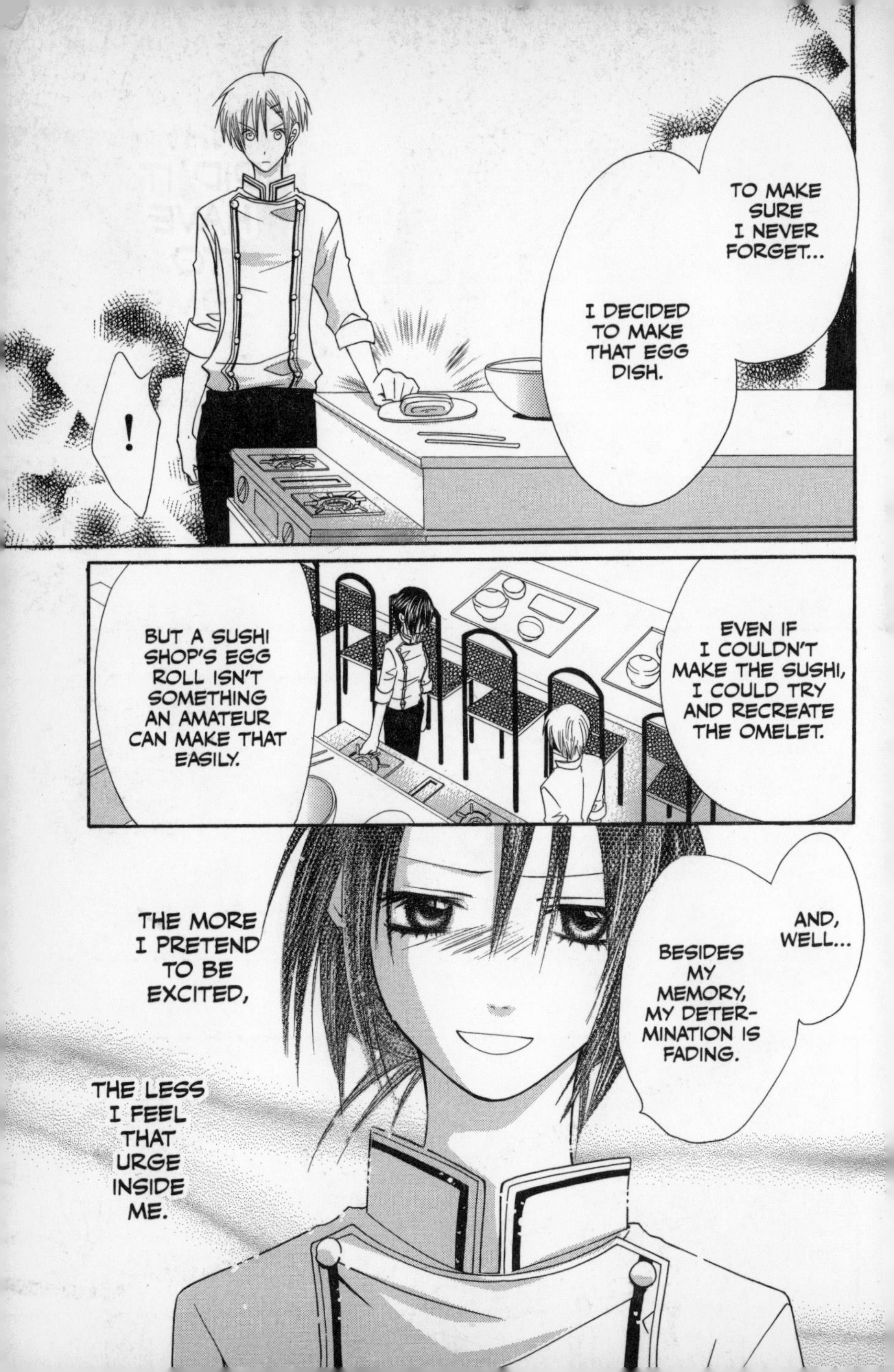
TO MAKE SURE I NEVER FORGET...
I DECIDED TO MAKE THAT EGG DISH.
!
EVEN IF I COULDN'T MAKE THE SUSHI, I COULD TRY AND RECREATE THE OMELET.
BUT A SUSHI SHOP'S EGG ROLL ISN'T SOMETHING AN AMATEUR CAN MAKE THAT EASILY.
AND, WELL...
BESIDES MY MEMORY, MY DETER-MINATION IS FADING.
THE MORE I PRETEND TO BE EXCITED,
THE LESS I FEEL THAT URGE INSIDE ME.

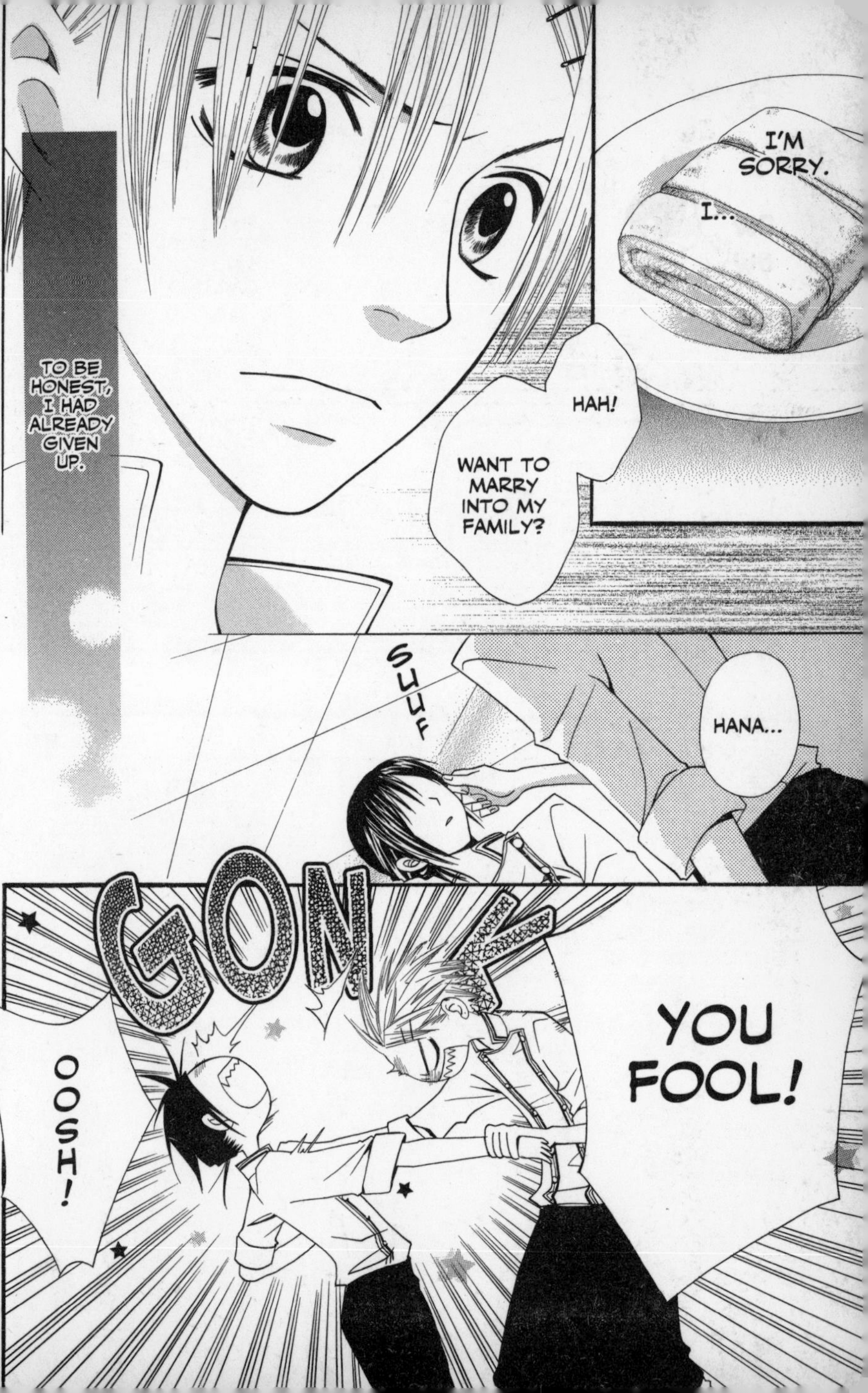
I'M SORRY.
I...
HAH!
WANT TO MARRY INTO MY FAMILY?
TO BE HONEST, I HAD ALREADY GIVEN UP.
HANA...
SHUUF
YOU FOOL!
GONK
OOSH!

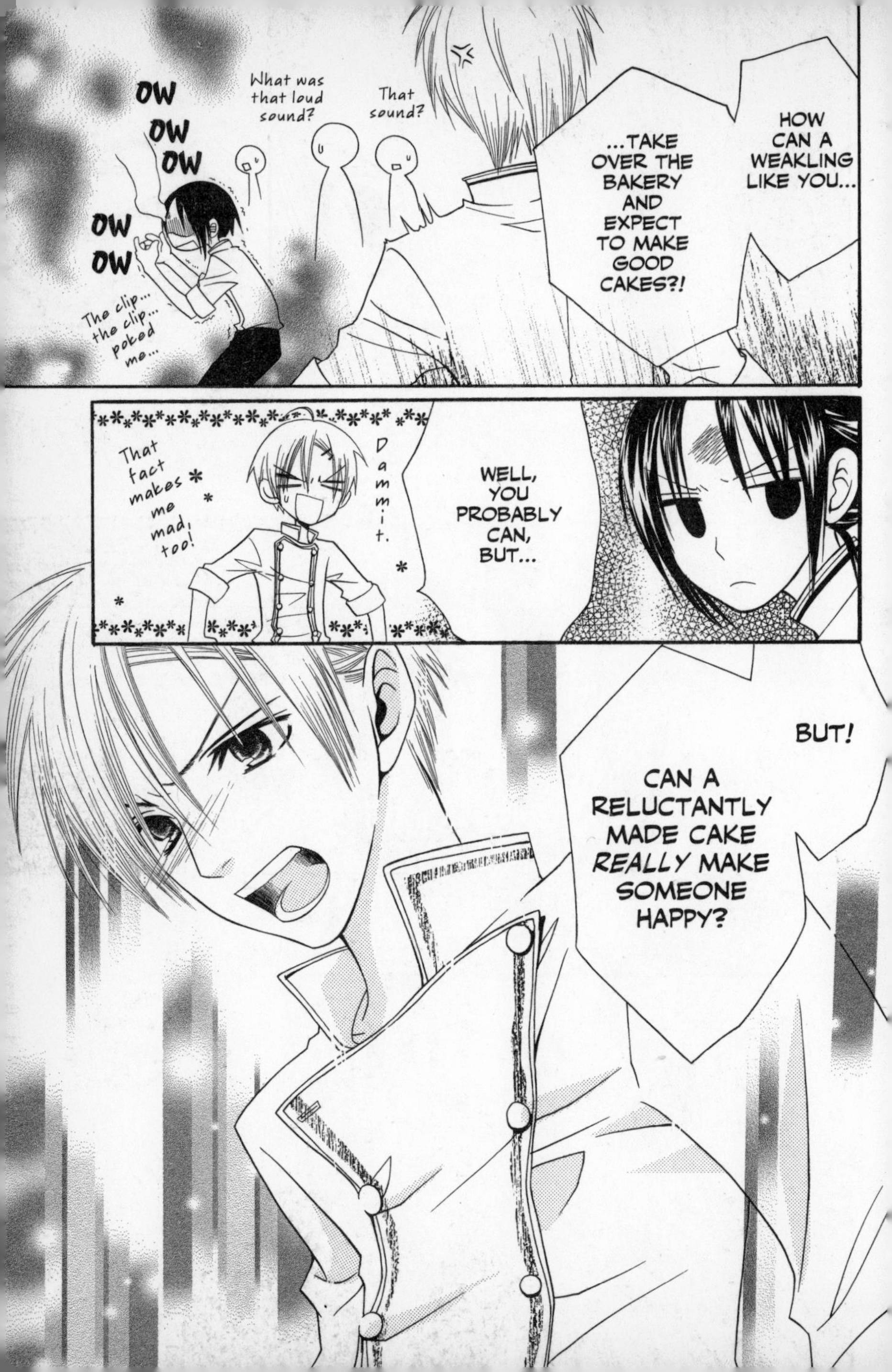
HOW CAN A WEAKLING LIKE YOU...
...TAKE OVER THE BAKERY AND EXPECT TO MAKE GOOD CAKES?!
What was that loud sound?
That sound?
OW OW OW
OW OW
The clip... the clip... poked me...
WELL, YOU PROBABLY CAN, BUT...
Dammit.
That fact makes me mad too!
BUT!
CAN A RELUCTANTLY MADE CAKE *REALLY* MAKE SOMEONE HAPPY?

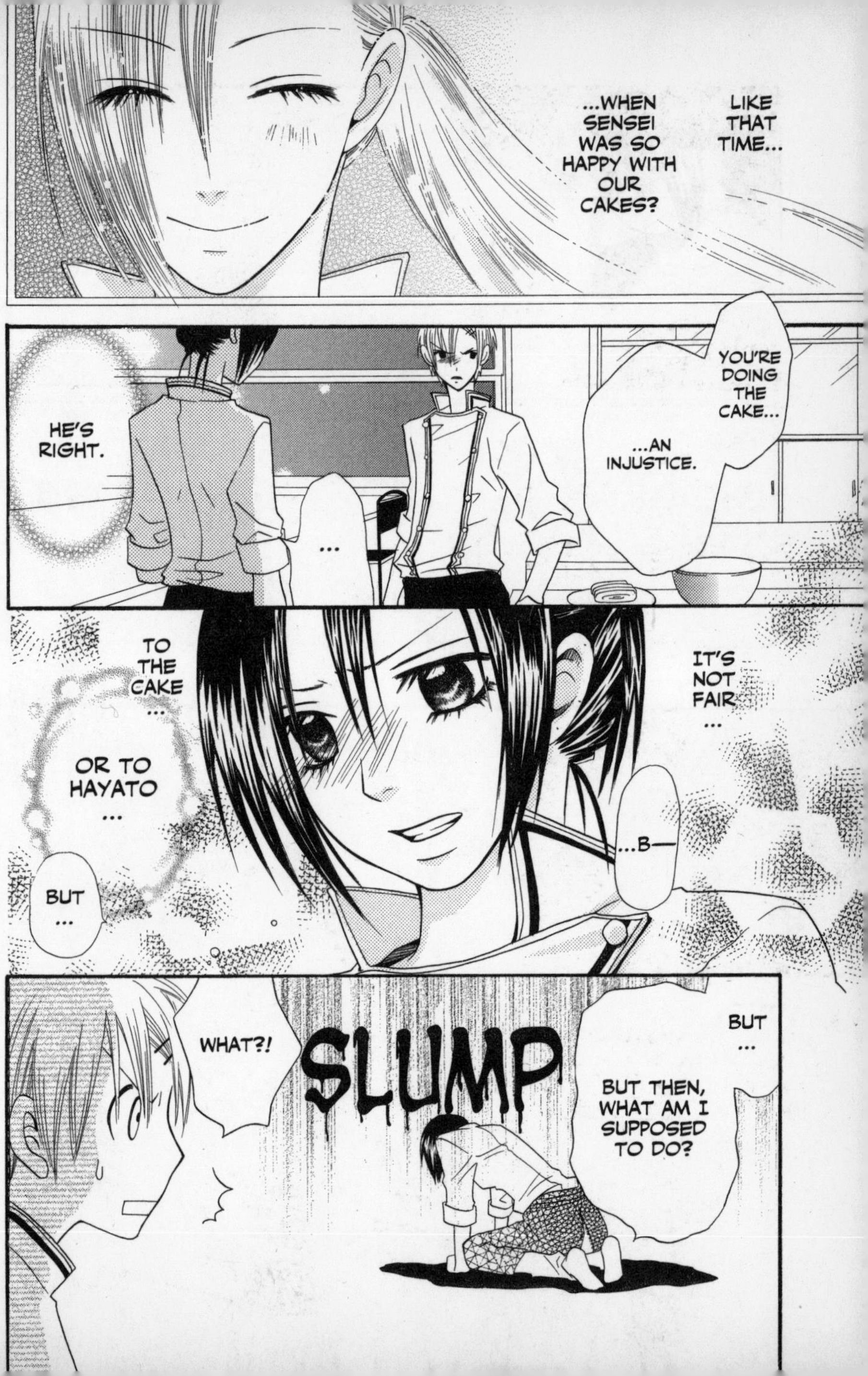
LIKE THAT TIME...
...WHEN SENSEI WAS SO HAPPY WITH OUR CAKES?
YOU'RE DOING THE CAKE...
...AN INJUSTICE.
...
HE'S RIGHT.
IT'S NOT FAIR ...
...B—
TO THE CAKE ...
OR TO HAYATO ...
BUT ...
BUT ...
BUT THEN, WHAT AM I SUPPOSED TO DO?
SLUMP
WHAT?!

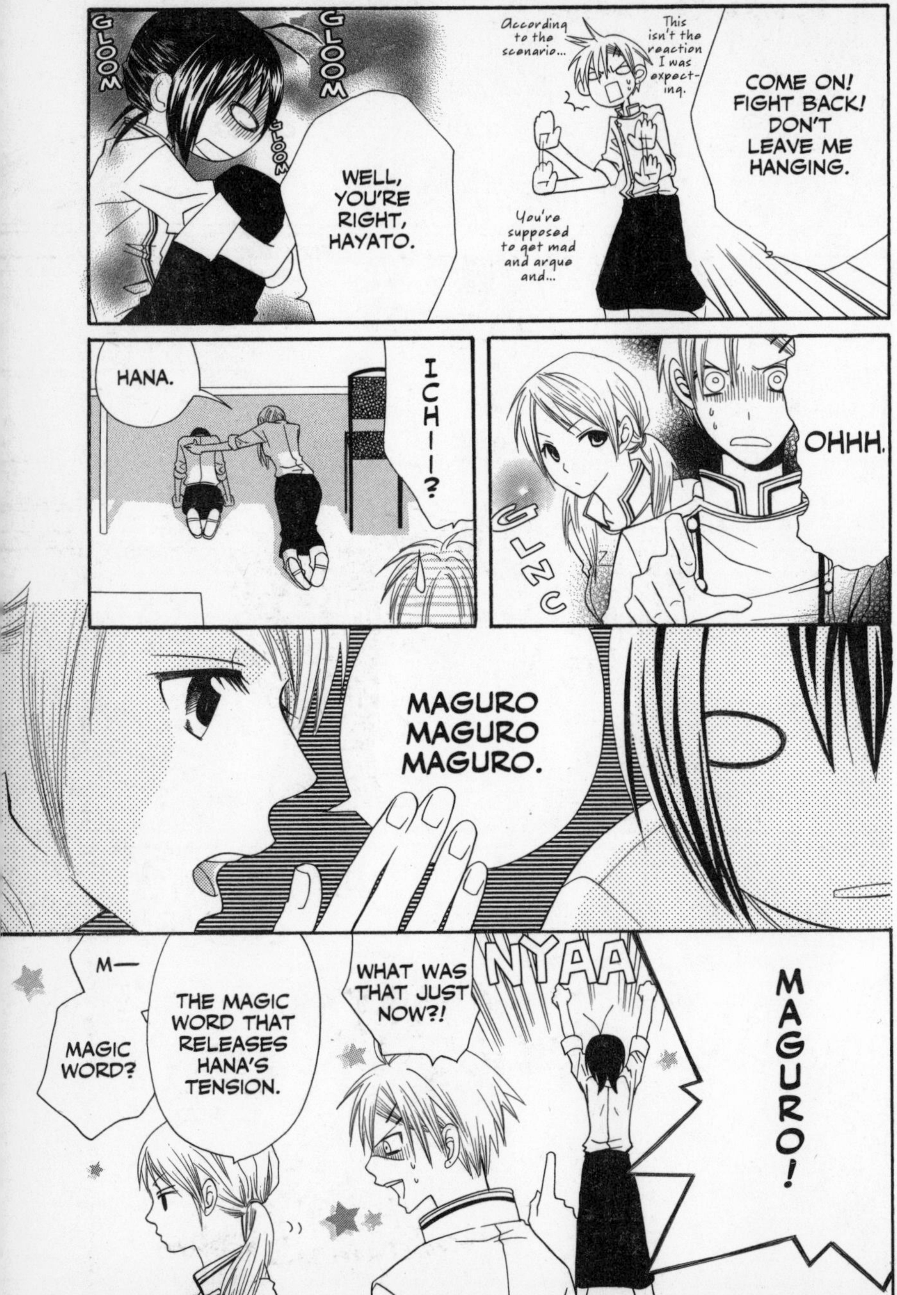
COME ON! FIGHT BACK! DON'T LEAVE ME HANGING.
This isn't the reaction I was expect-ing.
According to the scenario...
You're supposed to get mad and argue and...
GLOOM
GLOOM
WELL, YOU'RE RIGHT, HAYATO.
GLOOM
OHHH.
ICHI—?
HANA.
MAGURO MAGURO MAGURO.
MAGURO!
NYAA
WHAT WAS THAT JUST NOW?!
THE MAGIC WORD THAT RELEASES HANA'S TENSION.
M—
MAGIC WORD?

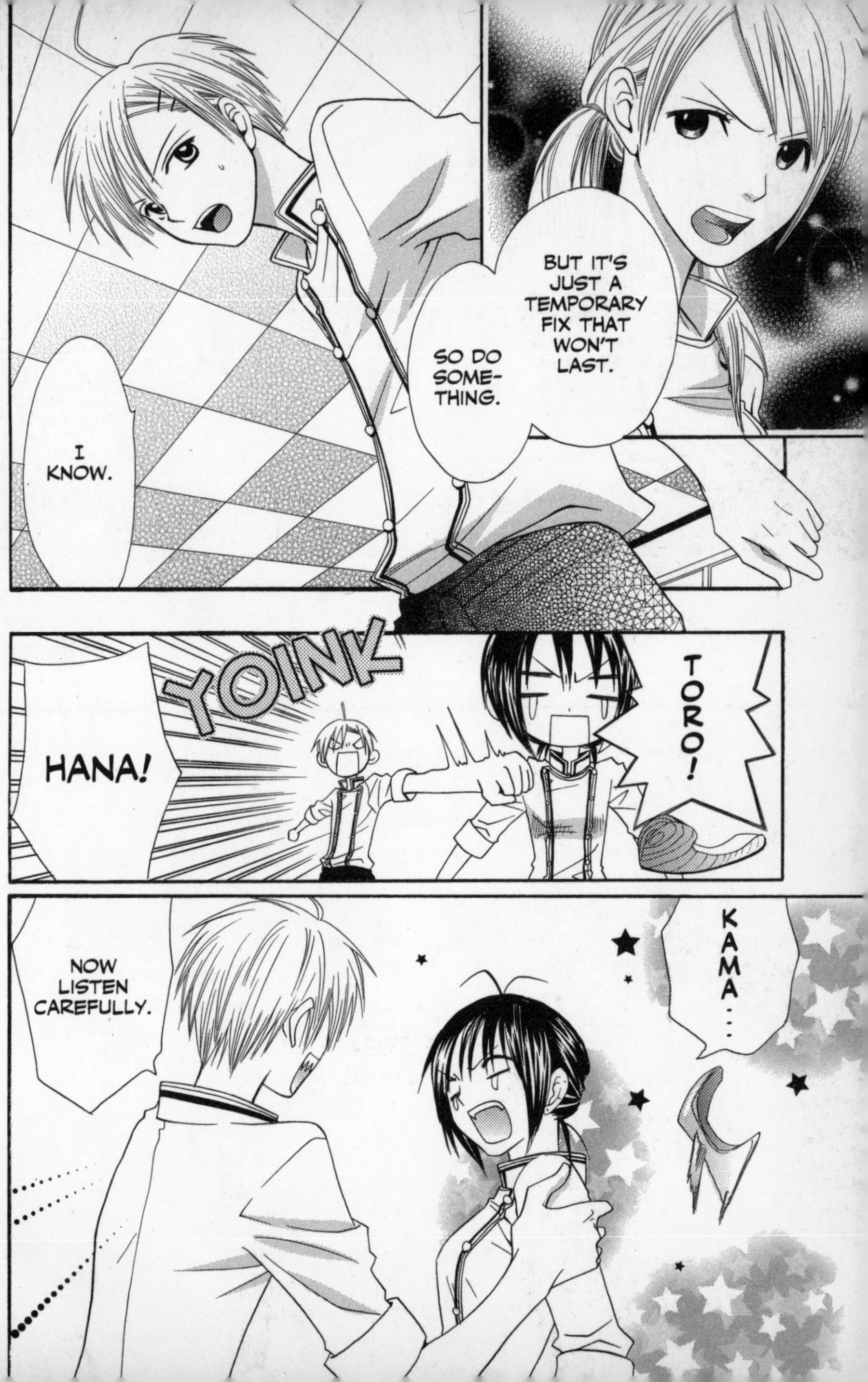
BUT IT'S JUST A TEMPORARY FIX THAT WON'T LAST.
SO DO SOME-THING.
I KNOW.
TORO!
YOINK
HANA!
KAMA...
NOW LISTEN CAREFULLY.

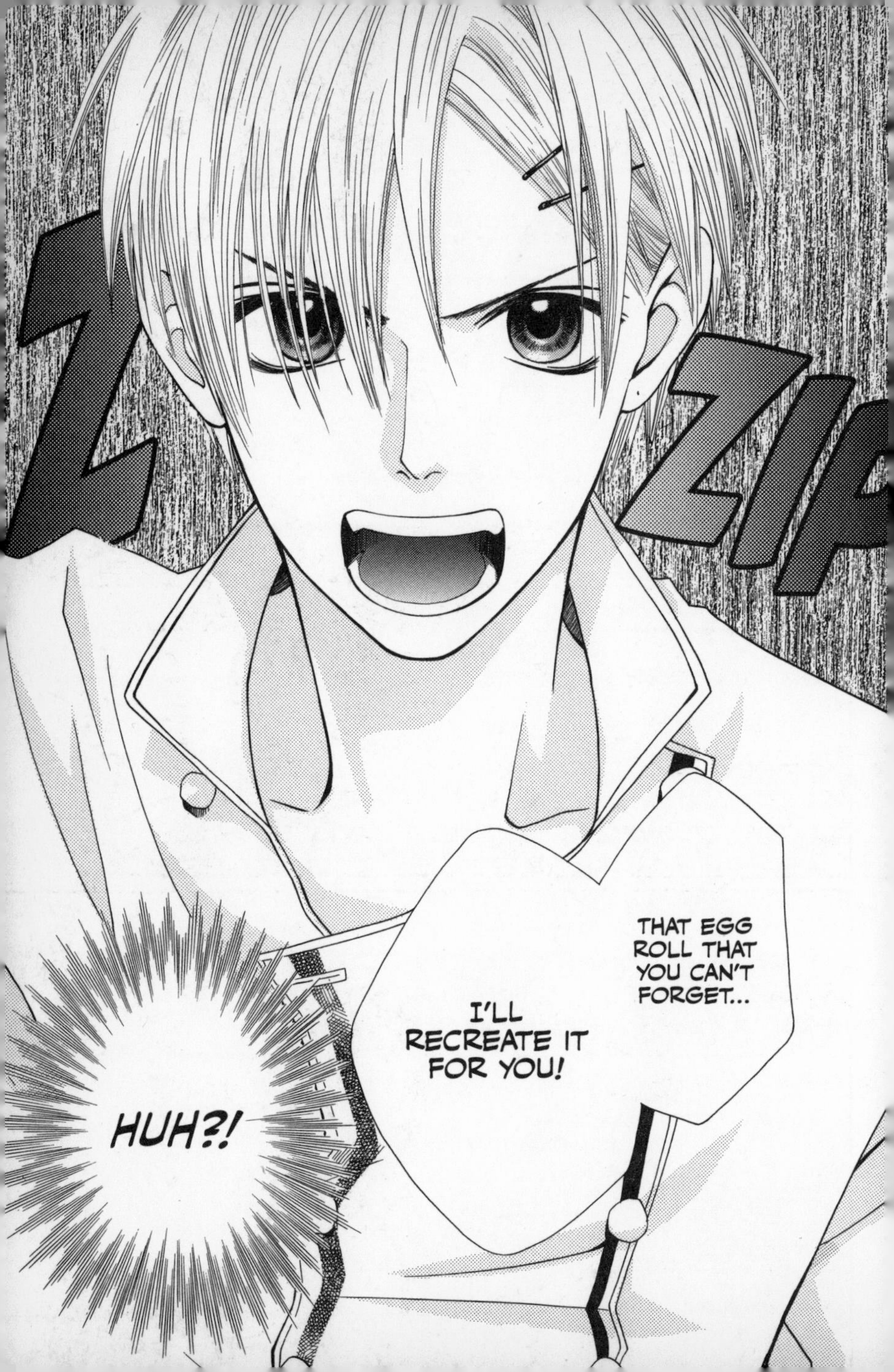
ZZIP
THAT EGG ROLL THAT YOU CAN'T FORGET...
I'LL RECREATE IT FOR YOU!
HUH?!

SIDE DISH Mixed Vegetables 6

THANK YOU VERY, VERY MUCH.

I REALLY WANT TO THANK YOU ALL VERY MUCH.
I CAN'T DO ANYTHING ALONE.

● MY EDITOR (CONGRATULATIONS ON THE CHIBA LOTTE MARINES' PENNANT VICTORY).

● THE EDITORIAL DEPARTMENT AT *MARGARET*.

● EVERYONE AT SHUEISHA.

● MY FELLOW MANGA ARTISTS (MS. SHIBATA, THANK YOU FOR PLAYING THE DEVIL'S ADVOCATE).

● ALL MY FRIENDS (THANK YOU FOR BRINGING ME THE VIDEO GAMES).

● EVERYONE AT THE VARIOUS RESTAURANTS WHO HELPED ME WITH MY RESEARCH.

● EVERYONE FROM THE PASTRY CLASS. (TO CAFE LUCKY CLOVER: YOUR COFFEE IS THE BEST!)

● MY FAMILY.

AND ABOVE ALL...
ALL OF YOU WHO READ MY MANGA!
ALL OF YOU WHO TAKE TIME TO WRITE! REALLY!
I'M SO HAPPY I COULD DIE! I'M SORRY I'M SO TERRIBLE
ABOUT ANSWERING YOUR LETTERS, BUT ONE THING
I PROMISE, I'LL DO MY BEST WITH THE MANGA!
SO PLEASE CONTINUE TO GIVE ME YOUR WARM SUPPORT.
IF YOU'RE INTERESTED, PLEASE SEND YOUR LETTERS
HERE. AND LET'S MEET AGAIN IN VOLUME 3.

AYUMI KOMURA
SHOJO BEAT MANGA/MIXED VEGETABLES
C/O VIZ MEDIA, LLC
P.O. BOX 77010
SAN FRANCISCO, CA 94107

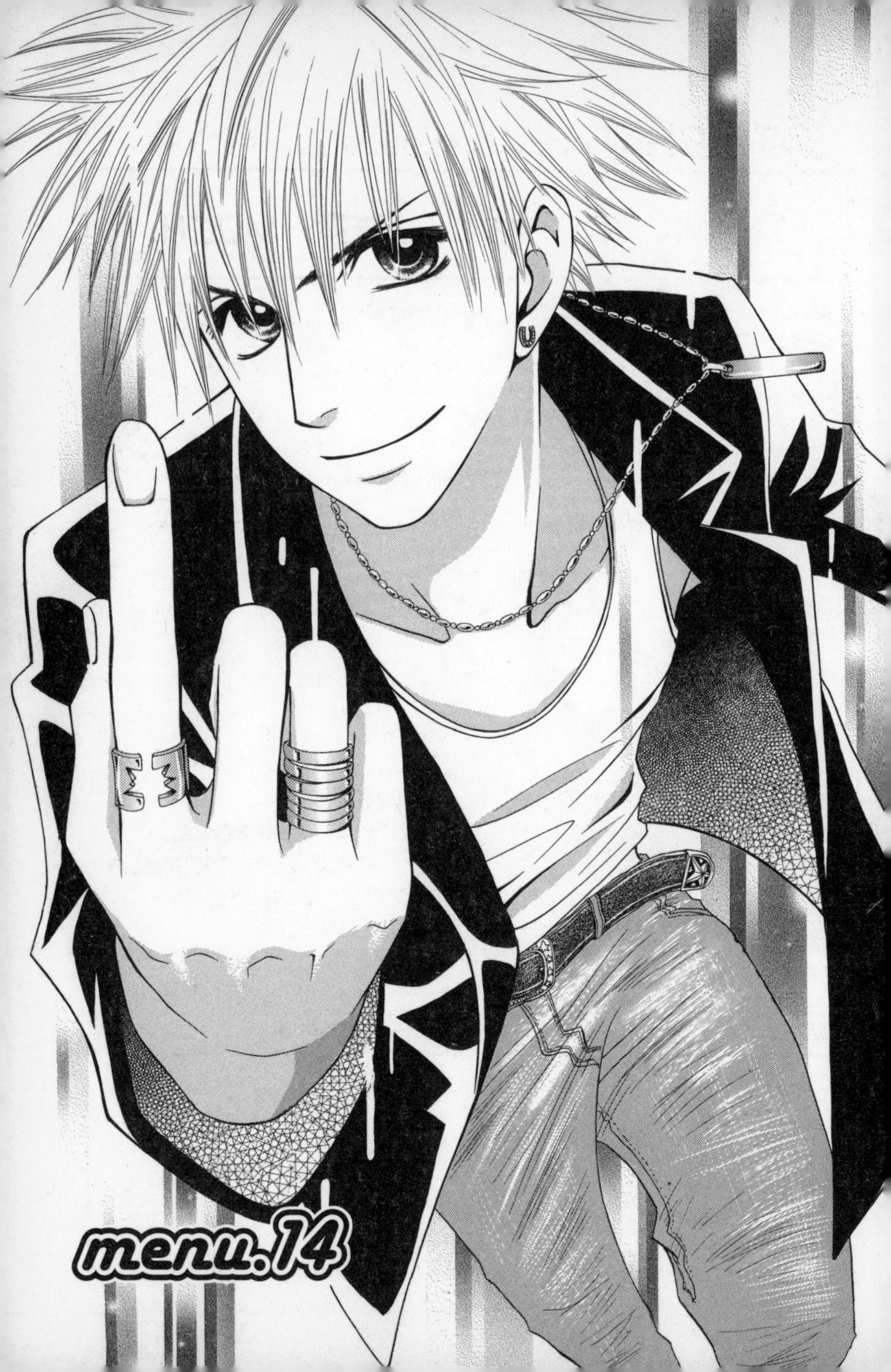
menu.14

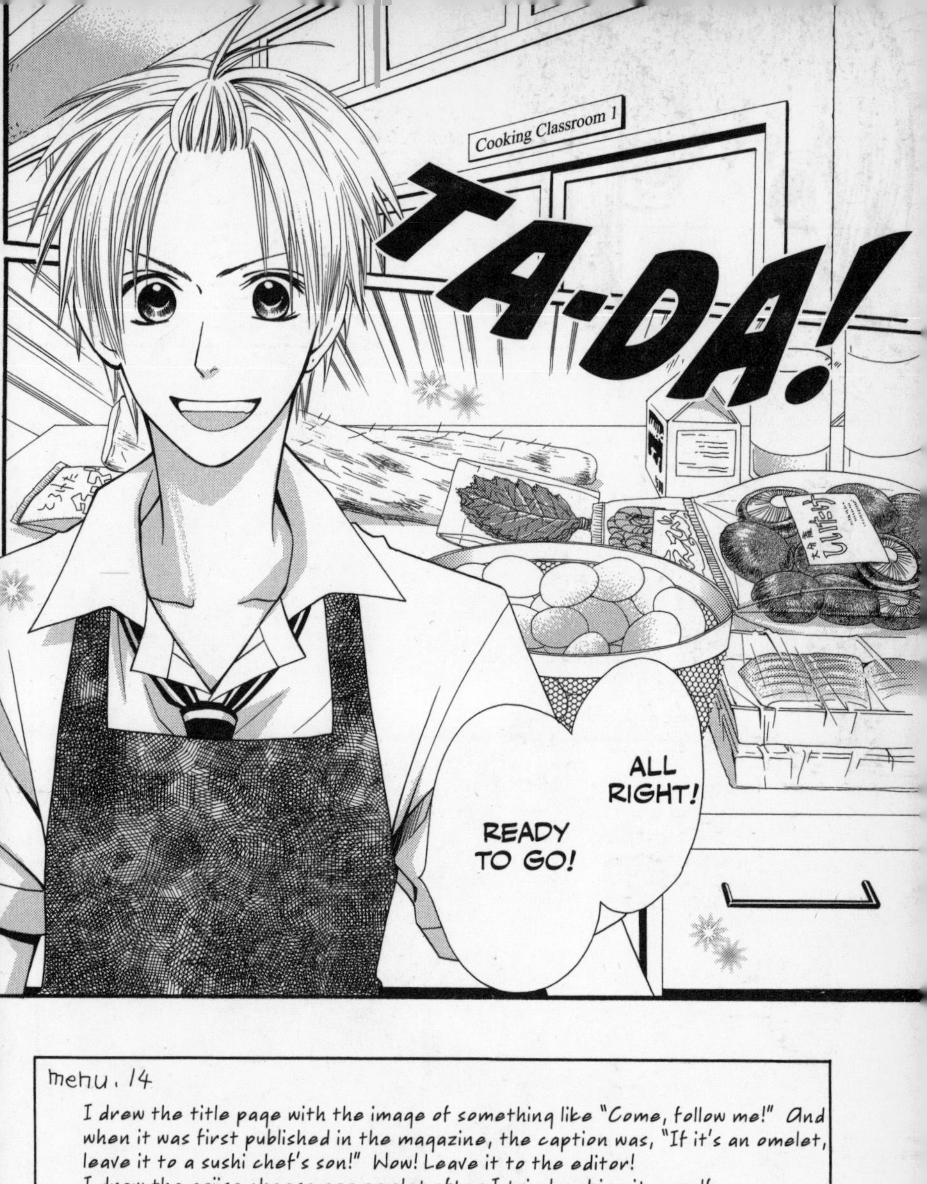
Cooking Classroom 1
TA-DA!
ALL RIGHT!
READY TO GO!

menu. 14

I drew the title page with the image of something like "Come, follow me!" And when it was first published in the magazine, the caption was, "If it's an omelet, leave it to a sushi chef's son!" Wow! Leave it to the editor!
I drew the aojiso cheese egg omelet after I tried making it myself.
But I used too much dashi, and it was really, really runny.
But it tasted good. It was good...
Hayato's father makes his debut! I love this character! Yay!
Volume 3 is about dads. And what a climax! (Who will be happy? Azumi will.)

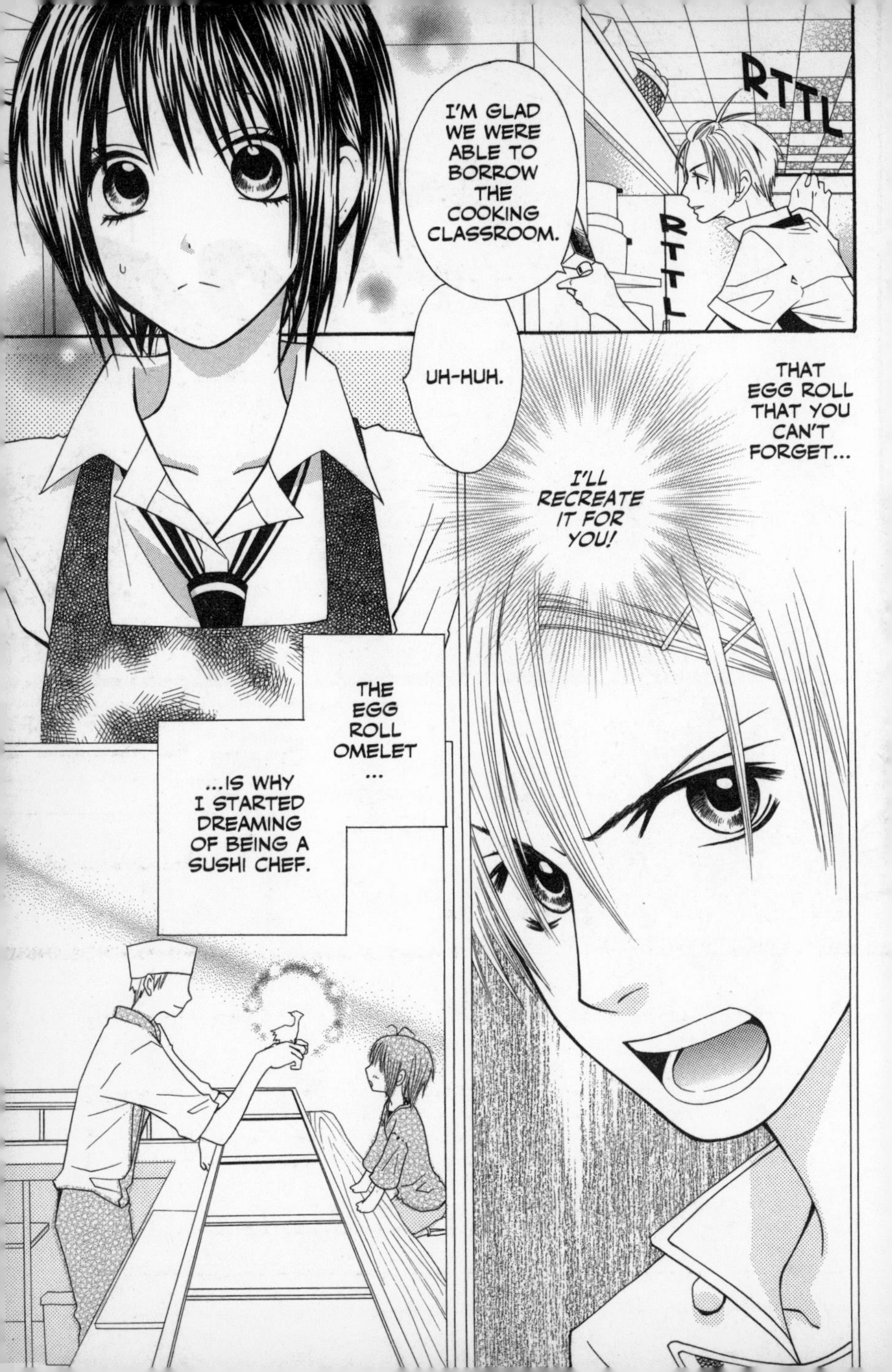
RTTL
RTTL
I'M GLAD WE WERE ABLE TO BORROW THE COOKING CLASSROOM.
UH-HUH.
THAT EGG ROLL THAT YOU CAN'T FORGET...
I'LL RECREATE IT FOR YOU!
THE EGG ROLL OMELET ...
...IS WHY I STARTED DREAMING OF BEING A SUSHI CHEF.

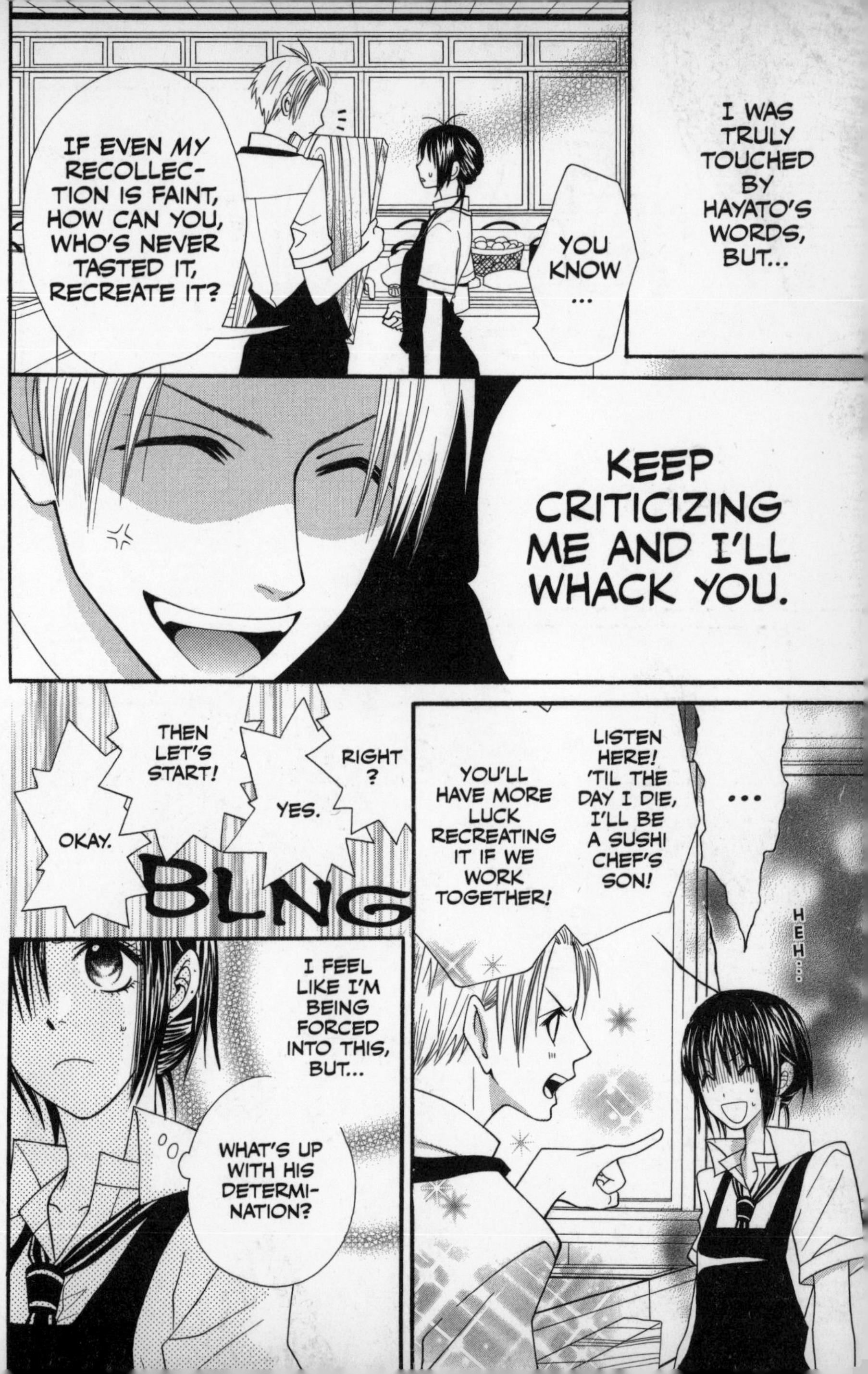
I WAS TRULY TOUCHED BY HAYATO'S WORDS, BUT...
YOU KNOW ...
IF EVEN MY RECOLLECTION IS FAINT, HOW CAN YOU, WHO'S NEVER TASTED IT, RECREATE IT?
KEEP CRITICIZING ME AND I'LL WHACK YOU.
...
LISTEN HERE! 'TIL THE DAY I DIE, I'LL BE A SUSHI CHEF'S SON!
YOU'LL HAVE MORE LUCK RECREATING IT IF WE WORK TOGETHER!
HEH...
RIGHT?
THEN LET'S START!
YES.
OKAY.
BLNG
I FEEL LIKE I'M BEING FORCED INTO THIS, BUT...
WHAT'S UP WITH HIS DETERMINATION?

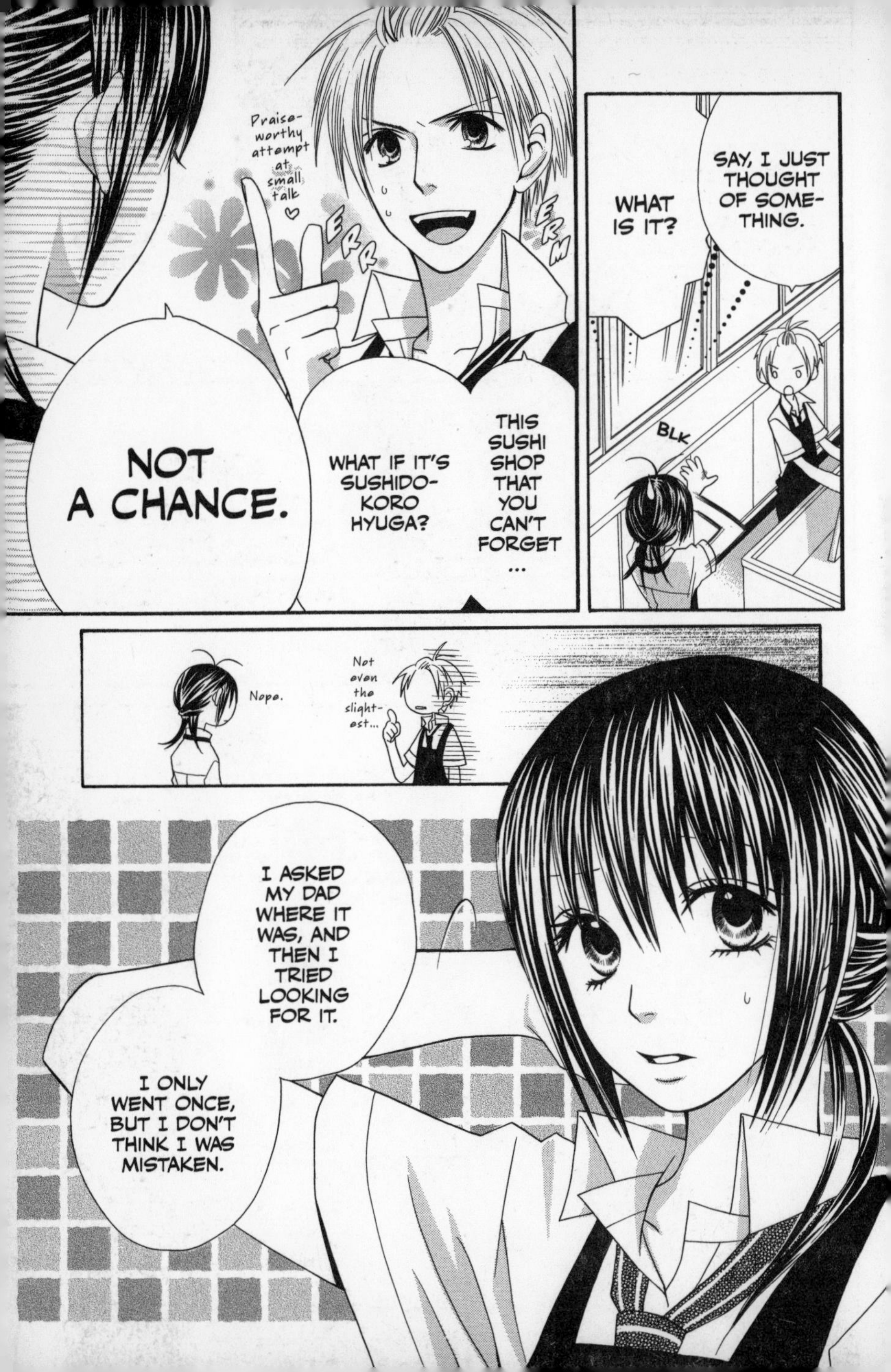
SAY, I JUST THOUGHT OF SOME-THING.
WHAT IS IT?
BLK
THIS SUSHI SHOP THAT YOU CAN'T FORGET...
WHAT IF IT'S SUSHIDO-KORO HYUGA?
ERM
ERR
Praise-worthy attempt at small talk ♡
NOT A CHANCE.
Not even the slight-est...
Nope.
I ASKED MY DAD WHERE IT WAS, AND THEN I TRIED LOOKING FOR IT.
I ONLY WENT ONCE, BUT I DON'T THINK I WAS MISTAKEN.

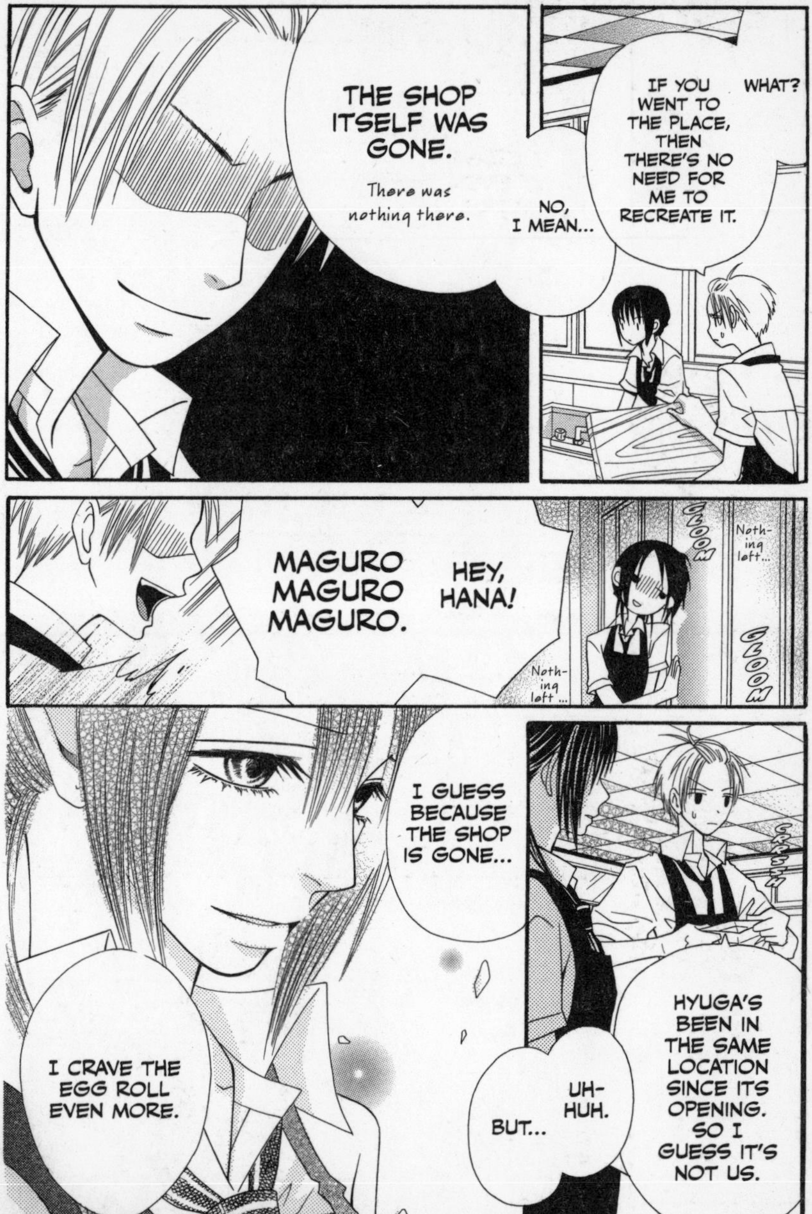
WHAT?
IF YOU WENT TO THE PLACE, THEN THERE'S NO NEED FOR ME TO RECREATE IT.
NO, I MEAN...
THE SHOP ITSELF WAS GONE.
There was nothing there.
Nothing left...
GLOOM
GLOOM
Nothing left...
HEY, HANA!
MAGURO MAGURO MAGURO.
HYUGA'S BEEN IN THE SAME LOCATION SINCE ITS OPENING. SO I GUESS IT'S NOT US.
UH-HUH.
BUT...
I GUESS BECAUSE THE SHOP IS GONE...
I CRAVE THE EGG ROLL EVEN MORE.

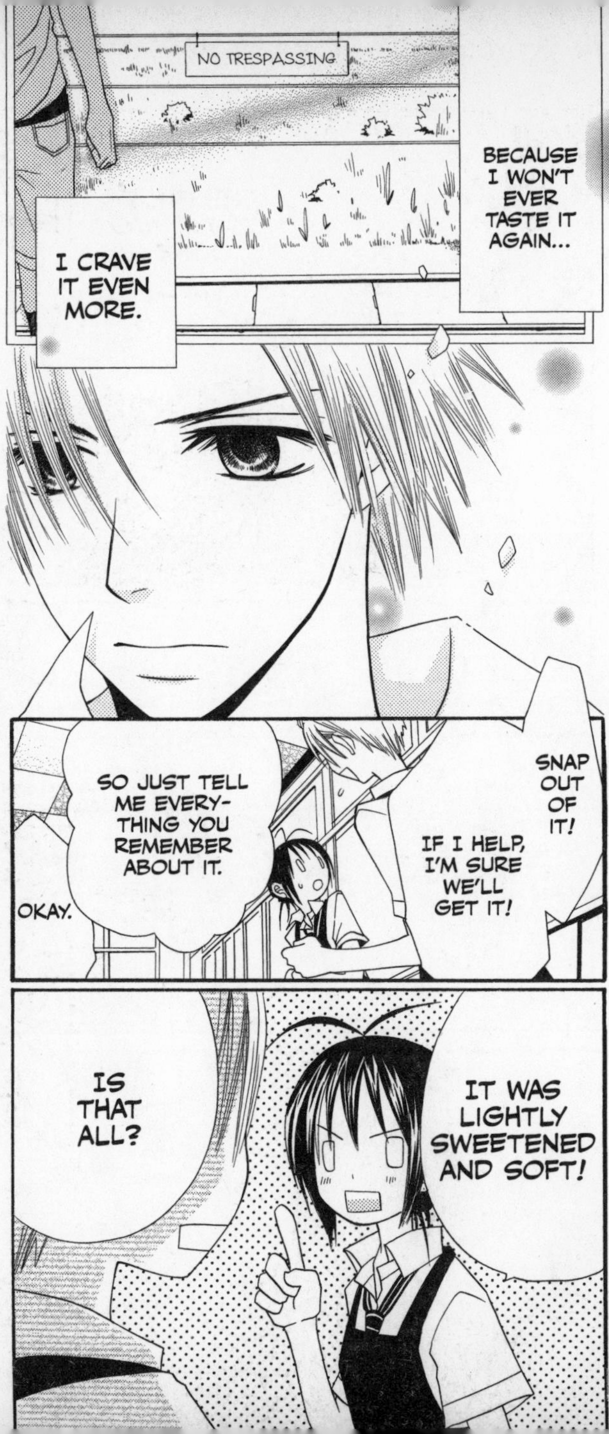
NO TRESPASSING
BECAUSE I WON'T EVER TASTE IT AGAIN...
I CRAVE IT EVEN MORE.
SNAP OUT OF IT!
IF I HELP, I'M SURE WE'LL GET IT!
SO JUST TELL ME EVERY-THING YOU REMEMBER ABOUT IT.
OKAY.
IT WAS LIGHTLY SWEETENED AND SOFT!
IS THAT ALL?
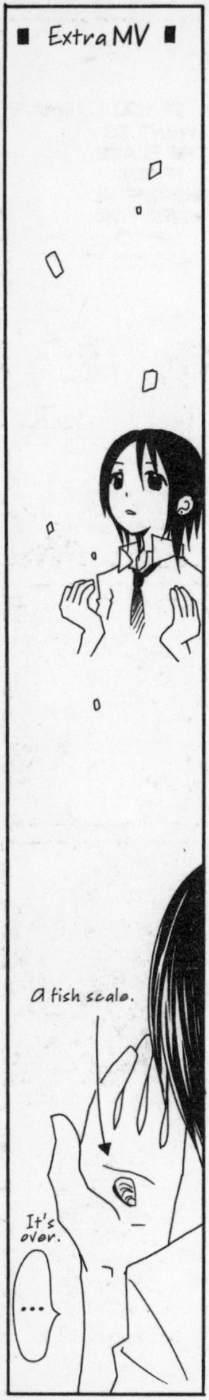
Extra MV
A fish scale.
It's over.
...

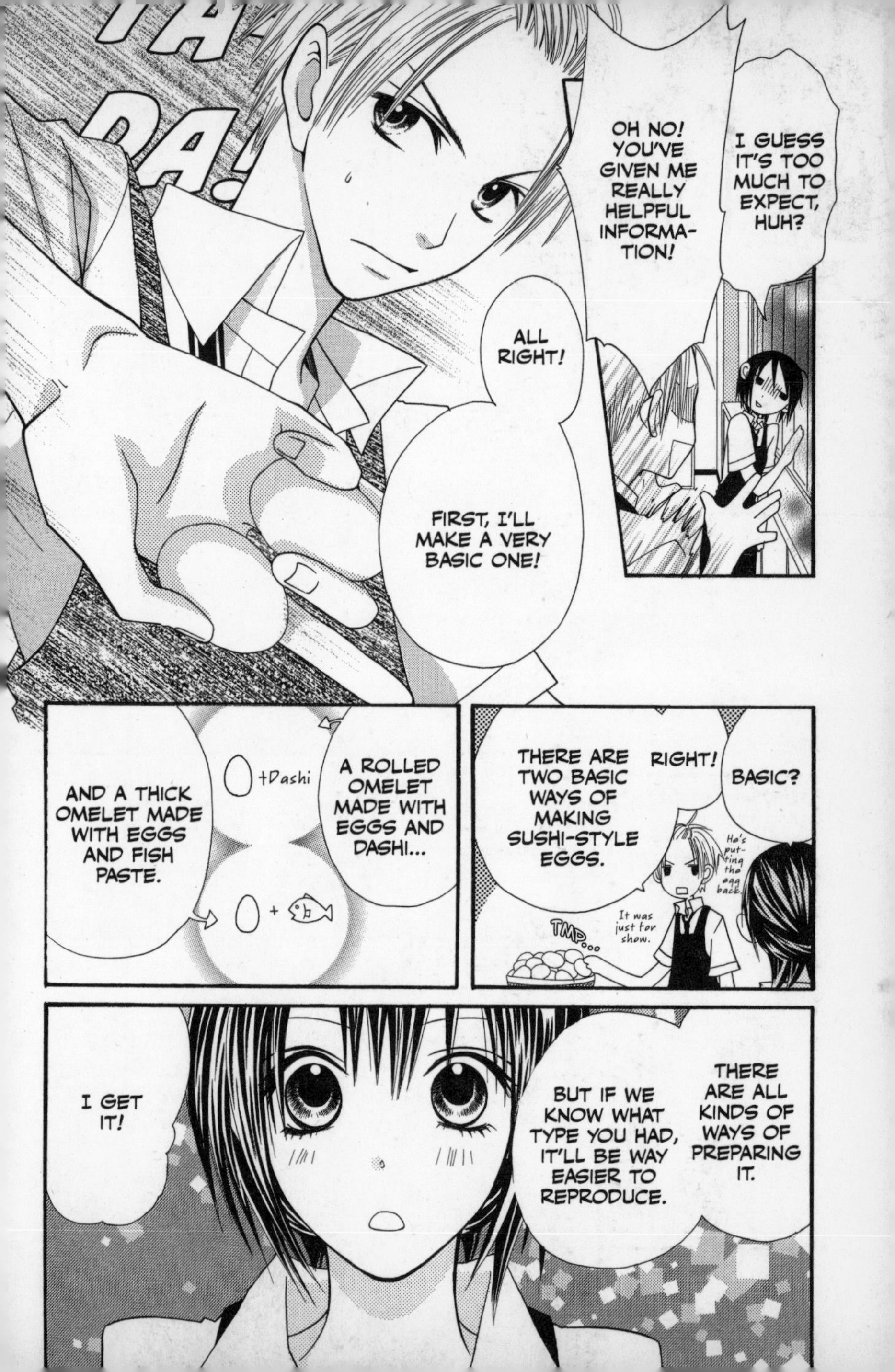
I GUESS IT'S TOO MUCH TO EXPECT, HUH?
OH NO! YOU'VE GIVEN ME REALLY HELPFUL INFORMATION!
TA-DA!
ALL RIGHT!
FIRST, I'LL MAKE A VERY BASIC ONE!
BASIC?
RIGHT!
THERE ARE TWO BASIC WAYS OF MAKING SUSHI-STYLE EGGS.
He's putting the egg back.
It was just for show.
TMP...
A ROLLED OMELET MADE WITH EGGS AND DASHI...
+Dashi
AND A THICK OMELET MADE WITH EGGS AND FISH PASTE.
+
THERE ARE ALL KINDS OF WAYS OF PREPARING IT.
BUT IF WE KNOW WHAT TYPE YOU HAD, IT'LL BE WAY EASIER TO REPRODUCE.
I GET IT!

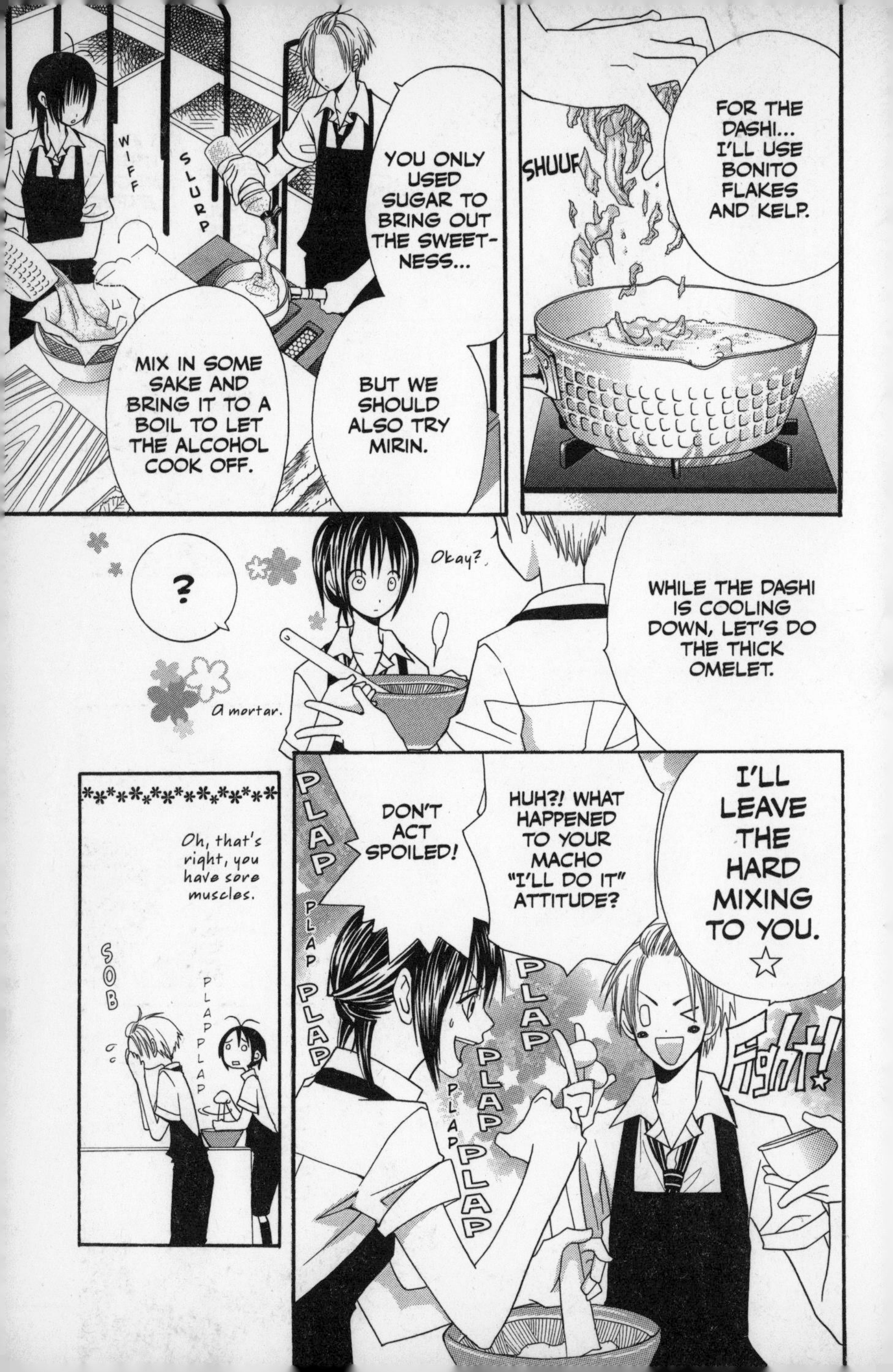
SHUUF
FOR THE DASHI... I'LL USE BONITO FLAKES AND KELP.
YOU ONLY USED SUGAR TO BRING OUT THE SWEETNESS...
SLURP
WIFF
BUT WE SHOULD ALSO TRY MIRIN.
MIX IN SOME SAKE AND BRING IT TO A BOIL TO LET THE ALCOHOL COOK OFF.
WHILE THE DASHI IS COOLING DOWN, LET'S DO THE THICK OMELET.
Okay?
?
A mortar.
I'LL LEAVE THE HARD MIXING TO YOU. ☆
HUH?! WHAT HAPPENED TO YOUR MACHO "I'LL DO IT" ATTITUDE?
DON'T ACT SPOILED!
PLAP PLAP PLAP PLAP PLAP PLAP PLAP PLAP
Oh, that's right, you have sore muscles.
SOB
PLAP PLAP PLAP

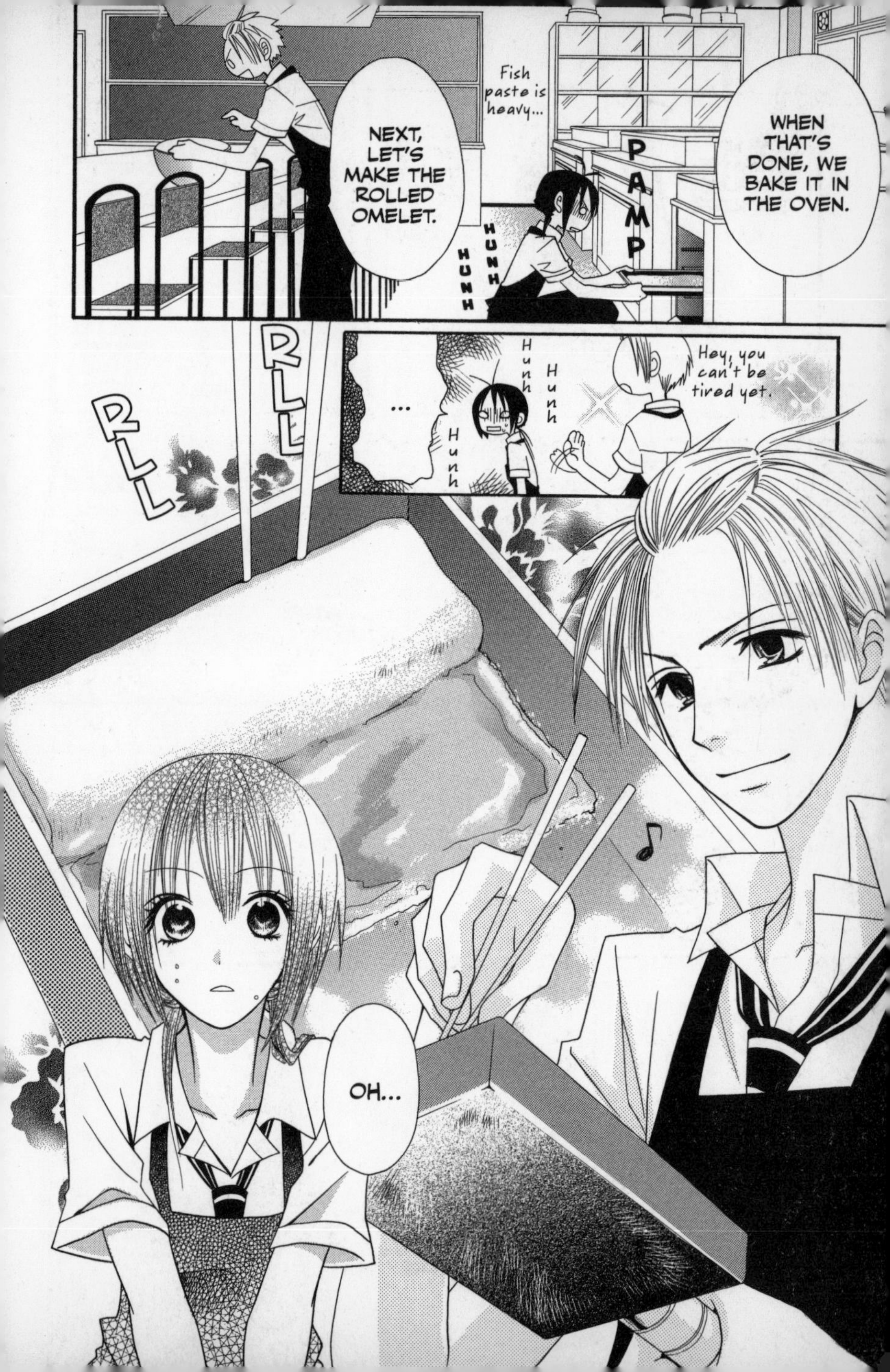
WHEN THAT'S DONE, WE BAKE IT IN THE OVEN.
PAMP
PAMP
Fish paste is heavy...
HUNH
HUNH
NEXT, LET'S MAKE THE ROLLED OMELET.
Hey, you can't be tired yet.
Hunh
Hunh
Hunh
...
RLL
RLL
OH...

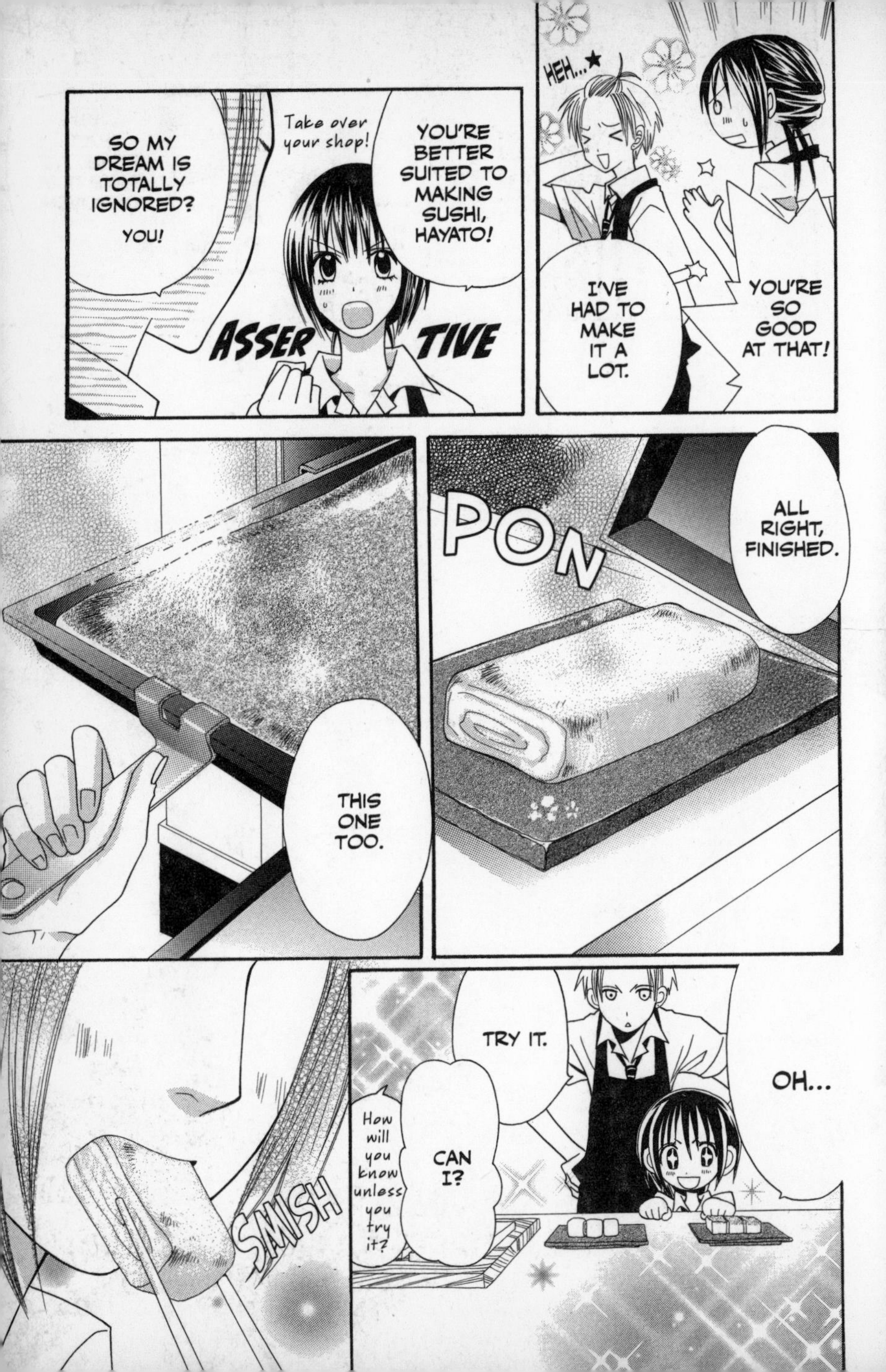
YOU'RE SO GOOD AT THAT!
I'VE HAD TO MAKE IT A LOT.
HEH...★
YOU'RE BETTER SUITED TO MAKING SUSHI, HAYATO!
Take over your shop!
ASSER TIVE
SO MY DREAM IS TOTALLY IGNORED?
YOU!
ALL RIGHT, FINISHED.
PON
THIS ONE TOO.
OH...
TRY IT.
CAN I?
How will you know unless you try it?
SMISH

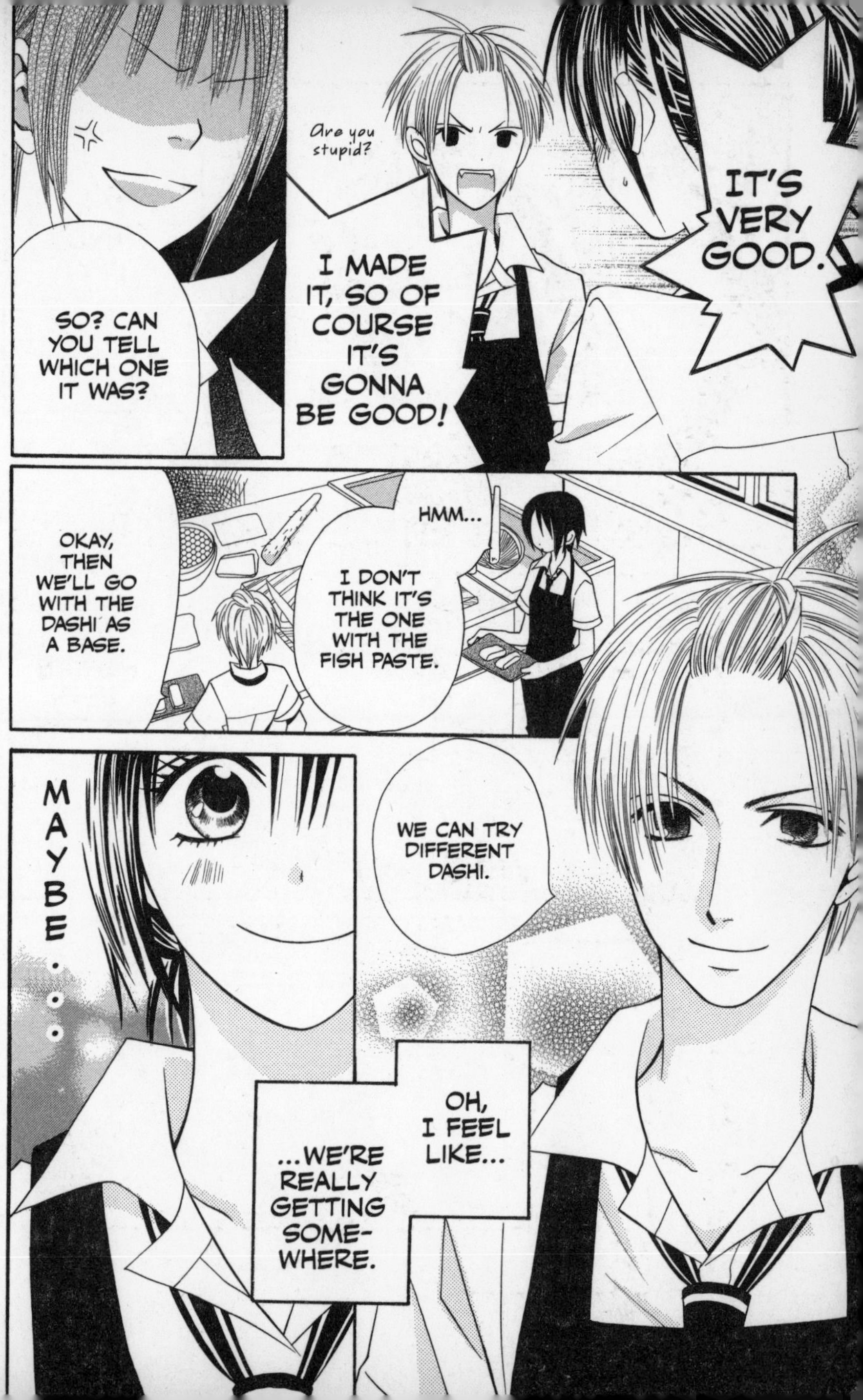
IT'S VERY GOOD.
Are you stupid?
I MADE IT, SO OF COURSE IT'S GONNA BE GOOD!
SO? CAN YOU TELL WHICH ONE IT WAS?
HMM...
I DON'T THINK IT'S THE ONE WITH THE FISH PASTE.
OKAY, THEN WE'LL GO WITH THE DASHI AS A BASE.
WE CAN TRY DIFFERENT DASHI.
MAYBE...
OH, I FEEL LIKE...
...WE'RE REALLY GETTING SOME-WHERE.

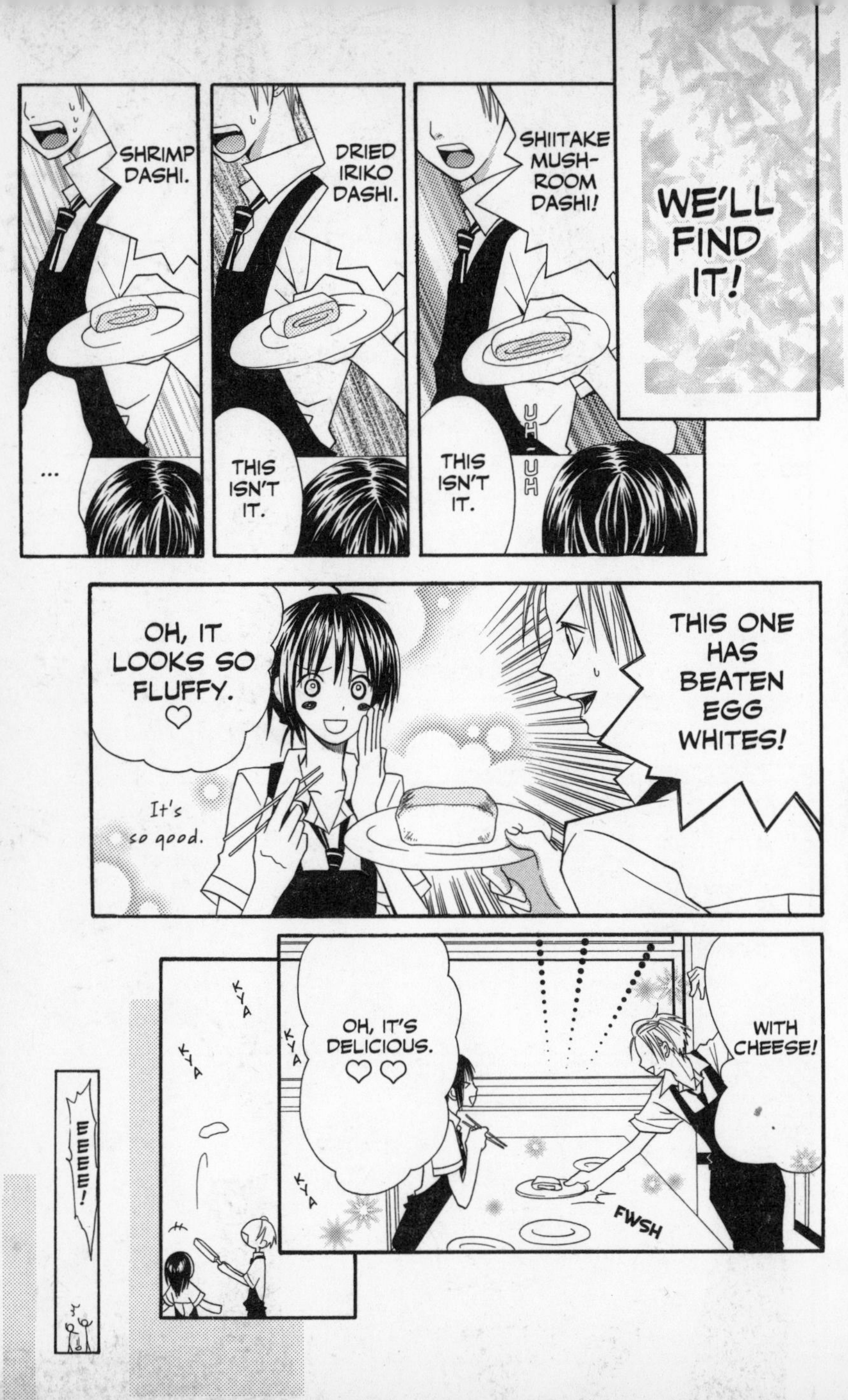
WE'LL FIND IT!
SHIITAKE MUSH-ROOM DASHI!
UH-UH
THIS ISN'T IT.
DRIED IRIKO DASHI.
THIS ISN'T IT.
SHRIMP DASHI.
...
THIS ONE HAS BEATEN EGG WHITES!
OH, IT LOOKS SO FLUFFY. ♡
It's so good.
WITH CHEESE!
OH, IT'S DELICIOUS. ♡♡
FWSH
KYA
KYA
KYA
KYA
EEEEE!

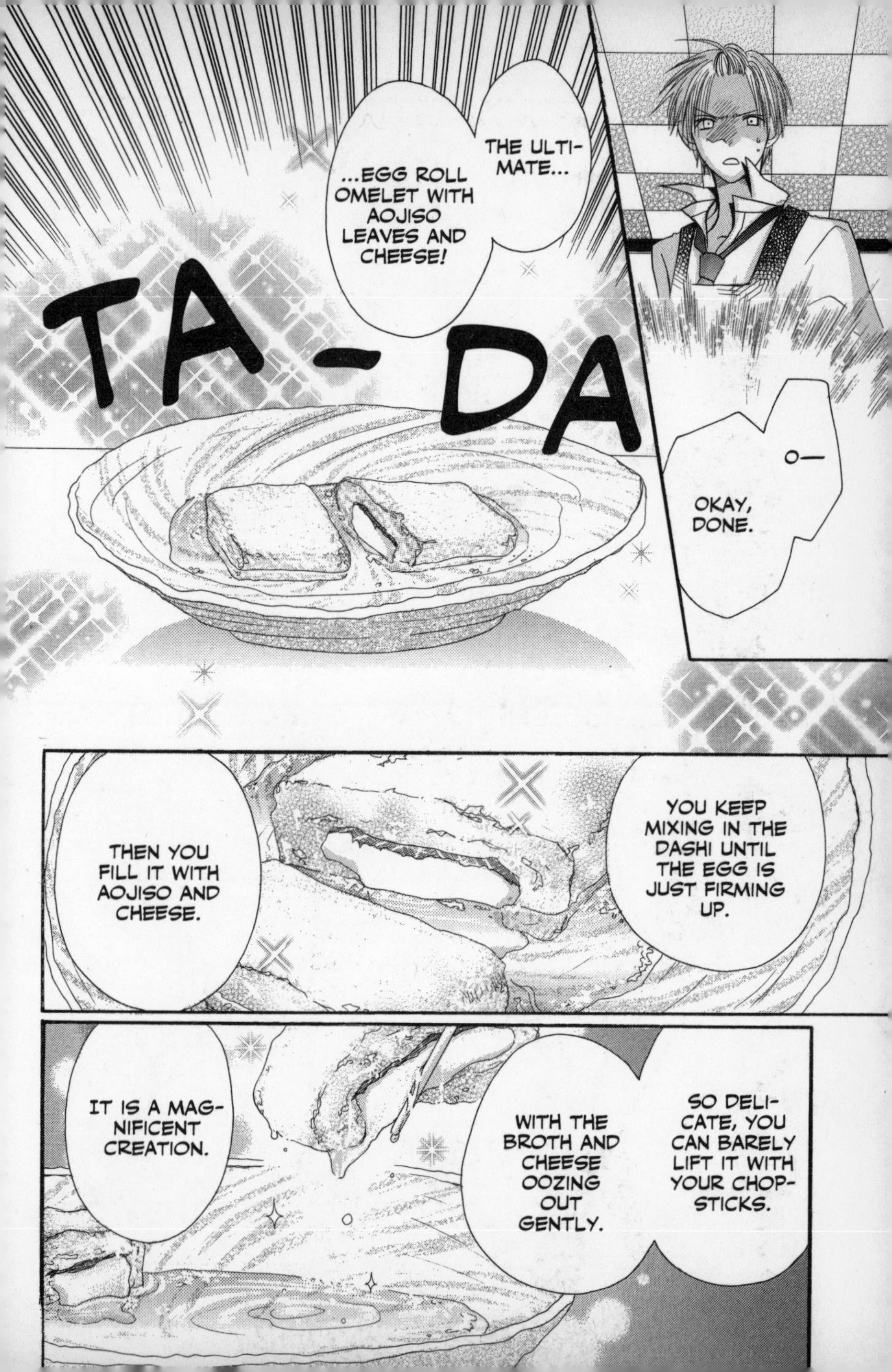
O—
OKAY, DONE.
THE ULTI-MATE...
...EGG ROLL OMELET WITH AOJISO LEAVES AND CHEESE!
TA-DA
YOU KEEP MIXING IN THE DASHI UNTIL THE EGG IS JUST FIRMING UP.
THEN YOU FILL IT WITH AOJISO AND CHEESE.
SO DELI-CATE, YOU CAN BARELY LIFT IT WITH YOUR CHOP-STICKS.
WITH THE BROTH AND CHEESE OOZING OUT GENTLY.
IT IS A MAG-NIFICENT CREATION.

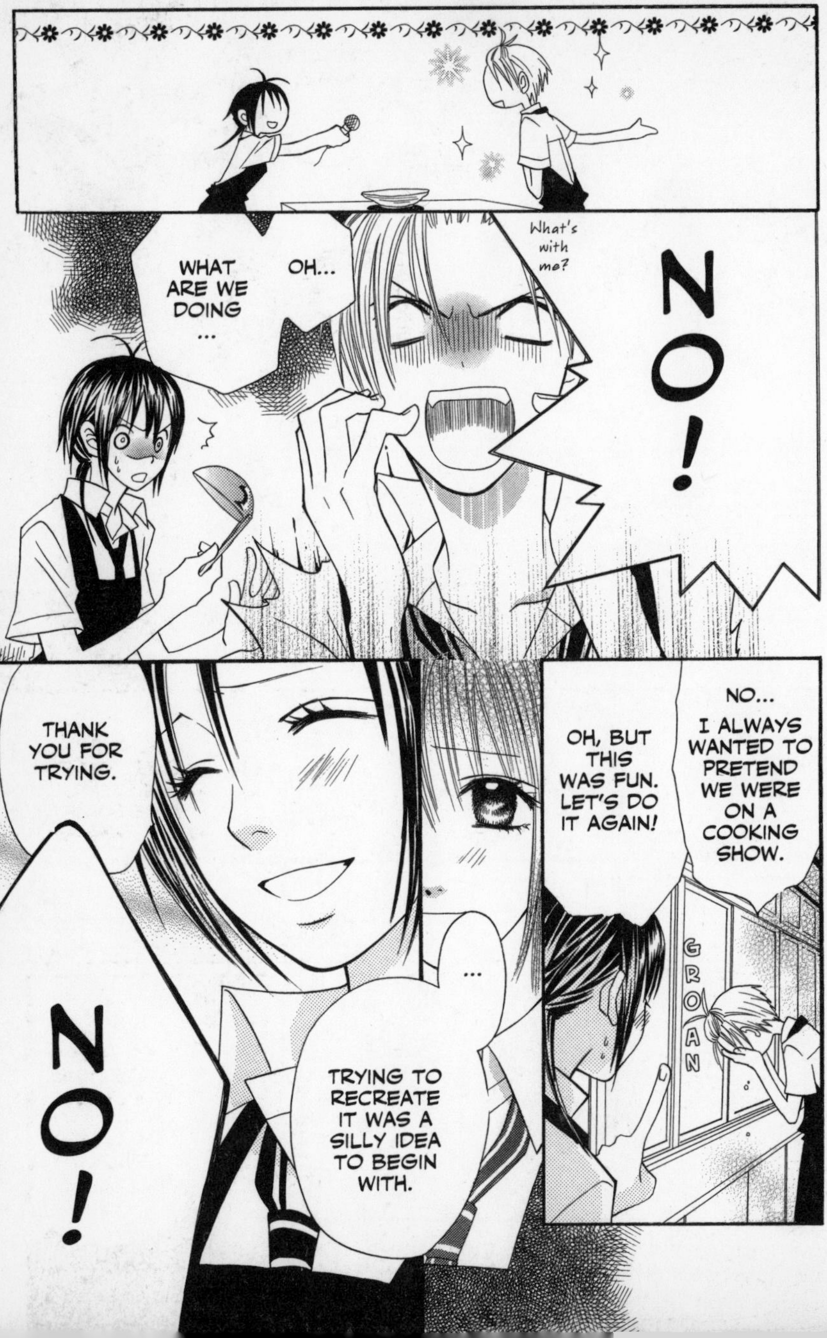
What's with me?
NO!
WHAT ARE WE DOING ...
OH...
NO... I ALWAYS WANTED TO PRETEND WE WERE ON A COOKING SHOW.
OH, BUT THIS WAS FUN. LET'S DO IT AGAIN!
GROAN
THANK YOU FOR TRYING.
...
TRYING TO RECREATE IT WAS A SILLY IDEA TO BEGIN WITH.
NO!

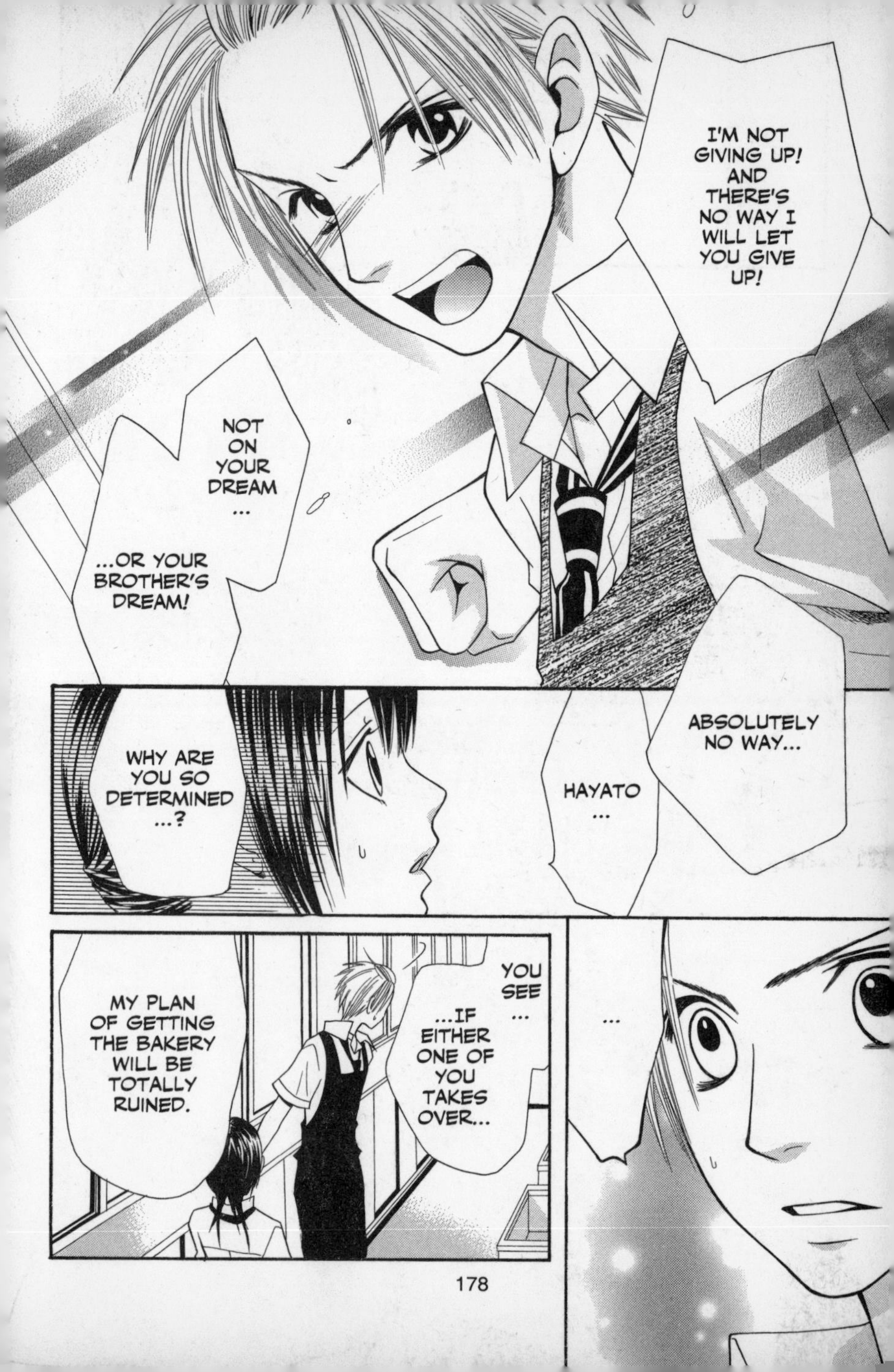
I'M NOT GIVING UP! AND THERE'S NO WAY I WILL LET YOU GIVE UP!
NOT ON YOUR DREAM ...
...OR YOUR BROTHER'S DREAM!
ABSOLUTELY NO WAY...
HAYATO ...
WHY ARE YOU SO DETERMINED ...?
...
YOU SEE ...
...IF EITHER ONE OF YOU TAKES OVER...
MY PLAN OF GETTING THE BAKERY WILL BE TOTALLY RUINED.

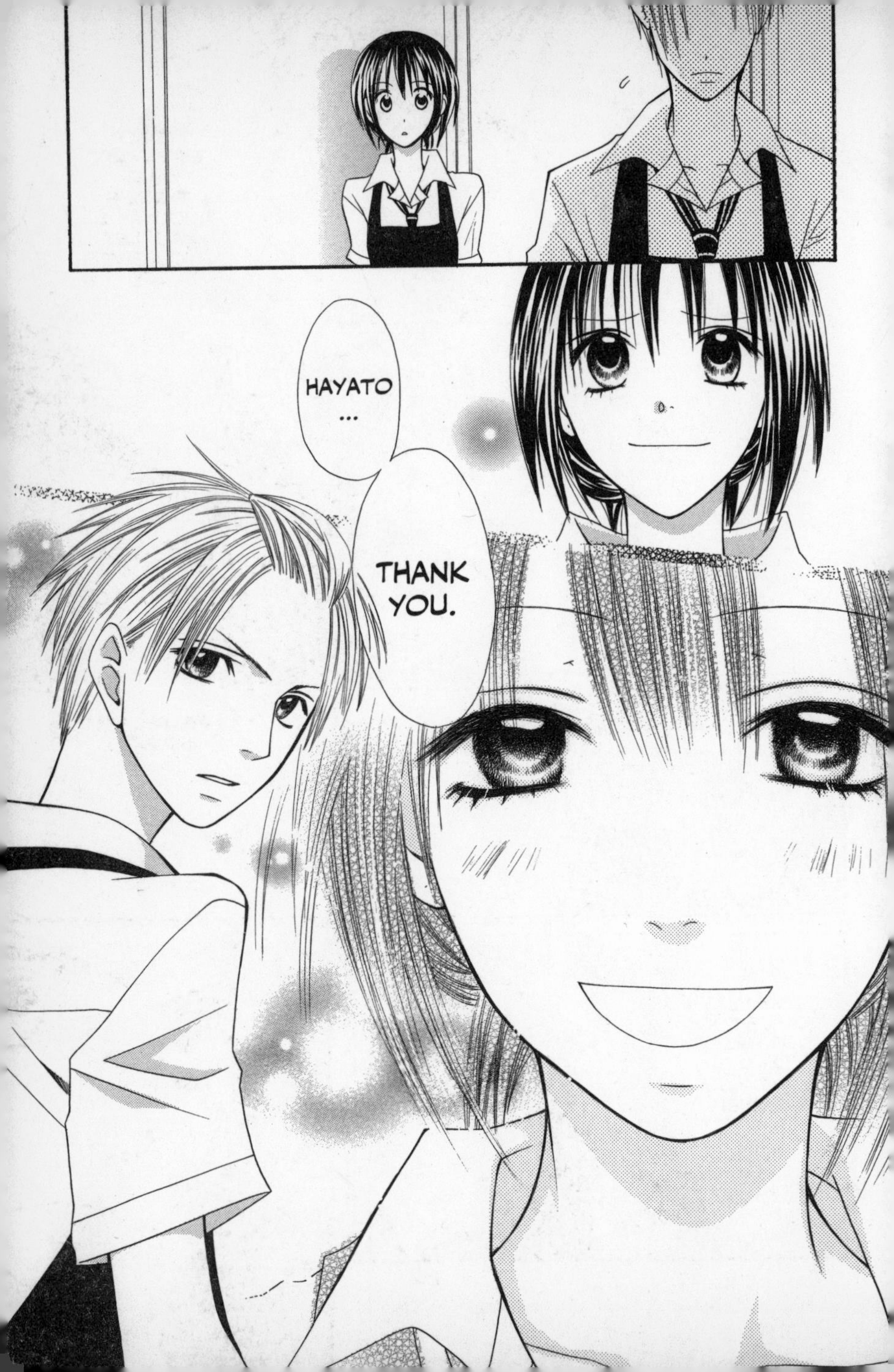
HAYATO ...
THANK YOU.

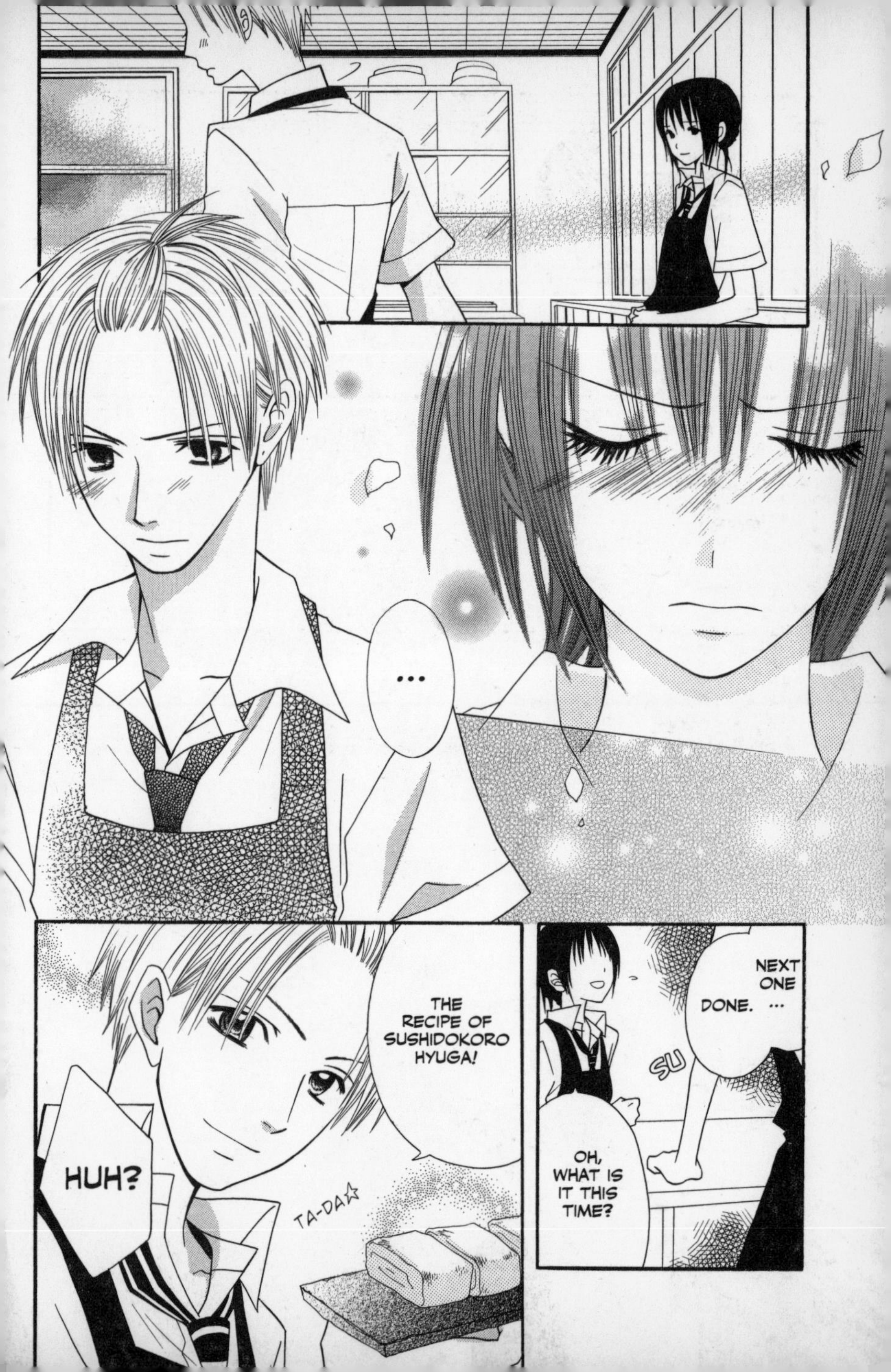
...
NEXT ONE DONE. ...
SU
OH, WHAT IS IT THIS TIME?
THE RECIPE OF SUSHIDOKORO HYUGA!
TA-DA☆
HUH?

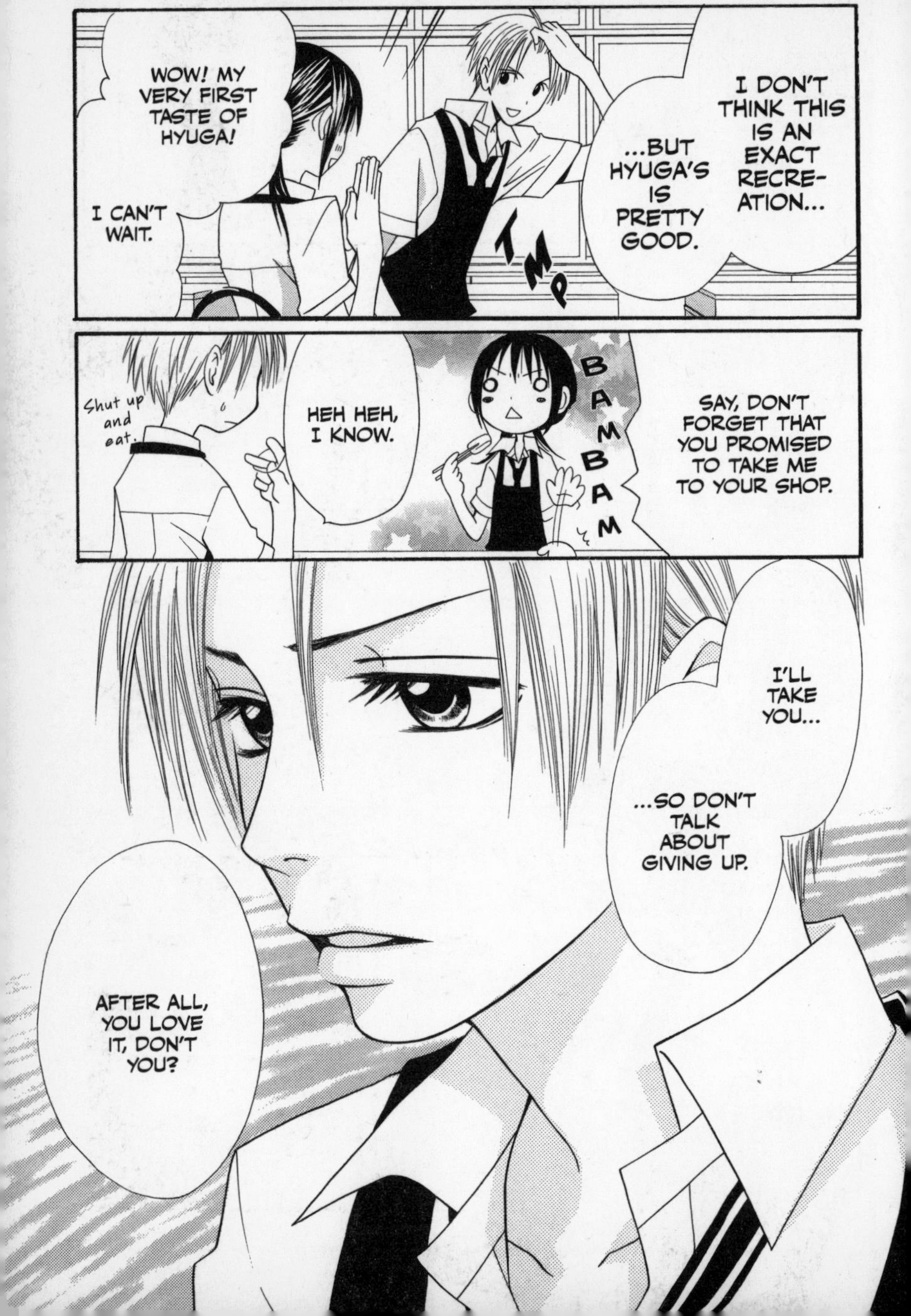
I DON'T THINK THIS IS AN EXACT RECRE-ATION...
...BUT HYUGA'S IS PRETTY GOOD.
TMP
WOW! MY VERY FIRST TASTE OF HYUGA!
I CAN'T WAIT.
SAY, DON'T FORGET THAT YOU PROMISED TO TAKE ME TO YOUR SHOP.
BAMBAM
HEH HEH, I KNOW.
Shut up and eat.
I'LL TAKE YOU...
...SO DON'T TALK ABOUT GIVING UP.
AFTER ALL, YOU LOVE IT, DON'T YOU?

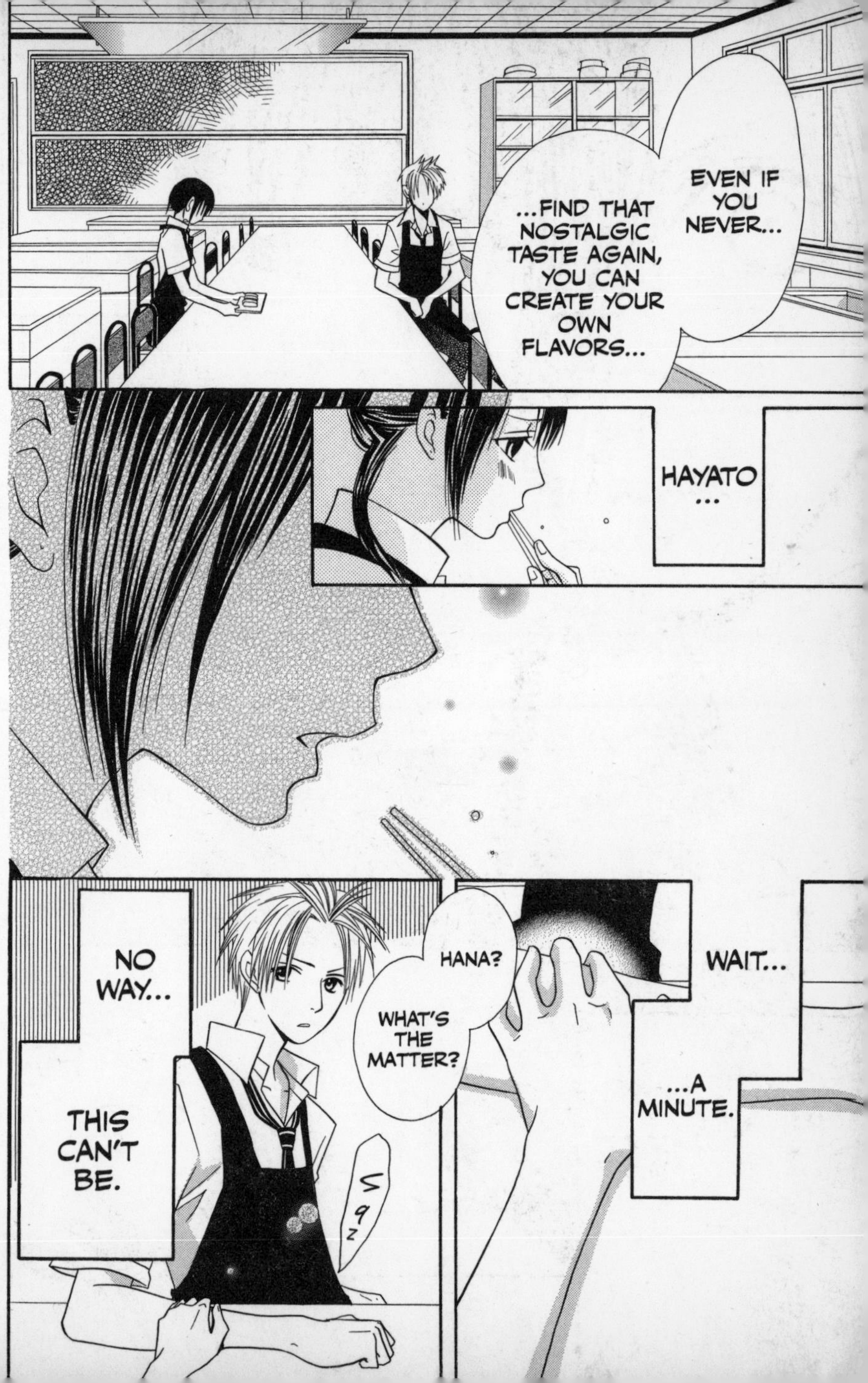
EVEN IF YOU NEVER...
...FIND THAT NOSTALGIC TASTE AGAIN, YOU CAN CREATE YOUR OWN FLAVORS...
HAYATO ...
WAIT...
...A MINUTE.
HANA?
WHAT'S THE MATTER?
NO WAY...
THIS CAN'T BE.
SQZ

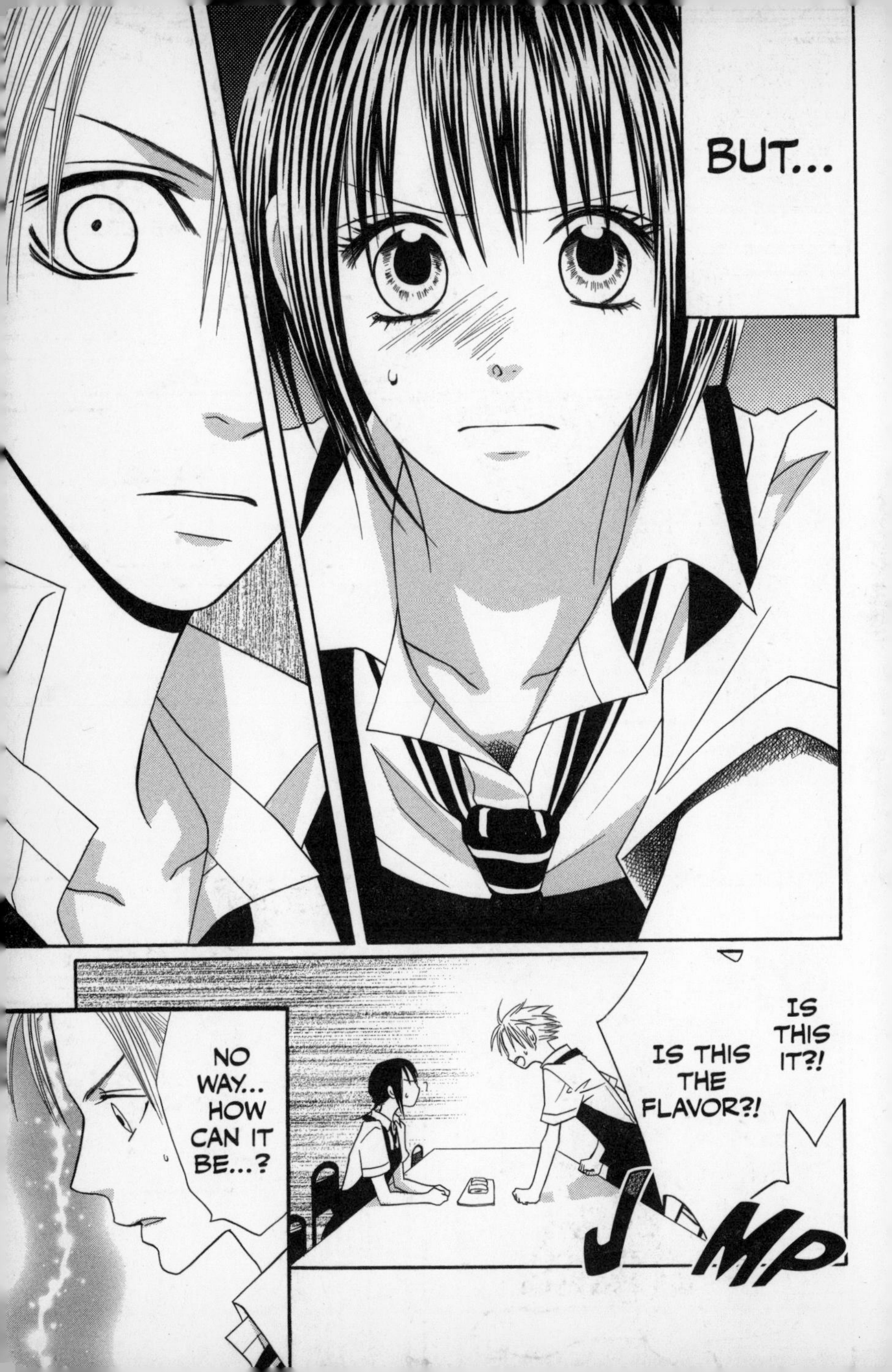
BUT...
IS THIS IT?!
IS THIS THE FLAVOR?!
NO WAY... HOW CAN IT BE...?

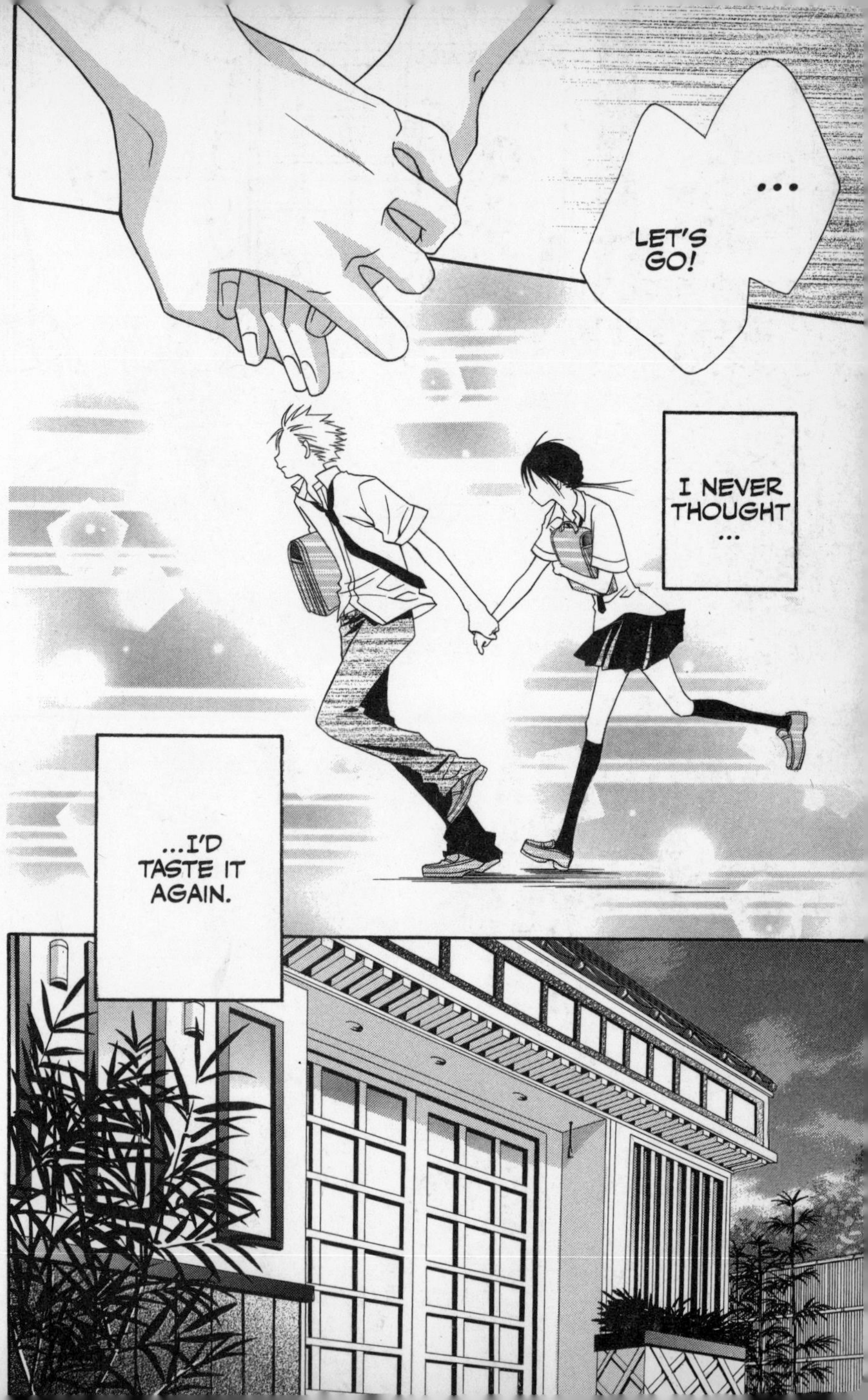
...
LET'S GO!
I NEVER THOUGHT ...
...I'D TASTE IT AGAIN.

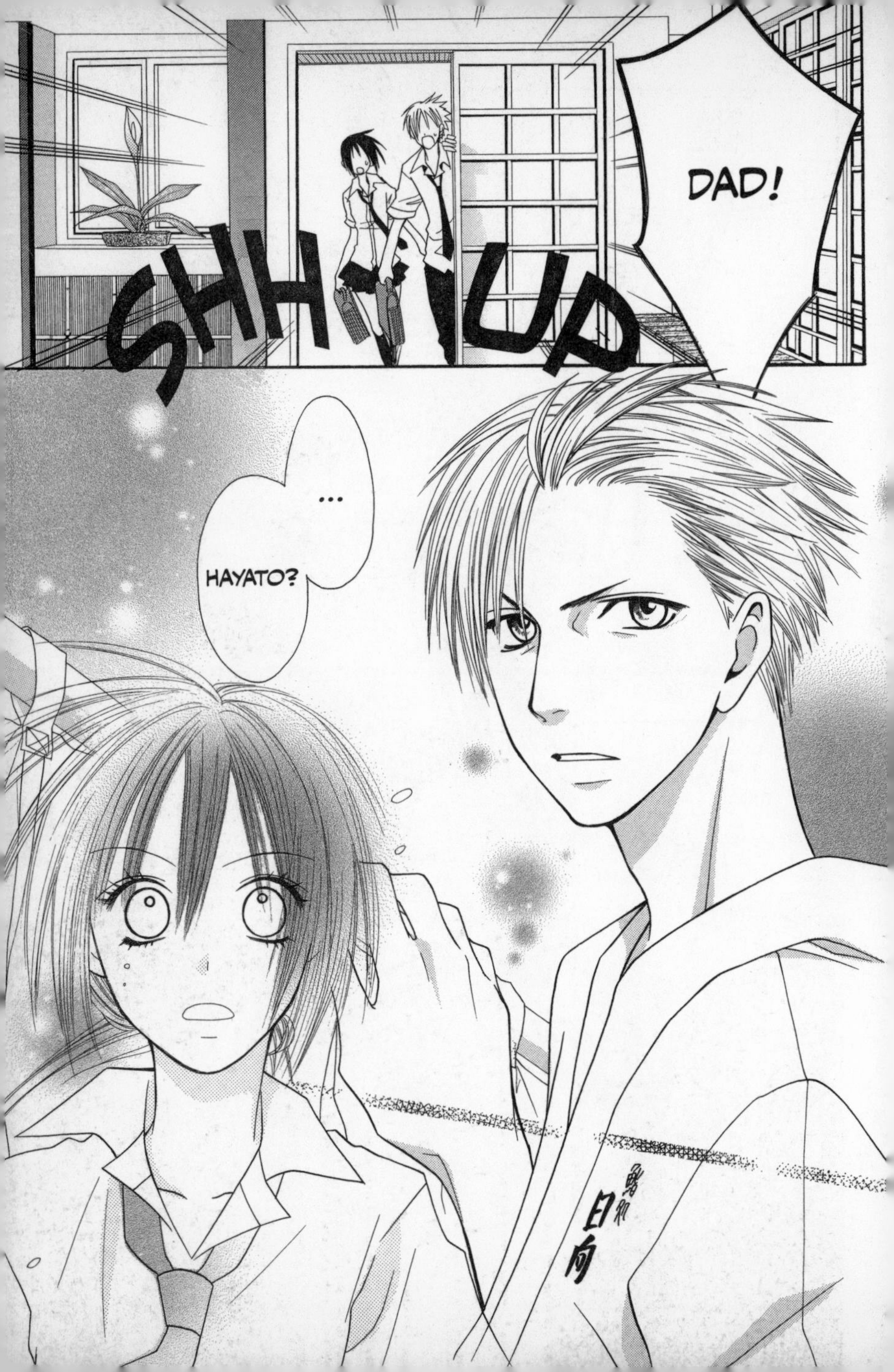
DAD!
SHH UP
...
HAYATO?
日向

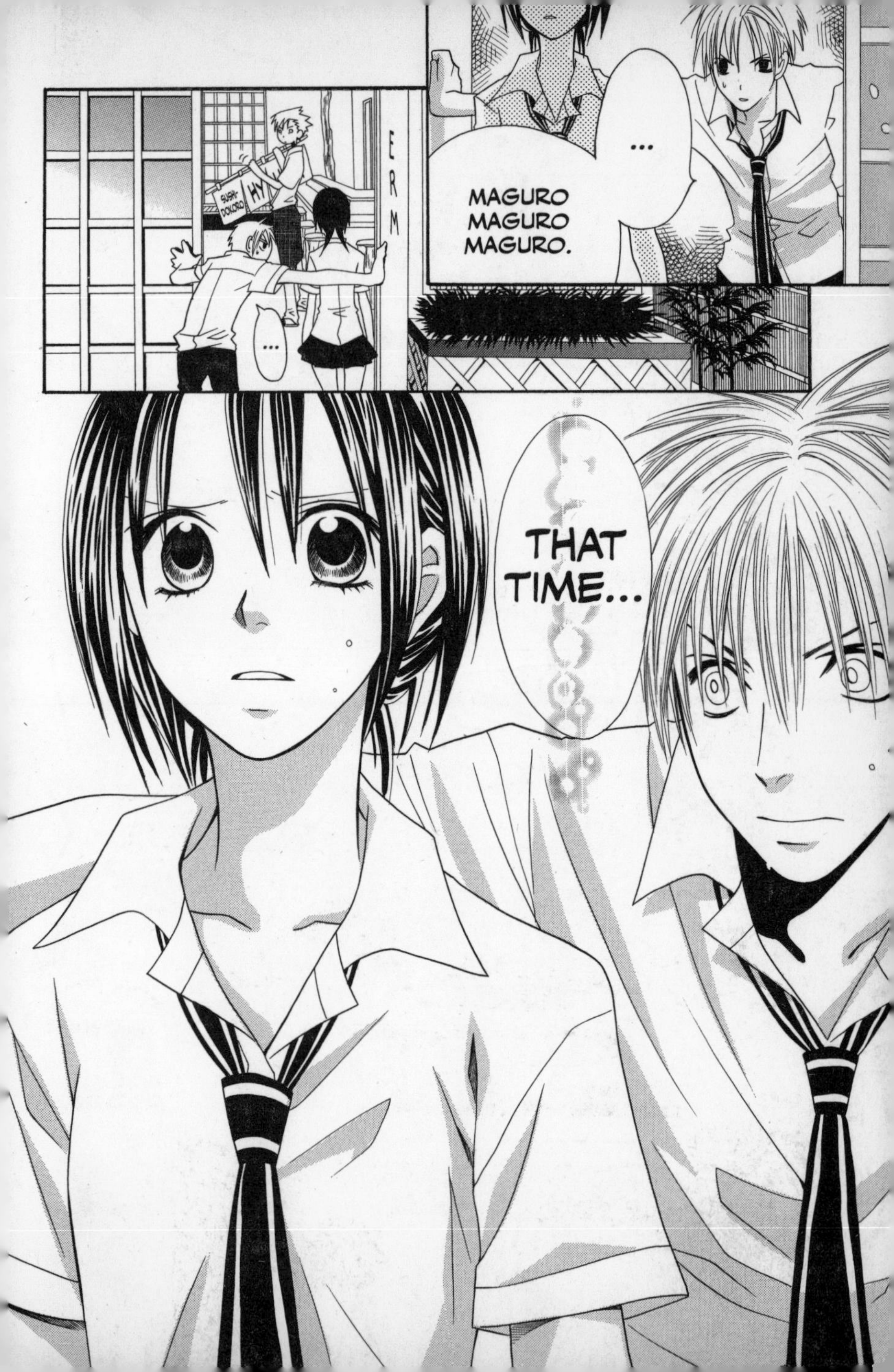
...
MAGURO MAGURO MAGURO.
SUSHI-DOKORO
HY
ERM
...
THAT TIME...

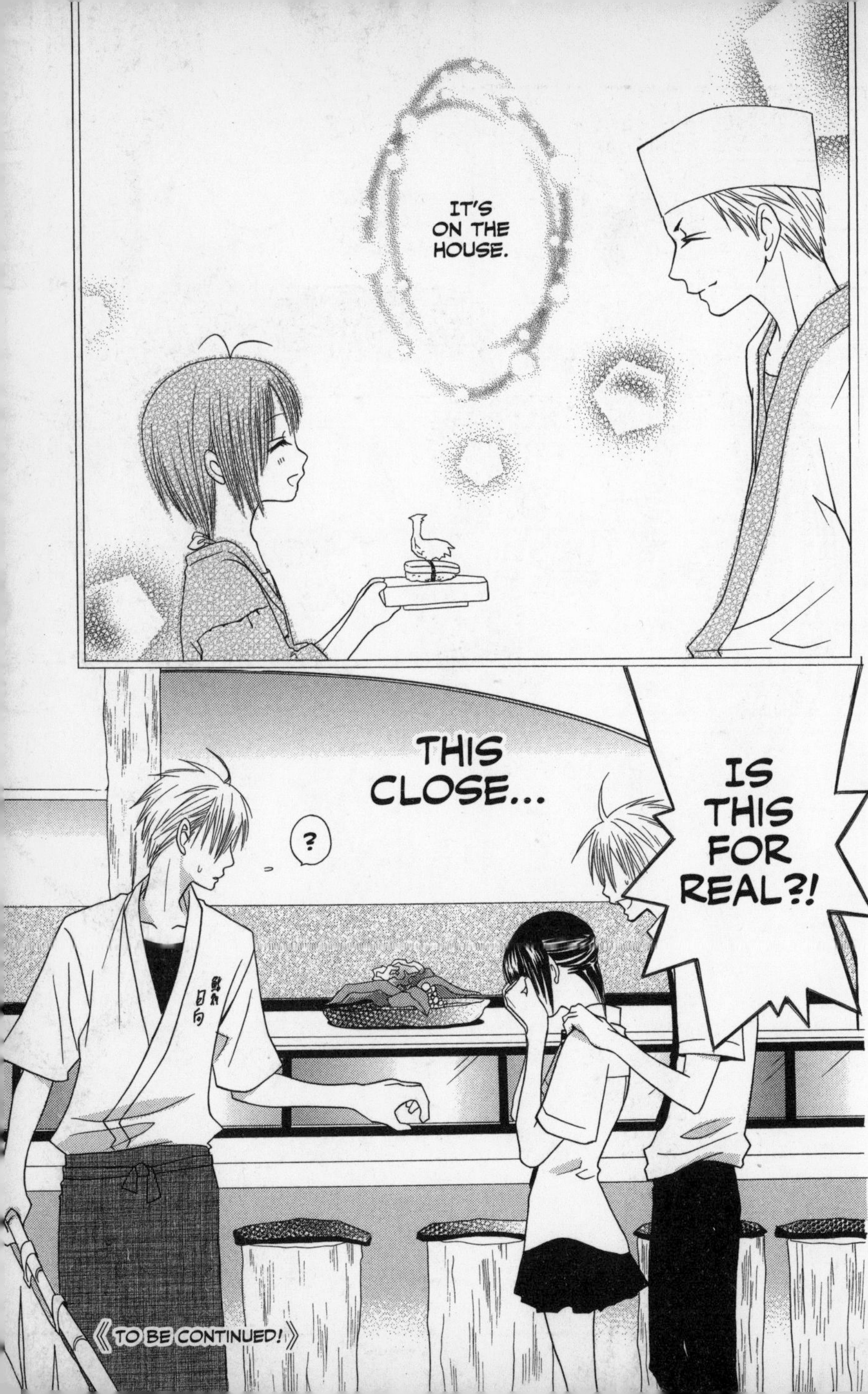
IT'S ON THE HOUSE.
IS THIS FOR REAL?!
THIS CLOSE...
?
《TO BE CONTINUED!》

SUPER SPECIAL Mixed Vegetables "Time Gap"

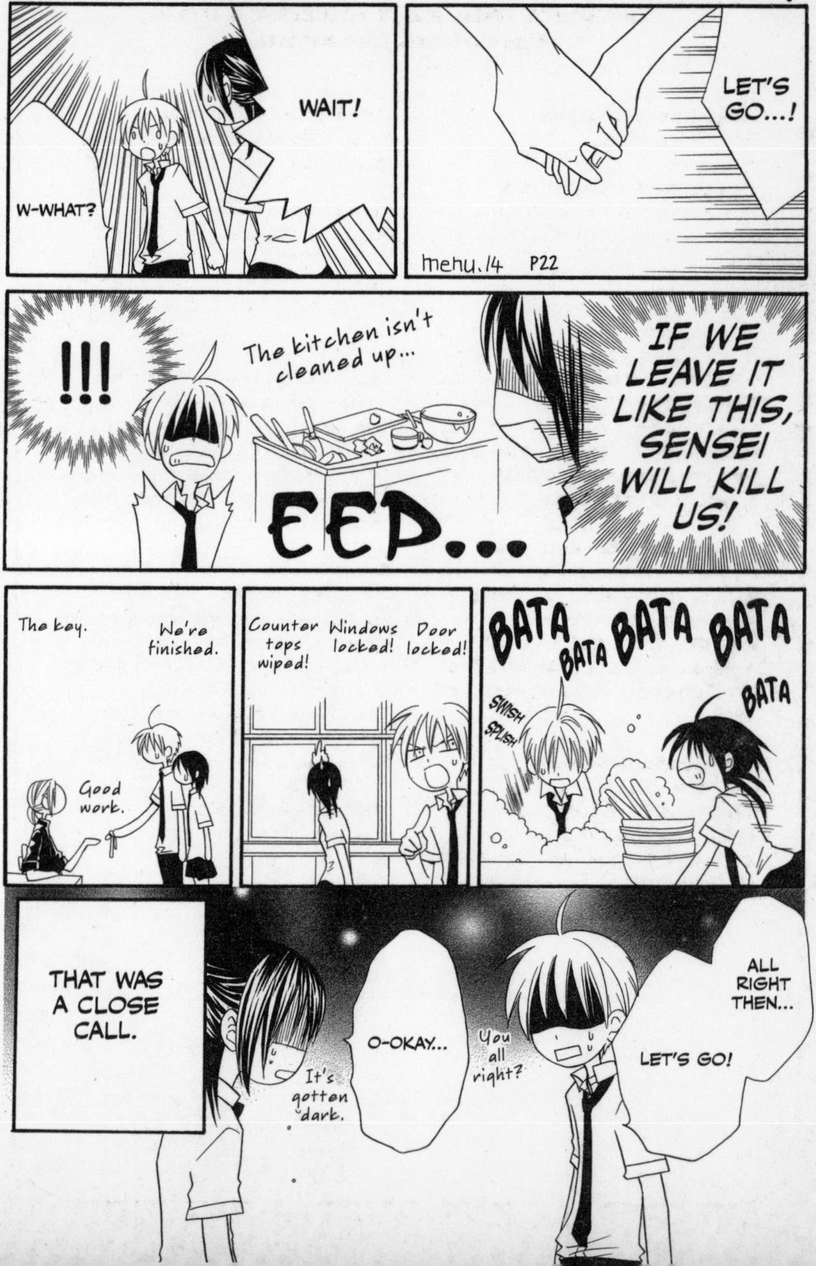
LET'S GO...!
menu.14 P22
WAIT!
W-WHAT?
IF WE LEAVE IT LIKE THIS, SENSEI WILL KILL US!
The kitchen isn't cleaned up...
!!!
EEP...
BATA BATA BATA BATA
BATA
SWISH SPLISH
Door locked!
Windows locked!
Counter tops wiped!
We're finished.
The key.
Good work.
ALL RIGHT THEN...
LET'S GO!
You all right?
O-OKAY...
It's gotten dark.
THAT WAS A CLOSE CALL.

Side Dish—End Notes

For those who want to know a little more about the menu.

Page 56, panel 1: Sashimi
Thinly sliced raw fish.

Page 56, panel 3: Egg and rice
In Japanese cuisine, pouring a raw, beaten egg over hot rice is a common practice.

Page 82, panel 1: Hitsumabushi
A dish of broiled eels served with rice, sauce, broth, and several garnishes. Hitsumabushi is typically eaten in three steps: First, one eats the eel with sauce and rice; second, one eats the rice along with garnishes like pickles and laver; third, one pours tea over the remaining rice and accompaniments.

Page 84, author notes: Cool Biz
An energy-saving campaign instituted by the Japanese Ministry of Environment in 2005 to promote short-sleeved shirts in lieu of suits, to lessen the use of air conditioning. That's why Komura drew Hayato wearing short sleeves.

Page 96, panel 2: Ribboning batter
The process of beating eggs and sugar together until the mixture piles up on itself in a flat, ribbon-like formation when the whisk or electric mixer beaters are held up to test the texture.

Page 108, panel 2: Kombu
A type of dried kelp seaweed, usually used in soups or in simmered dishes.

Page 112, panel 3: Yellowtail
Also known as Japanese amberjack. White-fleshed yellowtail is a popular sushi fish. In Japan it is called *hamachi* or *buri* and has a flavor and texture similar to tuna.

Page 143, panel 4: Oyako donburi
Bowl of rice topped with chicken and eggs. *Oyako* means "parent and child," as in chicken and egg. *Donburi* means "bowl." There are various *donburi* dishes topped with tempura, *tonkatsu* (deep-fried pork cutlet), etc.

Page 144, panel 2: Ayu
Also called "sweetfish", this delicate saltwater fish has a slightly golden, olive skin and a white belly. The sweetfish is so named because it has sweet-tasting flesh, which the author described in Volume 1 as tasting of watermelon. Others attribute a cucumber aroma to the fish's flesh.

Page 159, panel 4: Maguro
Bluefin tuna, one of the most common sushi fish.

Page 160, panel 3: Toro
The fatty, belly portion of tuna/maguro. Toro is more expensive than any other part of the tuna and is prized for its taste and texture.

Page 160, panel 4: Kama
The gill area of a fish, where the meat is considered to be the most succulent. The kama is difficult to extract raw, so it is usually grilled or simmered and the meat pulled out with chopsticks.

Page 164, author notes: Aojiso
The green variety of a strongly flavored herb known variously as *perilla* or *shiso* around the world. The herb can also be purple. Aojiso is eaten with sashimi or sliced into strips and used in salads and other dishes.

Page 164, author notes: Dashi
Soup stock made from a variety of ingredients, but commonly a combination of *kombu* and dried bonito tuna flakes. Some dashi is made by soaking dried shiitake mushrooms or dried sardines. Dashi with bonito flakes is often the base for miso soup.

Page 171, panel 2: Mirin
A sweet, low-alcohol rice wine and an essential ingredient in the Japanese kitchen.

Page 175, panel 2: Shiitake
A particularly meaty type of mushroom often used in Japanese cuisine, either fresh or reconstituted from dried.

Page 175, panel 3: Iriko
Dried anchovies or sardines.

A trial-and-error volume 2...I wonder?
I'm just hoping that whoever takes this book into
their hands will enjoy it.

-Ayumi Komura

Ayumi Komura was born in
Kagoshima Prefecture. Her favor-
ite number is 22, and her hobbies
include watching baseball. Her
previous title is *Hybrid Berry*,
about a high school girl who ends
up posing as a boy on her school's
baseball team.

MIXED VEGETABLES
VOL. 2
The Shojo Beat Manga Edition

STORY AND ART BY
AYUMI KOMURA

English Translation/JN Productions
English Adaptation/Stephanie V.W. Lucianovic
Touch-up Art & Lettering/HudsonYards
Design/Yukiko Whitley
Editor/Megan Bates

Editor in Chief, Books/Alvin Lu
Editor in Chief, Magazines/Marc Weidenbaum
VP, Publishing Licensing/Rika Inouye
VP, Sales & Product Marketing/Gonzalo Ferreyra
VP, Creative/Linda Espinosa
Publisher/Hyoe Narita

Published by VIZ Media, LLC
P.O. Box 77010
San Francisco, CA 94107

store.viz.com

Shojo Beat Manga Edition
10 9 8 7 6 5 4 3 2 1
First printing, December 2008

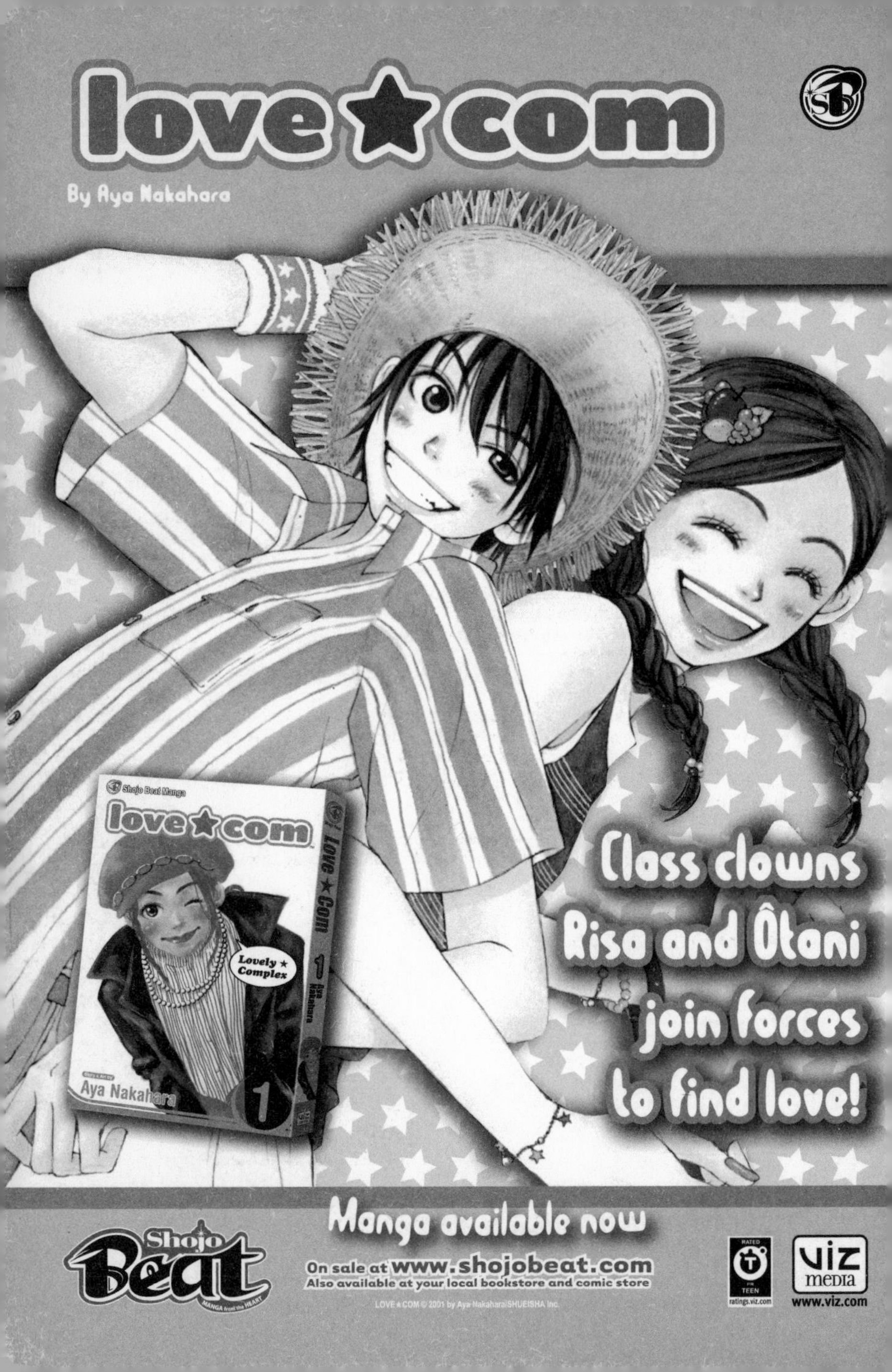

love★com
By Aya Nakahara
Shojo Beat Manga
love★com
Lovely ★ Complex
Aya Nakahara
1
Class clowns Risa and Ôtani join forces to find love!
Manga available now
Shojo Beat
MANGA from the HEART
On sale at www.shojobeat.com
Also available at your local bookstore and comic store
LOVE★COM © 2001 by Aya Nakahara/SHUEISHA Inc.
RATED T TEEN
ratings.viz.com
VIZ media
www.viz.com

High School DEBUT

By Kazune Kawahara

When Haruna Nagashima was in junior high, softball and comics were her life. Now that she's in high school, she's ready to find a boyfriend. But will hard work (and the right coach) be enough?

Find out in the *High School Debut* manga series—available now!

Art book featuring
216 pages of beautiful
color images personally
selected by Tanemura

Read where Mitsuki's
pop dreams began
in the manga—all 7
volumes now available

Complete your
collection with the
anime, now on DVD

www.viz.com

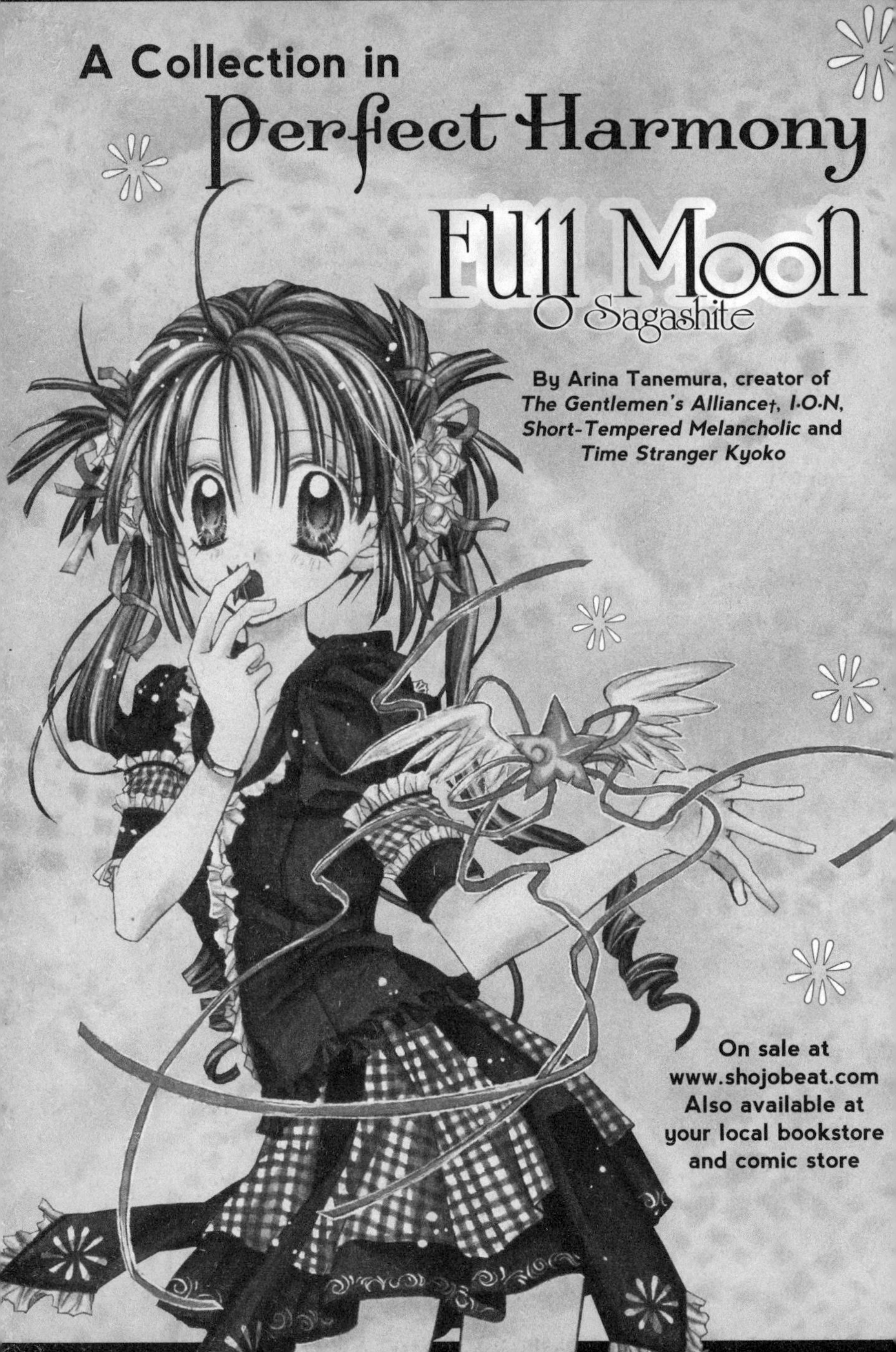
A Collection in
Perfect Harmony
Full Moon
O Sagashite
By Arina Tanemura, creator of
The Gentlemen's Alliance†, I·O·N,
Short-Tempered Melancholic and
Time Stranger Kyoko
On sale at
www.shojobeat.com
Also available at
your local bookstore
and comic store

Tell us what you think about Shojo Beat Manga!

Our survey is now available online. Go to:

shojobeat.com/mangasurvey

Help us make our product offerings better!

Shojo Beat™

MANGA from the HEART

The Shojo Manga Authority

12 GIANT issues for ONLY $34.99*

That's 51% OFF the cover price!

The most **ADDICTIVE** shojo manga stories from Japan **PLUS** unique editorial coverage on the arts, music, culture, fashion, and much more!

Subscribe **NOW** and become a member of the Sub Club!

- **SAVE** 51% OFF the cover price
- **ALWAYS** get every issue
- **ACCESS** exclusive areas of www.shojobeat.com
- **FREE** members-only gifts several times a year

Strictly VIP!

3 EASY WAYS TO SUBSCRIBE!

1) Send in the subscription order form from this book **OR**
2) Log on to: www.shojobeat.com **OR**
3) Call 1-800-541-7876

Save OVER 50%

The Shojo Manga Authority

This monthly magazine is injected with the most **ADDICTIVE** shojo manga stories from Japan. PLUS, unique editorial coverage on the arts, music, culture, fashion, and much more!

☑ **YES!** Please enter my one-year subscription (12 GIANT issues) to *Shojo Beat* at the LOW SUBSCRIPTION RATE of **$34.99!**

Over **300 pages** per issue!

NAME

ADDRESS

CITY   STATE   ZIP

E-MAIL ADDRESS   P7GNC1

☐ **MY CHECK IS ENCLOSED** (PAYABLE TO *Shojo Beat*)   ☐ **BILL ME LATER**

CREDIT CARD: ☐ VISA   ☐ MASTERCARD

ACCOUNT #   EXP. DATE

SIGNATURE

CLIP AND MAIL TO ➡

SHOJO BEAT
Subscriptions Service Dept.
P.O. Box 438
Mount Morris, IL 61054-0438

RATED
T+ OLDER TEEN
ratings.viz.com